ONE YEAR® OF

DINNER TABLE DEVOTIONS

& discussion starters

TYNDALE HOUSE PUBLISHERS, INC.
Carol Stream, Illinois

ONE YEAR® OF

DINNER TABLE

DEVOTIONS

& discussion starters

365 opportunities to grow closer to God as a family

NANCY GUTHRIE

Visit Tyndale's exciting Web site at www.tyndale.com

TYNDALE and Tyndale's quill logo are registered trademarks of Tyndale House Publishers, Inc.

One Year and *The One Year* are registered trademarks of Tyndale House Publishers, Inc.

One Year of Dinner Table Devotions and Discussion Starters: 365 Opportunities to Grow Closer to God as a Family

Designed by Jennifer Ghionzoli

Edited by Stephanie Voiland

Library of Congress Cataloging-in-Publication Data

Guthrie, Nancy.
    One year of dinner table devotions and discussion starters : 365 opportunities to grow closer to God as a family / Nancy Guthrie.
        p. cm.
    ISBN-13: 978-1-4143-1895-0 (sc)
    ISBN-10: 1-4143-1895-2 (sc)
1. Family—Prayers and devotions. 2. Devotional calendars. I. Title.
    BV255.G88 2008
    249—dc22   2008020548

Printed in the United States of America

14   13   12   11   10
 7   6   5   4   3

INTRODUCTION

Most modern Christian families live with a nagging sense of guilt that they don't have any kind of consistent family devotions. Or maybe I should say *my husband and I* have lived with a nagging sense of guilt that we have not had any kind of consistent family devotions! But I don't think we're alone in this.

Getting the kids to turn off the TV and computer and gather to read the Bible, to have a meaningful discussion everybody participates in, and to pray over anything other than a meal seems like too much of a daily hurdle for most families. Besides, most of us don't feel like we are authorities on the Bible, so we hardly know where to start. But we want to do something. And we want more than a daily chore that our children dread and can't wait to be done with. We're looking for something that won't be resisted or rejected as "totally lame." We want a meaningful and personal discussion about things that really matter, something everyone takes part in.

That's why I've written *One Year of Dinner Table Devotions and Discussion Starters*. Because we need it at our house, and I'm guessing you might need it at your house too.

One Year of Dinner Table Devotions and Discussion Starters helps families start in a natural gathering place—around the dinner table. As the meal comes to a close, family members can take turns reading the dinner table devotion for that day. Each day's devotion includes readings on a specific theme from two or three Scripture passages out of the accessible New Living Translation, a brief devotional thought, and three discussion-starter questions—all designed to be done together as a family in ten to fifteen minutes (before everybody helps with the kitchen cleanup!).

It is written for families with children in all stages—from elementary school to high school—who long for a way to have spiritual input in their children's lives and who want Scripture to be naturally woven into their family life and conversations.

What Makes *Dinner Table Devotions* Different?

Whereas most family devotionals focus on Bible stories or on practical moral lessons, *Dinner Table Devotions and Discussion Starters* focuses on biblical themes, concepts, and words, in ways that are understandable to children without talking down to adults or teens. It will help your family take a step back to look at the big picture of what God is doing in the world and his purposes and plans in creating and redeeming the world. Once you and your family have worked your way through this book, you will have discussed nearly every major attribute of God and a host of profound theological truths, such as justification, redemption, substitution, and sanctification—without all those daunting words. You will have looked into important concepts from the Bible, such as covenant, adoption, judgment, and redemption, as well as spiritual realities, such as hell, angels, resurrection, and glorification. This is not dry theology for theology's sake, but living theology that makes a huge difference in how we do battle against temptation, deal with disappointment, and determine our futures.

Over the course of the next year, your family will go deeper into developing an understanding of who God is, what he is like, what he expects, and what he is doing. Together you can embark on a journey of understanding who we are, why we need a Savior, and what it means to place our faith solely in Jesus. Holy living flows out of that.

The format of a short devotion followed by three discussion questions is designed to turn the devotional time into a family-wide discussion rather than a one-person lecture or reading. This is not a continuation of the school day or Sunday school but an opportunity to apply biblical truths to the most important areas of life.

How to Use *Dinner Table Devotions and Discussion Starters*

If you've rarely read and discussed God's Word together as a family, it can be awkward at first. But that initial awkwardness fades as conversations are sparked and understanding deepens. We have a treasure to pass on to our children—the Bible, which contains God's message to us and the answers to life's greatest questions. Because it is so important to us, we want to talk about it.

The goal of these devotions is to create an opportunity for dialogue and conversation. You as a parent set the tone as you allow yourself to be a learner and a seeker rather than a teacher or an authority. You do this as you are willing to say, "I don't think I really understand that completely" or "That is something I'd like to work on in my life to be more like Jesus." You do this as you affirm the input of every family member and maintain an atmosphere of acceptance and open participation.

Perhaps the most important way to encourage your dinner table devotions and discussions is something that happens away from the table. You want to make sure any confession of struggle or weakness expressed in your discussions is treated with respect and confidentiality. Nothing puts the lid on authentic sharing more quickly than when people's words are used against them. The best way to encourage vulnerability and openness is by creating a safe environment for sharing.

Each day's devotion is designed for everyone around the table to share and interact with it. You might choose to have different family members read the various verses, and you can encourage conversations by discussing the questions at the end of each devotion. The first question is answerable for family members of all ages, elementary and up. It is designed to draw family members in and to get everyone talking about their own thoughts and experiences. The next two questions are more thought provoking and in some cases more personal.

You may want to have different family members read the questions each time so that everyone has an opportunity to be on the asking end and the answering end. Many of the questions are "What do you think?" questions that may or may not have a "right" answer. Some are "Why do you think?" questions meant to encourage deeper thinking. And many are "How?" or "In what ways?" questions meant to draw out practical application of the truths presented. There are no answers in the back of the book! When you come to a question that is challenging to everyone around the table, this presents the opportunity to acknowledge that God is a mystery to be probed and a treasure to be mined, and that the things of God are not always simple to figure out. But the rewards for pursuing them are great.

The most personal questions are those that ask participants to identify ways they need to change or ways they would like to change. This can be new territory for families, but it also presents a meaningful opportunity for family members to connect with each other and with God. As a parent, you can set the tone and example here in terms of a willingness to be humble and to show others in the family that you are still an "unfinished project" when it comes to becoming all God wants you to be.

Starting the Conversation

In Deuteronomy 6:6-7, we read this instruction from God to the people of Israel: "You must commit yourselves wholeheartedly to these commands that I am giving you today. Repeat them again and again to your children. Talk about them when you are at home and when you are on the road, when you are going to bed and when you are getting up." What better place to practice "when you are at home" than around the dinner table?

The people of Israel were expected to understand Scripture well enough to talk about it with their children. They were to discuss the words of Scripture during their family activities and apply them to everyday life situations.

Our desire for our kids is that they develop a faith that is real and personal—not something they grow out of or leave behind. When they are pressed by the world, we want them to have the foundation to piece together what their faith really means and what makes Jesus worth knowing and following. We want them to be able to make an argument for him and feel comfortable talking about him as someone who is real, someone who matters in every area of their lives.

Now is the time to begin that conversation so it becomes as natural as breathing. It's by talking about him that we weave our understanding of God through all of life and through the life of our families. As we talk about him, he enters into not only our discussions around the dinner table but also our entertainment choices, our spending habits, our vacations, our time, and certainly our treatment of each other. By bringing him into our discussions around the dinner table, we saturate our lives with God. And isn't that what we really want?

Paul wrote, "Whether you eat or drink, or whatever you do, do it all for the glory of God" (1 Corinthians 10:31). I'm praying for you as you seek to glorify God around your dinner table—that he will be pleased, and that your family will have some laughs, perhaps shed some tears, and grow together toward God.

Nancy Guthrie
NASHVILLE, TENNESSEE

Everything New

It's a new year. And don't we love new? A new outfit, a car that still has that "new car" smell, a new recipe to fix for dinner, a new video game to conquer? But all around us, instead of new, we see things that are used and broken down—neighborhoods that are run down, relationships that fall apart, bodies that don't work as well as they used to. The reality is that everything on this earth is wearing out. Everything breaks down.

And in the midst of that reality, God says, "I am making everything new!" When we hear this we typically think new in terms of replacing something old. But God doesn't say he is making *all new things*. He is making *all things new*—in other words, he's making things better, fresher, brighter, and stronger.

And this is good news for those of us who want a fresh start, those who don't want to surrender to "that's just the way I am, the way I've always been. I can never change." Even now God is moving into our lives that are full of mistakes, and he's making us new. The process begins when God makes himself known to us in the deadness of our sin and we awaken to him. He touches our lives, and the dead places become alive again, fresh again. Right now, God is giving his people new thoughts, new hearts, new purpose, new energy for this new year ahead. And he wants to do something new in *you*, too.

 | **DISCUSSION STARTERS**

What are some new things you are enjoying now?
What things around you are old or broken?

How have you seen God's renewing work in your life and your family over the past year?

How do you hope he will work in this coming year?

The one sitting on the throne said, "Look, I am making everything new!"
REVELATION 21:5

Against its will, all creation was subjected to God's curse. But with eager hope, the creation looks forward to the day when it will join God's children in glorious freedom from death and decay.
ROMANS 8:20-21

This means that anyone who belongs to Christ has become a new person. The old life is gone; a new life has begun!
2 CORINTHIANS 5:17

Making Plans

A new year means a new calendar or daily planner. All those blank dates just waiting to be filled in! What are you planning for this year? Where will you go, and what do you hope to accomplish?

It is good to make plans. Jesus affirmed the person who made sure he had the needed resources before building a tower, and the king who made sure he had enough troops before entering into battle (SEE LUKE 14:28, 31). But there can also be a problem with making plans. The problem comes when we start assuming that we determine the course of our lives and the outcome of our plans, ignoring the fact that God is ultimately in control.

In the end, God is the one who determines the number of days we're on this earth. Everything is filtered through his hands—what we accomplish and whether we succeed or fail. And God wants us to make our plans and speak of our plans in a way that reflects our firm confidence that he is in control. So James tells us that instead of pronouncing what we are going to do as if we've given no thought to God, we should say, "If the Lord wants us to, we will live and do this or that." It is foolish to talk as if we chart our own destiny and determine the course of our lives. As wise Solomon says, "We can make our plans, but the LORD determines our steps" (PROVERBS 16:9).

Look here, you who say, "Today or tomorrow we are going to a certain town and will stay there a year. We will do business there and make a profit." How do you know what your life will be like tomorrow? Your life is like the morning fog—it's here a little while, then it's gone. What you ought to say is, "If the Lord wants us to, we will live and do this or that." Otherwise you are boasting about your own plans, and all such boasting is evil.
JAMES 4:13-16

Don't brag about tomorrow, since you don't know what the day will bring.
PROVERBS 27:1

But I will come—and soon—if the Lord lets me.
1 CORINTHIANS 4:19

| DISCUSSION STARTERS

What kind of plans do people write down on calendars?

Is the phrase "if the Lord wants us to" something we need to say out loud about all our plans, or is it more of a heart attitude we need to have? Or is it a little of both?

What goals do you have for this year that you want to submit to God's sovereign (all-powerful) plans?

Think Change

Our minds are not just computers that process data. We all have what we might call a mind-set (the way we think about life) and a viewpoint (the way we see the world). Our minds have attitudes and thought patterns that are ingrained in us—like habits. And our natural ways of thinking aren't perfect—they're fallen, like everything else in this world. None of us naturally think good and right thoughts about God. In fact, it's worse than that. On our own, we have thoughts about God that make him out to be less than he is, thoughts that set our hearts against him. Romans 1:28 says, "Since they thought it foolish to acknowledge God, he abandoned them to their foolish thinking."

So how do we change our minds? How do we begin to think differently? We feed them better food. We fill our minds with truth from Scripture, conversations about God, and ways of thinking about God and the things of God that are right and true and worthy of someone so great. We welcome the Holy Spirit to show us our old ways of thinking—*me first*; *got to get ahead*; *if it feels good, do it*; *I deserve it*; *I am the master of my own destiny*—and we invite the Holy Spirit to change how we think, what we want, and even how we feel.

The Holy Spirit can change our natural ways of thinking about things as he helps us understand and apply the Bible to our lives. The Bible gives us a new filter that all our thoughts run through—an eternal perspective that reshapes our value system, realigns our priorities, and reworks our personalities.

 | DISCUSSION STARTERS

Our society values an "open mind." What do you think that is? Is it valuable?

How do different people you know use their minds to please or glorify God?

In what ways would you like to use the intellectual ability God has given you?

> Let the Spirit renew your thoughts and attitudes.
> *EPHESIANS 4:23*

> Don't copy the behavior and customs of this world, but let God transform you into a new person by changing the way you think.
> *ROMANS 12:2*

> Those who are dominated by the sinful nature think about sinful things, but those who are controlled by the Holy Spirit think about things that please the Spirit. So letting your sinful nature control your mind leads to death. But letting the Spirit control your mind leads to life and peace.
> *ROMANS 8:5-6*

Knowing His Name

We interact with a lot of people without ever knowing their names. But when we learn people's names, they become more real to us as unique people, with their own unique personalities and histories.

God wants us to know him—not in a generic or shallow way (as in "the Man Upstairs"). He wants us to know him personally. He wants us to recognize that he has his own personality and character and preferences. So he has told us his name. He doesn't have a name like Joe or Christopher or Sarah or Emily. His name is unique and holy, just like he is. In fact, the Jewish people saw God's name as so holy they didn't say it out loud.

The name used most often for God in the Old Testament (almost seven thousand times) is a name that is translated into English as "I Am Who I Am." You will see this name written as *Lord* in all capital letters in your Bible. In Hebrew this name had four letters—YHWH—and was pronounced something like "Yahweh." Out of honor and reverence to how holy God is, Jewish people substituted the word *Adonai*, which means "my Lord," rather than saying "Yahweh." So when we read *Lord* in the Bible, it refers to God's proper name. When we see it, it tells us that God wants to be known—not as a vague, distant deity, but as a person. And then he took another step toward us when he became a human in the person of Jesus, who said, "Come to me!" By covering us in his own holiness, Jesus made it possible for us to be known by a holy God.

Moses protested, "If I go to the people of Israel and tell them, 'The God of your ancestors has sent me to you,' they will ask me, 'What is his name?' Then what should I tell them?"

God replied to Moses, "I Am Who I Am. Say this to the people of Israel: I Am has sent me to you." God also said to Moses, "Say this to the people of Israel: Yahweh, the God of your ancestors—the God of Abraham, the God of Isaac, and the God of Jacob—has sent me to you. This is my eternal name, my name to remember for all generations."

EXODUS 3:13-15

 | **DISCUSSION STARTERS**

Who are some people you are around often but you don't know their names? What difference might it make if you knew their names?

What does God's name tell us about who he is? How would things have been different if God had never told us his name?

What are some ways we can show appropriate respect for God's name?

Are You a Sinner?

Have you ever known someone who had the chicken pox? Maybe it started with one little, red, itchy spot. Pretty soon that person had several itchy spots and it became obvious that the person was sick. But there didn't have to be a bunch of visible spots to know it was the chicken pox. When there was just one spot, it showed that the chicken pox virus was in that person's system.

Sin is like that. Just thinking or doing one wrong thing shows you have the fatal disease of sin. Just one sin reveals that you're a sinner.

"Now, wait a minute," you might want to say. "I'm a good person. I may have made some mistakes, but I'm not a sinner." None of us want to think of ourselves that way. But until we see ourselves as sinners, we'll think we have no need for Jesus. Jesus came to save sinners, not good people. He actually resists people who think they're good, and he is drawn to people who recognize their own deep sickness of sin.

We are not sinners because we sin. We sin because we're sinners. It is inside us, running through our bloodstreams. Sin is not merely a matter of breaking the Ten Commandments or any other list of dos and don'ts. More than what we do, it is who we are. We are all natural-born sinners.

But that's not the end of the story—there is hope for sinners like us. God knew we'd never be good enough, and he knew we'd need someone to save us from our deadly disease of sin. So he sent Jesus to be the cure for us. The good news of the gospel is that we can be transformed from guilty sinners into forgiven sinners through faith in Jesus.

> When Jesus heard this, he told them, "Healthy people don't need a doctor—sick people do. I have come to call not those who think they are righteous, but those who know they are sinners."
> *MARK 2:17*

> The person who keeps all of the laws except one is as guilty as a person who has broken all of God's laws.
> *JAMES 2:10*

> Everyone has sinned; we all fall short of God's glorious standard.
> *ROMANS 3:23*

🥤 | DISCUSSION STARTERS

Think of a time when you were really sick. What were some of your symptoms? In what ways is sin like a sickness?

What remedy or cure does God offer to people who are sick with sin?

Does it discourage you or encourage you to realize that you sin because you are a sinner? Why?

JANUARY

6

I pray that your hearts will be flooded with light so that you can understand the confident hope he has given to those he called—his holy people who are his rich and glorious inheritance. I also pray that you will understand the incredible greatness of God's power for us who believe him.
EPHESIANS 1:18-19

We keep on praying for you, asking our God to enable you to live a life worthy of his call. May he give you the power to accomplish all the good things your faith prompts you to do.
2 THESSALONIANS 1:11

Better than Chatting

Some social situations call for the skill of "chatting," or the art of casual conversation. It's the ability to talk pleasantly with someone you don't know well about stuff that doesn't matter all that much.

If we're not careful, we can find ourselves reducing prayer to "chatting" with God, limiting prayers to superficial topics, surface issues, never getting to the heart of things. Have you ever noticed that when people offer prayer requests, they are usually about physical needs and rarely about spiritual needs? We ask God to heal physical ailments, to provide safe travel, and to "be with us." It's not that God doesn't care about these things. He cares about us, and what matters to us matters to him. But prayer is much more than that. It's a spiritual process toward a spiritual end. God wants to do a deep work in our inner lives, rubbing off the rough edges and cleaning up our character. So why do we settle for talking to him only about the shallow stuff?

When our prayers move from the superficial to the significant, we find ourselves inviting God to do no less than a deep, transforming, life-changing work in our lives and in the lives of those we're praying for. We talk to him about our fears, we invite him into our failures, we confess the ways we fall short. We open up our lives for him to do a significant spiritual work.

 | **DISCUSSION STARTERS**

What kinds of things do you talk about when you "chat" with a person?

What kinds of things do you talk about when you have a meaningful conversation with someone you trust?

What are some spiritual matters you'd like your family to pray about for you?

We've Never Heard Anyone Speak like This!

Some speakers are hard to listen to—sometimes it is something about the person's voice, and other times the speaker is just boring, or what he or she is saying seems unimportant. So we tune the speaker out and daydream rather than listen.

No one who listened to Jesus speak got bored and tuned him out. People listened to him all day, not even wanting to take a break to eat. They followed him wherever he went, wanting to hear more. It wasn't that he was humorous, although he did tell interesting stories. And it wasn't that he was always easy to understand. People were often mystified by what he said, trying to figure out what it meant. His messages often caused controversy and discomfort, and he asked people to do hard things.

The people were amazed at Jesus' teaching—no doubt they got goose bumps. There was a sense of reality and authority to what he said that made their hair stand on end. What he said was profoundly true and in some cases profoundly troubling. What Jesus says both convicts us and comforts us. He speaks both judgment and salvation. No one else speaks like Jesus. And no one's teaching matters as much as his does.

🧂 | DISCUSSION STARTERS

What do you think it was like to hear Jesus teach on the hillside or in the Temple?

What are some things Jesus said that are troubling to you? What things are difficult to understand?

What are some things Jesus said that comfort you? What things challenge you?

The people were amazed at his teaching, for he taught with real authority— quite unlike the teachers of religious law.
MARK 1:22

When the crowds heard him say this, some of them declared, "Surely this man is the Prophet we've been expecting." Others said, "He is the Messiah.". . . So the crowd was divided about him. Some even wanted him arrested, but no one laid a hand on him.

When the Temple guards returned without having arrested Jesus, the leading priests and Pharisees demanded, "Why didn't you bring him in?"

"We have never heard anyone speak like this!" the guards responded.
JOHN 7:40-41, 43-46

The one thing I ask of the LORD—the thing I seek most—is to live in the house of the LORD all the days of my life, delighting in the LORD's perfections and meditating in his Temple.

PSALM 27:4

Take delight in the LORD, and he will give you your heart's desires.

PSALM 37:4

In my inner being I delight in God's law.

ROMANS 7:22, NIV

What We Want

Do you know how to get what you want from your parents or a teacher or a boss or a friend? Is it all in how you ask or in choosing just the right timing?

When we read Psalm 37:4, "Take delight in the LORD, and he will give you your heart's desires," we're tempted to see it as a formula for getting what we want from God. We might read it as, "Get close to God, and then he'll give you what you want." We might think that if we give God our obedience and interest and compliments, we can get what we want from him in return.

But delighting in God is not a way to get what we want from him. That is manipulation or bribery. Genuine delight has no ulterior motive, no additional demands. Delight is saying thank you to God for his many blessings, such as good food to eat, a house to live in, people who love us, and a school or a job to go to. But delight also means saying to God, "I will not worship these things by making them more important than you. And I will not demand them from you."

If we see this verse as a formula for getting what we want from God, we're settling for much less than what God is offering. *God wants to change what we want.* He wants to free us from the slavery of wanting what will never completely satisfy us. He wants to give us what he knows will completely satisfy us forever: himself.

 | ## DISCUSSION STARTERS

What are some things you take delight in? What makes you happy?

What is something you really want or have been asking God for? Do you think God will give it to you?

God wants to change what we want instead of just giving us whatever we desire. Why is that better?

Knowing God versus Knowing about God

Do you know your mail carrier? How about your grandparents? How about the Queen of England? How about your best friend? There are different ways of "knowing" people, aren't there? Some people we actually just know about. And even among those we know personally, there are different levels of knowing—we know some more intimately than others.

The Bible says that we are made to know God. But a person can know a lot *about* God and not really *know* him. We can be interested in theology (which is a fascinating subject!) and know the books and stories of the Bible, and hardly know God at all. We can also go to church and read lots of Christian books and be up on the latest teaching and yet not know God at all.

We get to know other people through personal interaction and involvement, by sharing life with them. We listen to what they say, observe how they interact with others, see what they value, find out what they enjoy. And it is similar with God. God is so magnificent that he is worth spending the rest of our lives listening to and studying and enjoying, so that we are constantly getting to know him better. As we get to know God better, things that confused us before about how God works begin to make more sense. Knowing him better helps us trust him more.

 | ## DISCUSSION STARTERS

Who are some of the people you know best? How did you get to know them?

What is the difference between knowing about God and knowing him?

In what way would you like to know God better than you do right now?

Those who wish to boast should boast in this alone: that they truly know me and understand that I am the LORD who demonstrates unfailing love and who brings justice and righteousness to the earth, and that I delight in these things. I, the LORD, have spoken!
JEREMIAH 9:24

This is the way to have eternal life—to know you, the only true God, and Jesus Christ, the one you sent to earth.
JOHN 17:3

Everything else is worthless when compared with the infinite value of knowing Christ Jesus my Lord.
PHILIPPIANS 3:8

If you look carefully into the perfect law that sets you free, and if you do what it says and don't forget what you heard, then God will bless you for doing it.
JAMES 1:25

Let the message about Christ, in all its richness, fill your lives.
COLOSSIANS 3:16

The word of God is alive and powerful. It is sharper than the sharpest two-edged sword, cutting between soul and spirit, between joint and marrow. It exposes our innermost thoughts and desires. Nothing in all creation is hidden from God. Everything is naked and exposed before his eyes, and he is the one to whom we are accountable.
HEBREWS 4:12-13

Joined to Jesus

When two people get married, it's usually because they want to be together. They want to spend the rest of their lives talking and listening to each other, spending time with each other, and caring for each other. Can you imagine two people who go through a marriage ceremony and never talk to each other again? Would that even be a real marriage?

When we join ourselves to Christ, we're not just going through a religious ceremony or one-time experience. We're entering into a personal relationship, a love relationship. And if we want to have a real connection with God, then we will spend the rest of our lives talking to him, enjoying being with him, and listening to him. It's not that we expect to hear an audible voice when he speaks to us. We listen to him by reading, thinking about, and memorizing his Word, the Bible. We draw strength from it and rely on it to help us make decisions. It makes us happy, and we like to listen.

If you were married to Mr. Smith, you might call yourself Mrs. Smith to show you were connected to Mr. Smith. Calling yourself a Christian is the same idea: It means that you are intimately connected to Christ. And the ways we relate to Christ day by day are through his Word and prayer. These are the ways we stay connected to him in an authentic and not just a ceremonial way. We get close and stay close to God by talking to him through prayer and listening to him as we read the Bible.

 **| DISCUSSION STARTERS**

What would you think about two people who had a wedding but never talked to each other?

What does it mean to really listen to God's Word and not just read it?

What should a person do who doesn't especially like to read the Bible?

Do You Feel the Burn?

Have you learned in science class how muscles develop and get bigger? Muscles develop by being pushed beyond their limits, which causes them to actually break down. It is in the recovery process that they are rebuilt stronger, firmer, and larger.

What this means is that if we want to build up our physical muscles, we have to repeatedly lift more weight than what is really comfortable for us. We have to keep lifting until we can feel our muscles beginning to burn a little. This burn is a sign that the muscle is breaking down and will come back bigger and stronger.

It's the burn that is uncomfortable when we exercise our bodies. And it's the burn that makes us uncomfortable when we exercise our spirits and souls. The truth is, we want to become stronger spiritually without struggle or suffering or pain. We want to develop spiritual muscles without the burn. But it doesn't work that way.

Do you want to keep going and keep growing in your faith? Do you want to know God better and love him more next year than you do today? Do you want to be more like him and do more for him? If so, then you've got to keep building your spiritual muscles by trusting him in new and bigger ways—even when it burns.

 | **DISCUSSION STARTERS**

Who do you know who has big muscles? How did that person get that way?

Have you ever felt the burn as you grew in your faith? What was that like?

If we develop stronger spiritual muscles, what might we be able to do in the future that we haven't been strong enough to do in the past?

Train yourself to be godly. "Physical training is good, but training for godliness is much better, promising benefits in this life and in the life to come."
1 TIMOTHY 4:7-8

He holds the whole body together with its joints and ligaments, and it grows as God nourishes it.
COLOSSIANS 2:19

Mark out a straight path for your feet so that those who are weak and lame will not fall but become strong.
HEBREWS 12:13

The Holiness of God

You get a completely different answer when you add 100 + 100 + 100 than when you multiply 100 x 100 x 100. When the angels cry out that God is "holy, holy, holy!" they aren't just repeating themselves or adding up God's holiness like a sum. They're saying that God's holiness is like perfection to the nth degree. It's perfection times perfection times perfection!

Holiness is a biblical term that means "to be set apart." It also describes purity or freedom from sin. The Bible speaks of "holy ground" (EXODUS 3:5), a "holy nation" (EXODUS 19:6), "holy garments" (EXODUS 28:2, NASB), a "holy city" (NEHEMIAH 11:1), "holy hands" (1 TIMOTHY 2:8), a "holy kiss" (ROMANS 16:16, NIV), and "holy faith" (JUDE 1:20). Almost anything can become holy if it is separated from what is commonplace and if it is devoted to God.

What does it mean that God is holy? God's holiness is simply his God-ness in everything he is, everything he says, and everything he does. He is not like us. He's not just a bigger, stronger, or better version of human beings. He is in a different category from us altogether. He is one of a kind, completely separate. He is holy. His holiness is his perfect self, to the nth degree. His holiness is what he is as God, which no one else is or ever will be.

No one is holy like the LORD!
There is no one besides you;
there is no Rock like our God.
1 SAMUEL 2:2

Holy, holy, holy is the LORD of Heaven's Armies! The whole earth is filled with his glory!
ISAIAH 6:3

Who will not fear you,
Lord, and glorify your name?
For you alone are holy.
REVELATION 15:4

 | **DISCUSSION STARTERS**

Have you ever heard someone repeat him- or herself over and over? Why do you think the person does that?

What do you think it means that God is holy? How can knowing about God's holiness change your life?

First Peter 1:15 says that "you must be holy in everything you do, just as God who chose you is holy." What is one area in your life where you want God's holiness to be more evident?

That's Not Fair!

We live in a world that teaches us, "The early bird gets the worm," "No pain, no gain," "There is no such thing as a free lunch," and "You get what you pay for." We buy the idea that people get what they deserve, at least in theory. Whenever we experience hardship or difficulty, we quickly say, "I don't deserve this!" Believing we have a right to fairness, we feel violated when we think we haven't gotten what we deserve.

On the surface, a perfectly fair world appeals to us. But would we really want to live in such a world? In a completely fair world, there is no room for grace—receiving what you don't deserve. There would be no room for mercy either—being spared from getting the punishment you do deserve. We deserve punishment but receive forgiveness; we deserve judgment but experience love; we deserve death but get showered with God's mercy.

Since we live in a world where we don't always get what we deserve and where we sometimes get what we don't deserve, we will experience loss. But this also means we can receive mercy. Ultimately it is not "fairness" we want from God. If he gave us what is fair—what we really deserve—we would have to pay for our sins. What we really want from God is justice (doing what is right) and mercy (not giving us the punishment we've earned). And we can be confident that his abundant mercy will keep us from getting what we really deserve.

 | **DISCUSSION STARTERS**

Can you think of a time when you said, "That's not fair"? How do we know what is fair?

Are there ways God is not fair but is right?

Do you want other people to treat you with fairness or with grace and mercy? Why?

When God our Savior revealed his kindness and love, he saved us, not because of the righteous things we had done, but because of his mercy.
TITUS 3:4-5

Have mercy on me, O God, because of your unfailing love. Because of your great compassion, blot out the stain of my sins.
PSALM 51:1

God had mercy on me so that Christ Jesus could use me as a prime example of his great patience with even the worst sinners. Then others will realize that they, too, can believe in him and receive eternal life.
1 TIMOTHY 1:16

Who's in Charge?

Have your parents or your teachers ever left you in charge of things at your house or in your classroom? "You're in charge," they say as they walk out the door. *Authority* means power and privilege. When people have authority, that means they've been trusted to lead other people. They have been given more responsibility than others have. They are able to determine and decide things, to make judgments, and to oversee certain rights and privileges.

Jesus said that God gave him "all authority in heaven and on earth." Jesus is in charge of this world and every-thing in it, as well as everything beyond it! There is noth-ing Jesus doesn't have authority over—nothing he doesn't have the right and the power to do with as he pleases.

Jesus showed this when he walked the earth. He had authority over disease, healing the sick. He had authority over nature, telling the storm to be still. He had authority over demons, commanding them to leave a man and enter into a herd of pigs. He had authority to forgive sin. He had authority over his own life, giving it up on the cross when it was the right time, and taking it up again three days later when he rose from the dead.

Many people in this world don't recognize the authority of Jesus. They think they're in charge of their own lives. But that is just an illusion. The day is coming when "at the name of Jesus every knee [will] bow, in heaven and on earth and under the earth, and every tongue confess that Jesus Christ is Lord" (PHILIPPIANS 2:10-11). On that day, no one will question who's in charge.

Jesus came and told his disciples, "I have been given all authority in heaven and on earth."
MATTHEW 28:18

The Father . . . has given the Son absolute authority to judge.
JOHN 5:22

This is the plan: At the right time he will bring everything together under the authority of Christ—everything in heaven and on earth.
EPHESIANS 1:10

 | **DISCUSSION STARTERS**

Think of things that Jesus is in charge of. Then go around the table naming some of those things.

Think of the people in your life who are in authority. How did they get their positions of authority? And where did Jesus' authority come from when he was on earth?

What is something you can do this week to show that Jesus is in charge of your life?

What Makes Jesus Cry?

We cry for all kinds of reasons—when we watch sad movies, when we're celebrating joyous occasions, when we skin our knees, when our feelings get hurt, when we're reunited with people we love, and when we say good-bye.

The Bible tells us about several times that Jesus cried. Jesus was fully human, with emotions like ours. What brought Jesus to tears? Jesus wept when his friend Lazarus died. But in some ways that's strange, because Jesus knew he was about to raise Lazarus from the dead. So why would he cry?

It troubled Jesus deeply when he saw Mary's despair over her brother's death and when he saw the wailing mourners with her. Perhaps he could see in her weeping and hear in their wailing a kind of unbelief. This unbelief robbed them of being able to grieve with hope and left them with only despair. As followers of Christ, we can't escape the pain of grief. But it is different for the believer than it is for those who do not know Christ—at least it should be. Jesus' tears weren't just because he was frustrated over their despairing grief. Jesus wept because he was personally pained at the hurt that death caused to people he loved. His tears were tears of compassion for Mary and Martha, and tears of determination, perhaps, to finish the work he came to do—to win a victory, once and for all, over the power of death. It breaks the heart of God that death has so much power to hurt those he loves. We see tears on the face of God because he feels the hurt and emptiness that death leaves in its wake, and he longs with us for the day when death is destroyed forever.

When Jesus saw [Mary] weeping and saw the other people wailing with her, a deep anger welled up within him, and he was deeply troubled. "Where have you put him?" he asked them.

They told him, "Lord, come and see." Then Jesus wept.
JOHN 11:33-35

He will wipe every tear from their eyes, and there will be no more death or sorrow or crying or pain. All these things are gone forever.
REVELATION 21:4

🧂🧂 | DISCUSSION STARTERS

What makes you cry? What do tears mean?

Is it okay to cry? Is it okay not to cry?

How does it make you feel to know that there are sometimes tears on the face of God?

Not everyone who calls out to me, "Lord! Lord!" will enter the Kingdom of Heaven.
MATTHEW 7:21

Examine yourselves to see if your faith is genuine. Test yourselves. Surely you know that Jesus Christ is among you; if not, you have failed the test of genuine faith.
2 CORINTHIANS 13:5

Examine Yourself

Have you ever known someone with diabetes? Many diabetics have to prick their fingers several times a day to draw blood to test the level of sugar in their bloodstreams. It is not something they can know just by feeling. They have to test themselves.

The Bible says that we need to test ourselves. Not by pricking our fingers, but by examining ourselves for evidence of genuine faith.

One way we can examine ourselves is to ask this question: Am I trusting Christ right now to make me right with God? Or is there something else I am trusting in to save me (like doing good works or coming from a family of faith or attending church)? Trusting Christ to save you is not a one-time thing, and it's not about reciting details about a conversion experience in your past. The work he did to save us happened one time, but he keeps saving us each day. If your testimony of saving faith is real, it should be a testimony of ongoing trust in Christ to save you and keep you faithful today and every day.

A second question to ask yourself is this: Is there evidence of the Holy Spirit making me new? Do I see growth in my life as the Holy Spirit works in me, producing love, joy, and peace? Do I have a growing love for God's Word and an increasing desire to center my life around God?

God doesn't intend for us to go through life fearful of whether or not our relationship with him is real. He wants us to be confident in our relationship with him—confident that he has his grip on us and won't let go. But Scripture also says, "Examine yourselves to see if your faith is genuine." It is a good thing to do a checkup on ourselves to see if the faith we claim is a reality in our lives.

 | ## DISCUSSION STARTERS

We generally don't like to take tests. Why is that?

What kinds of things change when a person becomes a believer in Christ?

When you think about examining yourself by asking the questions in today's devotion, what is your reaction? What can hold us back from taking a good look at our lives?

Impossible to Understand?

Have you ever opened the pages of a book only to discover it is written in another language that you don't know? Or have you ever opened a high-level textbook about a subject you know nothing about and it seems completely impossible to understand?

Sometimes people can feel that way when reading the Bible—it seems like it's in a foreign language or it's written at a level they can't comprehend. It's true that the Bible is like a treasure of knowledge that can be opened over and over throughout your lifetime, offering deeper levels of understanding. But no advanced degree or special experience is required to understand the Bible. Everything we need for salvation and for living the Christian life is clear in Scripture.

Understanding the Bible is more of a spiritual ability than an intellectual ability. God is the one who opens our minds so we can grasp what we read in his Word. "People who aren't spiritual can't receive these truths from God's Spirit. It all sounds foolish to them and they can't understand it, for only those who are spiritual can understand what the Spirit means" (1 Corinthians 2:14).

God makes Scripture understandable for people who don't know him but are reading it to find him. And he makes Scripture understandable to people who do know him but need help making sense of what they read. So when we come to something in the Bible we don't understand, we know that we have a fresh opportunity to discover something about God. We can ask for God's help and search the Scripture intently, believing that God will show us what we need to learn.

> The teaching of your word gives light, so even the simple can understand.
> **PSALM 119:130**

> All Scripture is inspired by God and is useful to teach us what is true and to make us realize what is wrong in our lives.
> **2 TIMOTHY 3:16**

> Such things were written in the Scriptures long ago to teach us.
> **ROMANS 15:4**

| DISCUSSION STARTERS

When was the last time you learned something new? How did you go about doing it?

What is something in the Bible that is hard for you to understand?

What is something in the Bible you understand better than you used to?

Anyone who listens to my teaching and follows it is wise, like a person who builds a house on solid rock. Though the rain comes in torrents and the floodwaters rise and the winds beat against that house, it won't collapse because it is built on bedrock. But anyone who hears my teaching and doesn't obey it is foolish, like a person who builds a house on sand. When the rains and floods come and the winds beat against that house, it will collapse with a mighty crash.

MATTHEW 7:24-27

Don't just listen to God's word. You must do what it says. Otherwise, you are only fooling yourselves. . . . But if you look carefully into the perfect law that sets you free, and if you do what it says and don't forget what you heard, then God will bless you for doing it.

JAMES 1:22, 25

What Are You Building On?

Do you know the song "The Wise Man Built His House upon the Rock"? It says that when the rains came down and the floods came up, the house on the rock stood firm, while the house on the sand went *splat*.

So what was the difference between the wise person and the foolish person? When we read the parable Jesus told, we see that they had many things in common. Both of them heard God's Word. In modern terms, it is as if they both attended church and sat through the sermon Sunday after Sunday. And both of them experienced the storm. They each faced trouble and difficulty. But the story tells us that the wise person's house did not collapse, while the foolish person's house fell with a mighty crash.

What does it mean to build your house on solid rock versus unstable sand? The difference is in the way you respond when you hear God's Word. One Bible version says that the wise person not only hears God's words but also "puts them into practice" (MATTHEW 7:24, NIV). The foolish person heard God's Word but ignored it. It is as if this person thought being in church was good enough. Wise people let God's Word change and shape them, strengthen and prepare them for when the storms of life come.

 | ## DISCUSSION STARTERS

Can someone lead in singing the song based on this parable? (If you don't know the song, you can look on the Internet or in a songbook to find the words.)

What was the difference between the wise person and the foolish person?

What can you do now to prepare for the storms of life that will surely come?

God's Dream

On August 28, 1963, Martin Luther King Jr. stood in front of the Lincoln Memorial and said, "I have a dream that one day on the red hills of Georgia, the sons of former slaves and the sons of former slave owners will be able to sit down together at the table of brotherhood. . . . I have a dream that my four little children will one day live in a nation where they will not be judged by the color of their skin but by the content of their character." His was an amazing, God-honoring dream. But it was just scratching the surface of God's ultimate dream, his plan for the redemption of all races.

God's dream is really more than a dream. It is a sure and coming reality that all of history is moving toward—the restoration of all things. It's bigger than how people of different skin colors and backgrounds relate to each other. It's about people from every race, every language, every tribe on the planet worshiping together around the throne of God. God's desire is for people from "every tribe and language and people and nation" to be united by our worship of our one and only King.

When we overcome our natural prejudices and join hands with people of other races to glorify God together, we experience a little bit of heaven here on earth.

 | **DISCUSSION STARTERS**

Who do you know of another race who also worships King Jesus?

What do you think is at the root of racial prejudice? How does God feel when his children of different races look down on each other?

What is something you can do to live out God's vision for racial harmony right where you are?

They sang a new song with these words: "You are worthy to take the scroll and break its seals and open it. For you were slaughtered, and your blood has ransomed people for God from every tribe and language and people and nation. And you have caused them to become a Kingdom of priests for our God. And they will reign on the earth."
REVELATION 5:9-10

People will come from all over the world—from east and west, north and south—to take their places in the Kingdom of God. And note this: Some who seem least important now will be the greatest then, and some who are the greatest now will be least important then.
LUKE 13:29-30

Turn Around

Have you ever driven or ridden in a car with a GPS that uses a computerized voice to give the driver directions? "In 300 yards, turn left," it will say. When you're using a system like this and you go off course, it will say, "Turn around when possible."

Jesus had a similar message for people who needed to go in a different direction in life. His message was, "Repent of your sins and turn to God." He was telling them that they were headed in a direction away from God, and now was the time to turn around and start moving in his direction.

Some people think that repentance is something we do one time when we turn toward Christ. But for the believer, repentance is really a way of life. As we walk with Jesus, the Holy Spirit continues to show us areas of our lives where we are headed in the wrong direction. He calls us to turn toward him and enter into the rest and freedom of repentance.

The most godly people you know are godly not because they never sin. They are godly because they are quick to repent. Rather than resisting God's instruction to turn around, they listen for his voice and quickly respond to his instruction, running in his direction.

 | DISCUSSION STARTERS

Have you ever found yourself headed the wrong direction? What were your options when you discovered you were going the wrong way?

Is it better to repent right away or to wait until later? Why?

What is the opposite of repentance?

Jesus began to preach, "Repent of your sins and turn to God, for the Kingdom of Heaven is near."
MATTHEW 4:17

I have come to call not those who think they are righteous, but those who know they are sinners and need to repent.
LUKE 5:32

The kind of sorrow God wants us to experience leads us away from sin and results in salvation. There's no regret for that kind of sorrow. But worldly sorrow, which lacks repentance, results in spiritual death.
2 CORINTHIANS 7:10

An Easy Load

Have you ever worn a pair of shoes that were too tight? Ugh! You feel the squeeze and can't wait to get them off! Or have you had to carry a backpack or suitcase that is too heavy for you? You can't wait to set it down.

When God gave his people the law, it was a high standard, but it wasn't unreasonable. Then, over the years, Jewish religious leaders added to the law God had given them, heaping up ridiculous rules no one could keep. People began to see God's law as confining and uncomfortable, like shoes that are too tight, and burdensome, like a load that's too heavy to carry.

This is what Jesus had in mind when he said, "Come to me, all of you who are weary and carry heavy burdens, and I will give you rest. Take my yoke upon you. . . . For my yoke is easy to bear, and the burden I give you is light." A yoke isn't something we hear much about today, but the people listening to Jesus would have known exactly what he was talking about. A yoke is a bar of wood that attaches to farm animals so they can carry their load. Perhaps Jesus was thinking of his days as a carpenter and how a carpenter adjusted every yoke he made to the build of the ox. In Jesus' day a farmer brought his ox to a carpenter, who measured its shoulders and then made a yoke to fit. Jesus was saying that his expectations fit just right.

Jesus invites everyone who is suffering under the burden of meaningless religion, ridiculous rules, and defeating guilt to come to him. He promises that he will not place a heavy set of unreasonable rules on us, and that what he asks of us will lead us into rest, not misery.

> Come to me, all of you who are weary and carry heavy burdens, and I will give you rest. Take my yoke upon you. Let me teach you, because I am humble and gentle at heart, and you will find rest for your souls. For my yoke is easy to bear, and the burden I give you is light.
> *MATTHEW 11:28-30*

> Loving God means keeping his commandments, and his commandments are not burdensome.
> *1 JOHN 5:3*

📖 | DISCUSSION STARTERS

Have you ever been given a job that was too hard for you? How did you feel?

Yokes often bound two oxen together to pull the load. What difference does it make to be "yoked" to Jesus?

What are some things the world says make life easier but that actually become a heavy load to carry?

What Is Sin?

Everyone who sins breaks the law; in fact, sin is lawlessness.
1 JOHN 3:4, NIV

Everything that does not come from faith is sin.
ROMANS 14:23, NIV

The world's sin is that it refuses to believe in me.
JOHN 16:9

Remember the first day of school when you were given a list of class rules? No chewing gum. Raise your hand before you speak. No talking while the teacher is talking. Many people see sin as simply breaking God's list of rules. They look at the Ten Commandments and the teachings of Jesus and think they are doing pretty well.

But we have to define sin the way the Bible does—in relationship to God's law and his perfect character. John writes that "sin is lawlessness." This goes to the root of all sinful actions and attitudes—our failure to trust God. Lawlessness is more than breaking the rules. It is living as though our own ideas are superior to God's. At the heart of all sin is a lie that says to each of us, "What you are doing or thinking or feeling or wanting is not really that bad, because other people are doing things that are much worse. Besides, you can't help it."

Sin isn't just limited to our failure to live up to a list of dos and don'ts given to us by God. In fact, many people have been deceived into thinking that things are okay between them and God because they don't do the things from the "don't" list, and they do at least a few things from the "do" list. But what they don't realize is that this is just being moral or a good citizen or a nice person. It isn't faith. And that means it won't be enough to save them. Only Jesus can do that.

 | ## DISCUSSION STARTERS

What are some of the rules in your classroom or workplace or home? How hard is it to follow those rules?

How would you describe what sin is?

If everything that doesn't come from faith is sin, does that mean it's possible to do good things and still be sinning? What makes it sin?

Planting the Right Seeds

When you plant flower seeds in your garden, do you expect to grow a pumpkin patch? Or when you plant a field of corn, do you expect to harvest green beans? Of course not! You know that what you harvest depends on the seeds you've planted.

It works the same way in our lives. We harvest what we plant. Sometimes we're surprised by the conflict and pain that our lives produce. But it is often because we've planted seeds of sinful attitudes and actions, and we are simply experiencing the natural outgrowth of what we've sown in our lives. It works the other way too. When we are more patient with others, when we respond to challenges with faith instead of fear, when we love people who are not very lovable, it is an outgrowth of seeds planted by the Spirit of God in our lives.

This is why we have to be careful about what kind of seeds we're planting in our hearts. If we want our lives to produce a crop of attitudes and relationships and accomplishments that are pleasing to God, we have to ask him to help us plant the right seeds.

| DISCUSSION STARTERS

Have you ever planted something in a garden before? What was the hardest part about it? What part was the most fun?

What kind of seeds are planted in your life when you read the Bible? when you watch television? when you talk to your friends?

What seeds would you like to plant in your life that will result in a good harvest for God someday?

Don't be misled—you cannot mock the justice of God. You will always harvest what you plant. Those who live only to satisfy their own sinful nature will harvest decay and death from that sinful nature. But those who live to please the Spirit will harvest everlasting life from the Spirit. So let's not get tired of doing what is good. At just the right time we will reap a harvest of blessing if we don't give up.

GALATIANS 6:7-9

Those who are peace-makers will plant seeds of peace and reap a harvest of righteousness.

JAMES 3:18

You are the salt of the earth. But what good is salt if it has lost its flavor? Can you make it salty again? It will be thrown out and trampled underfoot as worthless. You are the light of the world—like a city on a hilltop that cannot be hidden. No one lights a lamp and then puts it under a basket. Instead, a lamp is placed on a stand, where it gives light to everyone in the house.

MATTHEW 5:13-15

You must have the qualities of salt among yourselves and live in peace with each other.

MARK 9:50

Live clean, innocent lives as children of God, shining like bright lights in a world full of crooked and perverse people.

PHILIPPIANS 2:15

Preserve! Shine!

When we say, "Pass the salt" at the dinner table, it's because we want to sprinkle some on our food to enhance the flavor. But in Jesus' day, long before refrigerators, salt was used not just to season food but to preserve it. By calling us salt, Jesus was saying that we are part of his ministry of preservation, part of his plan to keep people from spoiling in a decaying world. As Christians, we are to promote healing and wholeness in a culture that is going bad without God.

Jesus also called us light, saying that we are part of his work of piercing through the darkness in a world that often does not want God. We are to shine the light on truth and show people how to find their way home to God. We are to be living examples of the difference Jesus makes in people's lives.

Our ability to preserve and shine is dependent on our connection to the source of true light and true saltiness: Jesus. On our own we cannot save or sustain anything, but Jesus has drawn us into the task he is already doing. His work has become our work. That goal begins to define not only what we do but who we are. When we are salt and light, we get to play a part in God's plan to redeem this dark and decaying world.

 | ## DISCUSSION STARTERS

Have you ever been in a place where it was really dark? How did it feel to be in the dark like that?

Where do you see decay in your city or school or neighborhood that could use some salt?

Where do you see darkness in your city or school or neighborhood that needs light?

God's Agenda

When people hide what they really want or what they're really trying to accomplish behind something else, we say they have a hidden agenda. It is a compliment when we say that someone is straightforward and honest, with no hidden agenda. And that is something we can say about God. He has made his agenda clear from the beginning. God's agenda is this: He plans to bless us. In other words, he wants to give us a full, rich life. God wants to pour out his goodness on us. That's his agenda.

Our problem with God's agenda is not that it is hidden, but that it simply seems too good to be true. We don't deserve God's blessing, and we can't earn it; it is a gift. In fact, when God chose to bless Abraham, he was no saint-in-training; he was more likely an idol-worshiper-in-training since his father worshiped other gods (SEE JOSHUA 24:2). But in his promise to Abraham in Genesis 12, God declared his agenda for all of history: to bless people from all nations of the earth through Abraham and his descendants. The blessing promised to Abraham comes to us through the most important of Abraham's descendants: Jesus Christ. Jesus is the blessing of God, given to us with no hidden agenda.

 | **DISCUSSION STARTERS**

Have you ever found out someone wasn't being straightforward with you about what that person wanted or what he or she was doing? How did that make you feel?

What are some examples of God's blessing you've seen in your life?

How can hard times or a guilty conscience be blessings from God?

I will make you into a great nation. I will bless you and make you famous, and you will be a blessing to others. I will bless those who bless you and curse those who treat you with contempt. All the families on earth will be blessed through you.
GENESIS 12:2-3

From his abundance we have all received one gracious blessing after another. For the law was given through Moses, but God's unfailing love and faithfulness came through Jesus Christ.
JOHN 1:16-17

Through Christ Jesus, God has blessed the Gentiles with the same blessing he promised to Abraham.
GALATIANS 3:14

The instructions of the LORD are perfect, reviving the soul. The decrees of the LORD are trustworthy, making wise the simple. The commandments of the LORD are right, bringing joy to the heart. The commands of the LORD are clear, giving insight for living. . . . They are more desirable than gold, even the finest gold. They are sweeter than honey, even honey dripping from the comb. They are a warning to your servant, a great reward for those who obey them.

PSALM 19:7-8, 10-11

A Book Worth Rereading

Can you think of any book you'd want to spend your whole life reading over and over again? There probably aren't many books like that, but the Bible is no ordinary book! Psalm 19 gives us a list of good reasons why we'll never outgrow our need to keep reading and studying the Bible.

1. Reading the Bible brings life to our souls. It helps us come alive again when we feel dead toward God and weary about life.
2. It makes simple people wise. In other words, we don't have to be afraid that we can't understand the Bible or will be confused by it. When we are seeking to know him, God gives us more understanding than we could have on our own.
3. It brings joy to the heart. When we keep getting to know someone we love, it makes us happy. Studying the Bible helps us know God better.
4. It gives direction for how to live. Reading the Bible gets us thinking about what really matters and moves us beyond superficial stuff.
5. It is better than money. Reading God's Word feeds our contentment in God rather than our greed and our desire for more. It makes us want what will truly make us happy forever.
6. It is sweeter than honey. Reading the Bible isn't an unpleasant duty; it's an enjoyable privilege. It's a satisfying treat, not a boring chore.
7. It is rewarding. Reading God's Word pays off—now and in the future. It's a worthwhile investment we will never regret.

 | **DISCUSSION STARTERS**

How is the Bible different from other books you've read?

What good things have you learned from the Bible?

What could you do to add to your enjoyment of the Bible?

Our Last Breath

Have you ever thought about the question, What would you do if you found out you only had a few months to live? Some people say they would go on an extended exotic vacation. Others say they would spend all their time with people they love.

Many people are forced to face that question when they receive a diagnosis for a fatal illness. But the Bible says that asking ourselves that question—thinking about the reality of the shortness of life—is a wise way to live all the time. Understanding death is a healthy part of life.

When we are healthy and everyone we love is healthy, it is easy to avoid thinking about death. But when someone we know gets very sick or when someone we love dies, we are forced to face the reality that our bodies will die at some point too. While we tend to expect to live eighty or ninety years, there are no guarantees of how long we're given on this earth.

Thinking occasionally about dying is not a morbid, depressing thing. It can actually be a life-giving exercise. It forces us to remember what Christ has done for us on the cross, and it builds our confidence in his victory over eternal death. We exercise our faith muscles when we seriously consider our own deaths someday and, by faith, choose to believe that death will not be the end for us. Because of our connectedness with Jesus, we will take our last breath here and our next breath in his presence, where we will never have to face death again.

> Teach us to realize the brevity of life, so that we may grow in wisdom.
> **PSALM 90:12**

> Your life is like the morning fog—it's here a little while, then it's gone.
> **JAMES 4:14**

> Better to spend your time at funerals than at parties. After all, everyone dies—so the living should take this to heart.
> **ECCLESIASTES 7:2**

 | DISCUSSION STARTERS

What things come to mind when you think about death?

What fears do you have when you think about the end of your life?

What hope could you offer to someone who is ill and facing death?

We're All Poor

Is there something you really want? Something that you want so much that you are willing to work for it and save for it so you can buy it?

What if what you really want is to be in good standing with God? Can you save up enough good works, enough proper behavior, enough denying yourself to buy God's favor? Unfortunately not. God doesn't accept people who think they have some sort of spiritual currency or money to be able to buy his blessing. In fact, he says that the only people he accepts are those who recognize that they not only don't have enough to offer God but that they have absolutely nothing to offer God. "Blessed are the poor in spirit," Jesus said (MATTHEW 5:3, NIV). He wasn't talking about people who are financially poor but people who are spiritually poor, people who are spiritually bankrupt.

Only when we see that we have nothing to offer God to gain his favor—no family connections, no self-sacrifice, not even any natural tendency to love him—only then are we in a position to receive what God wants to give to us. And then he gives us everything. Jesus is the one who receives all things from God the Father, and he shares all those good things with us—when we come to him with empty hands and empty pockets, empty of our own efforts, with nothing to offer him.

No one is righteous—not even one. No one is truly wise; no one is seeking God. All have turned away; all have become useless. No one does good, not a single one.
ROMANS 3:10-12

God saved you by his grace when you believed. And you can't take credit for this; it is a gift from God. Salvation is not a reward for the good things we have done, so none of us can boast about it.
EPHESIANS 2:8-9

You say, "I am rich. I have everything I want. I don't need a thing!" And you don't realize that you are wretched and miserable and poor and blind and naked.
REVELATION 3:17

 | DISCUSSION STARTERS

What would be the most difficult part of being financially poor?

What does it mean to be poor in spirit? What is the opposite of being poor in spirit?

Why is it so difficult to admit that we're spiritually poor?

News Flash: You Were Dead!

Sometimes people will say, "I have good news and bad news; which do you want first?" And though Scripture is filled with good news (*gospel* actually means "good news"), it also contains some very bad news. In fact, the bad news may be worse than you think.

A number of people might think of themselves as spiritually sick and in need of assistance. They recognize that they are not who they need to be or want to be, and they admit that Jesus can help them become a better person and keep them out of hell. But the doctor's diagnosis on every one of us is much worse than "very sick." We're dead. We need much more than a self-improvement project or a boost of goodness. We need a miracle. The miracle of a dead person coming alive.

How can a dead soul come to life? Only God himself can do it. Just as God breathed into Adam the breath of life and formed the world out of nothing, God can make a dead person alive.

If you're a believer, the reality of your past is that you were dead and completely without hope. You had no spiritual pulse, and there were no signs of potential life. But then God breathed his life into you! Now you are alive to God—thinking about him, wanting him, listening to him speak to you through Scripture, allowing him to change you and shape you. And your future reality is no longer death; it's life—eternal life.

> Once you were dead because of your disobedience and your many sins. . . . But God is so rich in mercy, and he loved us so much, that even though we were dead because of our sins, he gave us life when he raised Christ from the dead.
>
> *EPHESIANS 2:1, 4-5*

> You were dead because of your sins and because your sinful nature was not yet cut away. Then God made you alive with Christ, for he forgave all our sins.
>
> *COLOSSIANS 2:13*

| DISCUSSION STARTERS

Tell about a time you went to the doctor when you were sick. How did the doctor help you?

What do you think it means to be spiritually dead?

Are there certain areas in your life that feel dead (something inside yourself, a relationship, a habit, a way of thinking)? How might God work to bring that dead part back to life?

Jesus replied, "I tell you the truth, unless you are born again, you cannot see the Kingdom of God."

"What do you mean?" exclaimed Nicodemus. "How can an old man go back into his mother's womb and be born again?"

Jesus replied, . . . "Humans can reproduce only human life, but the Holy Spirit gives birth to spiritual life."

JOHN 3:3-4, 6

You have been born again, but not to a life that will quickly end.

1 PETER 1:23

Born a Second Time?

The majority of people who live in the United States describe themselves as "Christian." But that means different things to different people. For some, since they are not Muslim or Buddhist or Jewish, and they believe there is a God and that Jesus was real, they call themselves Christians. But many of those people would not be willing to call themselves "born-again" Christians. This is a label given to believers who are a little more radical about Jesus than those who simply want to go to church and follow the teachings of Christ that fit comfortably into their lives.

But there's no such thing as a Christian who has not been born again. That's what Jesus said. He said that the only way anyone has any sort of genuine spiritual life is if he or she has experienced the miracle of being born a second time—not physically this time, but spiritually. Being born again is not just about changing—although a person who has been born again *will* change. It means the birth of a whole new life brought about by the Holy Spirit.

Jesus said that being born again is not just one form of saving faith or an addition to it; it is the *only* form of saving faith. He said that "*no one* can enter the Kingdom of God" without it (JOHN 3:5, emphasis added). It is impossible to become a baby and be born all over again. That would require a miracle.

And that's the point.

 | **DISCUSSION STARTERS**

Can you think of a time when you made such a mess of something that, rather than fixing it, you just wanted to start over again?

What do you think people mean when they describe someone as a "born-again Christian"? What do you think Jesus meant when he talked about being born again?

How is being born again spiritually a miracle?

Someone Is Lying to You

You know what it's like to really, really want something, right? There's nothing wrong with wanting; desire is a good thing. We all come equipped with desires we need for life—like the desire for food, relationships with other people, approval, greatness, rest. God gave us these desires for our good, to serve us.

But sin takes healthy desires meant to serve us, and turns them into unhealthy obsessions that make us slaves. Sin twists our healthy desires so they become liars. Our desires, when clouded by sin, lie to us with half-truths, like "It will feel good." And it might feel good—for a while. But eventually sinful desires turn on us and destroy us. Sin turns our God-given desire for food into the lie that eating more food than we really need will make us happier or that denying ourselves food will make us more acceptable. Sin turns our God-given desire for love into the lie that we have to do whatever someone wants us to do in order to get it. Sin twists our desire for security into an addiction for money and more stuff. Sin takes our healthy desire for success and makes it an obsession with work and competition. Sin twists the truth, and lies outright. So we have to recognize the voice of the liar and confront the lies of sin with the truth of Scripture. And the truth is God wants all our desires to be fulfilled—in him.

🧂 | DISCUSSION STARTERS

What are some of the things we want that are bad for us? How are they good desires that have been twisted by sin?

What are some lies people you know have bought into? What lies do you find yourself tempted to buy into?

What are some ways you can fight these lies?

Temptation comes from our own desires, which entice us and drag us away. These desires give birth to sinful actions. And when sin is allowed to grow, it gives birth to death.
JAMES 1:14-15

Live as God's obedient children. Don't slip back into your old ways of living to satisfy your own desires.
1 PETER 1:14

Take delight in the LORD, and he will give you your heart's desires.
PSALM 37:4

God's Tattoo

Have you ever seen someone with a person's name tattooed onto an arm or ankle? Some people tattoo the name of the person they love on their bodies as an expression of their devotion to the person, and as a constant reminder of this person who is precious to them.

When God's people complained to God that they thought he had abandoned them, God told them, "I have written your name on the palms of my hands." It's as if he held out his open hands to those who felt forgotten by him and said, "Look. You will see something—someone—too precious to me to ever forget."

If you could look at God's hands, you would see that he has tattooed your name there because he loves you. He wants to keep you in the center of his attention. He thinks about you all the time. He watches over you. When he sees your name there, your concerns become his concerns. He sees not only your name but every aspect of your life—every joy, every struggle, every need. You are never off his mind, out of his sight, or away from his loving care.

Jerusalem says, "The LORD has deserted us; the Lord has forgotten us."

"Never! Can a mother forget her nursing child? Can she feel no love for the child she has borne? But even if that were possible, I would not forget you! See, I have written your name on the palms of my hands. Always in my mind is a picture of Jerusalem's walls in ruins."
ISAIAH 49:14-16

They will see his face, and his name will be written on their foreheads.
REVELATION 22:4

 | ## DISCUSSION STARTERS

Do you think you would ever get a tattoo? Why or why not? Does your family have opinions or rules regarding tattoos?

Have you ever felt like God forgot about you? What are some things you know about God that can give you confidence that he will never abandon you?

Revelation 22:4 describes people in heaven having Jesus' name on their foreheads. Why do you think we will have this kind of "tattoo" in heaven?

God on Display

Some people say they can't believe in anything they can't see. But there are plenty of things we can't see but we still believe in—like the air we breathe to stay alive or the gravity that keeps us on the ground. Even though we can't see air, our lives depend on it. Even though we can't spot gravity, we feel its effects every day.

It's the same with God. We can't see him, but our lives depend on him and we experience evidence of him every day. Even though we can't see him with our eyes, the Bible says that he has made the truth about himself obvious to us. All people everywhere have been given a deep, inner sense that God is real. While many people reject this truth about God's existence, those who respond to it in faith discover that this inner awareness of God becomes stronger and more defined. That's how they can say they know God.

Along with the internal knowledge God gives to every person, nature offers clear evidence of God's existence. In some sense, every created thing proves that God is real and God is good. We look into the sky and see the sun and the clouds, the moon and the stars. By their very existence, they seem to shout that a powerful and wise Creator made them and sustains them. But nothing gives as clear a witness to the existence of God as we do. It only makes sense that an intricate, skillful, communicative, living creature like a human being only could have been created by an all-powerful, all-wise Creator.

 | **DISCUSSION STARTERS**

What are some things that amaze you about how your body works and how nature works? How do those things speak to you about the existence of God?

Naturalistic evolution is the belief that the universe evolved by the random forces of matter, time, and chance. What do you think?

If someone asked you how you know there's a God, what would you say?

> The heavens proclaim the glory of God. The skies display his craftsmanship. Day after day they continue to speak; night after night they make him known.
>
> **PSALM 19:1-2**

> They know the truth about God because he has made it obvious to them. For ever since the world was created, people have seen the earth and sky. Through everything God made, they can clearly see his invisible qualities—his eternal power and divine nature. So they have no excuse for not knowing God.
>
> **ROMANS 1:19-20**

FEBRUARY

3

You want what you don't have, so you scheme and kill to get it. You are jealous of what others have, but you can't get it, so you fight and wage war to take it away from them. Yet you don't have what you want because you don't ask God for it.

JAMES 4:2

When you call, the LORD will answer. "Yes, I am here," he will quickly reply.

ISAIAH 58:9

In my distress I prayed to the LORD, and the LORD answered me and set me free.

PSALM 118:5

Have you ever tried to talk to someone who was distracted? Maybe the person was listening to music or reading something or deep in thought, and you felt like he or she was ignoring you.

But what about God? Does he ever ignore us when we talk to him? When we pray, can we be confident God will listen and respond in some way, or does he sometimes ignore our prayers? We often wonder if prayer can really change anything. But the Bible promises us that God always listens, and it shows us that our prayers have an impact on what we receive from God.

When James said, "You don't have what you want because you don't ask God for it," he was implying that our failure to pray and ask God for what we need deprives us of what God would have given us if we'd asked. And when Jesus instructed us to "keep on asking, and you will receive what you ask for" (MATTHEW 7:7), he was making a clear connection between asking God for things and receiving them from him. So evidently, when we ask, God responds. This doesn't mean he's like a genie and he'll automatically give us whatever we want. But he does promise to hear us and respond—even if his response is not the response we were looking for.

God is happy when we depend on him. So he never ignores our heartfelt requests for his presence and his power in our lives. In prayer, we take a step in his direction, and he comes close to us. Through prayer, not only do we experience God's activity and involvement in our world, but we also have the opportunity to be involved in a significant way in the work of God's Kingdom. We can be confident that even though other people may ignore us, God never will.

 | **DISCUSSION STARTERS**

Have you ever tried to talk to someone only to have him or her ignore you? How did that feel?

Have you ever felt like God was ignoring you? When you feel that way, is that really true?

How have you experienced God's response to your prayers?

What Will Spill out of You?

Have you ever drunk out of a Styrofoam cup? If so, you know you have to be careful, because if you accidentally poke a hole in it, the liquid inside will come spewing out.

Our lives are a little bit like that cup. When problems poke a hole in our plans or when we feel pressured by our circumstances, whatever is inside of us comes spilling out. We can't help it. It just comes out. Sometimes it's words of frustration, and sometimes it is words of concern about someone else. So we have to ask ourselves, *What comes spilling out when I'm frustrated, made fun of, inconvenienced, or hurt? Is my natural response to be angry or defensive? Or am I finding that I can respond with joy, selflessness, patience, and kindness?*

The Bible teaches that the Holy Spirit actually comes to live inside us when we become believers. As we allow the Holy Spirit to fill us and control us, he will be what spills out of our lives. When we submit to the Holy Spirit, he changes our attitudes, alters our perspectives, and orders our steps. Then, when our lives are bumped by hard times, what comes spilling out is the work of the Holy Spirit on our attitudes and character. We find ourselves responding in kindness to those who are unkind to us, in compassion to those who are in need, and in gentleness to those who treat us harshly. And those are all good things to see spilling out of a person's life, don't you think?

The LORD is my strength and shield. I trust him with all my heart. He helps me, and my heart is filled with joy. I burst out in songs of thanksgiving.
PSALM 28:7

May you always be filled with the fruit of your salvation—the righteous character produced in your life by Jesus Christ.
PHILIPPIANS 1:11

Be filled with the Holy Spirit.
EPHESIANS 5:18

 | ## DISCUSSION STARTERS

If you poked a hole in a balloon, what would come out? How about a juice box? a bottle of glue? a bottle of chocolate syrup? a bag of beans?

Think about the last few days at your house. What has come out when various people have been poked by problems? Have you seen a natural reaction or the fruit of the Spirit?

Think of someone who spills out good things when facing tough times. In what ways would you like to be more like that person?

Are You Adopted?

Do you know any families who have experienced the miracle of adding to their family through adoption? Adoption is a legal process that creates a new, permanent relationship between a parent and a child where one didn't exist before.

God loves adoption! It was his good idea. The Bible says that even before the creation of the world, God decided he would adopt us into his own family. You see, God knew that every human being since Adam and Eve would sin and that we would need a way to be brought back into his family. And to all who believe in him, he gives the right to become his children.

But not everyone has been adopted into God's family. The Bible says that those who do not believe in Christ are called "children of wrath" and "sons of disobedience" (EPHESIANS 2:2-3, NASB). That's what we used to be. But God takes people who once wanted nothing to do with him—and he gives them the special privileges of being his children!

Something incredible happens when we are adopted: We go from being outsiders to being beloved children. Because God is our daddy, we can cry out to him, confident that nothing can cause him to stop loving and caring for us. He's our dad, and we've been permanently adopted into his family.

To all who believed him and accepted him, he gave the right to become children of God.
JOHN 1:12

You received God's Spirit when he adopted you as his own children. Now we call him, "Abba, Father."
ROMANS 8:15

God decided in advance to adopt us into his own family by bringing us to himself through Jesus Christ. This is what he wanted to do, and it gave him great pleasure.
EPHESIANS 1:5

 | **DISCUSSION STARTERS**

Do you know someone who is adopted?

Moses and Esther are two people in the Old Testament who were adopted. How does their adoption show God's divine role in adoption?

What do you think it means to be able to call God "Abba," or Daddy?

Something Has Come Between Us

What happens when a child disobeys his or her parents? Does it mean that the parents disown the child or kick him or her out of the house? Of course not! They're family. But there is a breakdown in their relationship. The disobedience has to be dealt with in order to get rid of the uncomfortable distance and invisible barrier that has come between them.

It is similar when we, as believers, disobey God. When we sin, we still have a place in God's family, and we're secure in his love. But our sin causes him deep sadness. It puts up a barrier between him and us until we admit we were wrong and then change our attitudes and actions.

But if there is no sense of loss or sadness over sin, and no desire to make things right with God again after a person sins, it should be a huge wake-up call. It indicates that there may be no real, saving relationship there at all. It might be easy to brush off our own sins or other people's sins as no big deal. But when a person sins and keeps sinning with no sadness about that sin—no tug toward change—there is definitely something broken in the person's relationship with God. Or perhaps there is no real relationship with him at all, just some form of being religious.

When you sin and you are pained by the distance your sin has brought between you and God, thank him for that pain. It is a sign to you of your saving relationship with him. And if you feel no sense of loss when your sin comes between you and God, perhaps you need to ask God to show you what it means to truly have him as your Father.

> Do not bring sorrow to God's Holy Spirit by the way you live. Remember, he has identified you as his own, guaranteeing that you will be saved on the day of redemption.
>
> *EPHESIANS 4:30*

> Listen! The LORD's arm is not too weak to save you, nor is his ear too deaf to hear you call. It's your sins that have cut you off from God.
>
> *ISAIAH 59:1-2*

 | ## DISCUSSION STARTERS

How does it feel when something has come between you and your parents or you and a friend?

How does a person know he or she is part of God's family?

What are some ways sin hurts a believer and those around him or her?

The Shadow of Death

Dr. Donald Grey Barnhouse was one of America's greatest preachers. His first wife died from cancer when she was in her thirties, leaving behind three children under the age of twelve. He had been searching for the words to help his children understand that death is not final for the person who knows Jesus, when a moving van drove by their car. As it passed, the shadow of the truck swept over the car. He turned to his children and said, "Would you rather be run over by the truck or by its shadow?"

His children said, "Well, of course, Dad, we'd rather be run over by the shadow. A shadow can't hurt us."

Then he explained that the truck of death ran over Jesus so that only death's shadow can run over us. He said, "Mommy went through the valley of the shadow of death. There is no pain there."

The "shadow of death" is the experience of physical death that sweeps over every person who lives and dies in this world. But the reason death is only a shadow for the believer is because the darkness of death is something we pass through, not something that destroys us. For the believer, death is just a passageway into a fuller, richer life in the presence of God.

Even though I walk through the valley of the shadow of death, I will fear no evil, for you are with me; your rod and your staff, they comfort me.
PSALM 23:4, NIV

He will remove the cloud of gloom, the shadow of death that hangs over the earth. He will swallow up death forever!
ISAIAH 25:7-8

The people who sat in darkness have seen a great light. And for those who lived in the land where death casts its shadow, a light has shined."
MATTHEW 4:16

 | **DISCUSSION STARTERS**

Think about the truck and its shadow. What is the difference between having the shadow cover you and the truck run over you?

Why do you suppose we think of death as a dark place?

What is God's promise to those who walk in the valley of the shadow of death? What does that promise mean to you?

Are You Changing?

People can change a lot of things about themselves. They can change their hair color, their names, and the people they spend time with. And there are some things they can't change—certain physical characteristics, the families they came from, and their natural personality types. When it comes to changing our habits or ways of thinking or the ways we respond to things, sometimes we feel powerless. *That's just the way I am,* we think. *I'll never change.*

But we are not on our own when it comes to change. If we are connected to God and open to the ways he wants to work on us and in us, he will change us from the inside out. Then we won't be stuck committing the same old sins and thinking the same destructive thoughts and feeling the same defeated feelings. Paul suggests that we are changed as we look at the face of Jesus. So if we want to change to be more like Jesus, we need to look toward him, think about him, and listen to him. This is the key to changing to become like him.

🧂🧂 | DISCUSSION STARTERS

How have you changed over the past year? How would you like to change in the coming year?

What things about yourself do you need to accept as part of the way God made you?

What things about yourself have you accepted as "just the way you are" that need to be changed to be more like Jesus?

All of us who have had that veil removed can see and reflect the glory of the Lord. And the Lord—who is the Spirit—makes us more and more like him as we are changed into his glorious image.
2 CORINTHIANS 3:18

The LORD your God will change your heart and the hearts of all your descendants, so that you will love him with all your heart and soul and so you may live!
DEUTERONOMY 30:6

This same Good News that came to you is going out all over the world. It is bearing fruit everywhere by changing lives, just as it changed your lives from the day you first heard and understood the truth about God's wonderful grace.
COLOSSIANS 1:6

Where Are You Planted?

The world looks very different from the window of an airplane, doesn't it? From the sky you can follow the pattern of farmland planted with crops as well as the crisscross of roads running through a city. You can trace a river or stream as it winds its way through the land. And along the edges of the river you usually see a lot of green growth. Sometimes plants far away from the river dry up due to lack of moisture, but the trees by the river have a ready supply of water that keeps them green and growing.

In Psalm 1 we see a picture of the kind of people who are especially happy and satisfied in life, the kind of people who are green and growing because of where they have put down roots. They're people who say no to things that are wrong—things that are underhanded or outright evil. They choose their friends carefully, resisting the influence of people who give no thought to God. They don't follow the crowd in making fun of faith or the faithful. But they say a glad yes to God. They read and think about God's Word in the morning, throughout the day, and as they go to sleep at night—not because they have to but because they want to. It makes them happy.

When we come to God, he plants us where we can draw from his stream of living water. As our roots go deep, we grow and get strengthened.

Oh, the joys of those who do not follow the advice of the wicked, or stand around with sinners, or join in with mockers. But they delight in the law of the LORD, meditating on it day and night. They are like trees planted along the riverbank, bearing fruit each season. Their leaves never wither, and they prosper in all they do. But not the wicked! They are like worthless chaff, scattered by the wind.
PSALM 1:1-4

I am like a tree whose roots reach the water, whose branches are refreshed with the dew.
JOB 29:19

 | ## DISCUSSION STARTERS

What do you know about how trees "drink" water?

How can you relate to the three things this happy person says no to in Psalm 1?

What do fruitfulness and growth look like in the life of a Christian?

God's Masterpiece

Do you sometimes struggle with the way God has made you—the shape or size of your body, the personality you have, the abilities you were given? It's easy to allow the way we look to define who we are, but Paul says we are God's masterpiece. What does he mean?

Antonio Stradivari made more than one thousand violins, harps, guitars, violas, and cellos during the seventeenth and eighteenth centuries. Each Stradivarius is a treasured masterpiece—no other instrument can compare to its sound. It is not made to sit on a shelf to be admired for its beauty but to be played—to be put into the hands of a master musician to create beautiful music.

You are a masterpiece, not like the Mona Lisa, which hangs in a museum behind thick glass. You are like a Stradivarius violin, whose true beauty and value are seen and experienced in its usefulness—especially when it is used by a master.

Being used by the Master, Jesus, in this hurting world is an exciting experience! The reason it feels so good to offer food to someone who's hungry, a coat to someone who's cold, friendship to someone who's lonely, a home to a child who's alone is because this is what we were made for. This is the joy of the Master making our lives into a masterpiece he can use.

 | ## DISCUSSION STARTERS

Has God ever used you to help someone else? What did that feel like?

Who have you seen God use to do his work in the world?

What are some ways God has created you that make you a masterpiece? How can he use those traits or abilities to help other people?

> We are God's masterpiece. He has created us anew in Christ Jesus, so we can do the good things he planned for us long ago.
> *EPHESIANS 2:10*

> All glory to God, who is able, through his mighty power at work within us, to accomplish infinitely more than we might ask or think.
> *EPHESIANS 3:20*

> I am certain that God, who began the good work within you, will continue his work until it is finally finished on the day when Christ Jesus returns.
> *PHILIPPIANS 1:6*

Not Your Final Destination

Imagine getting a letter telling you that you have been given the country of Japan. You hop on the next plane and go there, and you spend the rest of your life living there in a camper. Your kids live in the camper next door, and their kids live in the next camper over. You move from place to place, with no home, no citizenship, and no rights—always as an outsider.

This is what it was like for Abraham living in the land of Canaan that God had promised him. We might expect that if God had promised Abraham a new country he would have made sure Abraham felt at home there. But it wasn't like that. Instead, Abraham made his home in the Promised Land "like a foreigner." He lived in tents, as did his son and his son's son. In fact, the only land Abraham ever owned in Canaan was the cave in which he buried his wife, Sarah.

But Abraham didn't want to make himself at home there anyway. He was "looking forward to a city with eternal foundations." Evidently, Abraham's greatest hopes and dreams for a homeland were invested not in earthly Canaan but in his heavenly homeland, where there would be no more moving from place to place in temporary lodging. He would finally be home. Peter says we should live this way too—not putting down our roots too deep here on this earth, because our true focus is on our eternal home in heaven.

Even when he reached the land God promised him, he lived there by faith—for he was like a foreigner, living in tents. And so did Isaac and Jacob, who inherited the same promise. Abraham was confidently looking forward to a city with eternal foundations, a city designed and built by God.

HEBREWS 11:9-10

Dear friends, I warn you as "temporary residents and foreigners" to keep away from worldly desires that wage war against your very souls.

1 PETER 2:11

 | **DISCUSSION STARTERS**

What are your favorite things about your home? What do you miss most when you're away from home?

How do people live differently when they see themselves as "temporary residents and foreigners" during life on earth?

What disappointments or difficulties are you facing right now? How might it help us face these situations to remember that earth isn't our final destination?

A Messy Human like Us

Being human is messy. Bodies take in food and water, and in return produce fingernails and toenails, phlegm, that crusty stuff in your eyes, urine, blood, earwax, dandruff, and other things we don't need to discuss—especially at the dinner table!

Jesus was willing to be human in all its messiness. Jesus had to let Mary change his diaper. He went through puberty. He was susceptible to disease and had surging hormones. Jesus got hungry and sleepy, his muscles ached after a hard day in the carpenter's shop, his nose got sunburned, and his lips got chapped.

Jesus became absolutely human, not just in body, but in mind. Jesus went to school as a child. And he didn't sit in the front row with all the answers automatically programmed into him. The Bible says that Jesus learned just like we do: "Jesus grew in wisdom and in stature" (LUKE 2:52). He thought like a child before he thought like a man.

Jesus was also fully human in his emotions. He felt the range of human emotions that we feel. When Lazarus died, Jesus "was deeply moved in spirit and troubled" (JOHN 11:33, NIV), and he even wept at his friend's death (11:35). The Lord experienced joy (SEE JOHN 15:11) and anger (SEE MARK 3:5) and even surprise (SEE LUKE 7:9; MARK 6:6).

We had no choice about being made of flesh and blood, but Jesus chose to be human. While still being completely divine and completely holy, he also willingly took hold of the messiness of being a person. He entered into our reality: walking, breathing, and living in our world.

> The child [Jesus] grew up healthy and strong.
> **LUKE 2:40**

> For forty days and forty nights [Jesus] fasted and became very hungry.
> **MATTHEW 4:2**

> Jesus, tired from the long walk, sat wearily beside the well about noontime.
> **JOHN 4:6**

 | **DISCUSSION STARTERS**

What kind of normal human things do you think Jesus experienced?

What is a difficult experience or struggle you're facing right now? How does it help you to know that Jesus understands the struggles of being human?

Jesus didn't just live as a human; he also died and was resurrected as a human. How does that give us hope as human beings who will die one day?

Unfailing Love

"That's it! I can't take it anymore!" Your friend has hurt you one too many times and you've had it. You decide the friendship is over.

That's how we tend to love other people. Our love has limits. And when we reach our limit of another person's rudeness, coldness, rejection, or betrayal, our love comes to its end. As humans we are sinful, changeable, and unfaithful, and even though we want to love others well and love them faithfully, we fail.

But God is not like that. His love doesn't have limits—it's not like human love. Paul writes, "Love never gives up, never loses faith, is always hopeful, and endures through every circumstance" (1 CORINTHIANS 13:7). He's drawing a picture of ideal love—something we can never live up to. Only God can love this way. His is the only love we can completely count on. And we can be confident that it will not fail, now or in eternity.

Sometimes when something hard or painful happens in our lives, we think God's love has failed, that he has somehow stopped loving us. But that's when we have to look at our circumstances through the lens of our confidence in God's unfailing love rather than looking at God through the lens of our disappointing circumstances. As God's children, we can be confident that no matter what happens to us, God is loving us in and through it. His love will never fade away or fail.

Long ago the LORD said to Israel: "I have loved you, my people, with an everlasting love. With unfailing love I have drawn you to myself."
JEREMIAH 31:3

How precious is your unfailing love, O God! All humanity finds shelter in the shadow of your wings.
PSALM 36:7

The law was given through Moses, but God's unfailing love and faithfulness came through Jesus Christ.
JOHN 1:17

 | **DISCUSSION STARTERS**

Have you ever been tempted to stop loving someone? Why?

Think about the way people are hurt and disappointed when someone doesn't love them well or stops loving them. How is God's love different from human love?

How did God love you before you were born? How will he love you after you die?

True Love

Why is it that most songs are about love—the celebration of love, the need for love, the agony over the loss of love? Perhaps it's because music is a way we express our deepest feelings and desires, and all of us have a deep desire to love and be loved. But can we really expect to experience love that will never disappoint, never fade, and never leave?

If we expect the rush of romance with another person to be the most satisfying love we can ever know, we are doomed to disappointment, because no other human can ever love us fully, completely, perfectly, or forever. We're limited by our humanity and our sinfulness. But Jesus' love is greater than any other love in the universe. He shows us what love looks like.

Jesus' love is not like human love, which grows weary of our quirks and habits. Jesus is patient. He will not bring up your failures from the past and use them against you. He forgives and forgets your sins, casting them away as far as the east is from the west (SEE PSALM 103:12). Jesus will never fail to defend those he loves. Out of his love for you and his hatred for evil, he will take up your case and will make everything right one day. Do you think Jesus will give up on you, release his grip on you, or walk away from you? Absolutely not. That's not what True Love does.

 | ## DISCUSSION STARTERS

Can you think of a song about love that is either insightfully true or ridiculously false?

Why do you think God made us with such a deep desire to be loved?

How does it help you to know that Jesus' love is so strong and solid?

Love is patient and kind. Love is not jealous or boastful or proud or rude. It does not demand its own way. It is not irritable, and it keeps no record of being wronged. It does not rejoice about injustice but rejoices whenever the truth wins out. Love never gives up, never loses faith, is always hopeful, and endures through every circumstance.

1 CORINTHIANS 13:4-7

May you experience the love of Christ, though it is too great to understand fully. Then you will be made complete with all the fullness of life and power that comes from God.

EPHESIANS 3:19

An Impossible Debt

What's the largest bill you've seen? A fifty-dollar bill? A one-hundred-dollar bill? The man in Jesus' parable owed the king millions of dollars—which would mean thousands of one-hundred-dollar bills today! His debt was not just large; it was an amount of money he couldn't even comprehend, let alone repay.

But there are two debtors in this story, and there is a great difference in the amount they owe. The debt owed to the servant by another man was a few thousand dollars—not an insignificant amount—but nothing compared to the debt the servant had been forgiven.

In reality, however, this parable is not so much about the two debtors but about the character of the king. The generous forgiveness of the king shows how big and gracious God's forgiveness is—the kind of forgiveness that sets prisoners free from an unpayable debt.

In order for us to forgive others when they hurt us, we have to first see how big our wrong has been toward God—how much he has forgiven us. When we finally see the enormity of our sin and the generosity of God's forgiveness toward us, only then will we really be able to forgive someone else.

The king called in the man he had forgiven and said, "You evil servant! I forgave you that tremendous debt because you pleaded with me. Shouldn't you have mercy on your fellow servant, just as I had mercy on you?" Then the angry king sent the man to prison to be tortured until he had paid his entire debt.

That's what my heavenly Father will do to you if you refuse to forgive your brothers and sisters from your heart.
MATTHEW 18:32-35

Forgive us our sins, as we have forgiven those who sin against us.
MATTHEW 6:12

 | ## DISCUSSION STARTERS

Can you retell the parable of the debtors in modern terms, as if it were happening today?

How would you describe the size of your debt of sin that God has forgiven?

In this parable, the man who refused to forgive was handed over to torturers. How is refusing to forgive like being tortured?

A Higher Authority

Open up the newspaper, turn on the television, or look online and you'll read or hear strong opinions about the policies of our government or the people leading our government. It's likely there are also some strong opinions at your house about the current president or party in power.

But regardless of what we think about our government and its leaders, God calls us to submit to all rulers—including leaders we disagree with, unfair bosses, and corrupt governments. When Paul writes in Romans 13:1 that those in authority have been placed there by God, he knows from Daniel 2:21 that "[God] controls the course of world events; he removes kings and sets up other kings." All kings (and presidents) are under God's ultimate control. He allows them to be put into office, and he allows them to be taken out of office.

We might wonder why God would allow a particular person or party with a clearly ungodly agenda to be in power over us. But the Bible teaches that God has the power to guide the "king's heart" or to change any leader's mind or policy. While God puts all human authority in place, there is a higher authority. Jesus said, "I have been given all authority in heaven and on earth" (MATTHEW 28:18). And when we submit to earthly authority, we're submitting for his sake. "For the Lord's sake, respect all human authority—whether the king as head of state, or the officials he has appointed" (1 PETER 2:13-14). We submit to human authority because it honors a higher authority, Jesus Christ.

The king's heart is like a stream of water directed by the LORD; he guides it wherever he pleases.
PROVERBS 21:1

Everyone must submit to governing authorities. For all authority comes from God, and those in positions of authority have been placed there by God.
ROMANS 13:1

Jesus Christ . . . is the faithful witness to these things, the first to rise from the dead, and the ruler of all the kings of the world.
REVELATION 1:5

🧂🧂 | DISCUSSION STARTERS

Who is in authority over you? What does it mean to submit to authority?

How does submitting to the authority of the government show our faith in God?

Can we disagree with someone in authority and still submit? How?

Then Cain founded a city, which he named Enoch, after his son.

GENESIS 4:17

O Jerusalem, Jerusalem, the city that kills the prophets and stones God's messengers! How often I have wanted to gather your children together as a hen protects her chicks beneath her wings, but you wouldn't let me.

MATTHEW 23:37

He took me in the Spirit to a great, high mountain, and he showed me the holy city, Jerusalem, descending out of heaven from God.

REVELATION 21:10

The Big City

Have you ever been to a really big city, or do you live in one? You can get lost in a big city—you could even disappear in a big city and not be found for a long time, because cities are bustling and crowded and there are plenty of places to hide.

That's what Cain was doing when he built the very first city. His punishment for killing his brother was that he was to be a homeless wanderer, banished from God's presence. His response was to build a city, his own world, where he could get lost and try to find satisfaction apart from God. Cain's city was eventually destroyed in the Flood.

The second city mentioned in the Bible, Babel, was built by some people in an arrogant effort to get to God on their own terms. It ended in a pile of rubble when God confused their languages and they could no longer work together. In Revelation, when John describes judgment, he talks about it in terms of a city that is destroyed: "Fallen! Fallen is Babylon the Great!" (REVELATION 18:2, NIV).

So it's interesting that the Bible describes heaven as a great city, the new Jerusalem. This is even more interesting when we think about the old Jerusalem. Jerusalem had a history full of paganism and rejection of God. Jerusalem was the city that rejected Jesus. Isn't this the most unlikely of cities to serve as a model for heaven?

What this tells us is that God is redeeming our idol-loving, God-rejecting, God-avoiding version of a city. He is transforming this idea we humans have messed up, and he has a plan to make it into a place he wants to live in.

 | **DISCUSSION STARTERS**

What's the biggest or smallest city you've ever been to, and what did you like about it?

Think through the Old Testament and New Testament history of Jerusalem. What does this tell us about God's ability to redeem people and places?

What do you think will be the best parts of the "city of God"?

Do You Want More?

"I'm so full, I can't eat another bite," we sometimes say after a big meal. But what if we realized there was chocolate cake still to be served?

Some of us say to God by our attitudes or our choices, *I'm full. I've seen all of God I want to see; my love for him is as deep as I want it to go; my confidence in his promises is as serious as I want it to be; I've been changed as much as I want to be changed. I have as much of God in my schedule, my thoughts, and my heart as I need—and as much as I want.*

Jesus says that those who hunger and thirst for righteousness will be filled, or satisfied. Paul prays that we would be filled with all the fullness of God. Both Jesus and Paul seem to be talking about an ongoing pursuit of an ever-growing sense of satisfaction. They are talking about a hunger to get all that God has to give in terms of joy, understanding, and power. It's a desire to see more of God, to love him more, and to be used by him more.

No matter how far we go with God, there's always more to know and enjoy and live out. In our pursuit of God, we're like mountain climbers struggling to reach the top of a mountain peak, only to discover that there are more amazing mountain peaks left to climb. We lose out when we settle for only what we've experienced of God so far.

✂ | DISCUSSION STARTERS

Is there a certain subject in school that you are so interested in you want to keep learning more? Is there one that you never want to have to study again once you finish that class?

In what ways do you want to learn about or experience more of God?

What are some things you can do to experience more of God?

FEBRUARY

18

Don't be drunk with wine, because that will ruin your life. Instead, be filled with the Holy Spirit.
EPHESIANS 5:18

May you be filled with joy, always thanking the Father.
COLOSSIANS 1:11-12

How generous and gracious our Lord was! He filled me with the faith and love that come from Christ Jesus.
1 TIMOTHY 1:14

Prayer Masks

When people don't seem to live what they say they believe, we tend to think of them as hypocrites. The word *hypocrite* originally came from the ancient Greek theater and described a person who wore a mask.

Jesus says that we shouldn't pray like the hypocrites. In other words, we shouldn't use prayer to put on a spiritual show for people that doesn't line up with who we really are. Why does Jesus have to warn us not to pray like hypocrites? Because he knows that we enjoy the admiration of other people and we'll use anything—even prayer—to get it. He knows that we would much rather work on getting a reputation for praying than actually praying. And he sees us when we tell someone we will pray for him or her, knowing even as we say the words that most likely we will not.

Jesus says that when we pray to impress other people, we've already received our reward—their admiration—but that is such an empty and fleeting reward! We can make a big deal about public prayers or brag about private prayer and receive the applause of people, or we can go into our secret places, shut the door, and talk with God. There we find our best reward, not in making an impression on others, but in finding intimacy with him.

When you pray, don't be like the hypocrites who love to pray publicly on street corners and in the synagogues where everyone can see them. I tell you the truth, that is all the reward they will ever get. But when you pray, go away by yourself, shut the door behind you, and pray to your Father in private. Then your Father, who sees everything, will reward you.
MATTHEW 6:5-6

He went in alone and shut the door behind him and prayed to the LORD.
2 KINGS 4:33

Before daybreak the next morning, Jesus got up and went out to an isolated place to pray.
MARK 1:35

 | **DISCUSSION STARTERS**

What does it mean to pray in secret?

How can praying with other people be an encouragement?

What are the marks of humble public prayer?

Is God Happy?

Have you noticed that some people seem to smile all the time? They seem to be naturally happy. And then there are others who seem to have been given the grumpy gene. You'd be shocked to see them break out in a toothy grin.

How about God? Do you think he is strained and serious, with a furrowed brow, always a little annoyed? Or do you think of him with a smile on his face, full of contentment and joy? And if God is happy, what makes him that way?

God has many reasons to be happy. First, he is happy because he finds pleasure in just being himself. It is as if he looks in the mirror and is happy about what he sees. He loves the glory of his own nature—the infinite beauty of all he is and all he does. When he saw his reflection in Jesus, who "radiates God's own glory and expresses the very character of God" (HEBREWS 1:3), he said, "This is my dearly loved Son, who brings me great joy" (MATTHEW 3:17).

God is happy because he has the power to do as he pleases and because everything he does is right and good. Nothing can frustrate his happiness. God is so happy that his happiness spills out on us in the form of mercy. He showers goodness on us because he enjoys it. His greatest happiness is to share his happiness with us. We experience his overflowing happiness when we accept that everything we need to be happy is found in him. "The LORD's delight is in those who . . . put their hope in his unfailing love."

The LORD's delight is in those who fear him, those who put their hope in his unfailing love.
PSALM 147:11

They will be my people, and I will be their God. . . . I will find joy doing good for them.
JEREMIAH 32:38, 41

Because of the joy awaiting him, he endured the cross, disregarding its shame. Now he is seated in the place of honor beside God's throne.
HEBREWS 12:2

 | ## DISCUSSION STARTERS

Do others usually see a smile or a frown on your face?

What do you think makes God happy?

What are some of the things we think will make us happy? Why can these things never take the place of God as our source of lasting, real happiness?

Stones That Breathe

Have you ever noticed a large stone set in a prominent location on the outside of a building that is inscribed with the construction date of the building and the names of people who built it? This stone is a cornerstone, set in an important place in the building's structure. Cornerstones are important since all other stones will be set in reference to these stones, which determine the position of the entire building.

This is what it means when we read that Jesus is the cornerstone of the building God is working on. God is building his temple, not with rocks or cement, but with living stones—you and me and everyone else who loves Jesus. We are being fit together on the foundation of Jesus. It is Jesus who determines everything about this building.

As living stones, we are part of something God is doing that is bigger than we are as individuals, more important than our own agendas and preferences. Christianity is not so much about God saving a large number of individuals (although he will!). It is about what he is building us into together—his church. We are living stones that God is using to build his spiritual house—the people he wants to live inside.

You are coming to Christ, who is the living cornerstone of God's temple. He was rejected by people, but he was chosen by God for great honor. And you are living stones that God is building into his spiritual temple. What's more, you are his holy priests. Through the mediation of Jesus Christ, you offer spiritual sacrifices that please God.
1 PETER 2:4-5

Look! I am placing a foundation stone in Jerusalem, a firm and tested stone. It is a precious cornerstone that is safe to build on.
ISAIAH 28:16

Together, we are his house, built on the foundation of the apostles and the prophets. And the cornerstone is Christ Jesus himself.
EPHESIANS 2:20

 | ## DISCUSSION STARTERS

Have you ever seen a building under construction? What parts of the process did you find interesting?

What false cornerstones do some people try to build their lives on?

Based on the idea of Jesus as our cornerstone, what would you say to someone who believes in Jesus but doesn't see the need to be connected to other Christians?

In or Out?

A parent, frustrated by the door being left open as her kids come and go, might say, "We don't want to heat the whole outdoors! You're either in or you're out!" The train engineer prompts the person with one foot on the platform and one on the train steps, "You're either going or staying." In other words, there's a choice to be made, and the choice is clear. You can't be halfway.

When it comes to Jesus, there is a choice to be made, and it is a choice everyone has to make on a personal level. Are you in or out? Are you going where he's going, or are you staying where you are? Because of this choice, there is a dividing line between people. Some people are "in" Christ and some people are "outside" of Christ. Some people are still living under judgment because they are guilty of sin and have rejected the grace and forgiveness Jesus offers them. And there are others who are just as guilty, yet they don't experience that judgment. They have chosen to hide themselves in Christ, who faced judgment in their place.

Our culture doesn't like drawing the dividing line between people so clearly. Many people today want things to be less defined than that. They see the claim that some people are in Christ (while others are not in Christ) as superior or exclusive. But God has opened his invitation to all to come in to Christ. Sadly, some choose to stay out.

🥛 | DISCUSSION STARTERS

When have you felt on the outside of something? When have you felt like you were on the inside?

What does it mean to you that "now there is no condemnation" over your life?

How would you respond to someone who says that Christ's teachings are narrow, exclusive, or extreme?

Now there is no condemnation for those who belong to Christ Jesus.
ROMANS 8:1

The LORD will redeem those who serve him. No one who takes refuge in him will be condemned.
PSALM 34:22

I tell you the truth, those who listen to my message and believe in God who sent me have eternal life. They will never be condemned for their sins, but they have already passed from death into life.
JOHN 5:24

Still Growing

Imagine if a baby just stayed a baby—never growing up or getting bigger. Something would be terribly wrong with a baby who didn't grow. And something would be wrong with a Christian who never grew either—a Christian who stayed a baby in faith. As we grow in years, we want to grow in how we talk to, listen to, and trust God.

How do we grow in faith? It starts with how we "eat" spiritually—talking about, thinking about, and memorizing the Bible. First, we feed ourselves the "milk"—the basics about life in Christ, who God is, and what he has done for us. Then, just as babies go from drinking milk to eating solid food, we move on from the "milk" to the "meat"—the deeper truths and bigger picture of God. We can do this by "chewing on" and "swallowing" more challenging passages in the Bible and by going deeper in learning about God's Word.

While our physical bodies stop growing at some point, we never have to stop growing spiritually. We will always have more to learn, new ways to trust God, deeper truths to understand.

Let your roots grow down into him and draw up nourishment from him, so you will grow in faith, strong and vigorous in the truth you were taught. Let your lives overflow with thanksgiving for all he has done.
COLOSSIANS 2:7

When your faith is tested, your endurance has a chance to grow.
JAMES 1:3

Teach us to make the most of our time, so that we may grow in wisdom.
PSALM 90:12

 | **DISCUSSION STARTERS**

In what way(s) have you been growing in the past year?

What kind of spiritual food helps your faith grow?

Looking back, can you pinpoint ways your faith has grown from what it used to be?

Wishful Thinking?

Lots of people make wishes—when they blow out their birthday candles or when they cross their fingers or when they look at shooting stars. They say, "I *hope* it will happen" or "I *hope* I will get it." They are wishing for something but have no confidence that it will happen.

But we don't have to cross our fingers and hope as hard as we can that God will give us everything he has promised to give us or to do everything he has promised us he will do. We can be completely confident, totally sure, solidly convinced that God is at work in the everyday aspects of our lives. We can count on him to fulfill his promises to us. What promises? All his promises, including these: God works everything together for good for those who love him (ROMANS 8:28); he will follow us with goodness and mercy all our days (PSALM 23:6); he will not leave us or forsake us (HEBREWS 13:5).

You don't have to wish and wait, wondering if God will do what he has said he'll do in his Word. You may not have experienced the fulfillment of some promises yet, but if he has promised something, there is no question it will happen. We can entrust our lives to the One who holds the future, no matter what happens. Because God will do what he has promised to do.

🔔🔔 | DISCUSSION STARTERS

What promises have people made to you? What promises have you made to other people?

What promises of God do you find it easy to put your faith in? What promises are harder for you to be confident in?

How do we know God is trustworthy—that he will follow through on all the promises he has made?

Faith is the confidence that what we hope for will actually happen; it gives us assurance about things we cannot see.
HEBREWS 11:1

Abraham never wavered in believing God's promise. In fact, his faith grew stronger, and in this he brought glory to God. He was fully convinced that God is able to do whatever he promises.
ROMANS 4:20-21

I pray that God, the source of hope, will fill you completely with joy and peace because you trust in him. Then you will overflow with confident hope through the power of the Holy Spirit.
ROMANS 15:13

I take back everything I said,
and I sit in dust and ashes
to show my repentance.
JOB 42:6

God blesses those who mourn,
for they will be comforted.
MATTHEW 5:4

The kind of sorrow God wants
us to experience leads us
away from sin and results in
salvation. There's no regret
for that kind of sorrow.
But worldly sorrow, which
lacks repentance, results
in spiritual death.
2 CORINTHIANS 7:10

A Good Kind of Sad

Usually when someone is sad, we try to cheer the person up. We don't like anyone around us to feel sad, and we avoid anything that would make us feel down. But Jesus said there's a good kind of sadness. What kind of sadness is actually good for us?

It is good for us when we begin to really see the sin in our lives and then, instead of minimizing it or excusing it or comparing it to the sin of others, we become deeply sad over it. When we see what an offense our sin is to God, out of our love for him we become truly sorry about our sin. This is the kind of sadness that is part of real repentance. This kind of sorrow puts us on a pathway toward genuine, deep, lasting happiness.

Can you remember the last time you were truly sad about the sin in your life? Have you *ever* really been sad about your wrong actions, your ungodly reactions to other people, your sinful attitudes? Perhaps you need to spend some time alone with God asking him to show you what sins are holding you back from living the way he wants you to live. Godly sorrow over sin leads to freedom from the hold that sin has on our lives. Only then can we be really, really happy.

 | **DISCUSSION STARTERS**

Can you think of a time when you were sad recently? What caused that sadness?

Do you sometimes find it hard to come up with specific sins to ask forgiveness for? How can we identify the sins we need to feel sorrow over?

Do you think this sorrow over sin is a one-time thing? If not, how often do you think we should feel this way?

Bible Addition and Subtraction

Some people come to the Bible the way they shop at a store. They have a list of things they want, and they shop until they find them, ignoring all the stuff they don't want. And sometimes they're frustrated that the store doesn't have exactly what they're looking for.

But that's not the way we want to come to God's Word—as a consumer or a shopper, picking and choosing what we want to listen to or obey. And we can't conclude that the Bible is any way lacking because it doesn't have what we're looking for on the subject we're interested in.

The Bible warns us about adding anything to Scripture. One way people do this is by making other writings or teachings of equal authority to the Bible. Anytime people go beyond what Scripture says to promote new ideas about God, basing their teachings not on Scripture but on their own speculation or personal experience, we have to check their words against what the Bible says. We also need to be careful about adding extra rules to those clearly stated in Scripture, labeling something as sin that is not forbidden by Scripture.

We need to be content with Scripture as God has given it to us—emphasizing the same issues it emphasizes. There are some subjects God has told us little or nothing about in the Bible. But we can be confident that God has given us everything we need for knowing and following him.

 | **DISCUSSION STARTERS**

Is there anything in the Bible you sometimes wish weren't there?

What do you wish the Bible had more information about?

Are there books of the Bible you've never read? What has kept you from reading them?

> I solemnly declare to everyone who hears the words of prophecy written in this book: If anyone adds anything to what is written here, God will add to that person the plagues described in this book.
> **REVELATION 22:18**

> I tell you the truth, until heaven and earth disappear, not even the smallest detail of God's law will disappear until its purpose is achieved.
> **MATTHEW 5:18**

> The instructions of the LORD are perfect.
> **PSALM 19:7**

God loved the world so much that he gave his one and only Son, so that everyone who believes in him will not perish but have eternal life.

JOHN 3:16

Jesus told them, "This is the only work God wants from you: Believe in the one he has sent."

JOHN 6:29

The world's sin is that it refuses to believe in me.

JOHN 16:9

Believe Into

You can say that you believe an airplane will fly. But to live that belief is to fly in one. You can say that you believe it is important to exercise. But if you don't exercise, it is proof that you don't really believe it is important. It's not that different with faith. It's easy to say that you believe in Jesus. But the proof that you really believe is that you entrust your life to him and depend on him to satisfy you and take care of you.

Many people think that believing in Jesus is simply agreeing with a list of facts about who Jesus is and what he did on the cross. But that is just the beginning. Belief also involves accepting the truth about Jesus for yourself, then entrusting your whole self to Christ.

Actually, in the original language John wrote in, he didn't record Jesus as saying we should "believe *in*" him. Our Bibles say it that way because it would sound weird to our ears for the verse to read what Jesus literally said. Jesus' actual words were that we have to "believe *into*" him. John 1:12 equates "believing into" Jesus with *receiving him*. In John 6:35 Jesus says that believing into him is like *coming to him* to satisfy the hunger and thirst at the core of our beings. To believe into Jesus is to enter into Jesus as a new way of living life.

DISCUSSION STARTERS

What does the fact you are sitting in a chair say about what you believe about that chair? What other things or people do you put your faith in?

How would you explain the difference between believing in a list of facts about Jesus and believing *into* Jesus?

What are significant things you believe *about* Jesus that cause you to choose to believe *into* Jesus?

FEBRUARY 27

A Parent's #1 Job

What is the most important thing your parents have taught you? To look both ways before crossing the street? How to develop friendships? How to run a household or a business? How to show respect?

All those things are important. God is so good to us to give us parents who are willing to teach us the things we need to know to navigate living in this world. But there is one thing in particular God holds parents responsible for teaching to their children, one thing God wants children to learn more than anything else: how to trust God. He wants parents to teach their children how to put confidence in God rather than in themselves or in anything or anyone else.

Parents can't force their children to learn to trust God, but they can teach them about trusting God. Sometimes learning comes from direct instruction—talking through different aspects of our faith together. And it is important to study Scripture and talk about what it means to trust God. But teaching others to trust God is best done by example. Parents teach best by trusting God themselves and by welcoming rather than resenting opportunities to trust God in new ways.

 | **DISCUSSION STARTERS**

What are some important lessons you've learned from your parents? What have you observed or learned about trusting God from your parents?

What do you think it means to trust God?

What things do you find the hardest to trust God with?

We will not hide these truths from our children; we will tell the next generation about the glorious deeds of the LORD, about his power and his mighty wonders. . . . So each generation should set its hope anew on God, not forgetting his glorious miracles and obeying his commands.

PSALM 78:4, 7

Teach those who are rich in this world not to be proud and not to trust in their money, which is so unreliable. Their trust should be in God, who richly gives us all we need for our enjoyment.

1 TIMOTHY 6:17

Such things were written in the Scriptures long ago to teach us. And the Scriptures give us hope and encouragement as we wait patiently for God's promises to be fulfilled.

ROMANS 15:4

MARCH

1

For forty days and forty nights he fasted and became very hungry. During that time the devil came and said to him, "If you are the Son of God, tell these stones to become loaves of bread."

Jesus told him, "No! The Scriptures say, 'People do not live by bread alone, but by every word that comes from the mouth of God.'"

MATTHEW 4:2-4

When you fast, comb your hair and wash your face. Then no one will notice that you are fasting, except your Father, who knows what you do in private. And your Father, who sees everything, will reward you.

MATTHEW 6:17-18

Heart Hunger for God

"**B**reakfast is ready!" "Lunch is on the table!" "Dinnertime!" Don't you love the sound of those words? They mean it's time to eat! And while God gives food for us to enjoy and to keep us healthy, he also expects that we will sometimes choose not to eat or choose not to eat certain foods. It's called fasting. Fasting is when we go without food or without certain foods for a period of time, not for the purpose of losing weight but for spiritual reasons—because we want to develop our hunger for God. We want to connect with God in an intense way by denying ourselves the comfort or distraction of food. People sometimes choose to fast from other things besides food—like television or the Internet or shopping. Instead of tuning in or logging on or going out, they choose to tune in to God through his Word.

To draw close to God is a good reason to fast. But sometimes people fast for the wrong reasons. Sometimes people choose to fast in a subtle attempt to twist God's arm or to win his approval. But God doesn't respond to pressure. However, God does promise to reward those who fast. He says that those who fast secretly—out of hunger for God and not a hunger to impress other people with how spiritual they are—will be rewarded.

Jesus fasted for forty days before he launched his public ministry, and he expected that those who follow him would fast too, praying for his Kingdom to come in its fullness. Jesus said, "*when* you fast" not "*if* you fast." Jesus needed to fast, and he expects us to fast because he knows it is a discipline that draws us close to him and encourages our dependence on him.

 | **DISCUSSION STARTERS**

What would it be like to skip a meal or go a whole day without food?

Why do you think we tend to want other people to know when we are denying ourselves food or any other comfort or pleasure?

What are some good reasons to fast as well as some bad reasons to fast?

Does God Get Jealous?

Some people call it the "green-eyed monster." It ruins relationships and makes people miserable. What is it? Jealousy. To be jealous is to want what someone else has only for yourself. Paul lists jealousy with other "desires of your sinful nature," like being involved with the occult and getting drunk (GALATIANS 5:19-21).

So if jealousy is bad, how could God describe himself as jealous? Everything about God is perfect—so his jealousy must be part of that perfection. This tells us that his jealousy is not like our self-serving jealousy. He is not out of sorts or irritable because of envy, but he is passionate for our affection out of love. Think of the people you know who are married. There is an appropriate measure of jealousy that a husband and wife should have for each other because they love each other and want to keep their marriage as an exclusive relationship. It's not that different with God—he is right to jealously guard the relationship he has with the people who belong to him.

The fact that God is jealous shows us how passionate he is about us. This isn't just a businesslike relationship we have with him. It is a love relationship that stirs his deep desire to pursue us. Because he loves us, he doesn't want our affections to wander away from him.

 | **DISCUSSION STARTERS**

Have you ever felt jealous about the attention someone gave to another person? What was that like?

What are some differences between our jealousy and God's jealousy? (Think of both the reasons for the jealousy and the way it is expressed.)

What things in your life might make God jealous for your affection?

You must worship no other gods, for the LORD, whose very name is Jealous, is a God who is jealous about his relationship with you.
EXODUS 34:14

I am jealous for you with the jealousy of God himself. I promised you as a pure bride to one husband—Christ. But I fear that somehow your pure and undivided devotion to Christ will be corrupted.
2 CORINTHIANS 11:2-3

You adulterers! Don't you realize that friendship with the world makes you an enemy of God? . . . If you want to be a friend of the world, you make yourself an enemy of God. What do you think the Scriptures mean when they say that the spirit God has placed within us is filled with envy?
JAMES 4:4-5

Keep on Asking

"Please, mom! Pretty please?!" This is how little kids plead with their parents when there is something they want and think they need. And sometimes children keep repeating their requests, hoping to break down Mom or Dad's resistance and turn a no into yes.

When we read Jesus' teaching on prayer and his encouragement to "keep on asking," we might be tempted to think that the secret formula for getting what we want from God is to wear him down by repeating the request. Or maybe we think that the secret is to get as many people as possible to ask God for it. We think, *Surely if enough people are praying, God will give us what we're asking for.* But does God respond to repetition or group pressure?

Most parents don't want their kids to wear them down by repeating requests over and over. What they want is to have a conversation. And that's how it is with our heavenly Parent. He loves us and he cares about our needs. And while he values and invites our persistence in prayer, maybe he's saying, "Don't just pound on the door of heaven repeating your same request, refusing to listen to me. Come in and talk to me. Share your heart with me, and let me share mine with you." Prayer is about a two-way conversation with God, not about wearing him down to get what we want. Asking, seeking, and knocking have little to do with getting what we want from God and everything to do with enjoying the Spirit in our lives.

Keep on asking, and you will receive what you ask for. Keep on seeking, and you will find. Keep on knocking, and the door will be opened to you. For everyone who asks, receives. Everyone who seeks, finds. And to everyone who knocks, the door will be opened.

You fathers—if your children ask for a fish, do you give them a snake instead? Or if they ask for an egg, do you give them a scorpion? Of course not! So if you sinful people know how to give good gifts to your children, how much more will your heavenly Father give the Holy Spirit to those who ask him.

LUKE 11:9-13

 | ## DISCUSSION STARTERS

When you want or need something from your parents, how do you usually go about trying to get it? What's the best way to do that?

What is the point of asking other people to pray for us?

What does it mean to be persistent in prayer?

Just a Coincidence?

Good luck. Beginner's luck. Don't push your luck. You lucky dog! Tough luck. We talk about luck a lot—perhaps without giving much thought to what we're saying. And sometimes we see things happen in amazing ways and say, "What a coincidence!" But is there such a thing as luck or coincidence?

In truth, the things that come together in our lives are not influenced by luck, fate, fortune, destiny, or chance. Instead, the hand of God is involved in many apparent coincidences to bring about his purposes. He is at work behind seeming good luck to bring success, and he's behind seeming bad luck to bring discipline or lessons in trust.

Acts 17:28 says, "In him we live and move and exist." Every step we take, every word we speak, everywhere we go, everything we think and feel—it's all under God's direction. God is ruler over all the events of history so that they work together for good for the people who love him. We call this God's providence. Providence is one of those words that you can't find in the Bible and yet it is written into every theme and story. Providence is when God works behind the scenes to bring about the outcome he desires. No event or circumstance falls outside of his providence.

🧂🧂 | DISCUSSION STARTERS

When have you thought of yourself as "lucky" or "unlucky"?

How does a solid belief in God's providence affect how we understand and accept what others might call a coincidence or an accident?

Do you think it would be a good idea to take the word *luck* out of your vocabulary, or is using the word *luck* no big deal? Why?

We can make our plans, but the LORD determines our steps. . . . We may throw the dice, but the Lord determines how they fall.
PROVERBS 16:9, 33

He makes everything work out according to his plan.
EPHESIANS 1:11

The LORD was with Joseph, so he succeeded in everything he did as he served in the home of his Egyptian master. . . . The LORD began to bless Potiphar's household for Joseph's sake. All his household affairs ran smoothly, and his crops and livestock flourished.
GENESIS 39:2, 5

Does a clay pot argue with its maker? Does the clay dispute with the one who shapes it, saying, "Stop, you're doing it wrong!" Does the pot exclaim, "How clumsy can you be?"
ISAIAH 45:9

O Israel, can I not do to you as this potter has done to his clay? As the clay is in the potter's hand, so are you in my hand.
JEREMIAH 18:6

Don't let the world around you squeeze you into its own mould, but let God re-mould your minds from within, so that you may prove in practice that the plan of God for you is good, meets all his demands and moves towards the goal of true maturity.
ROMANS 12:2, PHILLIPS

Are You Moldable?

Have you ever made something out of clay or Play-Doh? Or have you ever seen a potter create something on a pottery wheel? The potter spins the lump of clay on the wheel, pressing and forming it here and there, transforming the shapeless clay into a work of art or a useful jar or bowl.

In the Bible, God describes himself as a potter who is shaping our lives into something he can pour his own glory into. We are in the hands of God right now, being shaped and formed, just as a potter shapes clay. And we have a choice about how we'll respond. We can resist his shaping through our rebellion or resentment, which makes us hard and unbending. Or we can be soft and moldable, open to whatever God wants to do in and through our lives.

God is making you and shaping you for his own unique purposes. And he's not done. You are still a work in progress, and God wants to keep refining his work of art. He wants to smooth out certain parts of you and grow you in other ways. He wants to redesign your inner life, reorganize your priorities, redirect the tendencies of your tongue, and rewire your thinking patterns. He's out to make something beautiful, and the softer you are toward him, the more beautiful your life will become.

 | **DISCUSSION STARTERS**

Do you have a piece of pottery at your house? What does it say about the person who created it?

What assumptions or attitudes tend to make us unmoldable?

What kinds of things does God use to mold us?

The Devil's Foothold

Do you ever find yourself "practicing" things you'd like to say to someone you're angry with? We want to be ready to win the war of words! Then we talk to other people about what and who has made us angry, asking them to take our side and feel outraged on our behalf. All the while, we keep throwing logs on the fire of our anger, building our case and assuming the worst about the other person's motives and actions.

Anger is a natural reaction when we feel threatened or injured. But then we have a choice about what we are going to do with that feeling. Will we replay our hurts over and over in our heads—and then plot and imagine how delicious it would be to put those people in their place? Or will we refuse to allow the poison of anger to rot us on the inside?

We do not have to let anger control us when someone does something that hurts us. We will be tempted to be consumed by this feeling, but we can refuse to give in to that temptation. While anger may be a natural reaction in many situations—and may even be justified by our circumstances—Jesus is all about transforming us on the inside so that we are no longer bound to do what comes naturally. The Holy Spirit in us empowers us to respond supernaturally. He gives us the strength we need to stop demanding what we think we deserve from other people.

Anger becomes sin as we allow it to stir our emotions and steer our actions. Don't let your anger stick around. Let it go.

> You must all be quick to listen, slow to speak, and slow to get angry. Human anger does not produce the righteousness God desires.
> *JAMES 1:19-20*

> "Don't sin by letting anger control you." Don't let the sun go down while you are still angry, for anger gives a foothold to the devil.
> *EPHESIANS 4:26-27*

> People with understanding control their anger; a hot temper shows great foolishness.
> *PROVERBS 14:29*

 | ## DISCUSSION STARTERS

What are some ways our anger comes out?

When someone is angry with you, what do you want him or her to do?

What do we need to do or tell ourselves in order to let go of anger?

Are All
Religions the Same?

Let's say your grandmother lives on the other side of the country, and you're going to take a trip in the car to see her. Imagine that you asked someone for directions, and that person told you that you could take any road you wanted to take and it would get you to her house. Would that make sense?

Many people in the world believe that all those who follow any religion with sincerity will eventually end up at the same place. They think that all religions are equally true, have the same basic goals, and get a person to the same destination—heaven. They claim that it's arrogant to try to convert people from one religion to another and that our common goal should be to make the world a better place by practicing our own various religions and viewing all other religions as equally true or valid.

But does it make sense that Buddhism, Hinduism, Islam, Judaism, and Christianity all represent valid paths to the same destination or that all these religions could be equally true? Of course not. All religions are not the same, and all religions do not point to the true God. At the heart of every religion is a particular way of defining who God is and why we're here. At the center of Christianity is the person and work of Jesus Christ. The one true God has declared that the one way to know him is through his Son, Jesus. This is the only path that will lead us to God.

 | **DISCUSSION STARTERS**

What are some beliefs you've heard from people of other religions that are different from what the Bible teaches?

Why is the suggestion that all paths lead to God appealing? Why is it impossible?

How can we stand firm in our belief that Jesus is the only way to know God, without arguing or coming across as rude?

There is salvation in no one else! God has given no other name under heaven by which we must be saved.
ACTS 4:12

Jesus told him, "I am the way, the truth, and the life. No one can come to the Father except through me."
JOHN 14:6

There is only one God and one Mediator who can reconcile God and humanity—the man Christ Jesus. He gave his life to purchase freedom for everyone. This is the message God gave to the world at just the right time.
1 TIMOTHY 2:5-6

When I Grow Up . . .

How many times have you been asked, "What do you want to be when you grow up?" Too many, right? Usually we come up with some sort of career we want so we can have an answer to this question. But Jesus told us what we all should want to be when we grow up: meek. It is not a job; it's a character trait, a way of responding to other people and especially to God. *Meekness* sounds like *weakness*. But really meekness is strength that is under control. Think of it like a Thoroughbred horse that is controlled by a bridle and bit in its mouth. The horse is strong but submissive. That's meekness. Meekness goes against everything the world tells us about getting what we want. We think we get what we want by standing up for ourselves and looking out for our own interests. But Jesus said that meek people will inherit the earth. They get it all. The only people who will get anything that lasts out of this life are people who learn to be meek.

In one of the few times Jesus spoke about his own personal character, he described himself as "meek and lowly" (MATTHEW 11:29, KJV). He is our example for what it is to be meek. It was his meekness—his strong submission to the plan of God—that led him to the Cross. At the Cross, we see clearly what meekness is supposed to look like.

Meekness is not about your personality type. We might think of meek people as those who are shy and quiet and never have an opinion. But strong, outgoing people can learn to be meek. Meekness is something God develops in us as we submit our strength to him. Without a spirit of meekness, it is impossible to submit to the work of God in our hearts and the plan of God for our lives.

> Blessed are the meek, for they will inherit the earth.
> *MATTHEW 5:5, NIV*

> Lay aside all filthiness and overflow of wickedness, and receive with meekness the implanted word, which is able to save your souls.
> *JAMES 1:21, NKJV*

> He was oppressed and treated harshly, yet he never said a word. He was led like a lamb to the slaughter. And as a sheep is silent before the shearers, he did not open his mouth.
> *ISAIAH 53:7*

 | **DISCUSSION STARTERS**

What kind of person do you want to be when you grow up?

What is the difference between meekness and weakness?

Who do you know who is meek? How have you seen meekness played out in that person's life?

In the beginning God created
the heavens and the earth.
GENESIS 1:1

By faith we understand that
the universe was formed
at God's command, so that
what is seen was not made
out of what was visible.
HEBREWS 11:3, NIV

By him all things were
created: things in heaven
and on earth, visible and
invisible, whether thrones
or powers or rulers or authorities; all things were created
by him and for him.
COLOSSIANS 1:16, NIV

Something out of Nothing

Nobody can make something out of nothing. Nobody, that is, except God. That's what the Bible teaches us about God's creation of the universe: God made something—everything—out of nothing.

This means that before God began to create the universe, nothing else existed except God himself. All that we see—the mountains, the oceans, the stars, the earth itself—came into existence when God created it, when he spoke it into being. And if God ever stopped speaking, "Be!" into your body and soul, you would cease to be. As Jesus said, "People do not live by bread alone, but by every word that comes from the mouth of God" (MATTHEW 4:4).

This means that everything God created and sustains has meaning and purpose. Everything that exists has a purpose, a goal, a reason for being. And the ultimate purpose of God in everything he created was and is to display his glory in all its fullness.

What does this mean for us now? It means that God can create faith where there is none in our minds or hearts. It means that God can generate love and forgiveness where there is none between two people in a hurting relationship. It means that God can speak into the emptiness in our lives and give purpose and meaning to them.

 | **DISCUSSION STARTERS**

What are some of the things Genesis 1 says God made out of nothing?

What can we learn about God from the things he has created?

Is there an area in your life where you would like God to create something out of nothing?

Reading
Your Own Obituary

In the newspaper every day there's a section called the obituaries—the listing of all the people who have died recently. Can you imagine opening up the newspaper and seeing your own obituary—the report of your own death?

Well, in a sense, that is what Paul wrote in several places in the New Testament. He wrote that if we have joined ourselves to Christ, we have died—that is, the old versions of ourselves have died, the old selves who lived only to please ourselves.

The moment you put your faith in Jesus, you became united with him. His death became your death. So really, your spiritual obituary could say that you died two thousand years ago on the day Christ died. But it could also say that you came alive again on the day Christ rose from the dead, because his resurrection is also your resurrection. The old you died and a new you is living in a whole new way. You are different now. Your connectedness to Jesus is changing you and making you new. And here's the best part about being dead: Because you have already died, you will never really die again. Your body will die one day, but you—the essence of who you are—will live forever in a resurrected body.

 | **DISCUSSION STARTERS**

Look at an obituary in the newspaper or on the Internet. If an obituary were about your spiritual life, what might it say about when you died and were given new life spiritually?

How can seeing your old self as dead and buried help you in the struggle against selfishness, inappropriate thoughts, pride, and anger?

In what ways can you tell that God is making you new?

MARCH

10

My old self has been crucified with Christ. It is no longer I who live, but Christ lives in me. So I live in this earthly body by trusting in the Son of God, who loved me and gave himself for me.
GALATIANS 2:20

You died to this life, and your real life is hidden with Christ in God.
COLOSSIANS 3:3

Since we have been united with him in his death, we will also be raised to life as he was. We know that our old sinful selves were crucified with Christ so that sin might lose its power in our lives. We are no longer slaves to sin.
ROMANS 6:5-6

Taking Faith for a Test Drive

These trials will show that your faith is genuine. It is being tested as fire tests and purifies gold—though your faith is far more precious than mere gold. So when your faith remains strong through many trials, it will bring you much praise and glory and honor on the day when Jesus Christ is revealed to the whole world.
1 PETER 1:7

Jesus soon saw a huge crowd of people coming to look for him. Turning to Philip, he asked, "Where can we buy bread to feed all these people?" He was testing Philip, for he already knew what he was going to do.
JOHN 6:5-6

It was by faith that Abraham offered Isaac as a sacrifice when God was testing him. Abraham, who had received God's promises, was ready to sacrifice his only son, Isaac.
HEBREWS 11:17

What's the first thing that comes to mind when you think of a test? Most of us probably think about a test in school—a measurement given out to see if we pass or fail. But what does it mean when God tests our faith? Does he put us in difficult situations and then stand back to see if we will pass or fail his test?

The kind of test God puts us through isn't really like a test in school. It's more like the test we put a car through when we are shopping for a new vehicle. We call it taking the car for a test drive. Are we looking to see if the car passes or fails? No. We are allowing the car to show us how it works and what it feels like—to demonstrate how it operates.

When God puts us to the test, he is giving us the opportunity to experience and demonstrate what it is like to live out our faith in him. It is our chance to live out what we say we believe. And God is not standing back to see if we've got what it takes. He is right beside us—even in us—giving us every ounce of faith we need to put his power on display in our lives.

 | **DISCUSSION STARTERS**

Would you rather take a test in school or test drive a car? Why?

When you consider the tests described in the verses above, do you think the tests were for God's benefit? for Philip's and Abraham's benefit? for our benefit?

How does a person's response to difficulty reveal if a person's faith is genuine or not?

Junk Food for the Soul

Your family is driving along the interstate, and everyone's stomach is starting to growl. You already had fast food for lunch, and now you want a nice meal. But as the exits pass and no good restaurants are in sight, you finally give in and go for what is easy and might satisfy the taste buds but isn't necessarily nourishing. Then sure enough, the next exit has your favorite sit-down restaurant. But by now you're all filled up with junk food!

Sometimes we wonder why we have no appetite to read the Bible, no hunger for getting to know God better, no desire to talk about Jesus. We know we should, but we just can't seem to work up an appetite for spiritual things. Often that's because we have filled up on something else—like when we fill up with chips before dinnertime. The noise of the television, the lure of the computer, the ring of the cell phone can so clutter our minds and fill up our days that we have no room left for quiet contemplation, thinking about Scripture, or listening for God. We filled up with other stuff, and now we can't work up a hunger for God.

God has given us a great deal of freedom in what we feed our schedules and our souls. Are you filling up on the junk of the world or working up a big appetite for God?

🧂🧂 | DISCUSSION STARTERS

In your opinion, what meal or restaurant is worth building up an appetite for?

Why do you think we sometimes fill up on other things besides God?

What "junk food" do you need to consider cutting out of your days so that you'll be more hungry for things of God?

God blesses those who hunger and thirst for justice, for they will be satisfied.
MATTHEW 5:6

When you open your hand, you satisfy the hunger and thirst of every living thing.
PSALM 145:16

They are headed for destruction. Their god is their appetite, they brag about shameful things, and they think only about this life here on earth.
PHILIPPIANS 3:19

They are pure in their own eyes, but they are filthy and unwashed.

PROVERBS 30:12

We are all infected and impure with sin. When we display our righteous deeds, they are nothing but filthy rags. Like autumn leaves, we wither and fall, and our sins sweep us away like the wind.

ISAIAH 64:6

They don't understand God's way of making people right with himself. Refusing to accept God's way, they cling to their own way of getting right with God by trying to keep the law.

ROMANS 10:3

My Goodness?

You've probably apologized to God for plenty of things you've done wrong. But have you ever thought of asking forgiveness for *good* things you've done? Sometimes we need to say we're sorry for doing certain good things because our motives for doing them have been wrong. If we've done them to try to impress God or other people, then that is self-righteousness. Self-righteousness is the goodness we've worked up on our own instead of the righteousness of Christ that is given to us as a gift.

Self-righteousness is the list inside our heads of what we've done or who we are that makes us acceptable to God and certainly, we think, better than the average person around us—our church attendance, our donations to charity, our self-sacrificial service. Self-righteousness keeps us thinking about *other* people who need to hear a sermon or shape up their lives, rather than seeing our own need for repentance. The opposite of self-righteousness is total dependence on the righteousness of Jesus—righteousness that is given to us to make us acceptable to God. When we agree with God's opinion of our efforts to be good—that they're all useless, all tainted with bad motives—we come to God and live before other people empty handed, with nothing good of our own to offer. And God gives us his own goodness.

 | **DISCUSSION STARTERS**

What are some of the good things people do that they believe will make them acceptable to God?

What's the difference between allowing God's righteousness to shine through your life and relying on your own righteousness?

Why would Isaiah say that our righteousness is like filthy rags?

Give Me a Break!

"Can't you just give me a break?" That's how we feel sometimes when we turn in a less-than-perfect research paper for class or a not-quite-good-enough project to a boss. It's what we want to say to the police officer when we get pulled over for driving a few miles over the speed limit. "Nobody's perfect!" we want to say, wishing our teacher or our boss or the police officer would just lower the standard so we could slip by.

That's what some people are hoping God will do someday—that he will lower his standard of perfection and let them slip into his good graces because of all their sincere efforts and good intentions. But God cannot and will not lower his standard.

The standard has been set. And the standard is holiness. It's a standard none of us can live up to. And while it might seem fair and reasonable to us that God could simply lower his standards to allow for a little sin, a little humanness, to do so would make him less than God. So how will any of us make it into his family, into his presence? We need someone perfect to take our place and live a perfect life so we can get the credit for it in God's eyes. And this is exactly what Christ has done for us! So instead of lowering the standard, he fulfills it for us. Jesus fulfills what the law demands in our place, and we get the credit for his righteousness.

 | **DISCUSSION STARTERS**

Are there times you wish your teacher or your boss or a police officer would lower the standard or change the rules for you? Would that be fair or just?

It seems like a loving God might give us a "pass" for some of our human weakness. Is that what God does when he forgives sin?

What would it tell us about God if he were to lower his standard or let some sin slip by unpunished?

MARCH

14

Don't misunderstand why I have come. I did not come to abolish the law of Moses or the writings of the prophets. No, I came to accomplish their purpose.
MATTHEW 5:17

I no longer count on my own righteousness through obeying the law; rather, I become righteous through faith in Christ. For God's way of making us right with himself depends on faith.
PHILIPPIANS 3:9

People are counted as righteous, not because of their work, but because of their faith in God who forgives sinners.
ROMANS 4:5

Do This to Remember Me

What do you do when you want to remember someone? Put the person's picture up in your room? Put his or her number in your cell phone? Add the person to your "friend list" online?

Jesus assigned us a specific and special way of remembering him—a way that honors him. It also strengthens us and helps us feel and know that he is close to us and even in us. It's called the Lord's Supper or Communion. But sometimes when we are celebrating Communion, our minds drift to other concerns, and sometimes our hearts just aren't moved by the sacrifice of Jesus for us. How can we truly remember him at this special celebration?

When we eat the bread, our thoughts focus on how the bread symbolizes Christ's life as a human being. We are taking his life into ours—inviting him in, asking him to flow through us. We reaffirm our deliberate choice to receive Jesus into every area of our lives. When we drink the wine or juice of Communion, we focus our thoughts on the blood of Jesus and its power to take away our sin. Just as we have blood pumping through our veins giving us life, we reflect on the power of the blood of Jesus pumping life in and through us. We thank God for his sacrifice that bought our freedom and gives us power to live for him. Before we drink the wine or juice, we should ask God to show us our sin and confess it.

Communion becomes meaningful to us as we consciously remember God's forgiveness and love, demonstrated by the price Jesus paid for us on the Cross. As we enter into Communion with our thoughts and emotions, we can feel and know God's closeness around us and in us.

On the night when he was betrayed, the Lord Jesus took some bread and gave thanks to God for it. Then he broke it in pieces and said, "This is my body, which is given for you. Do this to remember me." In the same way, he took the cup of wine after supper, saying, "This cup is the new covenant between God and his people—an agreement confirmed with my blood. Do this to remember me as often as you drink it." For every time you eat this bread and drink this cup, you are announcing the Lord's death until he comes again.

1 CORINTHIANS 11:23-26

 | **DISCUSSION STARTERS**

How do you usually remember the people who mean the most to you?

What kinds of things do you usually think about during Communion?

How can the Lord's Supper nourish us spiritually?

But I'm a Good Person!

Have you ever seen a TV interview of the friends and family members of someone who has committed a terrible crime? They often say to the interviewer, "I don't know how this happened! He's really a good person!" They see the greed that drove the person to steal or the hate that pushed him or her to harm someone as a surprising exception to the person's basic character and natural tendencies.

But is that really true? Are we basically good people who occasionally do bad things? Or are we thoroughly bad people who occasionally do good things?

The Bible is like a mirror that we look into, and it shows us how we really are. And while we want to think that we are basically good, so that we can save face and feel good about ourselves, the Bible says that we are "totally evil," "desperately wicked," and "corrupt."

But the Bible also has very good news for bad people. If you're a bad person—if even the best things you've done have been tainted by your own sinful motives and thoughts, then you are the kind of person Jesus saves. But if you see yourself as a basically good person who may have made a mistake or two—if you are a person who deep down believes that God is lucky to have someone like you on his team—you are saying that you really don't need a Savior. To believe you are a good person is to think you have no need for God. To acknowledge that you are no good on your own is the first step toward becoming someone who can enjoy receiving the goodness of Jesus.

 | ## DISCUSSION STARTERS

What does it mean to be a "good person"?

How good does a person have to be to be accepted by God?

Why do you think it is hard for us to accept that we are not really good?

The LORD observed the extent of human wickedness on the earth, and he saw that everything they thought or imagined was consistently and totally evil.
GENESIS 6:5

The human heart is the most deceitful of all things, and desperately wicked. Who really knows how bad it is?
JEREMIAH 17:9

The LORD looks down from heaven on the entire human race; he looks to see if anyone is truly wise, if anyone seeks God. But no, all have turned away; all have become corrupt. No one does good, not a single one!
PSALM 14:2-3

You can ask for anything in my name, and I will do it, so that the Son can bring glory to the Father.
JOHN 14:13

You didn't choose me. I chose you. I appointed you to go and produce lasting fruit, so that the Father will give you whatever you ask for, using my name.
JOHN 15:16

I tell you the truth, you will ask the Father directly, and he will grant your request because you use my name.
JOHN 16:23

Magic Words?

Do you remember when your parents told you to use the "magic word"? It was *please*, and when you said it, you received whatever it was you were asking for.

When Jesus says we should ask God for things using his name, is he saying that *in Jesus' name* are "magic words" that will get us whatever we want? Not at all. Adding "in Jesus' name" is not a special formula that adds effectiveness to our prayers. In fact, none of the prayers recorded in the Bible have "in Jesus' name" at the end of them. So why do we say it?

Coming in the name of someone means that person has given you the right to come on his or her authority, not your own. So praying in Jesus' name means praying with the authority of Jesus, on the basis of having Jesus as your mediator or go-between. The name of Jesus represents all that he is—his entire character. So praying in Jesus' name also means your request is consistent with his character. This means we would never ask for something that doesn't fit with who Jesus is and what he taught.

Prayer is a real conversation with someone who knows us better than we know ourselves. It never depends on using certain formulas or required words. It's a matter of our relationship to the one who makes it possible to come directly into God's presence through prayer: Jesus.

 | **DISCUSSION STARTERS**

What are some things you think Jesus would never pray for?

How can we be sure God hears our prayers?

What are other ways to pray "in Jesus' name" without using that phrase?

How Can I Help?

Usually when someone gives us a gift, it is for us to enjoy ourselves. But the Bible teaches that God gives each of us a spiritual gift—a special ability—not for our own enjoyment, but for the purpose of strengthening someone else's faith. These are gifts that are to be given away, not used for ourselves.

The Bible lists spiritual gifts in six different passages—each with a different list. But spiritual gifts aren't limited to these examples or categories. Spiritual gifts are any abilities the Holy Spirit gives a person in order to strengthen another person in his or her walk with God.

What does it mean to strengthen other people? To strengthen others using your spiritual gift means helping their faith not to fail under the pressures of life's difficulties. So when we see someone who is struggling in his or her faith, we can do or say what seems most helpful. And if the person is helped, then we may have discovered one of our spiritual gifts.

You don't necessarily have to be able to name your gifts. It is more important to be the kind of person who wakes up in the morning wondering how you can help other people become stronger in their faith, more confident in God's promises, and deeper in their love for Jesus because you've crossed their paths.

| DISCUSSION STARTERS

When has God used you to encourage someone else's faith?

What gifts do you see at work in other family members' lives?

What gift do you need to begin using to help others?

MARCH

18

A spiritual gift is given to each of us so we can help each other. To one person the Spirit gives the ability to give wise advice; to another the same Spirit gives a message of special knowledge. . . . It is the one and only Spirit who distributes all these gifts. He alone decides which gift each person should have.

1 CORINTHIANS 12:7-8, 11

God has given each of you a gift from his great variety of spiritual gifts. Use them well to serve one another.

1 PETER 4:10

Don't worry about anything; instead, pray about everything. Tell God what you need, and thank him for all he has done. Then you will experience God's peace, which exceeds anything we can understand. His peace will guard your hearts and minds as you live in Christ Jesus.
PHILIPPIANS 4:6-7

Give your burdens to the LORD, and he will take care of you.
PSALM 55:22

Give all your worries and cares to God, for he cares about you.
1 PETER 5:7

Don't Worry!

Do you know what it is like to wake up with a sick feeling of worry in the pit of your stomach? to have a sense of dread when the phone rings in the middle of the night? to fearfully wonder what's around the next corner?

When Paul wrote, "Don't worry about anything," the word he used for "worry" indicates choking or strangling. And that's what anxiety does. It puts a choke hold on us, wiping the joy off of our faces—and squeezing it out of the rest of our lives too. In its mildest form, we get a sick feeling in our stomachs. In its most severe form, we panic. This is no way to live.

We don't have to give in to being worriers, letting our minds continually feed on looming fears. Jesus offers those who suffer from worry and anxiety a new atmosphere of peace to live and breathe in. Rather than being consumed with fear, we can channel our energy into prayer. Believing there is no concern too small and no situation too big for God dissolves our worry into peace. We can feel safe, having our hearts guarded by the peace of God and our emotions guided by belief in God.

Though we're invited into this beautiful place of peace, we have to choose to enter in. Refusing to enter in is choosing to be emotionally bankrupt and spiritually paralyzed. What good does worry do? Why not surrender your worries and entrust your cares to God?

 | ## DISCUSSION STARTERS

What does it mean to worry? Can you think of a time when you were really worried?

Why do you think people tend to worry instead of trusting God?

What are some ways you can stop anxious thoughts when they creep into your mind?

The Good Shepherd

Shepherds—people who take care of sheep—are not usually famous. But there are a few famous shepherds—like the shepherds who saw the star when Jesus was born in Bethlehem. Another famous shepherd is David, who became king of Israel.

Since David grew up as a shepherd and knew what a good shepherd does, we listen to him a little more closely when he says that the Lord is his Shepherd. David knew from experience that a sheep's quality of life depended on how well the shepherd cared for it. Most likely he had seen neglected, suffering sheep in the care of lazy shepherds. And he had seen flocks thriving in the care of good shepherds. And because he was confident in the character, commitment, and compassion of God, he wanted to be under the care of this Good Shepherd.

But the most famous shepherd is Jesus himself. Isaiah prophesied about the Messiah this way: "He will feed his flock like a shepherd. He will carry the lambs in his arms, holding them close to his heart. He will gently lead the mother sheep with their young" (40:11). This shows us something about our Shepherd's heart. He will take care of us and tenderly carry us through the things that threaten our security, holding us close to his heart, because we are precious to him.

🧂🧂 | DISCUSSION STARTERS

What do you think a shepherd would do as part of his job? Do you think you'd want to be a shepherd?

We know that David experienced death threats from King Saul, defeats in battle, the death of a child, attempted murder by his own son, and the disappointment of not being able to build the Temple for God. With this in mind, what does it reveal about David that he could still say, "I have all that I need"?

What are the benefits of being a sheep in God's flock?

MARCH
20

The Lord is my shepherd; I have all that I need. He lets me rest in green meadows; he leads me beside peaceful streams. He renews my strength. He guides me along right paths, bringing honor to his name.
PSALM 23:1-3

Once you were like sheep who wandered away. But now you have turned to your Shepherd, the Guardian of your souls.
1 PETER 2:25

I am the good shepherd. The good shepherd sacrifices his life for the sheep. . . . I know my own sheep, and they know me.
JOHN 10:11, 14

Temptation comes from our own desires, which entice us and drag us away. These desires give birth to sinful actions. And when sin is allowed to grow, it gives birth to death.
JAMES 1:14-15

Do not let sin control the way you live; do not give in to sinful desires.
ROMANS 6:12

The sinful nature wants to do evil, which is just the opposite of what the Spirit wants. And the Spirit gives us desires that are the opposite of what the sinful nature desires. These two forces are constantly fighting each other, so you are not free to carry out your good intentions.
GALATIANS 5:17

How Did That Happen?

Have you ever gotten lost and tried to retrace your steps to figure out exactly where you took a wrong turn? Sometimes we end up where we don't want to be because of sin. And the Bible helps us retrace our steps by showing us exactly how sin happens, step by step.

Sin starts with temptation, or a strong desire for something we shouldn't have. We want this thing, so we try to rationalize and make excuses for why we are right to want what we want. At this point, we are deceived into believing that getting what we want will satisfy us and meet our need. The next step is when we make plans for getting what we want. Sin happens when we act on that plan.

It is not a sin to be tempted or to have a strong desire for something. Everyone experiences temptation—including Jesus, while he was on earth. When we're tempted, we have a choice to make about what we'll do with that desire. When we find ourselves taking the next step—rationalizing and making excuses for why we are right to want what we want—we have the chance to avoid going the wrong direction toward sin. But we can avoid sin only if we squash our excuses with the truth about how empty and unsatisfying sin is and how good and satisfying God is. A Christian is not a person who never has bad desires. A Christian is a person who says no to those bad desires and says yes to desires for God.

 | ## DISCUSSION STARTERS

Have you ever gotten lost? What helped you find your way back?

How did Jesus avoid taking the next step toward sin after he was tempted?

When you are tempted, what is the discussion like in your head that helps you say no to sin?

Is God Mad?

It never feels good when you know you've done something that has made someone really mad at you. Worse yet is being afraid of what someone is going to do to you because he or she is really mad at you!

A lot of people believe God is mad at them, and they fear what he is going to do to them. But is God angry and fuming, waiting to take out his anger on us?

The Bible says, "God is love" (1 JOHN 4:8, 16). It never says, "God is anger." But God's anger shows us how serious his love is. You see, God is mad about sin because sin hurts us and distances us from him. His anger is not like human anger. It is an appropriate and fair reaction to our indifference and disobedience. Because he cares about us and the way sin hurts us, he can't sit back and do nothing. And because he is perfectly holy and just, he has to pour out his anger on sin.

So here is how much God loves us: God offered up a willing substitute—Jesus—and poured out his anger over our sin not on us, but on him. We don't have to fear God's anger. Jesus experienced it in our place.

 | ## DISCUSSION STARTERS

When you're mad at someone, how do you treat the person?

How is your anger different from God's anger?

Why did God have to punish sin? Why couldn't he just excuse it?

Don't you see how wonderfully kind, tolerant, and patient God is with you? Does this mean nothing to you? Can't you see that his kindness is intended to turn you from your sin? But because you are stubborn and refuse to turn from your sin, you are storing up terrible punishment for yourself. For a day of anger is coming, when God's righteous judgment will be revealed.
ROMANS 2:4-5

Since we have been made right in God's sight by the blood of Christ, he will certainly save us from God's condemnation.
ROMANS 5: 9

God chose to save us through our Lord Jesus Christ, not to pour out his anger on us.
1 THESSALONIANS 5:9

MARCH

23

As they were eating, Jesus took some bread and blessed it. Then he broke it in pieces and gave it to the disciples, saying, "Take this and eat it, for this is my body."

MATTHEW 26:26

The kind of sorrow God wants us to experience leads us away from sin and results in salvation.

2 CORINTHIANS 7:10

I am glad to boast about my weaknesses, so that the power of Christ can work through me. That's why I take pleasure in my weaknesses, and in the insults, hardships, persecutions, and troubles that I suffer for Christ. For when I am weak, then I am strong.

2 CORINTHIANS 12:9-10

A Good Kind of Broken

Usually when something is broken, we get rid of it. We see it as useless. But that's not how God works. It is actually our brokenness that *makes* us useful to him. In fact, brokenness is required in order for us to be pleasing to God. "The sacrifice you desire is a broken spirit," David wrote (PSALM 51:17). If brokenness is what makes us useful and pleasing to God, what does it mean to be broken?

Brokenness is a lifestyle of agreeing with God about the true condition of our hearts. It means admitting that we aren't perfect—and we never will be. It means shattering our solid determination to get what we want and be who we want, so that the life and character of Jesus can spill out of our lives. It means humbly admitting our sin and being willing to change.

Jesus didn't just tell us we need to be broken—he was willing to be broken himself. But he wasn't broken because of his sin; he was broken because of his obedience to God. God used Jesus' broken body on the cross to bring about our salvation. Jesus showed us what it means to be broken and to be used by God in painful but beautiful ways.

 | **DISCUSSION STARTERS**

Have you ever broken something? What did you do with the item after it broke?

Is brokenness something that happens to us, or is it something we do?

In what ways did Jesus show us what it means to be broken?

A Deposit to Your Account

Let's say you're hungry, and you have a twenty-dollar bill. You have two choices. You can use the twenty-dollar bill to buy some lunch. Or you can eat the twenty-dollar bill. Yuck! Of course you wouldn't eat the money! You'd use the money to buy something good for lunch.

Faith is like that twenty-dollar bill. Faith is not what saves you. Faith is the channel by which you receive what saves you—kind of like money is a channel you get fed through. What saves you is the righteousness of Christ—a gift deposited into your spiritual bank account. People are not saved because they have faith, just as they are not fed by eating twenty-dollar bills. The only way a person is saved is by being righteous enough to enter God's presence. Faith is the channel by which we get that righteousness—the righteousness of Christ.

The important word that helps us understand this truth is the word *credited*. This is an accounting or bookkeeping term. If you have placed your faith in Christ, a deposit has been made to your spiritual account. Your account has been credited. But it wasn't you who made the deposit. It was someone else. When you turn to God in faith, that faith is the channel by which Jesus makes a deposit to your account. He credits you with his own perfect righteousness. Jesus is basically saying, "You need perfection so you can enjoy being in God's presence? I'll give you mine."

 | **DISCUSSION STARTERS**

What do you know about how a bank account works?

Based on what you've earned on your own, what do you think would be in your spiritual account?

Why do you think God would want to make such an expensive deposit in our accounts?

Abram believed the LORD, and he credited it to him as righteousness.
GENESIS 15:6, NIV

We who live by the Spirit eagerly wait to receive by faith the righteousness God has promised to us.
GALATIANS 5:5

I no longer count on my own righteousness through obeying the law; rather, I become righteous through faith in Christ. For God's way of making us right with himself depends on faith.
PHILIPPIANS 3:9

Oh, what joy for those whose disobedience is forgiven, whose sins are put out of sight. Yes, what joy for those whose record the Lord has cleared of sin.

ROMANS 4:7-8

Speak tenderly to Jerusalem, and proclaim to her that her hard service has been completed, that her sin has been paid for, that she has received from the Lord's hand double for all her sins.

ISAIAH 40:2, NIV

God Picks Up Your Tab

Do you know what it means for someone to "pick up the tab"? It's when one person pays the bill on behalf of someone else.

When King David said, "Oh, what joy for those whose disobedience is forgiven" (PSALM 32:1-2), he was celebrating that someone had "picked up his tab." He had run up a big debt from the sins he'd committed. Because God is perfectly just, the debt for sin has to be paid. And David knew that. He also knew that his record of sin included impure thoughts, unfaithfulness to marriage vows, and murder. So when he rejoiced that the long tab he had run up by his sin had been covered and would not be counted against him, it was no small celebration!

How was his debt covered? And just as important, how is *our* debt covered for the sins we commit? Do we have to pay for our sins ourselves? To settle our accounts with God, two things need to happen. We need the righteousness of Christ deposited into our accounts. But we also need someone to pay off the debt we owe because of our sin.

And that is what Jesus has done. We have racked up a big debt of sin that needs to be paid for. Jesus says, "Hand the bill to me—I'll pay it. It's a debt that you owe, but I will pay it myself." That's why Jesus went to the Cross. There he paid the debt for every wrong you've ever done. And that's what makes the gospel such good and almost unbelievable news: Jesus has paid the debt you owe.

 | **DISCUSSION STARTERS**

Have you ever known someone who had a big debt to pay off? How do you think this person would feel if someone paid his or her debt for them?

Are there any sins so big that Jesus is unwilling to pay the debt for them?

Knowing what a big debt Jesus paid for us, what do you think we can do or say in response?

Who Me? Holy?

We use the word *holy* in some very unholy ways: "Holy cow!" we say as an expression of surprise. "That child is a holy terror" we say about an out-of-control child. But the Bible takes holiness very seriously. In fact, God has set holiness as the goal of our lives—the target we're aiming for. God said, "You must be holy because I am holy" (LEVITICUS 11:45). So what does it mean to be holy?

Holiness involves doing what's right, but it is much more than that. To be holy is to be set apart *for* God and *to* God. The evidence that we are becoming holy is that our thoughts, actions, and desires become more centered on God and what is pleasing to him.

When God says that he wants us to be holy, that doesn't mean he expects us to be perfect here and now. He is moving us in that direction and will complete the process when he comes back for us. But even now, we can commit ourselves to becoming closer in reality to what he has already declared us to be through our connectedness to Christ: holy.

Some people think that because God is so generous with grace, holy living is optional—that God sets it out there but doesn't expect it. But God's grace is not a get-out-of-jail-free card for living apart from God. It makes us want to live lives that center around God and are pleasing to him. God's grace empowers us to become holy like he is.

🥛 | DISCUSSION STARTERS

What comes to mind when you hear the word *holy* or *holiness*?

Is holiness mostly about what we do, why we do it, or the way we do it?

What are some practical ways you can be holy in your everyday life?

MARCH

26

God loved us and chose us in Christ to be holy.
EPHESIANS 1:4

His Spirit has made you holy. As a result, you have obeyed him.
1 PETER 1:2

You must live as God's obedient children. Don't slip back into your old ways of living to satisfy your own desires. You didn't know any better then. But now you must be holy in everything you do, just as God who chose you is holy.
1 PETER 1:14-15

MARCH

27

Jesus took Peter and the two brothers, James and John, and led them up a high mountain to be alone. As the men watched, Jesus' appearance was transformed so that his face shone like the sun, and his clothes became as white as light.

MATTHEW 17:1-2

We saw his majestic splendor with our own eyes when he received honor and glory from God the Father. The voice from the majestic glory of God said to him, "This is my dearly loved Son, who brings me great joy." We ourselves heard that voice from heaven when we were with him on the holy mountain. Because of that experience, we have even greater confidence in the message proclaimed by the prophets.

2 PETER 1:16-19

A Glimpse of Glory

Sometimes when we're doing something scary, we lose our confidence. That's why it helps to have someone stronger assure us, "You'll be fine. I'm right here. I'll catch you if you fall."

Jesus told his disciples that he was going to Jerusalem, where he would be killed. That news must have been overwhelming and heartbreaking to the disciples—not at all what they'd had in mind when they left everything to follow Jesus. Six days later, Jesus took Peter, James, and John up on a high mountain. Perhaps Jesus knew they needed a confidence boost so they could accept this difficult message and the tough times that were coming.

So Jesus gave them a glimpse of his glory. It was as if he said, "Look at me," knowing that seeing him in all his real glory was what they needed to face their fears. Jesus let them see the powerful, radiant glory that had been poured into his flesh when he came to earth as a baby. They could see him for who he really is, and it made them want to stay there with him and worship him. But instead they followed their Master down the mountain and toward the Cross. And years later they could say that this experience gave them greater confidence in the truth and power of the gospel.

 | **DISCUSSION STARTERS**

Can you think of a time you needed confidence to face something difficult?

Read the story of the Transfiguration in Matthew 17:1-9. What do you think it would have been like to be there?

How do you think this experience on the mountain must have changed the disciples' outlook and level of confidence?

Walking with God

Some families have a family Bible or other keepsake that traces the lives of their grandparents and great-grandparents. They can read the birth dates and death dates of their family members going back many generations.

Genesis has a long list of descendents from Adam to Noah, where we read over and over that so-and-so lived X number of years. Until we get to Enoch. It doesn't say that Enoch lived three hundred sixty-five years; it says Enoch *walked with God* three hundred sixty-five years. So evidently there's a big difference between walking with God and merely living.

When we read of someone who "walked with God," someone who "pleased God," we tend to dismiss it as a possibility only for an elite superspiritual few—people who lived in Bible times. To be recognized as one who pleases God can seem out of our reach, can't it?

God does not require great acts of faith or some over-the-top commitment to service. He simply wants to walk with you day by day. He wants to begin and end the day with you; he wants you to be aware of his presence every moment in between. He wants us to walk with him in faith, simply and consistently, by talking with him, listening to him, and sharing our lives with him. He wants us to walk in step with him, not run ahead of him or drag our feet in doing what he has called us to do. And as we diligently seek him, he is pleased.

Enoch lived 365 years, walking in close fellowship with God. Then one day he disappeared, because God took him.
GENESIS 5:23-24

It was by faith that Enoch was taken up to heaven without dying—"he disappeared, because God took him." For before he was taken up, he was known as a person who pleased God. And it is impossible to please God without faith. Anyone who wants to come to him must believe that God exists and that he rewards those who sincerely seek him.
HEBREWS 11:5-6

🧂🧂 | DISCUSSION STARTERS

If your name were recorded in a long list of family names, what would you want to be remembered for?

What do you think it means to walk with God?

What do you think it takes to be pleasing to God?

MARCH

29

A farmer went out to plant his seed. As he scattered it across his field, some seed fell on a footpath, where it was stepped on, and the birds ate it. Other seed fell among rocks. It began to grow, but the plant soon wilted and died for lack of moisture. Other seed fell among thorns that grew up with it and choked out the tender plants. Still other seed fell on fertile soil. This seed grew and produced a crop that was a hundred times as much as had been planted!

LUKE 8:5-8

Testing the Soil

Did you know you can take a bucket full of dirt from your yard to a laboratory and have it tested to see what it needs to grow plants better? More important, did you know we are supposed to have the soil of our hearts tested?

Jesus described hearts as having different kinds of soil. And he said we need to examine or test the soil of our hearts if we want his Word to take root there and grow into a crop of right living.

For some people, the soil of their hearts has been hardened by disappointment and doubt. Their hearts become calloused when they are pricked over and over by the truth but they fail to respond. For others, the seed of God's Word falls on hearts with shallow, stony soil. These are people who respond enthusiastically to God initially but never allow his Word to run deep and take root in their lives. When the heat of hardship beats down on them, there is no deep inner strength to face it.

All of us find the soil of our hearts infected at times with thorns and weeds. Our lives become so easily cluttered with time-wasting and soul-absorbing things. We find ourselves sitting in church thinking about our plans for the afternoon or rushing through our devotions so we can get on with "more important things." This type of heart soil is dangerous and deceiving, as we may hardly notice the weeds of empty pleasure and activity growing up around us. The weeds choke out the true seed of God's Word before it can grow into something beautiful and fruitful in our lives.

 | **DISCUSSION STARTERS**

Read the story of the soils from Luke again. What are the four kinds of soil the seed can fall on?

Is it possible to change the soil of our hearts? If so, how?

What do you think God wants to grow in the soil of your heart?

Clearing the Pathway

If you live in a place where there are significant temperature changes, then you probably know what potholes are. Potholes are places on the surface of a road where a portion has broken away, leaving a hole.

Potholes can be annoying when we come across them on the road, but most of our roads today are luxurious compared to the roads in ancient times. Because the roads were so bad then, when a king was preparing to visit a certain area, a team of people went ahead of him to build smooth roads to make his journey as easy and direct as possible.

This is what the prophet Isaiah had in mind when he made the prophecy that John the Baptist would prepare the way for Israel's future King, the Messiah. John was the "voice shouting" for people to prepare not their roads but their hearts for the coming of Jesus. Preparing a pathway for King Jesus requires repentance—getting rid of anything and everything that puts a barrier between us and God. Repentance clears the pathway for him to come to us.

To prepare our hearts for the King means that we tear down mountains of stubborn opinions and fill up valleys created by shallow, pleasure-seeking habits. We clear away obstacles of meaningless rituals and lingering conflicts. We clean up everything that is cluttering the pathway between us and God. God wants to build a highway into our lives so he can come and dwell with us.

 | ## DISCUSSION STARTERS

When someone is visiting your house, what do you do to get ready?

What kinds of obstacles clutter the pathway between us and God?

How can we welcome Jesus into our lives and prepare the way for him?

John went from place to place on both sides of the Jordan River, preaching that people should be baptized to show that they had repented of their sins and turned to God to be forgiven. Isaiah had spoken of John when he said, "He is a voice shouting in the wilderness,

'Prepare the way for the Lord's coming! Clear the road for him!

The valleys will be filled, and the mountains and hills made level.

The curves will be straightened, and the rough places made smooth.

And then all people will see the salvation sent from God.'"

LUKE 3:3-6

Fear of the LORD is the foundation of wisdom.
PROVERBS 9:10

Get wisdom; develop good judgment. Don't forget my words or turn away from them.
PROVERBS 4:5

His Spirit searches out everything and shows us God's deep secrets.
1 CORINTHIANS 2:10

The Wisdom of God

If someone tells you, "Get some milk at the store," you know what you're looking for and where to get it. But when we read the instruction in Proverbs to "get wisdom," we're left to wonder, what exactly is wisdom? And how do we get it?

Wisdom is knowing what the greatest goal is in any situation and the best way to achieve it. It's different from knowledge, but you need knowledge to exercise wisdom.

Another way to describe wisdom is that it's knowing the right and best thing to do with the knowledge you have. There are many people who are brilliant but foolish. And there are many wise people who are not well educated.

So how does a person get wisdom? The only way to get wisdom is to receive it from God. "If you need wisdom, ask our generous God, and he will give it to you" (JAMES 1:5). Real wisdom doesn't come naturally. It is not something you are born with or can develop through study. It is supernatural. It is a gift from God. To get the wisdom of God, you don't need a certain level of intelligence, education, or experience. But you do need humility and a hunger for God. When we realize how big God is and how small we are, we are convinced that we don't have what it takes to make it through life on our own. And it's only then that we're ready to receive wisdom from God as a gift. So if you want to grow in wisdom, ask for it—beg for it. God has promised to give it to you when you ask.

 | ## DISCUSSION STARTERS

What's the difference between knowing a lot and having wisdom?

What are some ways a person can grow in wisdom?

What are some of the characteristics of people you know who have godly wisdom?

Foolishness

If we saw someone trade in a painting by a famous artist like Monet or Picasso for a painting by a first grader, we would think, *What a fool! That person must not understand how valuable that painting is!*

We tend to think of a fool as a person who doesn't have the brains to grasp the meaning of things, or someone who can't understand things. But foolish people are not unintelligent; they just have no sense of what is valuable and what is worthless, and that impacts how they live. They understand what they can have through the person and work of Christ but find it unnecessary, unsatisfying, perhaps even ridiculous. And instead of trading in their lives for something that will be satisfying and worthwhile in the end, fools trade in their time and energy and attention for what is worthless and won't last.

The Bible tells us that on our own we are all foolish. We simply can't see how valuable Jesus is. But as the Holy Spirit takes over our thoughts and our value systems, we begin to see the true value of things. We go from being bored by the Bible to enjoying God's Word. We go from seeing ourselves as the center of the universe to seeing God as worthy of all our worship. The Spirit enables us to see how worthless a life outside of Christ is and how precious it is to know and walk with Christ.

Only fools say in their hearts,
"There is no God."
PSALM 14:1

The wisdom of this world
is foolishness to God.
1 CORINTHIANS 3:19

People who aren't spiritual
can't receive these truths
from God's Spirit. It all sounds
foolish to them and they can't
understand it, for only those
who are spiritual can understand what the Spirit means.
1 CORINTHIANS 2:14

 | ## DISCUSSION STARTERS

What's the most foolish thing you've done or seen someone else do?

Do you think it's possible to be intellectually smart but foolish about spiritual things? Why or why not?

What can you do to become less foolish and more wise?

APRIL

2

Taking the twelve disciples aside, Jesus said, "Listen, we're going up to Jerusalem, where all the predictions of the prophets concerning the Son of Man will come true. He will be handed over to the Romans, and he will be mocked, treated shamefully, and spit upon. They will flog him with a whip and kill him, but on the third day he will rise again."

LUKE 18:31-33

Should I pray, "Father, save me from this hour"? But this is the very reason I came!

JOHN 12:27

Live a life filled with love, following the example of Christ. He loved us and offered himself as a sacrifice for us.

EPHESIANS 5:2

Walking toward Jerusalem

If you knew that certain suffering and death was at the end of the road you were traveling on, would you keep going down that road? Most of us would turn around and go the opposite direction as fast as possible. But not Jesus.

As Jesus traveled the road that led him into Jerusalem, he knew exactly what was waiting for him there. He told his disciples that he would be handed over to the Romans, made fun of, spit on, whipped, and killed. But Luke 9:51 says that instead of turning and going the other direction to escape what was ahead for him, "Jesus resolutely set out for Jerusalem."

Jesus was not a victim who was caught by surprise by cruel people out to get him. He walked into the death trap laid for him fully aware of what was ahead. Jesus offered himself willingly as a sacrifice for sin. "No one can take my life from me," said Jesus. "I sacrifice it voluntarily" (JOHN 10:18). Jesus' death was planned long before he was born in Bethlehem, so his death was not the failure of his plan, but the fulfillment of it.

 | DISCUSSION STARTERS

What emotions do you think Jesus felt as he went toward Jerusalem, knowing the suffering that was ahead for him there?

How was Jesus' suffering different from the suffering we usually experience?

When God calls us to do something uncomfortable or perhaps even dangerous, how can looking at Jesus' example help us?

The King's Arrival

Sometimes when we're waiting for something special, we begin to picture in our minds what it will be like. But sometimes when we finally get what we've been waiting for, it's different from what we'd expected.

The Jewish people had been waiting a long, long time for the Messiah. They knew from the prophets that the Messiah would be the king of Israel and that Jerusalem would be his capital city, where he'd rule the world in peace and righteousness. And they were right. What they didn't understand was that the victory Jesus would win over sin and Satan and death would be won by his own suffering and death. And the Kingdom they thought would be established immediately would, in fact, take thousands of years before being fulfilled completely.

Many of the people in Jesus' day were disappointed that Jesus was not the kind of king they were looking for. But he is the King. And in time his Kingdom will bring peace to all nations. In fact, another "Palm Sunday" is coming when "a vast crowd" will be "clothed in white robes" with "palm branches in their hands" before the throne of God (REVELATION 7:9). And we will be part of it—welcoming and worshiping King Jesus.

 | **DISCUSSION STARTERS**

How would you expect a king to enter a city? How did Jesus enter Jerusalem?

In what ways are we like the people of Jesus' day who expected Jesus to fulfill all his promises immediately?

Just a few days after hailing Jesus as King, many of the people cried out for his crucifixion. How do you think this could have happened?

The crowd was listening to everything Jesus said. And because he was nearing Jerusalem, he told them a story to correct the impression that the Kingdom of God would begin right away.
LUKE 19:11

A large crowd of Passover visitors took palm branches and went down the road to meet him. They shouted, "Praise God! Blessings on the one who comes in the name of the LORD! Hail to the King of Israel!"

Jesus found a young donkey and rode on it, fulfilling the prophecy that said: "Don't be afraid, people of Jerusalem. Look, your King is coming, riding on a donkey's colt."
JOHN 12:12-15

4

The LORD holds a cup in his hand that is full of foaming wine mixed with spices. He pours out the wine in judgment, and all the wicked must drink it, draining it to the dregs.

PSALM 75:8

He went on a little farther and bowed with his face to the ground, praying, "My Father! If it is possible, let this cup of suffering be taken away from me. Yet I want your will to be done, not mine."

MATTHEW 26:39

I will lift up the cup of salvation and praise the LORD's name for saving me.

PSALM 116:13

The Cup

Have you ever poured yourself a glass of milk and started to drink it only to discover that it is sour? It tastes so awful you have to spit it out. No one wants to drink a cup of sour milk. Now imagine a cup that is filled not with sour milk but with the white-hot, punishing anger of God against sin. Imagine the fury of God against everything evil put into liquid form and poured in a cup. Then imagine being asked to drink it.

That is what Jesus faced when he was in the garden of Gethsemane on the night before he was crucified. He didn't want to drink it. So he cried out to God three times, asking God to take the cup away, if possible. It wasn't primarily the physical pain of crucifixion that Jesus wanted to avoid. It was a much more significant suffering—the agony of drinking the cup of God's judgment and experiencing the break in relationship with his Father that would come from drinking that cup.

But drink it he did—every last drop—so that we won't have to drink it. In fact, because he drank the cup of wrath, we are handed another cup to drink from, filled not with judgment but with salvation. This cup can never be emptied. It is always full and overflowing.

Which cup will you drink from—the cup of God's judgment or the cup of salvation?

 | ## DISCUSSION STARTERS

What is the yuckiest drink you have ever tasted?

What do you think it meant for Jesus to drink the cup of God's judgment? What did it mean emotionally? physically? spiritually?

What does it mean to you to drink from the cup of salvation?

Betrayed with a Kiss

There are kisses—and then there are *kisses*. There is the quick peck on the cheek a toddler gives to his grandma. But that is nothing like the kiss a new husband gives his bride at the altar. While kisses have different meanings, we mostly think of kisses in terms of affection or romance.

In Jesus' time, there was another kind of kiss: a kiss of greeting. Men in that culture would kiss each other on the cheek much like we shake hands today. But Judas's kiss was different. His was a kiss of betrayal. Judas had been Jesus' close companion for three years. And while he walked and worked with Jesus, evidently he never truly followed Jesus. And when Judas saw that Jesus was not going to bring the political kingdom he had been counting on, he wanted out. More than that, he wanted payback for what he saw as three wasted years of poverty. So for about four months' worth of pay, he handed Jesus over to those who wanted to kill him.

Of all the pain Jesus experienced in the crucifixion, certainly this sting of betrayal cut his heart like a knife. It wouldn't have hurt so much if just anybody had set him up for arrest. But Judas was his trusted friend. And that place of closeness gave Judas the access to be able to wound Jesus deeply. But even at this low point in his life, Jesus showed us how to live, how to love, and how to forgive. He called Judas his friend (SEE MATTHEW 26:50), reaching out one more time to remind Judas of his mercy.

👥 | DISCUSSION STARTERS

What do different kinds of kisses mean today?

What thoughts or memories might have gone through Jesus' mind when Judas showed up with the crowd and kissed him?

What does Jesus' response to Judas show us about how to respond when we are betrayed by someone close to us?

Wounds from a sincere friend are better than many kisses from an enemy.
PROVERBS 27:6

Judas, one of the twelve disciples, arrived with a crowd of men armed with swords and clubs. They had been sent by the leading priests and elders of the people. The traitor, Judas, had given them a prearranged signal: "You will know which one to arrest when I greet him with a kiss."
MATTHEW 26:47-48

Judas walked over to Jesus to greet him with a kiss. But Jesus said, "Judas, would you betray the Son of Man with a kiss?"
LUKE 22:47-48

Spitting in His Face

I t is the ultimate insult, the ultimate expression of disrespect and disgust, to spit in someone's face. Now can you imagine the arrogance and the foolishness of someone who would actually spit in the face of God? Doesn't the very idea make you cringe?

But that is actually what people did. They spit in Jesus' face. This is the same face that had looked on thousands of people with compassion to heal their diseases and forgive their sins. It is the same face that was striped with tears as he looked over the city of Jerusalem, wishing he could gather the people like a mother hen gathers her chicks to love and protect them. What kind of people could look that kind of love in the face and spit at it?

Our kind of people. All people. The truth is, all of us are natural God-haters. Until the Holy Spirit reveals to us the beauty and value of Christ, our hearts are set against him. Until he makes our hearts new, our natural response is to spit in God's face. But when he reveals himself to us and changes our hearts, rather than spitting in his face, we bow before him to worship. Instead of spitting, we start submitting. He turns our hatred into love, and he forgives us for all our hateful ways.

I offered my back to those who beat me and my cheeks to those who pulled out my beard. I did not hide my face from mockery and spitting.
ISAIAH 50:6

They began to spit in Jesus' face and beat him with their fists. And some slapped him.
MATTHEW 26:67

God, who said, "Let there be light in the darkness," has made this light shine in our hearts so we could know the glory of God that is seen in the face of Jesus Christ.
2 CORINTHIANS 4:6

 | **DISCUSSION STARTERS**

How do you think you would feel if someone spit in your face?

What are some ways people "spit in Jesus' face" today?

If people spit in Jesus' face, how do you think people will act toward you for following Jesus? How should you respond?

The Silent Lamb

Has anyone ever accused you of doing something you didn't do? If so, what did you do? If you're like most people, you probably spoke up and defended yourself, telling everyone you were innocent. When someone says we did something wrong that we didn't do, we want people to know the truth.

But it is interesting to see how Jesus responded when he was in this situation. Even though people were lying about what he had said and done, and even though they were ready to kill him based on those false charges, Jesus didn't speak up to defend himself. He stayed silent.

What do we learn from the example of Jesus? Jesus shows us that we don't always have to defend ourselves or make sure we set the record straight about what we have and haven't done. We can be content that "God is pleased with you when you do what you know is right and patiently endure unfair treatment" (1 PETER 2:19).

But more important, we learn that when we are not innocent—when we have done something wrong and feel deep shame—we don't have to live under that burden of shame. You see, when Jesus took our sin on himself, he endured all the punishment of that sin. And shame is a part of punishment. Jesus was willing to take on our sin as well as our shame, so we don't have to bear the blame or the shame.

> He was oppressed and treated harshly, yet he never said a word. He was led like a lamb to the slaughter. And as a sheep is silent before the shearers, he did not open his mouth.
> *ISAIAH 53:7*

> The high priest stood up and said to Jesus, "Well, aren't you going to answer these charges? What do you have to say for yourself?" But Jesus remained silent.
> *MATTHEW 26:62-63*

 | **DISCUSSION STARTERS**

What does it feel like when someone says you did something wrong that you really didn't do? Why do we want others to know it isn't true?

What is shame? Is it a good thing or a bad thing?

When we still feel ashamed after asking God for forgiveness, how can it help us to know that Jesus took our shame on himself?

Really, Really Thirsty

O God, you are my God;
I earnestly search for you.
My soul thirsts for you; my
whole body longs for you in
this parched and weary land
where there is no water.

PSALM 63:1

Those who drink the water
I give will never be thirsty
again. It becomes a fresh,
bubbling spring within them,
giving them eternal life.

JOHN 4:14

To fulfill Scripture he
said, "I am thirsty."

JOHN 19:28

Have you ever seen a movie or TV program that shows people lost at sea, baking in the sun on their raft, desperately thirsty and surrounded by salt water that they can't drink? Drinking salt water only increases a person's thirst and causes even more intense dehydration. So even though it looks inviting when you're really thirsty, it will only make you thirstier.

In a sense, when we expect the things of this world—like experiences, entertainment, or success—to satisfy us, it is like we have put our heads down into salty water, only to find it causes us to dry up.

As Jesus hung on the cross he said, "I am thirsty." It is interesting that he said this, because throughout being whipped and beaten and nailed to the cross, he never complained about the physical torture and agony. So when he said, "I am thirsty," he probably wasn't talking about a physical thirst, even though he must have been desperately thirsty. More likely he was speaking as our substitute, as the one who became sin for us. He was saying that he felt the agonizing pain every sinner deserves to feel forever. And in our place, Jesus descended into hell—that place of unquenchable thirst and scorching fire. Jesus Christ experienced the agonizing thirst of eternal punishment on behalf of those who turn to God for the living water of life.

 | **DISCUSSION STARTERS**

When you are really, really thirsty, what drink best satisfies your thirst?

Why do you think Scripture uses the metaphor of thirst to describe intense longing?

How would you explain to someone what it means to drink the living water of Christ?

Passover

When you open an umbrella and walk in the rain, the rain keeps on falling, but you are protected and kept dry by the umbrella. God was preparing to "rain down" judgment on the Egyptians, causing the death of the firstborn son in every home where the true God was not feared and obeyed. But he provided a way for his people to be protected from this storm of death—a covering. He instructed the Israelites to kill a lamb and mark the doorframes of their houses with the lamb's blood. Death would "pass over" those houses marked with blood.

The phrase *pass over* has a deeper meaning than just the idea of skipping over something to avoid contact. The Hebrew word used here means spreading the wings over and protecting. This word tells us that God not only passed by the houses of Israelites but that he stood on guard, protecting each family behind the blood-marked doorways. The feast of Passover celebrates God's protection through the blood of the lamb.

God is still providing his people with the protection we need from eternal death. Out of his love and mercy, he protects those whose lives are marked by the blood of the true Passover Lamb—Jesus. He protects us when we put our faith in the power of his blood to shield us from judgment.

 | **DISCUSSION STARTERS**

Tell about a time you felt protected in a scary or dangerous situation.

How did the lambs that were killed at the first Passover point to the sacrificial death of Jesus?

What does the story of Passover show about God's judgment and mercy?

The whole assembly of the community of Israel must slaughter their lamb or young goat at twilight. They are to take some of the blood and smear it on the sides and top of the doorframes of the houses where they eat the animal. . . . On that night I will pass through the land of Egypt and strike down every firstborn son and firstborn male animal in the land of Egypt. I will execute judgment against all the gods of Egypt, for I am the LORD! But the blood on your doorposts will serve as a sign, marking the houses where you are staying. When I see the blood, I will pass over you.
EXODUS 12:6-7, 12-13

Christ, our Passover Lamb, has been sacrificed for us.
1 CORINTHIANS 5:7

Abandoned

Have you ever seen a story on the news about a baby who has been left on the doorstep of a church or a hospital or a police station? For whatever reason, the baby's mother couldn't take care of the baby and abandoned him or her.

It's hard to think about parents abandoning children they were meant to love. Now imagine God the Father abandoning his own Son. It's even more difficult to understand, isn't it? It sounds impossible, because we know how much God loves his Son. And yet there was a painful point in time when God turned his back on Jesus. *Why would he do that?* we wonder. And Jesus wondered too, crying out from the cross, "My God, why have you abandoned me?"

But God had to abandon Jesus. You see, all our sin—all the jealousy, anger, and rebellion, all the lying, stealing, and having bad attitudes, all the times we say things we know we shouldn't—it was all laid on Jesus. And because God cannot look upon sin, he had to turn away.

But Jesus was not completely abandoned by his Father. Jesus spoke to his Father again from the cross, shouting, "Father, I entrust my spirit into your hands!" (LUKE 23:46). Though Jesus was abandoned because of our sin, he was not abandoned forever. Once the price for sin was paid, he was welcomed into God's presence. And because Jesus was abandoned, it means we don't have to be. We, too, will one day be welcomed into the presence of God.

At about three o'clock, Jesus called out with a loud voice, *"Eli, Eli, lema sabachthani?"* which means "My God, my God, why have you abandoned me?"
MATTHEW 27:46

My God, my God, why have you abandoned me? Why are you so far away when I groan for help?
PSALM 22:1

No, I will not abandon you as orphans—I will come to you.
JOHN 14:18

 | ## DISCUSSION STARTERS

Have you ever felt abandoned or alone? Were you truly abandoned?

What does God's abandonment of Jesus on the cross tell us about how God feels about sin?

How do we know that God will never abandon us because of our sin?

Behind the Curtain

When you go to someone's house, you usually wait to be invited in. But there may be some people you know well enough that you don't even have to knock when you visit them. You are welcome to walk right in.

In Old Testament times there was a curtain in the Temple, and God's presence was behind the curtain. But people could not walk right in behind the curtain. According to the rules in the Old Testament, only one person—a priest—could go behind the curtain, and he could only go in once a year. Not just anyone could go directly into God's presence, because people's sins separated them from God.

But that changed the day—the very moment—Jesus died. That day the Temple curtain that had separated people from God was ripped from top to bottom. It wasn't ripped by any person, but by God himself. In that culture, people expressed their sorrow by tearing their clothes. It was almost as if the dwelling place of God was so saddened by the death of Jesus that it tore its clothing. At the same time, it was as if God was throwing open the door to his house and welcoming us in. Because of what Jesus accomplished on the cross in paying for our sin, there is no longer a barrier of sin between God and his people.

| DISCUSSION STARTERS

Are there any places in your house or school or church that are off limits? Why can only certain people go in these places?

What is the significance of the day and time the curtain was split?

How would worshiping God in Old Testament times have been different from the way we worship him now?

The LORD said to Moses, "Warn your brother, Aaron, not to enter the Most Holy Place behind the inner curtain whenever he chooses; if he does, he will die. For the Ark's cover—the place of atonement—is there, and I myself am present in the cloud above the atonement cover."
LEVITICUS 16:2

Jesus uttered another loud cry and breathed his last. And the curtain in the sanctuary of the Temple was torn in two, from top to bottom.
MARK 15:37-38

Dear brothers and sisters, we can boldly enter heaven's Most Holy Place because of the blood of Jesus. By his death, Jesus opened a new and life-giving way through the curtain into the Most Holy Place.
HEBREWS 10:19-20

APRIL

12

He isn't here! He is risen from the dead, just as he said would happen.
MATTHEW 28:6

Christ has been raised from the dead. He is the first of a great harvest of all who have died.
1 CORINTHIANS 15:20

The Lord himself will come down from heaven with a commanding shout, with the voice of the archangel, and with the trumpet call of God. First, the Christians who have died will rise from their graves.
1 THESSALONIANS 4:16

The First One Up

Who is usually the first one to get up in the morning at your house? Is there someone who likes to wake up before everyone else?

We celebrate the resurrection of Jesus at Easter because Jesus was the first one up in the house of God. Jesus didn't get out of bed first. He rose from the grave first. His was the first body to come back to life and never die again. But Jesus will not be the only one whose body will rise from its grave; he's just the first. He's leading the way. Observing his resurrection shows us what the resurrection of our own bodies will be like.

If you have joined yourself to Jesus, the moment your body dies, your spirit will immediately be in the presence of Jesus. Your body will be in the ground waiting for resurrection. And one day, when Jesus returns to this earth, your body will rise out of your grave and be like his.

We all have bodies that will die, because we're all descendants of Adam and Eve. Adam and Eve sinned and brought death down on all of us, and since then every other human being except Jesus has sinned too. But every believer who has ever died, every body belonging to someone who loved Jesus that is in the grave, is going to come out of the grave perfect someday—just like Jesus' resurrection body. Bodies die because of Adam's sin. Bodies live because of Christ's resurrection.

 | DISCUSSION STARTERS

What do you think will be the best parts about getting a new resurrection body someday?

What do we know about Jesus' resurrection body that gives us clues about what ours will be like?

How would you explain to a friend why we celebrate the Resurrection?

It's All about Me

Imagine pointing to a book that doesn't even have your name in it and saying, "It's all about me. All of it." It would be hard for someone else to understand how that could be true. But that's what Jesus said.

Jesus had just risen from the dead when he started walking beside two of his followers, although they didn't know it was Jesus. These disciples were leaving Jerusalem terribly disappointed. They had expected Jesus to start his earthly Kingdom immediately, and instead he had died on a cross. There were rumors going around that he'd risen from the dead. But these disciples just didn't get it. They couldn't see it. And so as he walked alongside them, Jesus started going through the Old Testament and showing them everything it said about the Messiah and how he fulfilled it perfectly. Perhaps he said something like this:

"Can't you see that I am the promised one who was to bruise the serpent's head, the descendant of Abraham through whom all nations were to be blessed? I am the substance of every Old Testament sacrifice commanded in the law of Moses. I am the true deliverer and King—the one all the judges and deliverers in Jewish history pointed to. I am the coming prophet greater than Moses. I am the Ark of safety from God's judgment, the scapegoat that took on the sin of others, the bronze serpent to look upon to be saved, the Lamb that was slaughtered, the High Priest to represent you before God. On every page, it's all about me!"

🧂🧂 | DISCUSSION STARTERS

If you could walk with Jesus like these followers did, what questions would you ask him?

What could have made it difficult for the two disciples to recognize Jesus?

What do you look forward to Jesus explaining to you about himself?

> You search the Scriptures because you think they give you eternal life. But the Scriptures point to me!
> *JOHN 5:39*

> Two of Jesus' followers were walking to the village of Emmaus. . . . Jesus himself suddenly came and began walking with them. But God kept them from recognizing him. . . .
>
> Then Jesus took them through the writings of Moses and all the prophets, explaining from all the Scriptures the things concerning himself.
> *LUKE 24:13, 15-16, 27*

Jesus told him, "You believe because you have seen me. Blessed are those who believe without seeing me."
JOHN 20:29

You love him even though you have never seen him. Though you do not see him now, you trust him; and you rejoice with a glorious, inexpressible joy. The reward for trusting him will be the salvation of your souls.
1 PETER 1:8-9

Faith is the confidence that what we hope for will actually happen; it gives us assurance about things we cannot see.
HEBREWS 11:1

Believing without Seeing

Some people say they'll only believe something if they can prove it or if they can see it with their own eyes. If they can't see it, touch it, hear it, or prove it some other way, they won't believe.

Did you know that Jesus is understanding when it comes to people who have a hard time believing in what they can't see? He showed us that when he was willing to give proof to his disciple Thomas. Thomas said he wouldn't believe that Jesus had risen from the dead unless he touched Jesus' hands where the nails had been and Jesus' side where the spear had wounded him. When Jesus appeared to Thomas, he said, "Put your finger here, and look at my hands. Put your hand into the wound in my side. Don't be faithless any longer. Believe!" And Thomas said, "My Lord and my God!" (JOHN 20:27-28).

Then Jesus responded that those who believe without seeing him are blessed. Jesus knew a time was coming when all who believed in him would do so without the benefit of seeing him with their eyes or touching him with their hands. So he gives us the gift of faith. Faith gives us the confidence to believe in a Jesus we have never seen with our physical eyes.

 | ## DISCUSSION STARTERS

Can you think of anything you believe in that you've never seen with your eyes? How about love? the law of gravity? What else?

What do you think Jesus meant when he said that those who believe without seeing are blessed?

How would you have expected Jesus to respond to Thomas's request for proof? How does it make you feel to know that Jesus responded this way?

Why Pay Taxes?

There's something satisfying about working hard and earning money for a job well done. But there's something annoying about having to give some of our hard-earned money to the government in the form of taxes. Nobody enjoys paying taxes.

Sometimes we dislike paying taxes because we don't agree with how the money is used or because we find it hard to respect those who make the decisions in the government—especially if those leaders make decisions that go against what we know is pleasing to God.

So why pay taxes? Jesus taught that we should pay everyone what we owe—if we owe taxes, we are to pay them. If we owe respect, we are to give respect. God is the one who made human governments as a way of running the world. We submit to our government and pay taxes and honor our leaders, not necessarily because they are worthy of it or because they have earned that honor, but because we want to please and obey God.

 | **DISCUSSION STARTERS**

What are some good things about our government you can thank God for?

Are there ever times it would please God for us to break the law?

Who is in authority over you? What difference does it make in your attitude and behavior to understand that all authority comes from God?

Give to Caesar what belongs to Caesar, and give to God what belongs to God.
MATTHEW 22:21

Everyone must submit to governing authorities. For all authority comes from God, and those in positions of authority have been placed there by God.
ROMANS 13:1

Pay your taxes, too, for these same reasons. For government workers need to be paid. They are serving God in what they do. Give to everyone what you owe them: Pay your taxes and government fees to those who collect them, and give respect and honor to those who are in authority.
ROMANS 13:6-7

Failed and Failed Again

There aren't many things worse than facing up to failure—a failed test, a failed business, or a failed relationship. Sometimes when we fail, we want to hide. We'd just rather not face the truth and feel the brunt of our disappointment.

Peter had failed Jesus, and failed again. He failed Jesus by denying that he knew him—even while Jesus was being beaten. Then after Jesus rose from the dead and instructed the disciples to wait in Galilee, Peter failed again. He and the disciples went to Galilee for a while. But then they got tired of waiting and went back to what they did before following Jesus—they went fishing.

When Peter heard Jesus calling to him from the shore, we might expect that Peter would hide, embarrassed by failure heaped on failure. That is what a lot of us try to do when we've let God down. We hide. We keep our distance. But Peter showed us what to do when we've failed God. He dove into the water in a rush to get back to Jesus. He didn't let his shame hold him back. And Jesus was there waiting for him, not with harsh words of criticism but with a comforting breakfast.

God is not looking for people who never fail. But he welcomes people who hurry to be restored when they fail—people who won't let anything get in the way of having their relationship with him restored.

Suddenly, the Lord's words flashed through Peter's mind: "Before the rooster crows tomorrow morning, you will deny three times that you even know me." And Peter left the courtyard, weeping bitterly.

LUKE 22:61-62

At dawn Jesus was standing on the beach, but the disciples couldn't see who he was. He called out, "Fellows, have you caught any fish?" . . . Then the disciple Jesus loved said to Peter, "It's the Lord!" When Simon Peter heard that it was the Lord, he put on his tunic, . . . jumped into the water, and headed to shore.

JOHN 21:4-5, 7

 | ## DISCUSSION STARTERS

When you fail at something, how do you usually react?

Why do you think Peter was willing to dive into the water to get back to Jesus?

What are we afraid of when we fail God? Do we need to be afraid?

Do You Love Me?

If you say, "I love ice cream" or, "I love riding my bicycle," most people will know what you mean. But what does it mean to say, "I love God"? Is it a feeling, or is it an action? Is it a choice we make or a gift we're given?

Some people say that loving God is an action, and no emotions or feelings are required. Some say loving God is the same thing as obedience to him, since Jesus said, "If you love me, obey my commandments" (JOHN 14:15). But while keeping Jesus' commandments flows out of our love for him, it is not the definition of our love for him. If we love Jesus, we will want to obey him and live the life he wants us to live. Beneath these actions will be strong feelings of awe about who Jesus is, enjoyment of his presence in our lives, gratitude for his love for us. Our love for God is not limited to an emotional feeling, but it is not empty of feeling either.

Jesus is worthy of being loved, not just through cold-hearted grit-your-teeth obedience (which could be defined as hypocrisy), but by warmhearted affection and admiration. Loving God is appreciating him, treasuring him, enjoying him. It's a reflex of the heart to all he is.

 | **DISCUSSION STARTERS**

How do you feel when you love another person? How do you show that love?

What role does obedience play in loving God?

What are some ways you can live out your love for God this week?

APRIL

17

If you love your father or mother more than you love me, you are not worthy of being mine; or if you love your son or daughter more than me, you are not worthy of being mine.
MATTHEW 10:37

Jesus told them, "If God were your Father, you would love me, because I have come to you from God."
JOHN 8:42

A third time he asked him, "Simon son of John, do you love me?"

Peter was hurt that Jesus asked the question a third time. He said, "Lord, you know everything. You know that I love you."

Jesus said, "Then feed my sheep."
JOHN 21:17

Praise the LORD, all you
nations. Praise him, all
you people of the earth.
PSALM 117:1

The Good News about the
Kingdom will be preached
throughout the whole world,
so that all nations will hear it;
and then the end will come.
MATTHEW 24:14

Go and make disciples of all
the nations, baptizing them
in the name of the Father and
the Son and the Holy Spirit.
MATTHEW 28:19

The Big Picture

Have you ever seen a mosaic picture? When you look at one closely, you see hundreds or thousands of smaller pictures or photographs. But when you step back and take in the big picture, these smaller images come together to make one main image.

When we read Jesus' final teaching, called the great commission (SEE MATTHEW 28:19), we hear his instruction to make disciples of all nations, and we see in our minds all the individuals who will come to Christ. But there is a bigger picture that emerges in Revelation 5:9 of Jesus' role in all of human history: "You were slaughtered, and your blood has ransomed people for God from every tribe and language and people and nation."

This is the big picture that all of history is moving toward. This is the big plan of God for the whole world—that people from all nations and tribes and languages will come to worship God through Jesus Christ. Jesus cares for all ethnic groups and will have disciples from every nation.

We sometimes think that the purpose of the gospel is individuals finding forgiveness and gaining the hope of eternal life. And it is. But that is not all it is. Making disciples is not just about winning individuals to Christ but about making communities of believers among all people groups, all around the world.

 | ## DISCUSSION STARTERS

What is a disciple? What do you think it means
to "make disciples"?

Is there a difference between evangelism and missions?
If so, what is it?

What part do you think God intends for you to play in this
big picture?

Pour On the Power

Picture a child walking along holding his father's hand. He is happy and secure in his father's love, but there is no powerful urge to talk about it. But then suddenly the father reaches down and sweeps the child into his arms, hugging and kissing him and telling him how much he loves him. Then he puts the child down, and they continue on their walk. The child believed his father loved him before, but now he can hardly contain himself—he wants to shout with joy over being so loved by his father.

This is a picture of what it's like when the Holy Spirit "comes upon" a person with power, as Jesus promised would happen to the disciples after he ascended and went to heaven. Before, they had a real but quiet knowledge of Jesus, but soon it would burst into an energetic outpouring of affection toward God—an overflowing joy coming from a complete confidence in him. Because the Holy Spirit filled their hearts and minds with a fresh passion for God, they couldn't resist praising him out loud and talking about him to anyone who would listen. This is what Jesus meant when he said they would receive power and be his witnesses.

 | ## DISCUSSION STARTERS

What do you think it means for us to be powerful? How does a person become powerful?

In what ways have you seen God's power in your life?

What do the verses above tell us about what the Holy Spirit wants to do in and through a believer's life?

I will pour out my Spirit upon the people of Israel. I, the Sovereign LORD, have spoken!
EZEKIEL 39:29

You will receive power when the Holy Spirit comes upon you. And you will be my witnesses, telling people about me everywhere—in Jerusalem, throughout Judea, in Samaria, and to the ends of the earth.
ACTS 1:8

By his divine power, God has given us everything we need for living a godly life. We have received all of this by coming to know him, the one who called us to himself by means of his marvelous glory and excellence.
2 PETER 1:3

The Most Famous Person in the World

In this world of reality TV, *American Idol*, and YouTube, it seems like everyone wants to be famous. Some people are famous for what they've done, some are famous for who they know, and some have figured out how to be famous just for being famous.

Would you believe that God wants to be famous? That sounds kind of strange to us, because it can sound like God is selfish or arrogant, just wanting to be the center of attention.

But God's passion for his own fame doesn't come from an out-of-control sense of pride; it comes from his perfection. His passion to be known and honored and worshiped isn't an expression of his love for himself; it's his loving us. He knows that his glory—the beauty of all he is—is the only thing that can ever make us truly happy forever. And he wants everyone to know him and to share in his eternal happiness.

What does God most want to be famous for? His mercy—his generous forgiveness of sinners. The mercy of God is the crown of his glory. He wants to be famous for showing mercy to people like you and me who deserve punishment. He gets the glory, and we get mercy.

O LORD, our Lord, your majestic name fills the earth! Your glory is higher than the heavens.
PSALM 8:1

LORD, we show our trust in you by obeying your laws; our heart's desire is to glorify your name.
ISAIAH 26:8

The Scriptures say that God told Pharaoh, "I have appointed you for the very purpose of displaying my power in you and to spread my fame throughout the earth."
ROMANS 9:17

 | ## DISCUSSION STARTERS

Would you want to be famous? What do you think would be the best and worst parts of being famous?

Why do you think being famous appeals to people? Do you think fame delivers what it promises?

In what ways can God use us to spread his fame?

Trampling on the Son of God

When you walk along a sidewalk and you look down and spot a dollar bill, you pick it up because you see it as something of value. But when you see a discarded gum wrapper or a used ticket stub, you don't pick it up; you just walk over it or step on it, because it is worthless to you.

Sometimes we keep chasing after something we know is sin, even after we've come alive to God and his goodness. When we do this, it's as if we see Christ's sacrifice for us on the cross and then just walk right over it, trampling it under our feet, because we see it as worthless. It's as if we say, "I know it's sin, but I am going to do it anyway." And in doing so, we're rejecting the sacrifice of Christ, saying, "I don't need you or your holiness. I want to live my way, not your way."

Once we become followers of Christ, we become more serious about how we deal with sin. We can't fool ourselves into thinking we can just keep walking toward sin after knowing and experiencing the truth. If we do, it's like we're trampling the Son of God.

As a believer you *will* sin, but if you find that you keep on choosing to sin without feeling sad about it, then you need to question if you have really placed your faith in Christ. But when you feel sad about your sin, you can celebrate that as confirmation that you want Jesus more than you want to go your own way.

🧂🧂 | DISCUSSION STARTERS

What is something that's worth a lot to you? What do you do to take care of that item?

Are there some sins we tend not to take very seriously in our society? in our churches?

How do you usually feel after you've sinned? In what way is conviction of sin a gift?

> If we deliberately continue sinning after we have received knowledge of the truth, there is no longer any sacrifice that will cover these sins. . . . Think how much worse the punishment will be for those who have trampled on the Son of God, and have treated the blood of the covenant as if it were common and unholy.
> *HEBREWS 10:26, 29*

> Should we keep on sinning so that God can show us more and more of his wonderful grace? Of course not! Since we have died to sin, how can we continue to live in it?
> *ROMANS 6:1-2*

> Anyone who continues to live in him will not sin. But anyone who keeps on sinning does not know him or understand who he is.
> *1 JOHN 3:6*

I will praise you as long as I live, lifting up my hands to you in prayer.
PSALM 63:4

Jesus led them to Bethany, and lifting his hands to heaven, he blessed them.
LUKE 24:50

In every place of worship, I want men to pray with holy hands lifted up to God.
1 TIMOTHY 2:8

Holy Hands

As children we are taught to fold our hands in prayer. But perhaps that has more to do with keeping our hands out of mischief than helping us approach God. So what do our hands have to do with the way we relate to God?

Throughout Scripture we are called to lift up our hands to God—in motions of asking and receiving, as well as motions of giving and blessing. When we lift our palms to God, that might express openness, invitation, and surrender. When we reach out our hands to God, that might signify asking him for something or depending on him. When we extend our open hands to God, that might symbolize blessing God.

Desperate for a response from God, David said, "I spread out my hands to you; my soul thirsts for you like a parched land" (PSALM 143:6, NIV). Our hands can mirror our souls as they stretch out to touch God. David also lovingly called to his faithful God with hands lifted up: "I will praise you as long as I live, lifting up my hands to you in prayer" (PSALM 63:4). Lifted hands reflect a connected heart.

Lifting hands is common in some church traditions and rare in others. But the lifting of hands isn't really about what kind of church you go to. And lifting up our hands to God should never become a meaningless habit or a spiritual show. If we're only lifting our hands in his direction to impress those around us, what an insult that would be to God! When our thoughts are about ourselves and our hearts feel cold toward God, we lift up our hands to him because of what we know about him. And that simple gesture can draw our hearts toward him.

 | ### DISCUSSION STARTERS

Is there a certain position that helps you to focus when you pray?

What is your church's view of the lifting of hands? Why do you think this is?

Have you ever lifted your hands in worship? If so, what does it mean to you? If not, what is holding you back?

A Good Trade

We all make trades all the time. We trade money for things like groceries. We trade time for a paycheck or watching TV. We trade energy for a tennis match or a service project. Every kid who has ever traded baseball cards knows that a good trade is defined by getting something back that is as valuable or more valuable than what was traded away, while a bad trade is getting something less valuable than what was traded away.

Jesus told us a story about two people who made trades—very expensive trades. He told about a man who discovered a hidden treasure in a field, and a pearl merchant who found a pearl of great value. They both traded everything they owned to have the treasure and the pearl. Jesus was saying that *he* is a treasure, a valuable pearl, and that it's worth trading everything you own so you can have him.

The psalm writers understand this concept when they say, "I would rather be a gatekeeper in the house of my God than live the good life in the homes of the wicked" (PSALM 84:10). The psalm writers see it as a good trade to give up the stuff of this world for a relationship with God. Paul was also willing to make what he saw as a good trade. He writes, "Everything else is worthless when compared with the infinite value of knowing Christ Jesus my Lord. For his sake I have discarded everything else, counting it all as garbage, so that I could gain Christ and become one with him" (PHILIPPIANS 3:8-9). Anything and everything you give up or give away to enjoy Jesus more will be a wise trade.

> The Kingdom of Heaven is like a treasure that a man discovered hidden in a field. In his excitement, he hid it again and sold everything he owned to get enough money to buy the field. Again, the Kingdom of Heaven is like a merchant on the lookout for choice pearls. When he discovered a pearl of great value, he sold everything he owned and bought it!
>
> *MATTHEW 13:44-46*

> They traded their glorious God for a statue of a grass-eating bull.
>
> *PSALM 106:20*

 | ## DISCUSSION STARTERS

What's the most significant thing you've traded? Was it a good trade or a bad trade?

What kinds of things do we need to trade away to have Jesus?

What have you traded so far for Jesus? Would you say it has been a good trade?

I am the LORD, who
makes you holy.
EXODUS 31:13

Make them holy by your
truth; teach them your
word, which is truth.
JOHN 17:17

May the God of peace make
you holy in every way,
and may your whole spirit
and soul and body be kept
blameless until our Lord Jesus
Christ comes again. God will
make this happen, for he
who calls you is faithful.
1 THESSALONIANS 5:23-24

Will I Ever Be Holy?

Have you ever been given a task that seemed too big for you? Did you think to yourself, *If it is up to me, I will never get this job done*?

When we understand that God wants us to be holy like he is, it can be very discouraging. We know ourselves and our weaknesses too well to think that we can do this job on our own. So some of us just give up on it altogether.

Fortunately, God gives us the ability to become what he commands us to be, and to do what he commands us to do. When God revealed himself in the Old Testament as "the LORD, who makes you holy," he was talking not only about his divine nature but also about his divine help. The same God who makes us right in his sight by paying for our sin and giving us Christ's righteousness is at work in us to renew our thinking and clean up our motives and capture our affections. His grace not only covers our sin of the past; it also gives us what we need to make headway in overcoming our sin, now and in the future. He is in the process of making us holy like he is.

The good news about God's desire for us to become holy is that he doesn't leave it up to us to accomplish this big job on our own. He is at work in us, chipping away at our selfishness, our lies, our hardened hearts. Holiness is not something that happens instantly. It's an ongoing project that God is doing in us.

 | **DISCUSSION STARTERS**

What jobs have you felt unable to do on your own and needed help to complete?

If there is absolutely no growth toward holiness in a person's life, what might that say about the person?

Knowing that it's God's job to make us holy, what is our part in the process?

Nobody Likes to Wait

We don't like to wait—not at traffic lights or in checkout lines or at bus stops. It is even harder to wait for someone who is far away to return home, for the money you need to pay the bills, for someone you love to come to faith, or for a loved one with a serious illness to be healed. Waiting on the Lord to act or to provide or to heal is hard. But waiting has a purpose. Waiting on God reminds us of how much we depend on him, and that's a good thing to be reminded of.

Think about all the people in the Bible who had to wait—Abraham and Sarah waiting for a child, Joseph waiting to be released from prison, the children of Israel waiting in the desert to enter the Promised Land, the Jewish people waiting for their Messiah to come.

When we're impatient and refuse to wait, it is actually a form of unbelief. By rushing to take things into our own hands, we're saying that we don't believe in God's timing or his guidance or his ability to provide the right opportunities.

But when we learn to wait patiently on God, he does something important inside our souls. Waiting teaches us dependence on God's promises. We confront the temptation to not wait by reminding ourselves of these promises. They convince our hearts that God's timing and guidance and power are enough to take this frustrated, boxed-in, unproductive situation and make something eternally valuable out of it. God is not trying to make us miserable when he makes us wait. He's working in us to make us holy, which will make us happy.

Be still in the presence of the LORD, and wait patiently for him to act.
PSALM 37:7

I waited patiently for the LORD to help me, and he turned to me and heard my cry.
PSALM 40:1

The Scriptures give us hope and encouragement as we wait patiently for God's promises to be fulfilled.
ROMANS 15:4

☕ | DISCUSSION STARTERS

When do you find it especially difficult to wait?

What good things can come from the process and time of waiting on God?

What are you waiting for now? What will it mean to wait patiently on God in this situation?

There are six things the LORD hates—no, seven things he detests: haughty eyes, a lying tongue, hands that kill the innocent, a heart that plots evil, feet that race to do wrong, a false witness who pours out lies, a person who sows discord in a family.

PROVERBS 6:16-19

God Hates

Every family has words that can't be used—inappropriate words, hurtful words. There are some families that don't allow the word *hate* because it is a very strong word and is often used in hurtful ways. But did you know that there are some things God hates? And we know that everything God does is perfect and right. Because God is so good, we want to love what God loves and hate what God hates. So what does God hate, and what does God love?

Solomon gave us a list of seven things God hates: (1) God hates pride that is so much a part of a person that others can see it in his or her eyes. He hates the way that person looks down on other people. God loves humility. (2) God hates lies and loves the truth. (3) God hates murder because he created life and made it sacred. (4) God hates hearts that are passionate about finding new ways to sin against him. God loves it when people enjoy pleasing him. (5) God hates feet that run toward sin—not those that trip and fall into it. God loves feet that run toward doing what is right. (6) God hates those who are willing to lie about someone else to make themselves look good. God loves to hear us lift others up. (7) God hates those who enjoy creating disagreements and carelessly hurt other people's feelings. God loves it when we love each other well.

 | ## DISCUSSION STARTERS

The first five things God hates are things that are done by parts of our bodies. What could you do with those body parts instead that would be pleasing to God?

Pick one of the things God hates. Why do you think he feels so strongly about that? How does it reveal his love for you?

What can you do to love others in your family well?

Is It Okay to Be Mad at God?

Mad at God. Have you ever felt that way? Were you disappointed that he didn't answer your prayer the way you'd hoped, or were you angry that he seemed to take away something or someone you love?

Sometimes people encourage us to express our anger toward God, assuring us that God understands and accepts our honest emotions. It's natural to be angry when you don't get your way, and God is an easy target for that anger. But do we really have a right to be angry with our Creator? Does God really owe us an explanation for what he does? When it comes down to it, isn't it pretty arrogant for us as limited, sinful creatures to disapprove of what God does and what he permits?

Does this mean that being honest with God about how you feel is sinful? No. When we feel it, we might as well admit it, since he knows anyway, and being fake about it only adds to our sin. You may *feel* angry with God at times, but as you work through your feelings and as you inform your feelings by what you know to be true about God, you can reject the temptation to turn your back on God. You can refuse to point a finger in the face of God, saying, "You are not good!" Instead, you can pour out your angry feelings before God, asking him to correct your wrong thoughts and change your strong feelings. He gives angry people grace and peace.

 | DISCUSSION STARTERS

How does your anger usually come out when you are mad at someone?

What is the difference between pouring out your disappointment before God and accusing God of doing something wrong?

Understanding that this world is broken because of sin, where should our anger be directed instead of at God?

This change of plans greatly upset Jonah, and he became very angry. So he complained to the LORD about it: "Didn't I say before I left home that you would do this, LORD? That is why I ran away to Tarshish! I knew that you are a merciful and compassionate God, slow to get angry and filled with unfailing love. You are eager to turn back from destroying people." . . .

The LORD replied, "Is it right for you to be angry about this?"

JONAH 4:1-2, 4

The people will declare, "The LORD is the source of all my righteousness and strength." And all who were angry with him will come to him and be ashamed.

ISAIAH 45:24

Ark of Safety

It would be hard to believe there was going to be a flood if you had never seen one before. But what if you'd never seen a thunderstorm? And what if you'd never even seen a raindrop?

Hebrews 11 says that Noah was warned about things not yet seen. He had never seen a flood or a thunderstorm, and he may have never even seen a raindrop. But he believed God. Even though this was all new to him, he took God at his word that there would be judgment on the earth in the form of a flood. He also believed that God would provide a way for him and his family to escape judgment. Noah had confidence that, just as God promised, the ark would protect them from the judgment that was about to fall on the earth in the form of raindrops.

Even though we all deserve judgment because of our sin against a holy God, that same God has provided an ark of safety where we can take refuge from the storm of judgment. Jesus himself is the ark, and all who believe can take refuge in him.

Look! I am about to cover the earth with a flood that will destroy every living thing that breathes. Everything on earth will die. But I will confirm my covenant with you. So enter the boat—you and your wife and your sons and their wives. Bring a pair of every kind of animal—a male and a female—into the boat with you to keep them alive during the flood.
GENESIS 6:17-19

They deliberately forget that God made the heavens by the word of his command, and he brought the earth out from the water and surrounded it with water. Then he used the water to destroy the ancient world with a mighty flood. And by the same word, the present heavens and earth have been stored up for fire. They are being kept for the day of judgment, when ungodly people will be destroyed.
2 PETER 3:5-7

 | ## DISCUSSION STARTERS

Tell about the biggest storm you've ever watched or experienced.

How do you think Noah must have felt before the storm as he was building the ark?

What if Noah's family had decided they didn't really need the ark? What will happen to people who decide they don't really need Jesus?

Hate My Family?

When we read the words of Jesus telling us that to be his disciples we need to hate father and mother, wife and children, brothers and sisters, it is shocking—and perhaps confusing. We wonder for a minute if Jesus forgot the fifth commandment: "Honor your father and mother."

But Jesus actually criticized the Pharisees for coming up with a way to get around the commandment to honor their parents (SEE MARK 7:9-13). So we know he hadn't forgotten it and he considered it important. What did he mean when he said we need to hate our families to be his followers?

Jesus likely meant for his words to be shocking. He wanted to startle his listeners into understanding what would be demanded from them if they were going to follow him, so they could count the cost. Jesus was not saying that we should neglect our families or dishonor our parents. The hate he was calling for has nothing to do with dislike or unkindness. Jesus was calling his disciples to such a radical devotion to him that their attachment to everything else—including their own families—would seem like hatred by comparison.

Jesus wasn't so much talking about how we care for our families as he was saying that he wants to be more than just another person we care about. He is calling us to have the kind of loyalty and devotion to him that we give to the people we love most.

🧂 | DISCUSSION STARTERS

How do you think Jesus treated his own earthly family?

How is the hatred Jesus was talking about different from hatred as we usually think of it?

What does Mark 10:29-30 promise to the person who loves Jesus more than anyone else?

APRIL

29

If you want to be my disciple, you must hate everyone else by comparison—your father and mother, wife and children, brothers and sisters—yes, even your own life. Otherwise, you cannot be my disciple.

LUKE 14:26

I assure you that everyone who has given up house or brothers or sisters or mother or father or children or property, for my sake and for the Good News, will receive now in return a hundred times as many houses, brothers, sisters, mothers, children, and property— along with persecution.

MARK 10:29-30

I will give them singleness of heart and put a new spirit within them. I will take away their stony, stubborn heart and give them a tender, responsive heart.
EZEKIEL 11:19

"Because your heart was tender and you humbled yourself before God when you heard His words against this place and against its inhabitants, and because you humbled yourself before Me, tore your clothes and wept before Me, I truly have heard you," declares the LORD.
2 CHRONICLES 34:27, NASB

The sacrifice you desire is a broken spirit. You will not reject a broken and repentant heart, O God.
PSALM 51:17

Are You Sensitive?

Have you ever had a section of skin that was very tender due to a burn or an injury? You probably didn't want anything to touch it or put pressure on it because it was so sensitive.

Having a heart that is sensitive to being touched—even though it might cause some pain—is something that God values and is even drawn to. As he works in us, his goal is not to give us thick skin so that nothing can hurt us. In fact, the Bible is filled with warnings about becoming callous, insensitive, and hard hearted.

The opposite of being tender is being cold and machine-like about the things of God and the hurts of others. Nothing can touch people who are like this. They pride themselves in their lack of tears. They carefully protect their hearts from being broken by the things that break the heart of God, and therefore they have little genuine closeness to him.

God wants us to stay soft and tender, moldable, and even vulnerable, because this is what we need to be responsive to him. We'll know we're being soft toward God when we're sensitive to sin, compassionate toward the hurts of others, and ready to listen for God's direction and guidance.

 | **DISCUSSION STARTERS**

What does it mean to be sensitive? Would you consider yourself to be a sensitive person?

Why do you think some people tend to be uncomfortable with sensitivity and tenderness?

What are some signs to watch for that indicate a growing insensitivity to the things of God?

Everything Changes

Styles change. Cultures change. Governments change. Scientific theories change. People change. Sometimes it seems like the only thing we can be sure of is that everything changes. But there is one thing that has never changed and will never change: the Word of God.

The gospel never changes. The way it's communicated might change, but the essential Good News that God saves sinners will never change or disappear. God's plans for this world will not change. His character will not change. Jesus will not change. His power over the universe will not fade, and his love for us will not grow cold. Styles of music may change and styles of preaching may change, and Bible versions may change to keep up with current language, but God's Word will never change. Christians may be harassed or persecuted, but God's Word will never go away. The gospel may be attacked, but it cannot be robbed of its saving power. The Bible can be misquoted and misused, rejected and ridiculed, but it cannot be corrupted.

We are unreliable, unsteady, and inconsistent. Even our good intentions come and go. We collapse under the heat of criticism and crumble underneath the weight of problems. But we have something solid and durable and dependable to build our lives on: the Word of God.

 | **DISCUSSION STARTERS**

As you look around the room, what do you notice that has changed since yesterday? What has changed since a year ago?

What things about God are you grateful to know will not change?

What difference does it make that God's Word has never changed and never will change?

People are like the grass. Their beauty fades as quickly as the flowers in a field. The grass withers and the flowers fade beneath the breath of the LORD. And so it is with people. The grass withers and the flowers fade, but the word of our God stands forever.
ISAIAH 40:6-8

Your eternal word, O LORD, stands firm in heaven.
PSALM 119:89

Jesus Christ is the same yesterday, today, and forever.
HEBREWS 13:8

Great Faith

There's a big difference between the people described in the first part of this list in Hebrews 11 and the people in the second part, isn't there? Everything seemed to go right for the people in the first part—they were victorious and saw God at work on their behalf. But when we read the second half of the list, we kind of wonder why God didn't show up and stop the people from being tortured, why God allowed these followers to face poverty and beatings and even death.

We could be tempted to think that the people in the first group had faith while those in the second didn't. But "all these people earned a good reputation because of their faith." There are some people who teach that the life of faith will bring health, wealth, and success, and that if those things are lacking it's because faith is lacking. But God does not necessarily reward faith with an easy life here. He rewards faith with the blessing of more of himself—in this life and in the life to come. He offers more of his presence and power, in the midst of good times and bad. It takes great faith to depend on God to do great things. And it takes tremendous faith to trust God and stand for him in the face of torture, hunger, and death. Faith says, "Whether I succeed or fail, live or die, I'm yours, God."

By faith these people overthrew kingdoms, ruled with justice, and received what God had promised them. They shut the mouths of lions, quenched the flames of fire, and escaped death by the edge of the sword. Their weakness was turned to strength. They became strong in battle and put whole armies to flight. . . .

But others . . . were jeered at, and their backs were cut open with whips. Others were chained in prisons. Some died by stoning, some were sawed in half, and others were killed with the sword. Some went about wearing skins of sheep and goats, destitute and oppressed and mistreated. They were too good for this world, wandering over deserts and mountains, hiding in caves and holes in the ground.

All these people earned a good reputation because of their faith.

HEBREWS 11:33-39

 | **DISCUSSION STARTERS**

How did the people in the first paragraph live out their faith?

How did the people in the second paragraph live out their faith?

How do you live out your faith?

Tempted like We Are

We're naturally skeptical of anyone who offers advice or opinions if they've never been where we are. What athlete wants coaching tips from someone who has never played the game? Who wants to trust a nurse who says, "It won't hurt a bit," if she has never had a shot?

Isn't it a relief to know that Jesus understands what it is like to live in this world with its temptations? Jesus was tempted in all the ways we are. Jesus was tempted to lie in order to make himself look good. Jesus was tempted to cut corners in the carpenter's shop to make a few extra bucks. Jesus was tempted to take a long, inappropriate look at a pretty girl when she walked by. Jesus was tempted to dishonor his parents when they didn't understand him. Jesus was tempted to be jealous of someone else's home when he had no home of his own. Jesus was tempted to seek revenge when someone he loved was senselessly murdered.

Jesus doesn't roll his eyes or wonder why we would consider giving in to temptation. He doesn't take lightly our struggles with sin, because he knows what it is like to be tempted. Jesus was tempted in all the ways we are—yet he never gave in to sin.

 | **DISCUSSION STARTERS**

Who do you usually take advice from? Why do you trust these people?

Is it possible to resist temptation? How?

Read Matthew 4:1-11. How does Jesus fight temptation in these verses? How can we use the same weapons to fight temptation?

> Jesus was led by the Spirit into the wilderness to be tempted there by the devil.
> *MATTHEW 4:1*

> Because he himself suffered when he was tempted, he is able to help those who are being tempted.
> *HEBREWS 2:18, NIV*

> We do not have a high priest who is unable to sympathize with our weaknesses, but we have one who has been tempted in every way, just as we are—yet was without sin.
> *HEBREWS 4:15, NIV*

Seeing Things That Can't Be Seen

We don't look at the troubles we can see now; rather, we fix our gaze on things that cannot be seen. For the things we see now will soon be gone, but the things we cannot see will last forever.

2 CORINTHIANS 4:18

We live by believing and not by seeing.

2 CORINTHIANS 5:7

Faith is the confidence that what we hope for will actually happen; it gives us assurance about things we cannot see.

HEBREWS 11:1

Have you ever watched a movie or read a book about a character who could become invisible? We might accept it for the world of fantasy, but if someone told us to look at something invisible in the real world, we would think he or she was either a little crazy or trying to trick us. But several times in the Bible we are told to "see" something that is invisible, so it must be possible.

Paul writes that "we live by believing and not by seeing" (2 CORINTHIANS 5:7). This means that the most precious and important realities in the world are beyond our five senses. So we "look" at these realities through what we know of Christ from the Bible. These truths about him were recorded by faithful witnesses who saw him and heard his voice and wrote down his message for us.

What are the things the Bible says we should "fix our gaze on" that cannot be seen? We have never seen Jesus with our physical eyes, and yet we fix our eyes of faith on him, and we believe. We can't see God's invisible hand working behind the scenes of history and in our lives, and yet by faith we believe it. We have never seen a place called heaven and can't find it on the map, and we can't imagine what it will be like. Yet we fix our eyes of faith on God's promises of the place he is preparing for us, and we believe.

This is faith—spiritually seeing God and recognizing him as the ultimate reality of the universe, the most solid truth in all creation, even though he cannot be seen with the human eye.

 | **DISCUSSION STARTERS**

What are some invisible things you wish you could see?

Is this kind of "seeing" a feeling or a decision or a gift?

What things do we have now to base belief on that the people of the Old Testament did not have?

Be Cut Back or Be Cut Off

Is there a set of pruning shears in your garage that are used for pruning the trees and shrubs in your yard? Pruning is when someone removes diseased, useless, or otherwise unwanted portions from a plant to shape it, keep it healthy, and increase its leaves, flowers, or fruits.

Just as trees and shrubs need the careful cutting of a gardener, our lives need the attention of our Father, the Gardener, if we want to be productive and healthy. God's strategy for coaxing a greater harvest out of his branches is to prune us—to cut away the things that hold us back.

It isn't easy getting pruned, is it? But it's what our Father does. And it isn't punishment. It isn't for fruitless people but for "the branches that do bear fruit." When the Father trims away things we like or things we're used to, he removes only what is keeping us from a fuller life in him. He might prune away relationships, beliefs, commitments, ambitions—anything that keeps us from going deeper with Jesus.

If you have ever asked God to make you more like him and to use you in a significant way, then his pruning is his answer to your prayers. The fact that he is cutting away things in your life reveals that he is carefully getting you ready to grow.

🥛 | DISCUSSION STARTERS

Have you ever pruned a plant or seen one pruned? How did it help the plant?

What's the difference between being cut off and being pruned?

Have you ever experienced spiritual pruning before? What was that process like?

> I am the true grapevine, and my Father is the gardener. He cuts off every branch of mine that doesn't produce fruit, and he prunes the branches that do bear fruit so they will produce even more. You have already been pruned and purified by the message I have given you.
>
> **JOHN 15:1-3**

> He will not crush the weakest reed or put out a flickering candle.
>
> **ISAIAH 42:3**

> No discipline is enjoyable while it is happening—it's painful! But afterward there will be a peaceful harvest of right living for those who are trained in this way.
>
> **HEBREWS 12:11**

What Has God Put in My Hands?

What are some things in your life that you're proud of? Maybe it's your intelligence, your athletic abilities, your social skills, your cash flow, or your musical talent. We tend to think of these things as ours—things we've earned, worked for, and deserve to do with as we please.

But the Bible indicates that everything in our hands—from our families to our reputations to our wealth—has been put there by God and is actually still God's. We are simply managers—temporarily taking care of these things. Everything belongs to him, but he entrusts gifts and resources to us to invest in this world for his purposes, not our own. This means that we should look at every resource we've been given and ask ourselves how we can be good managers of them to build up God's Kingdom. We should hold on to the things of this world loosely so that we can let go of them easily when they are needed for serving God's purposes. We can be confident that he will give us far more as a reward one day than whatever we've let go of.

What God entrusts to us is valuable to him. He expects and requires that we do all we can with what he has given us—time, talents, gifts, energy, personality, life experiences, money. When we do, we can be confident he will say to us one day, for all to hear: "Well done, my good and faithful servant. You have been faithful in handling this small amount, so now I will give you many more responsibilities. Let's celebrate together!" (MATTHEW 25:21).

When someone has been given much, much will be required in return; and when someone has been entrusted with much, even more will be required.
LUKE 12:48

The servant with the one bag of silver came and said, "Master, I knew you were a harsh man, harvesting crops you didn't plant and gathering crops you didn't cultivate. I was afraid I would lose your money, so I hid it in the earth. Look, here is your money back." But the master replied, "You wicked and lazy servant!"
MATTHEW 25:24-26

 | **DISCUSSION STARTERS**

Can you think of a time when someone entrusted you with an important job or a valuable item? What was that experience like?

Read Matthew 25:14-30. What was the basis for distributing the money? What reward was given to the wise investors?

What abilities, opportunities, and resources has God placed in your hands? How can you invest these things for his glory?

Spiritual Healing

Have you ever considered how amazing it is that our bodies can heal? Cuts mend, colds go away, and cancer can go into remission. But there are some sicknesses that people do not heal from without a miracle. This was especially true in the time of Jesus—long before antibiotics and other medications. So when Jesus healed someone, it got people's attention!

But Jesus wasn't trying to impress people with his ability to heal their bodies. He wanted them to see that the same power that enabled him to heal their bodies enabled him to heal their souls from the sickness of sin. And while the miracles Jesus performed revealed his love and compassion for hurting people, the greater purpose of each miracle was to show a picture of a deeper spiritual reality, a more significant spiritual power.

When Jesus healed a person from the skin disease leprosy, it illustrated his power to heal us from the crippling nature of sin. When he gave sight to those who were blind, he showed he could cause people with spiritual blinders to see God for who he is. When he cast out demons, he showed his power to rid us of our dominating sins. When he healed the woman with a bleeding problem, he showed that he can make us whole and clean. Through his miracles of physical healing, Jesus showed he can heal it all.

🔬 | DISCUSSION STARTERS

When your body heals naturally, would you say it's a miracle? Why or why not? When a doctor is involved in helping your body heal, would you say it's a miracle? Why or why not?

Why do we tend to value physical healing more than spiritual healing?

Have you experienced a healing of your body or your soul, or is there a particular way you want God to heal your body or soul?

> The Pharisees . . . asked his disciples, "Why does your teacher eat with such scum?"
>
> Jesus . . . said, "Healthy people don't need a doctor—sick people do." Then he added, "Now go and learn the meaning of this Scripture: 'I want you to show mercy, not offer sacrifices.' For I have come to call not those who think they are righteous, but those who know they are sinners."
>
> *MATTHEW 9:11-13*

> Jesus told him, "I entered this world to render judgment— to give sight to the blind and to show those who think they see that they are blind."
>
> *JOHN 9:39*

I have refined you, but not as silver is refined. Rather, I have refined you in the furnace of suffering.
ISAIAH 48:10

These trials will show that your faith is genuine. It is being tested as fire tests and purifies gold—though your faith is far more precious than mere gold. So when your faith remains strong through many trials, it will bring you much praise and glory and honor on the day when Jesus Christ is revealed to the whole world.
1 PETER 1:7

He will sit like a refiner of silver, burning away the dross. He will purify the Levites, refining them like gold and silver, so that they may once again offer acceptable sacrifices to the LORD.
MALACHI 3:3

Refined by Fire

In ancient times, a workman would take a piece of ore found in the ground, crush it into pieces, and place it in a pot. He would then put the pottery into a fire. The refiner would watch the fire carefully, knowing just how intense the flame needed to be to soften the ore. At a certain temperature, the impurities would rise to the top so they could be skimmed off, leaving a bubbling treasure of liquid metal.

The refiner was patient, knowing just how long the metal should stay in the fire so that more and more unwanted material would rise to the surface, until finally he could look into the liquid silver and see what he had been working for and waiting for: his own reflection.

God describes himself as a refiner. He puts us into the fire of suffering—not to hurt us, but to cause impurities in our lives to bubble to the surface so they can be removed. He knows just how hot to make the fire and how long to keep us there. He plunges us into the fire so he can shape us into his image. And he waits patiently until he can see his own reflection in us.

 | **DISCUSSION STARTERS**

What at your house is made of silver or another precious metal?

What kind of "impurities" does suffering bring to the surface in our lives?

How can suffering help us to look more like Jesus?

Finding Your Way Out

9

Before an airplane takes off, a flight attendant shows passengers how to buckle their seat belts and put on an oxygen mask. He or she usually points out lights that will come on along the floor of the aircraft in the event of a power failure or fire, pointing passengers to the nearest exit. It's good to have an exit strategy in place before things get hot! It's also wise to have an exit strategy for when the temptation to sin heats up in your life. We all need a practical plan for getting away from what will hurt us—and perhaps even destroy us.

The first strategy is to avoid what tempts you in the first place, if at all possible. "Hold on to what is good. Stay away from every kind of evil." (1 THESSALONIANS 5:21-22). Most of us know our own weaknesses, so we know what situations to avoid that bring us tremendous temptation. Second, quickly say a firm no to thoughts of temptation. Don't toss the idea around in your mind, fanning its flame. "Resist the devil, and he will flee from you" (JAMES 4:7). Talk back to the temptation with what you know is true, with what God has promised you. Focus your thoughts on the promises and joys of Christ until the temptation is exposed for the lie it is and until you want to please God more than you want to sin. Then get busy doing something productive and good. Replace your passion for something sinful with a passion for doing something pleasing to God.

 | **DISCUSSION STARTERS**

What's the closest you've ever been to a fire? Do you have a plan for getting out of your house in case of fire?

Give some examples of what it means to "talk back" to temptation.

Based on your experiences, how is pleasing God more satisfying than giving in to sin?

The temptations in your life are no different from what others experience. And God is faithful. He will not allow the temptation to be more than you can stand. When you are tempted, he will show you a way out so you can endure.
1 CORINTHIANS 10:13

Keep watch and pray, so that you will not give in to temptation. For the spirit is willing, but the body is weak.
MARK 14:38

Those who live only to satisfy their own sinful nature will harvest decay and death from that sinful nature. But those who live to please the Spirit will harvest everlasting life from the Spirit.
GALATIANS 6:8

Honor your father and mother. Then you will live a long, full life in the land the LORD your God is giving you.

EXODUS 20:12

Fear of the LORD is the foundation of true knowledge, but fools despise wisdom and discipline. My child, listen when your father corrects you. Don't neglect your mother's instruction. What you learn from them will crown you with grace and be a chain of honor around your neck.

PROVERBS 1:7-9

Give your father and mother joy! May she who gave you birth be happy.

PROVERBS 23:25

Mother Knows Best

What have you learned from your mother or other female role models in your life? How to bake a cake, ride a bike, balance a checkbook, read a book, write a letter? Your mom probably didn't have to teach you how to cry when you were born, but that's about it. After we're born we have to learn how to walk, how to talk, and how to eat, as well as how to know right from wrong. The family is the first school God gives us so we can learn what we need to know for life. Parents teach their children through modeling, counseling, explaining, correcting, and disciplining.

The Bible says the most important thing parents should teach their children is to fear God. A parent's job is to show children what it looks like to treat God with reverence, what it sounds like to talk over everything with him through prayer, what it means to worship him, and what it is like to trust him in good times and bad.

Solomon knew something about how we interact with our parents. We are often tempted to rebel by not listening when our parents give us instruction, so he told us to listen when they correct us. We're also tempted to forget about what we've learned when we leave home, so he said, "Don't neglect your mother's instruction." When children learn from their parents' teaching and example to fear God, they have learned the most important lesson in life.

 | **DISCUSSION STARTERS**

What are some specific things you learned from your mother or another female role model?

What do you think the promises in Exodus 20:12 and Proverbs 1:7-9 mean?

What are subtle ways people dishonor mothers in our society?

Run to Win!

The Olympic Games took place in Greece every four years without interruption from 776 BC until AD 393. That's 1,169 years! Since everyone in Corinth knew about the Games, Paul's readers could picture exactly what he was talking about when he wrote about running in a race to win. And so can we.

But Paul doesn't just want us to imagine athletes running in the race. He wants us to consider all the discipline and effort that go into training for the race. Olympic runners don't approach their training by trying to figure out the least amount of work they can do to get by. They do whatever needs to be done to bring about their best performance on the track.

And so should we in this race called the life of faith. Rather than putting in the least amount of effort toward godliness, we give our full attention and energy to the task of becoming like Christ and living for the glory of God. We ask ourselves, *What will make me most useful for the Kingdom? What will stir up my passion for God most? What will make me more genuine in prayer? What will trigger more hunger for God's Word? What will strengthen my commitment to love others? What will give me a greater desire for holiness?* And then we run in that direction.

 | ## DISCUSSION STARTERS

Do you think you would ever want to run a marathon or compete in the Olympics? Why or why not?

How is the prize an Olympic runner gets different from the prize won by a person who runs the race of faith?

What kinds of things weigh people down or trip them up in their faith race?

Let us strip off every weight that slows us down, especially the sin that so easily trips us up. And let us run with endurance the race God has set before us. We do this by keeping our eyes on Jesus, the champion who initiates and perfects our faith.

HEBREWS 12:1-2

Don't you realize that in a race everyone runs, but only one person gets the prize? So run to win! All athletes are disciplined in their training. They do it to win a prize that will fade away, but we do it for an eternal prize. So I run with purpose in every step. I am not just shadow-boxing. I discipline my body like an athlete, training it to do what it should.

1 CORINTHIANS 9:24-27

MAY

12

The LORD replied to Moses, "I will indeed do what you have asked, for I look favorably on you, and I know you by name."
EXODUS 33:17

I knew you before I formed you in your mother's womb.
JEREMIAH 1:5

I am the good shepherd; I know my own sheep, and they know me.
JOHN 10:14

It's Not Who You Know, but Who Knows You

Imagine standing outside the White House as the president of the United States walks by. You call out to him, and while he may look in your direction, he doesn't know you, so he doesn't respond to you. So while you may say you know the president, it doesn't really mean anything unless you have a relationship with him—unless he knows you and chooses to get to know you better.

Similarly, you could never know God if he didn't choose to know you. He's the one who initiates the relationship. Even before you were born, God knew your name and loved you personally. God doesn't relate to us as a nameless, faceless group of people, but as individuals. He knows our names.

So the good news is that God knows you. The bad news is that God really does *know* you. Every thought, every feeling, every experience—everything you are and do is known by God! In fact, he knows you better than you know yourself. He knows your intentions and motivations that you may not be consciously aware of. He knows your greatest fears, your deepest hurts, and your most cherished dreams. The good news is that God's love for you is based on knowing the worst about you and choosing to love you anyway. So no discovery can ever stop him from loving you or change his desire to bless you. You don't have to hide anything from God (as if you could!). He knows you. It's not about who you know, but about who knows you.

 | ## DISCUSSION STARTERS

If you could meet any famous person in the world, who would you choose? What would you want to tell that person?

What does it say about God that he knows his children by name?

Recognizing that God knows you better than you know yourself, how might that affect the way you talk to him about your concerns?

You're Not the Boss of Me!

Have you ever heard a kid being told what to do by an older brother or sister, until finally the kid shouts back, "You're not the boss of me!"?

That is what Paul says we should shout to sin. "Sin, you're not the boss of me. You don't control me anymore. I don't have to do what you tempt me to do!" This puts an end to our excuses. It means it just isn't true that we can't help it. We *can* keep our eating habits under control. We *can* stop ourselves from watching trashy TV shows and movies. We *can* keep our mouths shut when the gossip session starts.

Sin is not just an action; it's a power that wants to control our lives. The only way we can escape being controlled by the power of sin is to be in Christ. When we are united with him, the power of sin is broken. So we do not have to give in to what our bodies or minds tell us to do. Instead, we give ourselves—our bodies, minds, wills, and emotions—to God and say, *You're in charge. I'm yours.*

If you have the Holy Spirit, then sin is not the boss of you! Sin doesn't have the power over you it once had before you were in Christ.

| DISCUSSION STARTERS

Who do we naturally like to be "the boss" of us? Why?

If sin is no longer controlling us, what or who should control us?

What should we do when we feel powerless to overcome sin?

You . . . should consider yourselves to be dead to the power of sin and alive to God through Christ Jesus. Do not let sin control the way you live; do not give in to sinful desires. Do not let any part of your body become an instrument of evil to serve sin. Instead, give yourselves completely to God, for you were dead, but now you have new life. So use your whole body as an instrument to do what is right for the glory of God. Sin is no longer your master, for you no longer live under the requirements of the law. Instead, you live under the freedom of God's grace.
ROMANS 6:11-14

You are a slave to whatever controls you. And when people escape from the wickedness of the world by knowing our Lord and Savior Jesus Christ and then get tangled up and enslaved by sin again, they are worse off than before.
2 PETER 2:19-20

O God, you are my God;
I earnestly search for you.
My soul thirsts for you; my
whole body longs for you in
this parched and weary land
where there is no water.
PSALM 63:1

The LORD will guide you
continually, giving you
water when you are dry
and restoring your strength.
You will be like a well-
watered garden, like an
ever-flowing spring.
ISAIAH 58:11

Anyone who believes in
me may come and drink!
For the Scriptures declare,
"Rivers of living water will
flow from his heart."
JOHN 7:38

Desert Times

Has there ever been a drought where you live—a period of time when there is not enough rain, so everything dries up and turns brown? Just as nature goes through times of dryness, most Christians go through some times of dryness in their relationship with God. In times of spiritual drought, our souls feel lifeless, with no sense of nourishing connection to God. There's no new growth. We feel like we're just going through the motions of our faith.

The reality is that almost every person in the Bible who was used significantly by God went through a dry, desert time. Think about it: Moses in the desert with God's people for forty years (SEE EXODUS 16:1-3). Elijah sitting under the broom tree in the desert wanting to die (SEE 1 KINGS 19:3-5). Jesus being tempted in the desert wilderness (SEE MATTHEW 4:1-3). Being in a place where we are dry—waiting, wanting, praying, examining—is often a place of getting prepared and proving our faith.

Sometimes God is preparing us for hardship, sometimes for blessing. Usually he is preparing us so he can use us. Spiritual dryness calls for perseverance and persistence in seeking after God. In the desert, we wait for him to pour out on us new joy, new intimacy, new insights, and a fresh experience with him.

 | **DISCUSSION STARTERS**

Have you ever been in a desert before or seen one on TV? What was it like?

Why do you think God uniquely uses times of spiritual dryness to prepare us to be used by him?

What should a person who feels spiritually dry do?

Does God Need Your Help?

A grandpa climbs up onto a tractor, and his grand-daughter says, "Can I help drive?" He agrees, and she sits in his lap and "drives" the tractor. All the while it's really his hands that are guiding the machinery. Her "help" actually makes the job more challenging, but because he loves her and she loves him, he invites her to join him in his work.

This is how it is with us and God. He doesn't need our help. God is completely independent and self-sufficient. He has no needs and depends on no one. He doesn't need helpers. But he stoops to work in and through his believing and obedient children anyway. He gives us the pleasure of joining him in his work in the world.

So what does he need from us? Companionship? People sometimes think God created human beings because he was lonely and needed fellowship. But God is not lonely. God the Father enjoys perfect fellowship with the Son and the Spirit. Knowing that God doesn't need us, we might wonder if we're important at all. But the truth is, God created us and determined that we would be meaningful to him. That's the very definition of significance.

🧂🧂 | DISCUSSION STARTERS

What part of God's work in the world are you most excited about being involved in?

Jesus gave those who believe in him a commission to go into all the world and preach the gospel. Does he need us for that?

If God does not need us to work for him, keep him company, or defend him, then what is our purpose in the world?

He is the God who made the world and everything in it. Since he is Lord of heaven and earth, he doesn't live in man-made temples, and human hands can't serve his needs—for he has no needs. He himself gives life and breath to everything, and he satisfies every need.

ACTS 17:24-25

Who has given me anything that I need to pay back? Everything under heaven is mine.

JOB 41:11

God decided in advance to adopt us into his own family by bringing us to himself through Jesus Christ. This is what he wanted to do, and it gave him great pleasure.

EPHESIANS 1:5

Get Over It

Have you experienced a hurt or disappointment that's so difficult you think you'll never get better, never stop hurting, never "get over it"?

Joseph had a hurt like that. His brothers sold him into slavery. Then he was falsely accused and suffered in prison for years. He had every right to be bitter and believe he would never be able to get over the betrayal and cruelty and injustice he'd experienced.

But Joseph wasn't just depending on himself to feel better or get better. Joseph had a deep confidence that God was active in his life and could heal him and use him. And God did use him in amazing ways. Joseph got out of prison and ended up saving many of his people—including the brothers who had betrayed him! To celebrate and broadcast what God had done in his life through his suffering, Joseph gave his two sons very special names. He named his firstborn son Manasseh, which means, "God has made me forget all my troubles and everyone in my father's family." God not only enabled Joseph to forgive, he also helped him forget, so his brothers' betrayal no longer caused a sting in his soul. Joseph named his second son Ephraim, which means, "God has made me fruitful in this land of my grief." In spite of the hardships he had experienced, Joseph saw that God was blessing his life by using him in significant ways.

This is how God helps us "get over" our hurts. He works in us to give us faith so we can forgive and forget, and then be fruitful for him.

Joseph named his older son Manasseh, for he said, "God has made me forget all my troubles and everyone in my father's family." Joseph named his second son Ephraim, for he said, "God has made me fruitful in this land of my grief."
GENESIS 41:51-52

I focus on this one thing: Forgetting the past and looking forward to what lies ahead, I press on to reach the end of the race and receive the heavenly prize for which God, through Christ Jesus, is calling us.
PHILIPPIANS 3:13-14

 | **DISCUSSION STARTERS**

What's something you had to forgive a family member or friend for? How did that compare to what Joseph's brothers did to him?

What do you think Joseph meant by saying God made him "forget"?

In what ways did God make Joseph fruitful?

A Step of Faith

Imagine you are invited to live in a big, beautiful mansion, but you are too afraid to go inside so you just live in a tent on the front lawn. There's a cozy, comfortable room waiting for you in the house, but you refuse to go in.

That's what it's like when a person finds out about the gospel—hears the invitation and understands it, sees other people entering in and enjoying it—but circles around it refusing to walk through the door of belief and trust. The person isn't willing to grab hold of it or commit to entering in.

This was what it was like for the children of Israel. They had heard the good news from Caleb and Joshua that the land God had promised them was theirs for the taking. But their response to that good news was lacking. They had seen the Red Sea part and the pillars of cloud and fire; they had eaten manna supplied by God every day. But now as they were faced with a new challenge, they simply didn't trust God. They wouldn't take the step of faith to enter the Promised Land God was inviting them into.

When we combine active trust with simple belief, we can find real rest. It does no good to hear the gospel if we don't believe it, if we don't respond to it in faith, if we don't go to Christ for salvation. Faith that pleases God is belief that's more than just a mental acceptance that something is true. It is a belief that blossoms into trust and plays out in the way we live our lives.

MAY

17

God's promise of entering his rest still stands, so we ought to tremble with fear that some of you might fail to experience it. For this good news—that God has prepared this rest—has been announced to us just as it was to them. But it did them no good because they didn't share the faith of those who listened to God. For only who believe can enter his rest. . . . Let us do our best to enter that rest. But if we disobey God, as the people of Israel did, we will fall.

HEBREWS 4:1-3, 11

 | **DISCUSSION STARTERS**

How is a refusal to trust God like sitting in front of a banquet and not eating or being offered a treasure and not taking it?

Why do you think people sometimes choose not to trust God?

What is the evidence that a person wholeheartedly trusts God?

I tell you the truth, all sin and blasphemy can be forgiven, but anyone who blasphemes the Holy Spirit will never be forgiven. This is a sin with eternal consequences.

MARK 3:28-29

It is impossible to bring back to repentance those who were once enlightened— those who have experienced the good things of heaven and shared in the Holy Spirit, who have tasted the goodness of the word of God and the power of the age to come—and who then turn away from God. It is impossible to bring such people back to repentance.

HEBREWS 6:4-6

Anyone who speaks against the Son of Man can be forgiven, but anyone who blasphemes the Holy Spirit will not be forgiven.

LUKE 12:10

Unforgivable Sin?

Along the highway, the driver sees sign after sign pointing to gas stations at every exit, but he keeps on going, ignoring the invitations to stop for gas. Finally a sign says, "Last gas for 23 miles." The gas gauge is already below *E*, yet the driver keeps on driving because he's unwilling to stop going in the direction he has been going and turn toward what he needs: gasoline.

In a sense, this illustrates what Jesus meant when he said there is a sin that cannot be forgiven—blasphemy of the Holy Spirit. Blasphemy of the Holy Spirit is not a single event that is impossible to undo. It is not simply making an insulting remark about Jesus or the Holy Spirit. It is an ongoing act of resistance toward the Spirit's convicting power. Anyone who turns toward God in repentance will be forgiven, but those who keep on driving away from him forfeit that offer.

The Holy Spirit holds up signs of warning and direction in our lives that point us toward Jesus and invite us into salvation. If we ignore those signs and continue to ignore them, we can't expect to enter into God's gracious forgiveness. The Holy Spirit opens our eyes to the goodness of Christ and our need to turn away from a life on empty, without God. Then he turns us toward a life of fullness and satisfaction in God.

 | **DISCUSSION STARTERS**

What signs on the road would be dangerous to ignore?

Why do some people put off responding to the Holy Spirit?

How can a person be sure to avoid committing the unforgivable sin of blaspheming the Holy Spirit?

Who Will
Pay Your Ransom?

In May 2001, American missionaries Martin and Gracia Burnham were taken hostage by the Abu Sayyaf in the Philippines. At the beginning of their yearlong ordeal, their captors admitted they believed they could get a million-dollar ransom payment because the Burnhams were Americans. But as other hostages arranged for ransoms and were released, the Burnhams remained in captivity.

Sitting around the fire in the jungle one day, Gracia told the other hostages, "I'm glad that when Jesus paid a ransom for us, we didn't have to wait for it to arrive or wait for him to decide if he was going to do it. Before the foundations of the world, he knew he would ransom us and that it would cost him everything."

Jesus paid a ransom so we would no longer be held captive by sin and its consequences. This ransom wasn't paid with mere money but with the precious blood of Christ.

Eventually someone paid a ransom for Martin and Gracia's release, but their captors decided it wasn't enough and asked for more.[1] You never need to fear that the ransom Jesus paid for you isn't enough. The blood of Christ is sufficient, and you are forever free.

 | ## DISCUSSION STARTERS

What do you think it would feel like to be taken hostage, waiting for someone to pay your ransom?

Who or what can hold us hostage in our daily lives?

Why do we need the blood of Jesus to buy our freedom?

M A Y

19

Even the Son of Man came not to be served but to serve others and to give his life as a ransom for many.
MATTHEW 20:28

You know that God paid a ransom to save you from the empty life you inherited from your ancestors. And the ransom he paid was not mere gold or silver. It was the precious blood of Christ, the sinless, spotless Lamb of God. God chose him as your ransom long before the world began.
1 PETER 1:18-20

You are worthy to take the scroll and break its seals and open it. For you were slaughtered, and your blood has ransomed people for God from every tribe and language and people and nation.
REVELATION 5:9

---

1. To find out more about the Burnhams' story, see Gracia Burnham and Dean Merrill, *In the Presence of My Enemies* (Carol Stream, IL: Tyndale House Publishers, 2003).

You are my strength; I wait for you to rescue me, for you, O God, are my fortress. In his unfailing love, my God will stand with me. He will let me look down in triumph on all my enemies.

PSALM 59:9-10

If you want to be a friend of the world, you make yourself an enemy of God.

JAMES 4:4

The last enemy to be destroyed is death.

1 CORINTHIANS 15:26

Who Are My Enemies?

When we think about enemies, we might think of classmates or coworkers who seem out to get us, competitors who want to ruin us, rivals who want to defeat us, or people who have hurt us. We might think of those who disagree with our ideas and oppose our agendas.

The Bible talks about enemies a lot—especially in Old Testament stories about Israel's battles. When we read the Psalms, it can be confusing to figure out who the enemies are that the psalmists ask God to protect them from. Some of the things the biblical writers ask God to do to their enemies we wouldn't wish on anyone!

It helps to understand that the children of Israel and their God-appointed leaders were God's chosen people. Friends of the children of Israel were friends of God. Enemies of Israel were enemies of God. But there were also times when Israel itself, through its disobedience, became God's enemy. Today God's enemies are those who love themselves more than God, those who reject and refuse the gift of God in his Son, Jesus.

God wants to give us victory over our enemies. But our true enemies are not usually people. Unbelief is an enemy. Our worldly desires are enemies. Our ultimate enemy is sin, which has the power to keep us in slavery. But God empowers us to overcome all these enemies—anything that would turn us away from him.

 | **DISCUSSION STARTERS**

Are there certain people you think of as enemies at times? Are there some people you once thought of as enemies who are now your friends?

According to Romans 5:6-11, who are God's enemies? What has God done for them?

Are there any spiritual enemies you need to keep up your guard against?

A Good Good-Bye

When you love someone, it's hard to say good-bye. Have you ever witnessed the parting of two people in love at an airport, or seen parents as their son or daughter moves into a college dorm?

It is interesting to note that when Jesus said good-bye to his closest friends and followers before he ascended into heaven, they "returned to Jerusalem filled with great joy." We might have expected it to be a tearful parting—and perhaps there were tears. But evidently the sadness of physical separation was outweighed by joy.

Those who loved Jesus were filled with joy because they believed him when he said, "When everything is ready, I will come and get you, so that you will always be with me where I am" (JOHN 14:3). They believed there would one day be a reunion, because Jesus promised it.

Perhaps they were also filled with joy because they knew that Jesus was going home! He was going to be in heaven with his Father, where he had been since before the world was made and until he came to earth as a man. Perhaps they imagined the joy in heaven when Jesus returned, having defeated sin and Satan, ready to sit down at God's right hand to rule over all his enemies.

 | DISCUSSION STARTERS

When have you been sad to say good-bye to someone?

What do you think the celebration was like when Jesus returned to heaven?

Read 1 Thessalonians 4:13-18. How does Jesus' ascension show us what ours will be like?

Jesus led them to Bethany, and lifting his hands to heaven, he blessed them. While he was blessing them, he left them and was taken up to heaven. So they worshiped him and then returned to Jerusalem filled with great joy.
LUKE 24:50-52

He was taken up into a cloud while they were watching, and they could no longer see him. As they strained to see him rising into heaven, two white-robed men suddenly stood among them. "Men of Galilee," they said, "why are you standing here staring into heaven? Jesus has been taken from you into heaven, but someday he will return from heaven in the same way you saw him go!"
ACTS 1:9-11

Oh, what joy for those whose disobedience is forgiven, whose sin is put out of sight! Yes, what joy for those whose record the Lord has cleared of guilt, whose lives are lived in complete honesty!

When I refused to confess my sin, my body wasted away, and I groaned all day long. Day and night your hand of discipline was heavy on me. My strength evaporated like water in the summer heat.

Finally, I confessed all my sins to you and stopped trying to hide my guilt.

I said to myself, "I will confess my rebellion to the Lord." And you forgave me! All my guilt is gone.

PSALM 32:1-5

No More Secrets

Nothing is more miserable than carrying around a secret when that secret involves a hidden sin or wrongdoing. But of course it's not really a secret—God already knows about it. And he has promised that "if we confess our sins to him, he is faithful and just to forgive us our sins and to cleanse us from all wickedness" (1 JOHN 1:9).

Confession is coming clean with God—making no excuses, naming our sin for exactly what it is, and rejecting our sin as something we want no part of. We admit the truth: "I've been greedy and haven't been giving like I should." "I've treated her unfairly because I'm jealous." "I've allowed inappropriate thoughts to get the best of me again."

We need to confess our sin to God in order to be forgiven, but it's also important to confess our sin to another person. This can give us some of the encouragement and accountability we need to leave that sin behind for good. Sometimes the reason we don't want to confess our sin to someone else is not just because we feel embarrassed but because we don't really want to become accountable to anyone. We want to leave our options open to commit that sin again without someone calling us on it. But keeping quiet about your struggle with lies or alcohol or food or anger leaves you on your own. James says to "confess your sins to each other" (JAMES 5:16). He knew that sometimes saying it out loud to another person forces us to see it for what it is—in its ugliness and destructiveness—and gives us momentum toward letting it go for good.

 | ## DISCUSSION STARTERS

Does confessing something you've done wrong give you a good feeling, a bad feeling, or both?

What are some strategies for keeping short accounts with God? How often should you examine your heart for sin to confess?

What makes a person "safe" for confessing your sins to?

From a Trickle to a Tidal Wave

The South Fork Dam was located on Lake Conemaugh, near South Fork, Pennsylvania. On May 31, 1889, the dam broke, sending 20 million tons of water racing fourteen miles downstream, causing the Johnstown Flood. Prior to that time, the people living downstream had enjoyed trickles of runoff from the dam and used water from the dam's spillways for their crops. But it was nothing like the wall of water that erupted when the dam failed.

This is a picture of how the people of God experienced the presence and power of the Holy Spirit before and after Pentecost. From the beginning of history, the Holy Spirit has worked in the lives of those who trust God. His job has always been to teach and counsel and bring new life to God's people. But while the Holy Spirit was active in the lives of people in Old Testament times, it was more like a trickle or a small stream.

So what was different after Pentecost? Pentecost was like the day the dam broke—except instead of bringing destruction, it flooded God's people with power. God's Spirit poured over his people, filling them, changing them, empowering them to spread the gospel to the ends of the earth.

🧂🧂 | DISCUSSION STARTERS

What's the difference in power between a spray bottle and a fire hose? How about between a flashlight and a spotlight?

Can you think of any people in the Old Testament who were empowered by God's Spirit to do incredible things?

How can we experience the power of the Holy Spirit in our lives?

The LORD replied, "Take Joshua son of Nun, who has the Spirit in him, and lay your hands on him."
NUMBERS 27:18

I can never escape from your Spirit! I can never get away from your presence!
PSALM 139:7

You sent your good Spirit to instruct them. . . . In your love, you were patient with them for many years. You sent your Spirit, who warned them through the prophets.
NEHEMIAH 9:20, 30

Who can be compared with the LORD our God, who is enthroned on high? He stoops to look down on heaven and on earth.

PSALM 113:5-6

Oh, that you would burst from the heavens and come down! How the mountains would quake in your presence!

ISAIAH 64:1

No one has ever gone to heaven and returned. But the Son of Man has come down from heaven.

JOHN 3:13

God Comes Down

Members of a royal family rarely mingle with commoners. They may wave from the balcony of a palace, but you would never expect a king to spend time at the mall or move in next door or come over for coffee. So could we ever expect that the King of the universe would enter into our world? Could we be bold enough to ask that the King of heaven would come to earth and do a work in us and in this world that only he can do? That's exactly what he wants us to ask him to do. No, he wants us to *beg* him to do it. He longs to hear us pray the prayer of Isaiah: "Oh, that you would burst from the heavens and come down!"

What happens when God comes down? People change their minds about him, and their hearts warm up to him. We become bold for him and willing to suffer for him. We treasure him and enjoy him instead of taking him for granted. Our uncaring attitudes turn into passion. We can't get enough of God's Word, and we can't stand to be at odds with other people. Our hearts are captured by spiritual things rather than the things of this world.

Many Christians are content to keep God at a safe distance, not expecting much from him and not longing for him. But God responds to heartfelt, desperate prayers for him to make his presence known in new ways in our lives. He wants us to pray for that—to pray that he will come down to us in a fresh way and do awesome things that only he can do!

 | ## DISCUSSION STARTERS

How does it make you feel when someone special or important comes to your school, your church, or your house?

Have you ever had a special sense of God's presence? What was that like?

Why do you think God wants us to invite him to invade our world?

The Keys of Death

Have you ever locked yourself out of your house or locked the keys in your car? You wonder, *Where did I put that extra key?* Because having a key means you have access—it allows you to get in and out.

So what does Jesus mean when he says, "I hold the keys of death and the grave"? Jesus is saying, *I'm in charge of death. So you don't have to fear physical death. I have the keys in my hand to that bitter, dark place of the dead. I hold the keys because I died and I defeated death. I came back with the keys in my hand. I'm going to be alive forever, so I can open the gates to death for those who don't want me. And I can shut the gates to death and open heaven for those who love me and want to live with me after they die.*

What does this truth mean for us? It means that when that person we love dies, it may have surprised us, but it didn't surprise God. Even though it seems to us that people we love die too soon, we can trust that God is in control and has perfect timing. Knowing that Jesus himself controls life and death means that when we face the death of someone we love, we don't have to surrender that person to an unknown, uncaring nothingness. We can rest, confident that everyone who knows Jesus is safely under his care. Jesus holds the keys. And as we face our own deaths, we can be comforted by hearing what Jesus is saying: *Don't be afraid. I'm in control here. Death cannot catch me off guard or sneak up on me. I hold the keys.*

As for me, God will redeem my life. He will snatch me from the power of the grave.
PSALM 49:15

I am the living one. I died, but look—I am alive forever and ever! And I hold the keys of death and the grave.
REVELATION 1:18

Jesus told her, "I am the resurrection and the life. Anyone who believes in me will live, even after dying."
JOHN 11:25

| DISCUSSION STARTERS

What do you have keys for? What do you *wish* you had keys for?

What do you think it means that Jesus holds the keys to death? Does this bring comfort or raise questions?

How does it give you comfort and courage to know that Jesus is in charge of life and death?

26

Everyone knows that you are obedient to the Lord. This makes me very happy. I want you to be wise in doing right and to stay innocent of any wrong.
ROMANS 16:19

I thank my God through Jesus Christ for all of you, because your faith in him is being talked about all over the world.
ROMANS 1:8

Do everything without complaining and arguing, so that no one can criticize you. Live clean, innocent lives as children of God, shining like bright lights in a world full of crooked and perverse people.
PHILIPPIANS 2:14-15

Famous for Obedience

Turn on the TV or go online or look at the headlines on magazines, and what are you swarmed by? Stories and photographs of celebrities. We're a society obsessed with famous people. We love to read about their secrets, their daily habits, and their conflicts with other people. Things that should bring them shame just get bigger headlines and more attention.

The Bible tells us that there is something we should be known for—something that might not make headlines but should identify those of us who call ourselves Christians. Our faithful obedience. We should be famous for living pure lives that stand out from the way people around us live without any thought of God.

Jesus said, "Let your good deeds shine out for all to see, so that everyone will praise your heavenly Father (MATTHEW 5:16). You see, when we deny ourselves or forgive others because of our love for Jesus, people notice. And when they do, it's God who gets the glory. As we live day to day in dramatic contrast to the way everyone around us lives—as we break free from the power of sin—people pay attention. The genuineness of our faith gets talked about, and God gets the praise he deserves.

 | **DISCUSSION STARTERS**

What kinds of things do people do that make them famous?

Who do you know who is "famous" for being obedient to God?

In the long run, what are the results of worldly fame? What are the results of obedient living?

God's Mirror

What do you see when you look in the mirror? Do you see someone who is growing up or growing old? Do you see in your reflection someone who is changing or simply staying the same?

Moses was someone whose face changed dramatically. He went up on Mount Sinai to be with God, and after he saw and experienced the glory of God on the mountain, the skin on his face literally glowed with God's glory. When he came down from the mountain, the glory began to fade with each passing day.

But the glory doesn't have to fade this way for us. We have something Moses didn't have. We have the Holy Spirit living inside us—changing us from the inside. The Spirit of God is at work, making us into mirrors so we can clearly reflect the radiance and beauty of God's glory.

We don't want to stay the same spiritually. We want to change—not just on the outside, but on the inside. We want the Holy Spirit to take away everything in our lives that doesn't look like Jesus. A year from now, if we are the same as we are today—if there has been no change in our character, no progress toward holiness, no development toward a clearer reflection of Jesus in our attitudes and actions—then something has gone wrong. God wants to change us, making us into better reflectors of him.

 | **DISCUSSION STARTERS**

What do you see about yourself when you look in a mirror?

What caused Moses to radiate God's glory? What does that tell us about how we can radiate his glory?

What are some ways you see Jesus reflected in other people?

When Moses came down Mount Sinai carrying the two stone tablets inscribed with the terms of the covenant, he wasn't aware that his face had become radiant because he had spoken to the LORD. When Moses finished speaking with them, he covered his face with a veil.

EXODUS 34:29, 33

Whenever someone turns to the Lord, the veil is taken away. For the Lord is the Spirit, and wherever the Spirit of the Lord is, there is freedom. So all of us who have had that veil removed can see and reflect the glory of the Lord. And the Lord—who is the Spirit—makes us more and more like him as we are changed into his glorious image.

2 CORINTHIANS 3:16-18

Never pay back evil with more evil. . . . Do all that you can to live in peace with everyone. Dear friends, never take revenge. Leave that to the righteous anger of God. For the Scriptures say, "I will take revenge; I will pay them back," says the LORD.

ROMANS 12:17-19

You have heard the law that says the punishment must match the injury: "An eye for an eye, and a tooth for a tooth." But I say, do not resist an evil person! If someone slaps you on the right cheek, offer the other cheek also.

MATTHEW 5:38-39

Getting Even

"I'll get you back!" we shout out loud or say under our breath to the person who has hurt or embarrassed us. We want those who hurt us to pay with pain—the kind of pain they caused us. This is what comes naturally to us.

But as believers we are not bound to do what comes naturally. The Holy Spirit supernaturally enables us to let go of that burning desire for revenge. We can let go of our plans to hurt someone back, confident that God notices the wrong done to us, that he sees the motives of those who hurt us more clearly than we do, and that he will settle all accounts with perfect justice.

Jesus taught that people should actually *love* their enemies. That's hard! On the surface, it seems that Jesus was suggesting we choke back the basic sense of justice inside of us. But when Jesus said not to seek revenge, he wasn't saying that justice won't be done. He meant that God will take care of it.

And this is not something Jesus just said to do; it's what he lived himself. "[Christ] did not retaliate when he was insulted, nor threaten revenge when he suffered. He left his case in the hands of God, who always judges fairly" (1 PETER 2:23). The most innocent man who ever lived suffered the most outrageous injustice ever experienced, and yet he refused to seek revenge. Instead, he turned it over to God because he knew God would do what is right. Jesus is our example to follow.

 | DISCUSSION STARTERS

How does it feel to get revenge against someone who hurt you?

What do you have to do to leave justice up to God?

What are some ways you can respond when you feel a passion to seek revenge?

The First and the Best

There's usually an order to it when we give away things like food or clothes or money. First, we want to make sure we have enough for ourselves of whatever it is we're giving away—enough to meet our own needs or wants. Then, when we figure we have enough, we're willing to give away what we don't need.

In the Old Testament, God's people were asked to bring an offering of grain or fruit every year at harvesttime. This offering was called a firstfruits offering, because it was the first part of their crops. They gave to God even before they knew they would have enough for themselves. They were to bring to the Temple the very best of their harvest. But instead of waiting until the full harvest was collected and choosing from what was left over, they were to bring the very best of what was gathered first, before they even knew if more would be harvested. The firstfruits offering was a step of faith, a way of trusting God with their first and best. It was an expression of their belief that God would take care of them, whether the rest of the harvest was much or little.

God is pleased when we offer up to him our firstfruits—giving him the best of our days rather than only what we can squeeze in around other activities and appointments. He smiles when we give money for his causes right after we get paid instead of waiting to see if there's anything left over after we take care of other expenses. These things show we really trust him to take care of us.

| DISCUSSION STARTERS

When you have two of something and need to give one to someone else, do you tend to give away or keep the best one?

What sets a firstfruits offering apart from other kinds of offerings?

Paul wrote that "Christ has indeed been raised from the dead, the firstfruits of those who have fallen asleep" (1 Corinthians 15:20, NIV). What did he mean?

> As you harvest your crops, bring of the very best of the first harvest to the house of the LORD your God.
> *EXODUS 23:19*

> We promise to bring the first part of every harvest to the LORD's Temple year after year—whether it be a crop from the soil or from our fruit trees.
> *NEHEMIAH 10:35*

> You must then say in the presence of the LORD your God . . . "And now, O LORD, I have brought you the first portion of the harvest you have given me from the ground."
> *DEUTERONOMY 26:5, 10*

God Sees

Doctors use X rays or ultrasounds to see inside our bodies. They can look for broken bones or growths that shouldn't be there. God sees inside us too, but he doesn't need an X-ray machine to see what's in our hearts.

Genesis tells us the story of Cain and Abel, who both brought offerings to God. But for some reason, Cain's offering offended God. When we read the story, it's hard to see what the problem was. It's not obvious to us. But God could see through both of these people, and he saw a difference in their offerings—a difference in their hearts toward him. Evidently, while Cain brought his leftovers to God, Abel brought his very best. Cain brought what he could comfortably afford; Abel risked everything on God by his gift. That's faith. God could see through to their hearts, and he saw religious effort in one heart and true worship in the other.

When we go through the motions of religious activity—going to church, singing, praying, giving—God sees. When we put in the minimum required, with no heart toward wanting to express to God our love, devotion, and gratitude, God sees. People around us probably can't tell the difference, but we can't hide our hearts from God.

When it was time for the harvest, Cain presented some of his crops as a gift to the LORD. Abel also brought a gift—the best of the firstborn lambs from his flock. The LORD accepted Abel and his gift, but he did not accept Cain and his gift. This made Cain very angry.
GENESIS 4:3-5

It was by faith that Abel brought a more acceptable offering to God than Cain did. Abel's offering gave evidence that he was a righteous man, and God showed his approval of his gifts.
HEBREWS 11:4

The LORD detests the sacrifice of the wicked, but he delights in the prayers of the upright.
PROVERBS 15:8

 | **DISCUSSION STARTERS**

What would it be like to be able to hear another person's thoughts?

How did Abel's gift of the firstborn lamb show faith?

What can you do when you find yourself going through the motions of worship with a cold heart?

A Harvest of Souls

Imagine sitting down with your family for a big holiday dinner. Just as you're getting ready to eat, you hear the roar of a tornado . . . only instead of being outside, the sound is inside the dining room! Before you've figured out where the noise is coming from, you look around and notice that small fires have erupted over the head of every person at the table! Then people start talking all at once, and you realize they're speaking Italian, Arabic, Japanese, Greek—languages they've never spoken before!

That's what happened fifty days after Jesus ascended into heaven. It was a Jewish holiday called Pentecost, when Jewish pilgrims from all over the known world came to Jerusalem for a feast to celebrate the harvest. But that Pentecost proved to be about a harvest much more significant than the harvest of crops. It was about the harvest of souls. On the day of Pentecost, three thousand people started following Jesus—you could say they were "harvested" for God.

When God poured out his Spirit at Pentecost, the people of God experienced an overwhelming sense of the greatness of God. That awe spilled over as courageous, passionate praise to God and as a witness to those who didn't know Jesus. By giving people the supernatural ability to speak languages they didn't know, God showed that his Spirit was empowering them to spread the gospel to the ends of the earth.

🧂🧂 | DISCUSSION STARTERS

What do you think it would have been like to be in that room at Pentecost?

As we think about God pouring out this kind of power for spreading the gospel, what does this tell us about his priorities?

In what ways and for what purposes does God pour out his Spirit today?

> You will receive power when the Holy Spirit comes upon you. And you will be my witnesses, telling people about me everywhere.
> *ACTS 1:8*

> On the day of Pentecost all the believers were meeting together in one place. Suddenly, there was a sound from heaven like the roaring of a mighty windstorm, and it filled the house where they were sitting. Then, what looked like flames or tongues of fire appeared and settled on each of them. And everyone present was filled with the Holy Spirit and began speaking in other languages, as the Holy Spirit gave them this ability.
> *ACTS 2:1-4*

The LORD said to Abram, "You can be sure that your descendants will be strangers in a foreign land, where they will be oppressed as slaves for 400 years. But I will punish the nation that enslaves them, and in the end they will come away with great wealth."

GENESIS 15:13-14

The LORD said to Moses, "Return to Pharaoh and make your demands again. I have made him and his officials stubborn so I can display my miraculous signs among them. I've also done it so you can tell your children and grandchildren about how I made a mockery of the Egyptians and about the signs I displayed among them—and so you will know that I am the LORD."

EXODUS 10:1-2

For Everyone to See

These days, if you want the world to know all about you, you might put up a Web site on the Internet or set up your profile—indicating your likes, dislikes, interests, and abilities—on a social networking site. When God wanted the world to know about him, he expressed himself not on an Internet page but in history—particularly in his dealings with his people, the Israelites.

Through an amazing series of events—from spectacular miracles to devastating tragedies—God showed his character and purposes to the human race. We wonder why God poured out ten plagues on Egypt and then delivered his people through the incredible act of dividing the Red Sea. More significantly, why did he allow his people to become slaves in the first place—something he seemed to have planned ahead of time since he told Abram it would happen centuries before the people became slaves (SEE GENESIS 15:13-14).

In Exodus 9:16, God told Moses to explain to Pharaoh why God had not destroyed Egypt: "to show you my power and to spread my fame throughout the earth." The parting of the Red Sea was not a hidden act of God. It was front-page news. It was done for all the world to see, so that hearts might fear and melt before the great and powerful God of Israel. God uses history to put his glory on display in the world.

When hard-to-explain and hard-to-understand things happen in our own lives, we can be confident that God wants to show us and show the world something significant about himself through our circumstances. He wants to put himself on display through his work in our lives.

 | **DISCUSSION STARTERS**

Listen again to the three verses above. What purposes are given in these verses for the slavery and deliverance of the Israelites?

Do these purposes seem worth it to you for the years of slavery and the suffering of the ten plagues? Why or why not?

Read Joshua 2:9-10. How did God's deliverance of his people impact Rahab, many years later?

Keeping a Soft Heart

When you have a spot of skin—maybe on your hand or foot—that gets rubbed over and over, the skin gets thick and hard, creating a callous. After the callous develops, you don't feel the rubbing so much anymore because of the hardness that has formed.

The same thing can happen to our hearts. God speaks to us through a sermon we hear, a passage of Scripture we read, or something a friend shares with us, and our hearts are pricked. Maybe they get pricked and pricked. Sometimes our hearts have been pricked so many times and we've ignored it so long that we don't even feel the prick anymore. We've built up a callous to conviction. Our hearts have become hard.

Have you found yourself ignoring the prompting of the Holy Spirit, hoping that feeling of conviction will just go away? It will with time . . . but that's not a good thing. If you keep ignoring it, your heart will become hard and you won't feel the prick anymore. And when you realize that has happened, it will be the saddest day of your life. Don't let your heart become hard by ignoring it when the Holy Spirit convicts you of sin in your life.

 | ## DISCUSSION STARTERS

When have you had a callous or seen someone else with a callous before? What caused it to form?

Why should we feel glad when we feel convicted of a sin in our lives?

How can we make sure our hearts stay soft toward God?

Today when you hear his voice, don't harden your hearts as Israel did when they rebelled, when they tested me in the wilderness . . . You must warn each other every day, while it is still "today," so that none of you will be deceived by sin and hardened against God.

HEBREWS 3:8, 13

The hearts of these people are hardened, and their ears cannot hear, and they have closed their eyes—so their eyes cannot see, and their ears cannot hear, and their hearts cannot understand, and they cannot turn to me and let me heal them.

MATTHEW 13:15

The LORD passed in front of Moses, calling out, "Yahweh! The LORD! The God of compassion and mercy! I am slow to anger and filled with unfailing love and faithfulness."

EXODUS 34:6

I will pour out my fury on them, consuming them with the fire of my anger. I will heap on their heads the full penalty for all their sins. I, the Sovereign LORD, have spoken!

EZEKIEL 22:31

He was merciful and forgave their sins and did not destroy them all. Many times he held back his anger and did not unleash his fury!

PSALM 78:38

God as He Is

There are some ice cream parlors where you can make your own flavor. You ask the person behind the counter to add a lot of fudge, a few nuts, perhaps a dash of cinnamon—and you have your own unique flavor.

Some people think God's character is like that ice cream—a mixture of various qualities in various amounts, with more of some ingredients than others. Some think of him as mostly love with a little justice thrown in. Others might think of him as mostly a giver who also makes a few demands. But God is not a bunch of traits mixed together in varying amounts. While it's true that some actions of God show certain characteristics more obviously, God's whole being includes every one of his attributes. He is love. He is mercy. He is justice. He is truth. He is beauty. He is completely all of those things, and much more. Every attribute of God that we can find in the Bible is true of all of God, all the time. No single attribute is more important or more influential than all the others. His love is not more important than his justice. His righteousness does not take precedence over his patience. We have a hard time seeing God as he truly is in his completeness. Paul says, "All that I know now is partial and incomplete, but then I will know everything completely, just as God now knows me completely" (1 CORINTHIANS 13:12). Someday we'll see and know God in the fullness of all that he is.

 | **DISCUSSION STARTERS**

How would you answer if someone asked you what God is like?

Which attributes of God do we usually emphasize?

Which attributes do we tend to ignore or pay less attention to?

A Living Sacrifice

Old Testament God-followers brought sheep, bulls, or pigeons to sacrifice on the altar as offerings to God. But God no longer requires the killing of animals as an expression of worship. The holy sacrifice that pleases God is a living person with a will that is surrendered to God. God wants us to offer our bodies—our whole lives—to him as living sacrifices.

Thinking about what happened to the animal sacrifices helps us understand more about what is being asked of us. When you are a living sacrifice, it means you are willing to die to the life you've been living. You want the will of God to be done in your life more than you want life itself. It means you are willing to go through the fire, to experience all that the altar represents—giving up yourself and your rights—for the one purpose of pleasing God. Being a living sacrifice means that you please God not through your death but in the way you live. It means you use the life God gave you, the personality and abilities God gave you to live all out for him.

Are you willing to place yourself on the altar as an offering, to become a living sacrifice? Ask God for the faith and courage you need to die to your desires and live for his. Offer yourself to him, saying, *I'm yours. You can do whatever you want to do with me.* This is pleasing sacrifice and holy surrender. This is what it really means to worship God.

 | ## DISCUSSION STARTERS

What do you think it would have been like to watch the sacrifices that were made in Old Testament times?

Why do you think God wants us as living sacrifices more than he wants animal sacrifices?

What kind of sacrifices could you make that would be acceptable to God?

I plead with you to give your bodies to God because of all he has done for you. Let them be a living and holy sacrifice—the kind he will find acceptable. This is truly the way to worship him.
ROMANS 12:1

The sacrifice you desire is a broken spirit. You will not reject a broken and repentant heart, O God.
PSALM 51:17

Don't forget to do good and to share with those in need. These are the sacrifices that please God.
HEBREWS 13:16

Faith: How Much Is Enough?

Have you ever run through an obstacle course—maybe crawled through a barrel or jumped over a bar or stepped through a series of tires to cross the finish line?

Some people see the life of faith in God kind of like an obstacle course—they think they have to prove to God that they've got what it takes in terms of faith. But does God really set up hoops for us to jump through? And in terms of faith, how much is enough? How do you measure it?

When the disciples asked Jesus how to get more faith, he didn't give them a formula for increasing the amount of their faith. He told them that it isn't the *amount* of faith that matters but the *object* of faith. In fact, the only thing that matters about your faith is who you put your faith in. Jesus showed what he meant by telling them all they needed was faith the size of a mustard seed—a tiny seed no bigger than a freckle on your nose. He was saying that if faith in God is present at all, even if it is no bigger than a mustard seed, it can accomplish wonders because of who God is.

It's not up to us to work up enough faith and get rid of all doubt so that God will be convinced we're worthy of whatever it is we're asking for. That's putting our faith in faith, and not in God.

 | **DISCUSSION STARTERS**

If you had to pick a size to describe your faith, how big would you say it is? Why?

What do the two verses from Romans (on the left) say about faith and where we get it?

What's the difference between depending on your faith in God to make something happen and depending on God to do something?

I tell you the truth, if you had faith even as small as a mustard seed, you could say to this mountain, "Move from here to there," and it would move. Nothing would be impossible.
MATTHEW 17:20

Faith comes from hearing, that is, hearing the Good News about Christ.
ROMANS 10:17

Don't think you are better than you really are. Be honest in your evaluation of yourselves, measuring yourselves by the faith God has given us.
ROMANS 12:3

Jesus:
The Softer Side of God?

Find a penny or a nickel or a quarter. What do you see? The face of Abraham Lincoln? Thomas Jefferson? George Washington? The image on the coin perfectly corresponds to the mold that was used to make it.

This is the same idea the Bible is talking about when it says Jesus is the "exact representation" of God. Jesus is completely the same as the Father even though they exist separately—like the mold and the coin. Jesus is the perfect, personal imprint of God in time and space. But some people see the God of the Old Testament and Jesus of the New Testament as two dramatically different beings— a sort of good cop/bad cop scenario. They like the idea of a gentle, nonjudgmental Jesus on the hillside teaching and healing, but they reject the vengeful version of God they've picked up from selected Old Testament stories.

Jesus is not the softer side of God, a slightly friendlier version. Somehow he is completely full of justice and completely full of grace at the same time. And he offers us an up close glimpse of God. Jesus shows us God from a different perspective, like taking a photograph of something from a new angle and seeing it differently, even though the object in the photograph hasn't changed.

Jesus is God's full personality and power and purpose in the form of a person. He's a precise copy, a perfect imprint, the exact image of God. He is no less than God himself in human form. Jesus shows us exactly what the God of the universe is like.

Christ is the visible image of the invisible God.
COLOSSIANS 1:15

The Son is the radiance of God's glory and the exact representation of his being.
HEBREWS 1:3, NIV

Anyone who has seen me has seen the Father!
JOHN 14:9

📖 | DISCUSSION STARTERS

When you picture Jesus, what is he doing? When you think about God the Father, what does he look like in your mind's eye?

What do you think people in Jesus' day saw in Jesus that they might not have expected from God?

What things about Jesus' character make you grateful God is like that?

JUNE

7

Your name will no longer be Jacob. From now on you will be called Israel, because you have fought with God and with men and have won.
GENESIS 32:28

The nations will see your righteousness. World leaders will be blinded by your glory. And you will be given a new name by the LORD's own mouth.
ISAIAH 62:2

I will give to each one a white stone, and on the stone will be engraved a new name that no one understands except the one who receives it.
REVELATION 2:17

Your New Name

Have you ever met someone who has changed his or her name? Many women change their names when they get married to take their husbands' last names. Some people change their names because they don't like their birth names or because they want to officially go by their nicknames instead.

One of the early followers of God was named *Abram*, which means "father of many." Now if you think about it, Abram had a name that just didn't fit. He had only one son, and his wife was way past the age of having children. People probably laughed at the irony of his name. But then God changed his name to one that seemed even more ridiculous: Abraham, which means "father of many nations."

In Hebrew there is a single shortened character that represents the name of God. When God changed Abram to Abraham, he simply added the character for his own name into Abram's name. He did the same thing with Abram's wife when he changed her name from Sarai to Sarah. When God gave them new names, he literally placed his own name in theirs.

This is an outward sign of what God does on the inside of people. He changed Jacob's name to Israel, and he changed Simon's name to Peter. God puts his personal stamp on us and his Spirit in us so we are not the same people we once were apart from his power. When you are truly in Christ, he puts himself *in* you.

 | **DISCUSSION STARTERS**

If you were going to change your name, what would you change it to? Why?

How was God's power evident in the lives of other people whose names were changed by God? (Think of Jacob and Simon.)

Revelation 2:17 says that God is going to give all of us new names in heaven. What do you think that might mean?

God's Words

If you wanted to get a message to someone you couldn't see in person, how would you do it? Would you call on the phone? send an e-mail or text message? write a letter? ask someone to deliver the message for you? Well, God had something he wanted to tell us, and that message was recorded before the days of phones and computers. His words are written down for us in the Bible—recorded by more than forty writers over a 1,500-year time span.

God used a variety of ways to communicate to the writers of the Bible what he wanted written. In some places he seemed to use dictation—telling the writers directly what to write. For example, near the end of John's life, Jesus spoke these words to him: "To the angel of the church in Ephesus *write* ..." (REVELATION 2:1, NIV, emphasis added). We know that Luke used ordinary historical research for writing his Gospel, which says, "Having carefully investigated everything from the beginning, I also have decided to write a careful account for you" (LUKE 1:3). In some cases Scripture writers speak of having dreams or visions, or hearing the Lord's voice. In other cases people who were with Jesus observed his life, and they documented his words and deeds based on personal experiences and the perfecting work of the Holy Spirit. This was just as Jesus had promised it would be: "When the Father sends . . . the Holy Spirit—he will teach you everything and will remind you of everything I have told you" (JOHN 14:26).

Ultimately, it is only by the power of the Holy Spirit that we can believe that the words of the Bible are God's words. The Holy Spirit speaks in and through the Bible to our hearts and gives us an inner assurance that it is God's Word.

> When you received his message from us, you didn't think of our words as mere human ideas. You accepted what we said as the very word of God—which, of course, it is.
> *1 THESSALONIANS 2:13*

> Jesus responded, "Then why does David, speaking under the inspiration of the Spirit, call the Messiah 'my Lord'?"
> *MATTHEW 22:43*

👥 | DISCUSSION STARTERS

Who are some of the people who wrote books of the Bible?

How did Jesus show that he viewed Scripture as God's Word?

When have you sensed God was speaking to you through the Bible?

You saw me before I was born. Every day of my life was recorded in your book. Every moment was laid out before a single day had passed. How precious are your thoughts about me, O God.
PSALM 139:16-17

This is the day the LORD has made. We will rejoice and be glad in it.
PSALM 118:24

You keep track of all my sorrows. You have collected all my tears in your bottle. You have recorded each one in your book.
PSALM 56:8

Written in His Book

What dates are significant in your life? The day you were born? The day an accident happened that changed your life or the life of someone you care about? The day someone you love died? We all have dates that are significant to us because of what happened on those particular days.

David thanked God that "every moment was laid out before a single day had passed." In other words, David was saying that God had arranged every experience and event in David's life—he planned in advance what David would do, who he would be, and how long his life would last.

On the days when life seems good, it is easy to say to God, "Every day of my life was recorded in your book." We can celebrate that God has planned out the days that bring us joy. But on the days that tragedy strikes, on the days our lives are changed forever by loss, we wonder, *Was this day of my life written in your book, by your hand? Is this the story you intended to write for my life, or has there been a terrible mistake?*

We can take comfort in knowing that God's plans for our lives are specific and complete. We don't have to be filled with fear about the future or regret over the past. Nothing happens in our lives that is outside of his plans for us. And his plans for us are for our ultimate good, even when they don't seem that way on the surface.

 | ## DISCUSSION STARTERS

What are some significant days or dates in your life?

What does it mean to you that God planned out the days in your past? What does it mean to you that he has planned out the days in your future?

Does the fact that God has power over every day in your life mean that you have no control over your life, no responsibility for your actions?

God Hears

Have you ever tried to tell a family member or friend something important, but you could tell that person really wasn't listening to you? Maybe he or she nodded and said, "Uh-huh," but you knew you weren't really getting through.

Sometimes we feel that way when we pray. We wonder if God is listening. We don't just wonder if he hears the words we say; we also wonder if he sees how we hurt, what we want, what we need.

God is never too busy to listen to you. He's never too distracted to really hear you. And he's always able to truly understand what we say to him. In fact, when we stop pretending and are just ourselves with him—when we're real about our sin, our needs, and our struggles to share our concerns with him—he bends down to listen to us.

So when it *feels* like God is not listening to your prayer, you have to tell yourself that it is just a feeling that isn't true. You can always be confident that God can hear you, even when it doesn't feel like it.

 | ## DISCUSSION STARTERS

How do you know when someone is really listening to you?

Do you think there is anything that could cause God not to hear our prayers?

What do you think God wants to hear most from his children?

Don't worry about anything; instead, pray about everything. Tell God what you need, and thank him for all he has done.
PHILIPPIANS 4:6

While Jesus was here on earth, he offered prayers and pleadings, with a loud cry and tears, to the one who could rescue him from death. And God heard his prayers because of his deep reverence for God.
HEBREWS 5:7

God says, "At just the right time, I heard you. On the day of salvation, I helped you." Indeed, the "right time" is now. Today is the day of salvation.
2 CORINTHIANS 6:2

[Command]: Don't let your hearts be troubled. Trust in God, and trust also in me.
JOHN 14:1

[Promise]: I am the resurrection and the life. Anyone who believes in me will live, even after dying. Everyone who lives in me and believes in me will never ever die.
JOHN 11:25-26

[Proverb]: You will always harvest what you plant.
GALATIANS 6:7

Command, Promise, or Proverb?

Your mom says, "You need to finish your dinner." Or she might say, "I will give you dessert after dinner." Or maybe she says, "I give dessert to children who finish their dinners." What's the difference? The first one is a command—an instruction to be followed. The second one is a promise—a commitment made no matter what. And the third one is a proverb—something that is generally true but has exceptions. In the Bible God speaks in all these ways, and we have to examine what we read to figure out which way God is speaking. This will help us understand what he wants us to do, what he wants to do for us, and how we can gain the wisdom he offers us.

For example, in Deuteronomy 6:5 God says, "You must love the LORD your God with all your heart, all your soul, and all your strength." That's a command. It's something we are to do all the time, no matter what. In Deuteronomy 31:6, God says, "He will neither fail you nor abandon you." That's a promise. It's not dependent on our doing anything. It's God's promise to us, and there are no exceptions. Proverbs 22:6 says, "Direct your children onto the right path, and when they are older, they will not leave it." That might sound like a promise, but it isn't. Some parents claim it as a promise concerning their children—a promise that their children will eventually follow Christ if they are raised in a Christian home. But it is a proverb—something that is generally true about the way a child's upbringing affects who he or she becomes. And while it is not a promise we can claim, it is wisdom we can embrace.

God is good to speak to us in all these ways—giving us commands to obey, promises to claim, and proverbs to show us how to live.

 | **DISCUSSION STARTERS**

How does a child know the difference between a parent's instruction and a parent's suggestion?

Read Proverbs 1:1-6. What does it say about the value of proverbs?

What commands, promises, and proverbs are in Proverbs 1:7-9; 3:5-7; 10:19; 15:1-5?

In the Guts

What does it mean if someone says, "I hate your guts," or "That felt like a kick in the guts"? *Guts* is another word for our insides, something deep within us. It's the same word the Gospels use when talking about how Jesus experienced the pain of others. Many of these stories record times when Jesus encountered hurting people and "had compassion on them." The Greek verb Matthew uses for compassion is *splanchnizomai*, which doesn't mean much unless you've been to medical school. It concerns the study of internal organs or, you could say, the "guts" of a person.

What this means is that Jesus didn't feel pity on people in a casual way. He was not working solely from his thoughts about the people's conditions, with no emotions. It means that Jesus felt the hurts of others in his gut. The pain of others felt like a sock in the stomach to him. He felt the brokenness of the crippled person, the physical suffering of the diseased person, the loneliness of the leper, the embarrassment of the scandalous sinner.

We can be confident that Jesus is not untouched by what hurts us and what weighs on us. When you feel sad, he is moved by your sadness. When you feel confused, disappointed, hurt, afraid, frustrated, Jesus has compassion on you. He feels it too.

> Jesus saw the huge crowd as he stepped from the boat, and he had compassion on them and healed their sick.
> **MATTHEW 14:14**

> When he saw the crowds, he had compassion on them because they were confused and helpless, like sheep without a shepherd.
> **MATTHEW 9:36**

> You must be compassionate, just as your Father is compassionate.
> **LUKE 6:36**

 | ## DISCUSSION STARTERS

Do you have a friend who has been hurt physically or emotionally? In what way did you feel his or her pain too?

How does it help you to know that Jesus has compassion on you and is hurt by what hurts you?

Many times when Jesus had compassion on people, he himself was hurting. For example, when he was dying on the cross, he asked his disciple John to care for his mother. What does his example show us about caring for others who hurt?

Jesus always used stories and illustrations like these when speaking to the crowds. In fact, he never spoke to them without using such parables. This fulfilled what God had spoken through the prophet: "I will speak to you in parables. I will explain things hidden since the creation of the world."

MATTHEW 13:34-35

To those who listen to my teaching, more understanding will be given, and they will have an abundance of knowledge. But for those who are not listening, even what little understanding they have will be taken away from them. That is why I use these parables,

For they look, but they don't really see. They hear, but they don't really listen or understand.

MATTHEW 13:12-13

Speaking in Stories

What do mustard seeds and fig trees, wine containers and oil lamps, seeds and treasures, lamps and baskets, wedding parties and children's games have in common? They're all ordinary things that Jesus talked about in his parables to help people understand who God is and what his Kingdom is like.

Jesus used simple word pictures, called parables, to help people know God better and get a glimpse into the way he works. He used images and characters taken from everyday life to create a miniature play or drama to illustrate his messages. His stories appealed to young and old, poor and rich, educated and uneducated.

Some parables are humorous and others are tragic; they are all simple yet thought provoking. Their deepest meaning and significance can be found in what they tell us about the Storyteller himself. At the same time, they seem to nail us for who we are and how we live. When we read a parable, we are sometimes bothered, sometimes confused, and sometimes encouraged, but we are always deeply challenged.

 | **DISCUSSION STARTERS**

What is your favorite story or parable that Jesus told?

Though parables are simple stories, they also have hidden meanings. Why do you think Jesus used this kind of story to teach people?

Why do some parables make people comfortable and uncomfortable at the same time?

Washed in Blood

When you want to get a piece of clothing really clean, what do you do? Maybe you rub in some spot remover or pour some bleach in the washer along with the detergent. How about when you want a clean conscience? How do you wash away regret and shame? How do you get rid of the stains that inappropriate thoughts, bad attitudes, jealousy, and fear have left on the record of your life?

The Bible says, "The blood of Jesus, his Son, cleanses us from all sin" (1 JOHN 1:7). It seems strange, doesn't it? We think of blood as something that causes stains rather than washing them. But the blood of Jesus is the only thing that can clean a guilty conscience. The blood of Christ takes away our desire to hide the spots and stains sin has left on our hearts and minds. When the blood of Jesus covers our hearts, it washes our sins away and makes us completely clean before God. So we don't have to carry around the guilt of what we've done and who we've been. All of that is gone. The cleansing power of Christ's blood sets us free. With his own blood, Jesus writes in large red letters across our lives, "Forgiven! Clean! Mine!"

All the animal sacrifices in the Old Testament were just a shadow of the final sacrifice of God's Son. The blood of Jesus reaches back to cover all the sins of God's people before Jesus' death and all the sins that come after. That's how valuable and powerful and necessary the cleansing power of Jesus' blood really is.

JUNE

14

Purify me from my sins, and I will be clean; wash me, and I will be whiter than snow.
PSALM 51:7

Our guilty consciences have been sprinkled with Christ's blood to make us clean.
HEBREWS 10:22

These are the ones who died in the great tribulation. They have washed their robes in the blood of the Lamb and made them white.
REVELATION 7:14

🥛 | DISCUSSION STARTERS

What does it mean to have a guilty conscience?

How is having your conscience a good gift from God?

What do you think it means that the blood of Jesus covers us?

Your God is coming to destroy your enemies. He is coming to save you. And when he comes, he will open the eyes of the blind and unplug the ears of the deaf. The lame will leap like a deer, and those who cannot speak will sing for joy!

ISAIAH 35:4-6

John the Baptist, who was in prison, heard about all the things the Messiah was doing. So he sent his disciples to ask Jesus, "Are you the Messiah we've been expecting, or should we keep looking for someone else?"

Jesus told them, "Go back to John and tell him what you have heard and seen—the blind see, the lame walk, the lepers are cured, the deaf hear, the dead are raised to life, and the Good News is being preached to the poor. And tell him, 'God blesses those who do not turn away because of me.'"

MATTHEW 11:2-6

Are You Who I Think You Are?

Have you ever played a game where you had to guess a person's identity based on asking yes or no questions? It was no game when John the Baptist, Jesus' cousin, sent some friends to ask if Jesus was the Messiah. At the time, John was in prison.

John had baptized Jesus and called him "the Lamb of God who takes away the sin of the world!" So he seemed to understand that Jesus was the Messiah. But like many other Jewish people of his day, he expected the Messiah to do some things Jesus just wasn't doing. He had expected fire and judgment from the promised Messiah. But instead of leading a political revolution or shaping up the religious system, Jesus was far from Jerusalem carrying on a ministry of healing. So John sent some of his friends to ask Jesus if he was the Messiah.

But Jesus didn't give them a yes or no answer. He told John's friends to report what they saw: "The blind see, the lame walk, the lepers are cured, the deaf hear, the dead are raised to life, and the Good News is being preached to the poor." John's question was answered. John knew the Scriptures and recognized this quote from Isaiah about the Messiah. He recognized that Jesus was saying he was the fulfillment of the prophecy.

 | **DISCUSSION STARTERS**

Perhaps you want to play a "Who am I?" game around the table, with everyone assuming the identity of a biblical character. Take turns asking each other yes or no questions until you can guess who each person is pretending to be.

What do you think John's reaction was when he got his disciples' report in prison?

In what ways is Jesus different from what people today might expect God to be like?

The Perfect Parent

Nobody likes to get in trouble and face the consequences from a parent. Sometimes we think the discipline we get is unfair—that it is too harsh or lasts too long. And the truth is, nobody has perfect parents. While most parents want to be fair and loving in the discipline they give their children, they aren't perfect.

We might think it's not fair to get certain privileges taken away; we might rather have to do extra chores than be grounded. We don't always know what discipline is right for us. But God does. He is the perfect Parent, and he always does what is right. He doesn't look the other way and ignore it when we do something wrong, but he also doesn't punish us unfairly or inappropriately.

We might feel like the discipline he is using in our lives—like hard times or loss—is unfair or random. But we can be confident that he knows just what we need. He knows we need to learn from the natural consequences of our bad choices. And he knows that facing difficulties or not getting everything we want can be good for us in the long run. Because he's our Father who loves us, he will discipline us in the exact way and amount we need.

🎲🎲 | DISCUSSION STARTERS

How does a parent show love by disciplining his or her child?

What kinds of things does God use in our lives as tools of discipline?

How can we respond to God's discipline in a way that will help us grow?

> I will discipline you, but with justice; I cannot let you go unpunished.
> *JEREMIAH 30:11*

> Our earthly fathers disciplined us for a few years, doing the best they knew how. But God's discipline is always good for us, so that we might share in his holiness. No discipline is enjoyable while it is happening—it's painful! But afterward there will be a peaceful harvest of right living for those who are trained in this way.
> *HEBREWS 12:10-11*

> Your heavenly Father already knows all your needs.
> *MATTHEW 6:32*

Satan's Rebellion

In the creation story recorded in Genesis, God said that everything he had made was "very good." And then the serpent—Satan—showed up to tempt Eve. So we can't help but wonder, *Where did he come from?*

God created a host of holy angels, and some of them, including Satan, who is called the serpent, sinned—or as Jude 1:6 says, they "did not stay within the limits of authority God gave them." Their sin was rebellion; they wanted more power and authority than God had given them. They put themselves above God. And so, "God did not spare angels when they sinned" (2 PETER 2:4, NIV).

Why did God allow evil to enter the world in the first place? Was this introduction of evil something God was unable to control? Or was this rebellion against him actually part of his plan? We don't really know how the sin of rebellion entered Satan's heart—that isn't clear in the Bible. But we do see over and over again in Scripture that Satan has to ask permission from God to do what he wants to do. God has the right and the power to restrain him anytime he chooses to do so.

God permitted Satan's fall, not because he was helpless to stop it, but because he had a purpose for it. And if he chooses to permit something, he does so for a reason—an infinitely wise reason. This gives us confidence that when God allows Satan to hurt us in some way, God intends to use it to build our faith and confidence in him.

[Jesus] replied, "I saw Satan fall like lightning from heaven."
LUKE 10:18, NIV

He was a murderer from the beginning. He has always hated the truth, because there is no truth in him.
JOHN 8:44

This great dragon—the ancient serpent called the devil, or Satan, the one deceiving the whole world—was thrown down to the earth with all his angels.
REVELATION 12:9

 | ## DISCUSSION STARTERS

How do we know that Satan is real?

What are some examples of Satan asking God's permission to do evil (see Job 1:6-12; 2:1-6; and Luke 22:31-34)?

What do we know about what will happen to Satan in the end?

So That You May Believe

JUNE

18

Have you ever seen a real miracle—something only God can do that goes against the laws of nature? Imagine what it must have been like in Jesus' day to see his miracles with your own eyes!

John says that the miracles Jesus performed were signs that pointed people to an important reality: that Jesus is the Messiah, the Son of God. John describes seven miracles in his Gospel. Each one shows us something about who Jesus is and points to a deeper spiritual reality.

When Jesus turned water into wine at the wedding in Cana, he showed us that he fills ordinary lives with extraordinary joy. When he healed the son of the government official, he demonstrated how he moves us from using God to trusting God. When Jesus healed the lame man, it illustrated how he offers wholeness to those who will walk in faith. With the feeding of the five thousand, Jesus pointed to the way he satisfies our deepest desires with himself. When Jesus walked on water in the middle of the storm, we see his power over the desperate circumstances in our lives. When he healed the man blind from birth, he showed how he removes the spiritual blinders in our lives so we can see him. And when Jesus raised Lazarus from the dead, it showed us that Jesus brings to life what was dead—just by the power of his word.

The miracles themselves were not what Jesus wanted people to see about himself. His miracles gave him credibility. So when he said he had the power to heal sin-sick souls, open eyes that are blind to truth, bring peace to troubled lives, and bring life to dead places in the heart, we can believe it and trust him to do it.

The disciples saw Jesus do many other miraculous signs in addition to the ones recorded in this book. But these are written so that you may continue to believe that Jesus is the Messiah, the Son of God, and that by believing in him you will have life by the power of his name.

JOHN 20:30-31

| DISCUSSION STARTERS

Which of the miracles described in the book of John would you have liked to see most?

Which of these spiritual miracles have you experienced?

Why do you think we don't see as many miracles today?

Abraham's Children

Some people can trace their family trees back many, many generations to a well-known figure, such as George Washington or Robert E. Lee. They discover who their great-grandparents and great-great-grandparents were to establish that they are a descendant of that famous person.

But according to the Bible, being a descendant of Abraham does not require that we trace our genetic ancestry back through the Jewish people to Abraham. Jews and non-Jews can be children of Abraham. Protestants of European descent can become children of Abraham; Hispanics and Laotians and Cambodians can become children of Abraham; black African Muslims can become children of Abraham.

Getting in on the blessings promised to Abraham's descendants is not based on being in his bloodline. It is based on being like him in terms of faith, on trusting God the way he did. "Abram believed the LORD, and the LORD counted him as righteous because of his faith" (GENESIS 15:6). If you are banking all your happiness on Christ, then you have an Abraham kind of faith, and you stand to inherit everything God promised to Abraham's family.

Not all who are born into the nation of Israel are truly members of God's people! Being descendants of Abraham doesn't make them truly Abraham's children.
ROMANS 9:6-7

"Abraham believed God, and God counted him as righteous because of his faith." The real children of Abraham, then, are those who put their faith in God.
GALATIANS 3:6-7

Now that you belong to Christ, you are the true children of Abraham. You are his heirs, and God's promise to Abraham belongs to you.
GALATIANS 3:29

 | **DISCUSSION STARTERS**

How far back can you trace your ancestry? Do you know the names of your great-grandparents? your great-great-grandparents?

Since we have characteristics of the people we're related to, what characteristics of Abraham's should we have if we are his descendants?

What do we stand to inherit as descendants of Abraham?

What Brides Do

Have you ever spent some time around a bride or a bride-to-be? A bride is a busy person. And she is a passionate person. She is busy making herself beautiful for her groom on their wedding day because she loves him and wants to please him.

The Bible uses the image of a bride and a groom to describe the relationship between Christ and his church. Anyone who is a Christian is "engaged" to Jesus, waiting for and preparing for the wedding that will happen when our Groom, Jesus, comes for us.

A bride loves to show off her engagement ring. As believers, we also make a statement to the world about our love and connectedness to Jesus when we are baptized. It is a sign of our commitment to him. A bride talks about her groom. She is enamored of him and wants to spend time with him. One of the best things about her life is that she is loved and chosen by him, and nothing makes her happier than knowing this. Nothing makes a Christian happier than knowing he or she is loved and chosen by God.

A bride likes to count down the days until her wedding. She can hardly wait because she knows that day will be the beginning of a whole new life and a new intimacy with the groom she has been longing for. As the bride of Christ, we wait with great anticipation for the day when we will be united with our Groom. Until then, we stay faithful to him and say, "Come, Lord Jesus!" (REVELATION 22:20).

> Your new name will be "The City of God's Delight" and "The Bride of God," for the LORD delights in you and will claim you as his bride.
> *ISAIAH 62:4*

> I saw the holy city, the new Jerusalem, coming down from God out of heaven like a bride beautifully dressed for her husband.
> *REVELATION 21:2*

> I promised you as a pure bride to one husband—Christ.
> *2 CORINTHIANS 11:2*

 | ## DISCUSSION STARTERS

What do you think are the best and worst parts about being a bride?

What does it mean to be a "pure bride"?

What has Christ done to make his bride beautiful (see Ephesians 5:25-27)?

When he finally came to his senses, he said to himself, "At home even the hired servants have food enough to spare, and here I am dying of hunger! I will go home to my father and say, 'Father, I have sinned against both heaven and you, and I am no longer worthy of being called your son. Please take me on as a hired servant.'"

So he returned home to his father. And while he was still a long way off, his father saw him coming. Filled with love and compassion, he ran to his son, embraced him, and kissed him.

LUKE 15:17-20

Your Father Is Waiting

What is the picture of God like in your head? Is he a no-nonsense judge? a boring teacher? an impossible-to-please boss?

Jesus wanted us to see a picture in our minds of what God is really like, so he told a story about a proud, rebellious son who took his part of the inheritance from his father and went his own way. Ultimately, he ended up at the bottom of the barrel—feeding pigs that were eating better than he was. So he decided to go back to his father—never expecting to be accepted as a son, but just hoping to be taken on as one of the servants. On his way home he worked up a speech to give his father, but he never got the chance to give it. His father was waiting on the front porch, and when he saw his son he ran out to greet him, brought him a robe and a ring, and welcomed him back, not as a servant but as his son.

This is how Jesus wants us to see God, our Father. He wants us to see how giving and loving and forgiving he is. Even when we're running away from him, wasting the resources he has given us, never thinking of him, God is still loving us and getting ready to welcome us back into closeness with him. He's not preparing a lecture. He's preparing a party.

If the day comes when you wake up to realize you've made a terrible mess of things and you think you've failed so miserably that you can't face God, let alone ask his forgiveness, remember this picture of God. Then come running in his direction.

 | DISCUSSION STARTERS

How do you picture God in your mind?

Why is it hard to turn to God when we've sinned? Should it be?

How can seeing God as a forgiving Father help you when you fail?

Your Father's Child

When people look at your family, can they see a resemblance in your physical features or mannerisms? Even adopted children often resemble their parents and siblings in many ways—hand gestures, facial expressions, speech patterns. When someone looks at you or listens to you, can they tell what family you come from?

Jesus said that there's a way to live that makes you immediately recognizable as one of his children. It's when you are a peacemaker. Because God, your Father, is a peacemaker too. "God was in Christ, reconciling the world to himself, no longer counting people's sins against them" (2 CORINTHIANS 5:19). "He made peace with everything in heaven and on earth by means of Christ's blood on the cross" (COLOSSIANS 1:20).

People will recognize us as God's children when we are willing to make sacrifices for peace the way God did, when we do everything we can to reconcile or restore relationships between people and God and between some people and other people.

Do you always seem to be at the center of a conflict? Are you always angry with someone? Do you get easily offended? If so, you are not carrying the family resemblance. Or do people see your peace with God and with other people? When people know they can count on you to offer words of wisdom and peace rather than anger or criticism, it's because they've seen that you are a peacemaker, just like your Father.

God blesses those who work for peace, for they will be called the children of God.
MATTHEW 5:9

Let the peace that comes from Christ rule in your hearts. For as members of one body you are called to live in peace.
COLOSSIANS 3:15

Christ himself has brought peace to us.
EPHESIANS 2:14

| DISCUSSION STARTERS

What do you think it means to be a peacemaker?

Who have you observed being a peacemaker?

How is sharing Christ with someone being a peacemaker?

Have the people of Israel build me a holy sanctuary so I can live among them. You must build this Tabernacle and its furnishings exactly according to the pattern I will show you.
EXODUS 25:8-9

In the first room were a lampstand, a table, and sacred loaves of bread on the table. This room was called the Holy Place. Then there was a curtain, and behind the curtain was the second room called the Most Holy Place. In that room were a gold incense altar and a wooden chest called the Ark of the Covenant, which was covered with gold on all sides. . . . Above the Ark were the cherubim of divine glory, whose wings stretched out over the Ark's cover, the place of atonement.
HEBREWS 9:2-5

Building God's House

When you're putting something together, like a bike or a game or a piece of furniture, do you carefully follow the directions step by step? Or do you use the directions as a last resort?

God gave instructions to Moses for building a Tabernacle, where he would meet with his people and live among them. These were very specific instructions about its size, materials, layout, and furniture. The people were to follow the directions exactly. Why did God do that? Is he just picky? God gave such specific instructions because this Tabernacle was much more than a meeting place. Every aspect of it said something about our need for God and the way those needs are provided for in Jesus.

The Tabernacle was a vivid illustration of the work of Jesus to bring people to God. The curtain showed the separation between us and God, a separation that was overcome when Jesus died and the curtain was torn in two. The priests sprinkled the blood of sacrifices on the cover of the Ark that held the tablets of the Ten Commandments. This was a symbol of Christ's blood coming between the presence of God and our sin so we can receive mercy. The container with manna God had provided in the wilderness was a picture of Jesus as the Bread that came from heaven, and the lampstand revealed him as the true Light that came into the world. The real point of the Tabernacle was who it pointed to: Jesus.

 | **DISCUSSION STARTERS**

What is the most significant item you've built or put together? Did you follow the directions?

Why was it important for the Tabernacle to be built exactly right?

How did the three items inside the Ark—the stone tablets with the Ten Commandments, the jar of manna, and Aaron's staff—remind the people of their need and God's provision (see Deuteronomy 10:1-2; Exodus 16:32-34; Numbers 17:10-11)?

The People of God

When we study ancient history, we learn about all kinds of civilizations. Have you ever wondered why God's history book—the Bible—focuses on one small group of people and God's dealings with them?

The Old Testament story of God's dealings with Israel is like a lesson book for all the world to read. It shows us who God is, what he expects, how he shows mercy, and how we can know him. Here are a few things the Israelites' history helps us understand:

- our need for a Savior—*they were delivered from slavery in Egypt*
- what it looks like to live by faith—*Abraham believed God and was made right with him*
- the need for payment for sin—*the priests made sacrifices to cover people's sins*
- our opportunity to approach God—*the Tabernacle was built as a place to meet with God*
- the provision of God—*God gave the Israelites manna, and water from a rock in the desert, and he led them to victory in battle*
- a place of eternal rest being prepared by God—*after many years in the desert, they were led to the Promised Land*

Israel's history shows us how God deals with his people. And today we, as the people of God—the church—are a living history book, showing those around us what God is like and what it means to live as his child, in his family.

🎎 | DISCUSSION STARTERS

When you think of stories you've heard or read about the children of Israel in the Old Testament, what do you remember about them?

From what you know about the Israelites, how are we like them?

What do the verses in 1 Corinthians 10 tell us about why God focuses his history book on the children of Israel?

JUNE

24

You have been set apart as holy to the Lord your God, and he has chosen you from all the nations of the earth to be his own special treasure.

DEUTERONOMY 14:2

Our ancestors . . . were guided by a cloud that moved ahead of them, and all of them walked through the sea on dry ground. In the cloud and in the sea, all of them were baptized as followers of Moses. All of them ate the same spiritual food, and all of them drank the same spiritual water. For they drank from the spiritual rock that traveled with them, and that rock was Christ. Yet God was not pleased with most of them, and their bodies were scattered in the wilderness. These things happened as a warning to us, so that we would not crave evil things as they did, or worship idols as some of them did.

1 CORINTHIANS 10:1-7

JUNE

25

You must love the Lord your God with all your heart, all your soul, all your mind, and all your strength.

MARK 12:30

Jesus told them, "If God were your Father, you would love me."

JOHN 8:42

Those who obey God's word truly show how completely they love him. That is how we know we are living in him.

1 JOHN 2:5

How Do You Love God?

Have you ever met a couple in love? They can't get through a conversation without talking about the other person. They see everything about their lives in relationship to that person. They not only talk fondly about the one they love, but they also look forward to talking to him or her—not out of any sense of duty, but because they want to share the ups and downs of their days, their deepest thoughts and feelings. They look to the future and smile with a sense of satisfaction and anticipation about life together. They can't stand it when something comes between them, and they'll do whatever is necessary to make things right again.

This kind of love helps us understand what the greatest commandment in the Bible means—love the Lord your God with all your heart, soul, mind, and strength. In other words, we are to love God with every part of our beings—our emotions, our thoughts, our speech, and our actions. God knows what our souls need most and what will satisfy our souls most—to love God freely and deeply.

What does it mean to love God? Loving God includes obeying all his commands, believing everything in his Word, thanking him for all his gifts, enjoying all that he is. To love God means that we want to express our love for him in ways that matter to him—and that means obedience.

 | **DISCUSSION STARTERS**

What does it mean to say you love another person?

How is loving God similar to loving another person? How is it different?

How can you learn to love God more? What are some specific ways you can show that love?

Happy to Lose?

Nobody likes to lose. We don't like to lose sports competitions. We don't like to lose our money or our possessions. We don't like to lose jobs, elections, or friends. Can you imagine anyone being happy when he or she loses?

In the Bible we read about people who were actually happy when they lost. It tells about a group of Christians who lost their businesses, homes, good reputation, and security. And yet they accepted these losses "with joy." How could they do that? The Bible says it was because they "knew there were better things waiting for [them] that will last forever." They were confident that there was something better than everything they'd lost, something that was already waiting for them that they would one day enjoy.

But actually the "better things" are not really things. The better things are the person of Jesus and the salvation he offers. God offers us a relationship of acceptance, fellowship, and enjoyment for eternity, and that's going to make everything we've lost here worth it. That's why we can be happy when we lose here. It's why we can live free from the fear and greed that could have kept us chained to security, safety, ease, and comfort. All our losses here remind us that we have something better than what we've lost, something better that's waiting for us in heaven when we see Jesus.

 | ## DISCUSSION STARTERS

What is the most precious thing you've ever lost?

How do we know there are better things waiting for us? How can we increase our confidence in this truth?

Is there anything in your life you're afraid to lose? Is that thing holding you back from serving God?

When troubles come your way, consider it an opportunity for great joy.
JAMES 1:2

I will rejoice even if I lose my life, pouring it out like a liquid offering to God. . . . And I want all of you to share that joy.
PHILIPPIANS 2:17

Think back on those early days when you first learned about Christ. Remember how you remained faithful even though it meant terrible suffering. . . . You suffered along with those who were thrown into jail, and when all you owned was taken from you, you accepted it with joy. You knew there were better things waiting for you that will last forever.
HEBREWS 10:32, 34

JUNE

27

I carried you before you were born. I will be your God throughout your lifetime—until your hair is white with age. I made you, and I will care for you. I will carry you along and save you.

ISAIAH 46:3-4

You brought me safely from my mother's womb and led me to trust you at my mother's breast. I was thrust into your arms at my birth. You have been my God from the moment I was born.

PSALM 22:9-10

Even before he made the world, God loved us and chose us in Christ to be holy and without fault in his eyes. God decided in advance to adopt us into his own family by bringing us to himself through Jesus Christ.

EPHESIANS 1:4-5

Before You Were Born

It's a scene that plays itself out daily at school recess: two team captains picking their teams for a game of kickball or softball. Everybody lines up, hoping to be chosen for the team.

Some people see our relationship to God something like that team selection scenario. Except we sometimes think God, the team captain, is standing there hoping we'll choose to be on his team. We think the choosing is completely up to us. But the truth is, God is not standing idly by, hoping we will choose him. He has made the first move to give us the desire to move in his direction.

Ephesians 1:11 from *The Message* says it this way: "Long before we first heard of Christ and got our hopes up, he had his eye on us, had designs on us for glorious living, part of the overall purpose he is working out in every-thing and everyone." Long before you were born, God determined that you would be his. He is not sweating it out on the sidelines, wondering if you will choose him. He made the first move by choosing you. He didn't choose you *because* you chose him; he chose you so that you *could* choose him. Paul said it this way: "By His doing you are in Christ Jesus" (1 CORINTHIANS 1:30, NASB).

 | **DISCUSSION STARTERS**

How does it feel to be chosen—for the team, for a play, as a friend?

What do you think about God's character that he chooses us?

How does it make you feel to know that God knew you before you were born?

The Master Switch

Somewhere in your house is an electrical box of circuit breakers. And at the bottom of that box, you'll likely find a master switch. With a flip of that master switch, you can control the power for your whole house.

You have a master switch in your life too—something with a great deal of power even though it is relatively small. It's your tongue. It can be used to encourage and bless, or it can be used to hurt and harm. It can open up life, or it can destroy a reputation or relationship. What we say reveals what's in our hearts. Our tongues are like tattletales that tell on the heart. Jesus said, "Whatever is in your heart determines what you say" (MATTHEW 12:34).

While what you say reveals what is in your heart, controlling your tongue is also a way to guard your heart from sin. If we speak loving, true, and thoughtful words—words of humility, wisdom, peace, and gratitude—these words will influence our attitudes and our actions. Likewise, if we control our tongues and refuse to speak words of self-pity, bad language, and angry insults, then the destructive fire of these things is put out before it becomes a blaze in our lives. The master switch has cut off the power of our words to lead us into sin.

 | ## DISCUSSION STARTERS

How have someone's words helped you? How have someone's words hurt you?

Can you think of a time your words either revealed what was in your heart or helped shape what was in your heart?

If we want to grow in holiness, what are some limits we may want to set on what we allow to come out of our mouths?

> If you claim to be religious but don't control your tongue, you are fooling yourself, and your religion is worthless.
> *JAMES 1:26*

> If we could control our tongues, we would be perfect and could also control ourselves in every other way. . . . The tongue is a flame of fire. It is a whole world of wickedness, corrupting your entire body. It can set your whole life on fire, for it is set on fire by hell itself.
> *JAMES 3:2, 6*

> I said to myself, "I will watch what I do and not sin in what I say."
> *PSALM 39:1*

29

Let us come boldly to the throne of our gracious God. There we will receive his mercy, and we will find grace to help us when we need it most.
HEBREWS 4:16

All of us can come to the Father through the same Holy Spirit because of what Christ has done for us.
EPHESIANS 2:18

Dear brothers and sisters, we can boldly enter heaven's Most Holy Place because of the blood of Jesus. By his death, Jesus opened a new and life-giving way through the curtain into the Most Holy Place.
HEBREWS 10:19-20

All-Access Pass

When you go to a big concert or event, there are usually some people working there who have a special tag hanging around their necks that says, "All Access." This means they are free to go wherever they want—behind the curtain, backstage, wherever. The security guard at the gate will not turn away people with an all-access pass like he does to those without one.

Usually you have to know somebody to get a backstage pass—someone with connections, someone who is willing to give you his or her credibility to get you in. Likewise, to gain access into the presence of God, you have to know somebody. Not everybody has access—only those with connections to Jesus. Jesus is willing to give us his credibility—his righteousness—so that we can have free and open access to God.

Some people who are connected to Jesus never take advantage of the access he has given to them. But he gave us this access so that we won't have to relate to God from a distance. He has granted us access and invites us in. He wants to know us—and he wants us to come backstage into the presence of God with him.

 | **DISCUSSION STARTERS**

What is the difference between seeing your favorite artist perform while you're sitting in the back of the auditorium and meeting that artist backstage or in his or her home?

What do you think it means to have "all access" to God?

What keeps us from using the access to God that Jesus has given to us?

Secret Things

It can be fun to know a secret. When someone shares a secret with you, it's like giving you a gift of something precious and important, and you feel special just for knowing.

God has secrets. And he doesn't have to tell us his secrets. But because he loves us, he has chosen to reveal to us his most precious secret—his secret plan for us. Colossians 2:2 says that God's secret plan is "Christ himself." What makes this secret so significant is that it is not just a secret we know with our minds. It is a secret we experience and enter into. Colossians 1:27 says, "God wanted them to know that the riches and glory of Christ are for you Gentiles, too. And this is the secret: Christ lives in you. This gives you assurance of sharing his glory."

God's secret is Jesus himself living inside us, changing us, making us new, bringing us safely home to himself. But it's not a secret anymore! God has entrusted his secret to us so that we can tell everyone who has not yet heard.

 | DISCUSSION STARTERS

What is one of the best secrets someone ever told you?

How would you explain God's secret plan in a sentence or two?

Why do you think God has let us in on his secret plan for us?

The LORD our God has secrets known to no one. We are not accountable for them, but we and our children are accountable forever for all that he has revealed to us, so that we may obey all the terms of these instructions.
DEUTERONOMY 29:29

His disciples came and asked him, "Why do you use parables when you talk to the people?" He replied, "You are permitted to understand the secrets of the Kingdom of Heaven, but others are not. To those who listen to my teaching, more understanding will be given, and they will have an abundance of knowledge.
MATTHEW 13:10-12

God has now revealed to us his mysterious plan regarding Christ, a plan to fulfill his own good pleasure.
EPHESIANS 1:9

1

Don't rejoice because evil spirits obey you; rejoice because your names are registered in heaven.
LUKE 10:20

I saw the dead, both great and small, standing before God's throne. And the books were opened, including the Book of Life. And the dead were judged according to what they had done, as recorded in the books.... And anyone whose name was not found recorded in the Book of Life was thrown into the lake of fire.
REVELATION 20:12, 15

What Do the Books Say about You?

Imagine the scene in your mind. Jesus, the Judge, is on his throne in heaven. And in front of him on one side is a tall stack of books. On the other side of him is one book. This is the scene at the end of time described in Revelation 20. The large stack is the books with everything we've done during our lives recorded in them. The single book is the Book of Life—a list of the names of all those who are in Christ.

The Book of Life is a record of the names of all those God calls his own. It is a list of all those who know him and love him. Ephesians 1:4-5 tells us whose names are in this book: "Even before he made the world, God loved us and chose us in Christ to be holy and without fault in his eyes. God decided in advance to adopt us into his own family by bringing us to himself through Jesus Christ. This is what he wanted to do, and it gave him great pleasure."

So if your name is in the Book of Life, does that mean the record of your life in the books is irrelevant? No. What is written there provides confirmation that you are connected to Christ in a saving, transforming way. Our deeds are not the basis of our salvation—they are the evidence of our salvation. The books provide an accounting of all the things God's grace has empowered us to do and become because of our connectedness to Jesus.

What's written in the stack of books will not determine where you will spend eternity. What matters is that your name is in the Book of Life—written there by the hand of God, never to be erased.

 | ## DISCUSSION STARTERS

If you read what was written about your day today in "the books," what would it say?

What or who determines if your name is in the Book of Life?

What would you like to have written in the books about your life?

Righteous Clothes

Have you ever been in a wedding party and had to buy the right dress or maybe wear a tuxedo? Jesus told a story about a wedding where not only the people in the wedding party were expected to wear matching clothing, but all the guests were too. In the parable, a king invites people to a wedding. Evidently, when they get to the wedding, each person is offered the appropriate clothes for entering the king's presence—clothes that have been supplied by the king himself. But one guy just doesn't want to wear the clothes supplied by the king. He wants to be in charge of his own wardrobe. He doesn't want to do things the king's way—he insists on his own way. And when the king sees him, he throws the guy out.

Jesus is saying that we can't enter God's presence wearing our own righteousness. To be in his presence, we have to accept the gift of perfect righteousness that he offers us—the righteousness of Jesus. Some people insist on wearing their own clothes—their own moral life (which seems good enough in comparison to people around them), church membership, church activities, and good deeds toward other people.

But Isaiah described these things—all our own attempts at righteousness apart from Jesus—as "filthy rags" (ISAIAH 64:6). That's why we need to make an exchange. Jesus takes our clothes of sin and gives us his own clothes—clothes of righteousness—so we can be in his presence.

> I am overwhelmed with joy in the LORD my God! For he has dressed me with the clothing of salvation and draped me in a robe of righteousness.
> *ISAIAH 61:10*

> When the king came in to meet the guests, he noticed a man who wasn't wearing the proper clothes for a wedding. "Friend," he asked, "how is it that you are here without wedding clothes?" But the man had no reply. Then the king said to his aides, "Bind his hands and feet and throw him into the outer darkness, where there will be weeping and gnashing of teeth."
> *MATTHEW 22:11-13*

🧂 | DISCUSSION STARTERS

Do you like to wear what someone else says you should wear, or would you rather choose your clothes yourself?

What types of "clothing" do people tend to think will make them good enough in God's eyes?

What are the benefits of coming to God dressed in Christ's clothes of righteousness rather than your own? What are the results if you don't?

JULY

3

The Lord did not set his heart on you and choose you because you were more numerous than other nations, for you were the smallest of all nations! Rather, it was simply that the Lord loves you.

DEUTERONOMY 7:7-8

You didn't choose me. I chose you.

JOHN 15:16

God chooses people according to his own purposes; he calls people, but not according to their good or bad works.

ROMANS 9:11-12

The Way God Chooses

"Pick me, pick me!" All of us know what it is like to want to be chosen—for the team, as a dance partner, as a friend, as a mate—and in many other ways. We put our best foot forward and talk up our good qualities, sometimes even show off.

How does God choose the people he will use for his purposes in the world? Well, we know he doesn't choose the way we choose. Remember that when he was looking for a king for Israel, he passed on the strong, good-looking sons of Jesse. "The Lord said to Samuel, 'Don't judge by his appearance or height. . . . The Lord doesn't see things the way you see them. People judge by outward appearance, but the Lord looks at the heart'"(1 Samuel 16:7). God does not choose based on talent or looks or family background. God chooses as he desires, and his choosing does not always make sense to us. We don't understand why he chooses someone we see as less gifted or less qualified to fill a particular role and passes over someone who seems just right to us. God turns our system of evaluating people upside down.

That's why Paul could say in 1 Corinthians 1:26-27, "Remember, dear brothers and sisters, that few of you were wise in the world's eyes or powerful or wealthy when God called you. Instead, God chose things the world considers foolish in order to shame those who think they are wise. And he chose things that are powerless to shame those who are powerful."

 | ## DISCUSSION STARTERS

What things do you consider when you are choosing teammates or friends?

Think through some of the people in the Bible. How did God's choosing to use those people go against how we might think God would choose people to use? (Consider Abraham, Jacob, Moses, David, Mary, Peter, and Paul.)

Are there people in your life God has chosen to use in surprising ways?

Celebrate Dependence Day

JULY
4

"I can do it myself! I don't need any help!" This is the voice of independence. It is inside each one of us, and it has run in our families as far back as Adam and Eve, who wanted to be like God rather than being dependent on God for everything. They had their own ideas about what they needed for a good life, and their rebellion lives on in us.

In Matthew 18:3 Jesus says, "I tell you the truth, unless you turn from your sins and become like little children, you will never get into the Kingdom of Heaven." What does it mean to become like little children? It means that we are dependent on God as our heavenly Father, rather than stubbornly and independently thinking we can take care of ourselves. The independent person says, "I'm in charge of my life. I'm free to do what I please and choose what I want. I will take care of myself. I really don't need God's provision or protection. And I really don't need Christ's righteousness. Mine is good enough."

The world tells us to give ourselves a pep talk, saying, *I can do it. I just need to believe in myself.* But Jesus says, "Apart from me you can do nothing" (JOHN 15:5). Rather than seeking to become more self-confident, we need to strive to become more God-reliant. Rather than seeking and celebrating independence, it is actually dependence that is worth celebrating.

 | ## DISCUSSION STARTERS

What are some things you can't do for yourself?

How can prayer encourage our sense of dependence on God?

What types of experiences help to deepen our dependence on God?

We think you ought to know, dear brothers and sisters, about the trouble we went through in the province of Asia. We were crushed and overwhelmed beyond our ability to endure, and we thought we would never live through it. In fact, we expected to die. But as a result, we stopped relying on ourselves and learned to rely only on God, who raises the dead.
2 CORINTHIANS 1:8-9

This is what the LORD says: "Cursed are those who put their trust in mere humans, who rely on human strength and turn their hearts away from the LORD."
JEREMIAH 17:5

The LORD is good to those who depend on him, to those who search for him.
LAMENTATIONS 3:25

I want you to understand this mystery, dear brothers and sisters, so that you will not feel proud about yourselves.
ROMANS 11:25

The kind of sorrow God wants us to experience leads us away from sin and results in salvation.
2 CORINTHIANS 7:10

Even if we feel guilty, God is greater than our feelings.
1 JOHN 3:20

God Changes How We Feel

Is it right or wrong to sneeze? That might seem like a ridiculous question. Sneezing is just something we do that isn't right or wrong. And that's how some people view feelings—not really right or wrong—they just are what they are, and we can't help them.

But the Holy Spirit doesn't just cause us to act and think differently. He causes us to *feel* differently. He changes how we think about him and therefore how we feel about him and about our circumstances. The clearer our view of God and his provision becomes, the more our feelings are centered in joy and peace. And while negative emotions that threaten our joy may never completely disappear, they lose their total power over us. We are no longer at their mercy.

When we feel afraid and forgotten, we hear God say, "I am with you." And we begin to believe he is by our side when we're in the operating room, at the graveside, in the courtroom, in our aching loneliness. We feel peaceful in his presence. When we feel angry, instead of making demands, we remind ourselves that all our deepest needs are met in Christ and that we can trust him to protect and defend us. Anger gives way to rest. When we feel jealous, instead of nurturing our thoughts of resentment that God has not given us what he has given to someone else, we look at all God has given to us in Jesus, and gratitude begins to blossom where jealousy threatened to control us. And we realize it's true: God *is* greater than our feelings.

 | ## DISCUSSION STARTERS

Can you decide to sneeze or not sneeze? Can you decide to be happy?

How does God change our feelings of anger or sadness?

What is the secret to not letting your feelings control your life?

Few Find It

Most of us like to be in step with the crowd. We want to dress the way people around us dress, talk the way they talk, and even think the way they think about different topics. We don't like to feel out of step at every turn with everyone around us. But Jesus says that if we want to be connected to him in a saving, eternal way, we have to be willing to go against the crowd—willing to be in the minority rather than the majority.

But being in the majority is usually more comfortable than being in the minority, isn't it? Along with the seeming safety of the majority come strength in numbers and a sense of "rightness." Jesus' statement that only a few will find their way into the Kingdom of God challenges our assumptions about the rightness of the majority. It shows us that huge numbers of people in our world are wrong about how to have a life-giving relationship with God and about what makes life worth living.

Some people suggest it is arrogant to believe that only a small number of people have a grasp on truth and the gift of eternal life. But actually it takes great humility to recognize our complete unworthiness and inability to earn a place in God's family. It requires humility to admit that we are desperately in need of a Savior.

 | **DISCUSSION STARTERS**

Have you ever been in the minority because of your gender, age, cultural background, interests, opinions, or something else? What was that like?

How would you respond to the criticism that Christianity is exclusive, or limited to certain people?

Why do you think Jesus said only a few will find life?

You can enter God's Kingdom only through the narrow gate. The highway to hell is broad, and its gate is wide for the many who choose that way. But the gateway to life is very narrow and the road is difficult, and only a few ever find it.
MATTHEW 7:13-14

Jesus told him, "I am the way, the truth, and the life. No one can come to the Father except through me."
JOHN 14:6

There is salvation in no one else! God has given no other name under heaven by which we must be saved.
ACTS 4:12

7

The serpent was the shrewdest of all the wild animals the LORD God had made. One day he asked the woman, "Did God really say you must not eat the fruit from any of the trees in the garden?"

"Of course we may eat fruit from the trees in the garden," the woman replied. "It's only the fruit from the tree in the middle of the garden that we are not allowed to eat. God said, 'You must not eat it or even touch it; if you do, you will die.'"

"You won't die!" the serpent replied to the woman. "God knows that your eyes will be opened as soon as you eat it, and you will be like God, knowing both good and evil."
GENESIS 3:1-5

That Sneaky Serpent

Dogs bark. Kittens purr. Birds chirp. You can hear them and you know they're there. But how about snakes? Snakes glide silently. They're dangerous because they can attack before you hear them coming.

This is what the devil did in the Garden of Eden—and what he still does today. He sneaks up on us and speaks lies to us when we don't even realize he's the one talking. He hates us, and he wants to use us to humiliate God. Just like he did in the Garden of Eden with Eve, he tries to convince us that God is withholding something good from us when really God is loving us by setting limits around us. The devil tries to manipulate us into looking out for ourselves rather than trusting God to look after us. He twists the truth to trick us into reaching for what looks good and what we think will feel good. But those things really only taste good or feel good for a short time, and then they go sour and hurt us.

The good news is that we are not forever at the mercy of the sneaky snake Satan. Right in the Garden after Adam and Eve sinned, God promised that a descendant of Eve would one day fight Satan to the death. That descendant would suffer but ultimately win (SEE GENESIS 3:15). The rest of the Bible tells the story of this promise—how a second Adam came to earth and overcame Satan's temptations. As God foretold in the Garden, Satan struck Jesus' heel, by working through people's evil actions to put Jesus on the cross; but Jesus crushed Satan's head, by overcoming death. He took away Satan's power to hurt us for good.

 | DISCUSSION STARTERS

Why do we think of snakes as sneaky? Why do they sometimes scare us?

How did Satan twist, question, and weaken what God had said to Adam and Eve?

What does Satan use to get us to turn on God rather than trust him?

Proof of Love

What would you think if someone told you he or she loved you but never did anything that showed that he or she cared at all? You would realize pretty soon that these were just empty words or fleeting emotions, but not real love. Love is not just an emotional feeling. Real love is something that is lived out.

Fortunately, God was not content just to tell us that he loves us. His love was lived out for us in ways we could see and experience and know. He proved it when he came to our earth and became one of us, when he touched and healed people, when he pointed out the sin that destroys us. But nothing put God's love for us on display like Jesus' death on the cross. Ultimate love was expressed in the ultimate sacrifice—the God of the universe on a cross dying for people who didn't even care about him or take an interest in him.

On the cross God showed us what it really means to love without limits, expecting nothing in return. He showed us what real love costs. This is our example to follow in loving others beyond just empty words. If we want to love, we need to be prepared to demonstrate—not just discuss—sacrificial love.

 | DISCUSSION STARTERS

What kinds of things keep us from demonstrating love to other people with our actions?

Read Titus 3:4-7. According to these verses, what are the ways God has demonstrated his love toward us?

Who are some people in your world who really need to be loved? How can you show them real love?

Long ago the LORD said to Israel: "I have loved you, my people, with an everlasting love. With unfailing love I have drawn you to myself."
JEREMIAH 31:3

God showed his great love for us by sending Christ to die for us while we were still sinners.
ROMANS 5:8

May you have the power to understand, as all God's people should, how wide, how long, how high, and how deep his love is. May you experience the love of Christ, though it is too great to understand fully. Then you will be made complete with all the fullness of life and power that comes from God.
EPHESIANS 3:18-19

JULY

9

You know the generous grace of our Lord Jesus Christ. Though he was rich, yet for your sakes he became poor, so that by his poverty he could make you rich.

2 CORINTHIANS 8:9

Teach those who are rich in this world not to be proud and not to trust in their money, which is so unreliable. Their trust should be in God, who richly gives us all we need for our enjoyment.

1 TIMOTHY 6:17

Just a Little Bit More . . .

In the late 1800s, the world's richest man was John D. Rockefeller, founder of the Standard Oil Company. One time he was asked the question, "How much money is enough money?" His answer says a lot about human nature: "Just a little bit more." Most of us struggle to be satisfied with what we have and the amount of money that comes our way. We tend to think that if we had a little bit more, then we'd be satisfied. But it never seems to work that way.

What is important about money is not how much or how little we have but how much more we *want* to have. A poor person can be a slave to money, and a rich person can be sold out for God. It's how we think and feel about money that has the power to destroy our souls. Paul writes that "people who long to be rich fall into temptation and are trapped by many foolish and harmful desires that plunge them into ruin and destruction. For the love of money is the root of all kinds of evil" (1 TIMOTHY 6:9-10). And the most evil thing that grows from the root of the love of money is a dissatisfaction in God. Paul is not condemning the desire to earn money in order to meet our needs and the needs of others. He is warning against the insatiable desire to have more and more money, and acknowledging the way it chokes out our desire for God.

Jesus understood this conflict. That's why he said, "No one can serve two masters. For you will hate one and love the other; you will be devoted to one and despise the other. You cannot serve both God and money" (MATTHEW 6:24).

 | ## DISCUSSION STARTERS

Why do you think it feels good to have a stash of money in your pocket, piggy bank, or bank account?

In what way(s) did Jesus' becoming poor make us rich (see 2 Corinthians 8:9)?

How can we learn to love money less and trust God more?

Growing Up

Nobody wants to suffer. In fact, most of us would have to admit that we spend a lot of energy doing everything we can to avoid pain. But suffering should not surprise us. Scripture tells us over and over to expect it.

We might think that the best method to grow up spiritually is to attend Bible studies and accumulate spiritual knowledge. But God's method of choice to make us spiritually mature seems to be suffering. However, suffering itself doesn't do the job. It is how we respond to the suffering that determines if the pain will become fertile ground for real growth. Growth comes when we respond to the major heartaches and minor difficulties in our lives with an attitude of endurance. Growth comes when we can say in the face of suffering, "This will not diminish my faith or trust in God. It will only cause me to dig deeper in my faith and trust him more fully."

So when we struggle, how will we look at our pain? Will we see it as God falling down on the job of keeping our lives pain free? Or will we see it for what it is—a tool God is using to strengthen our faith?

🎲 | DISCUSSION STARTERS

When parents discipline their children, what is their goal?

Why do you think people tend to see their suffering as a sign that God doesn't care instead of as a sign that God loves them?

Do you know anyone who is stronger in his or her faith in God because of an experience of suffering?

Christ will make his home in your hearts as you trust in him. Your roots will grow down into God's love and keep you strong.
EPHESIANS 3:17

Since Christ suffered physical pain, you must arm yourselves with the same attitude he had, and be ready to suffer, too. For if you have suffered physically for Christ, you have finished with sin. You won't spend the rest of your lives chasing your own desires, but you will be anxious to do the will of God.
1 PETER 4:1-2

You know that when your faith is tested, your endurance has a chance to grow. So let it grow, for when your endurance is fully developed, you will be perfect and complete, needing nothing.
JAMES 1:3-4

Because of their unbelief they were not able to enter his rest.
HEBREWS 3:19

Despite all the miraculous signs Jesus had done, most of the people still did not believe in him.
JOHN 12:37

The father instantly cried out, "I do believe, but help me overcome my unbelief!"
MARK 9:24

The Ultimate Insult

What would you think if you offered to do something for a friend, promising to see it through, and your friend said something like, "No, thanks. I've decided I just can't trust you anymore." It would be an insult to your integrity, and your relationship with that person would be damaged. And if you'd never failed to live up to what you'd promised, the insult would be even greater.

This gives us a sense of how ugly and offensive our sin is to God. God is infinitely wise and infinitely dependable, and he has paid an infinite price. This price was to give himself to us so he could work in our lives for our good. So what an insult and offense it is when we say to God by our choices and behavior, "I don't really think you can be counted on to know what's best for me. I'm not sure you can really make a better future for me than I can create for myself."

When we refuse to trust in the promises of God and to find our joy in his provision for our future, it's a tremendous insult to God. Unbelief is not merely refusing to accept the truths of the Bible; it is refusing to trust in the promises of God, refusing to enjoy the provision of God. This unbelief is the root of all our sin. We disobey God because deep down we don't really believe his commandments are life to us. We disobey because we don't believe he knows more than we do about what will ultimately make us happy. What an insult.

 | ## DISCUSSION STARTERS

How do you feel when someone doesn't believe what you say?

Think through various sins people might be tempted by—greed, pride, cheating, lying, etc. What promise of God are people not believing when they sin in one of these areas?

What promise of God do you want to focus on believing?

He Bought Us Back

Have you ever spent time in an arcade, earning tickets or coupons out of the games and machines as you play them? When you're done, you usually take the tickets up to the counter and use them to purchase a prize to take home. This is redemption. You redeem that toy from the arcade with your tickets and bring it home with you.

A redeemer is someone who pays to buy something that needs to be delivered or rescued. Throughout the Bible, God is described as the Redeemer of Israel because he delivered the Israelites out of slavery in Egypt. In this same way, Jesus is our Redeemer. He paid the price so that we could be delivered from slavery to sin and brought home to live with him. What form of payment did Jesus use to buy us? His own blood. Peter writes, "You know that God paid a ransom to save you from the empty life you inherited from your ancestors. And the ransom he paid was not mere gold or silver. It was the precious blood of Christ, the sinless, spotless Lamb of God" (1 PETER 1:18-19).

When God created the human race in the Garden of Eden, we were his. But then Adam and Eve sinned and we became hostages or slaves to sin. So God sent someone to redeem us, someone who was willing to pay the ultimate price to buy us back. Now, because we've been redeemed, we can live with him in his home forever.

 | **DISCUSSION STARTERS**

How do you "redeem" a coupon at a grocery store?

How would someone who was once a slave feel and act toward the person who paid for his or her release?

Who did Christ redeem with the payment of his blood? Why did he make this payment?

I am the LORD. I will free you from your oppression and will rescue you from your slavery in Egypt. I will redeem you with a powerful arm and great acts of judgment.
EXODUS 6:6

"The Redeemer will come to Jerusalem to buy back those in Israel who have turned from their sins," says the LORD.
ISAIAH 59:20

Jesus gave his life for our sins, just as God our Father planned, in order to rescue us from this evil world in which we live.
GALATIANS 1:4

The Healer

Most doctors take a formal, public promise when they begin to practice medicine. This promise is called the Hippocratic oath. Doctors affirm that they will always use the practice of medicine to help and to heal, and not to hurt.

God has no need to take an oath to heal. Healing is not just an activity God may choose to do or not to do. Healing is who he is; it is his very nature, reflected in his name. One of the names he called himself is Yahweh-Rophi, which means "the Lord who heals you." God is our Healer. He heals our bodies from disease and heals our minds from twisted thinking. He heals our emotions from hurtful disappointments and heals our affections from harmful desires. He heals our relationships and restores our hope for the future.

Resting in this truth about who God is, we can be confident that even when pain comes into our lives, God has a purpose of greater healing. It's kind of like when we feel the sting of antiseptic on an open wound. It may hurt, but it's an agent of cleansing and healing.

Jesus is moved by the pain in our lives. We can come to him and ask him to touch us with his hand of healing, and because he is our Healer, we can be confident he will do it.

 | **DISCUSSION STARTERS**

What are some things a doctor does that sometimes hurt before they heal?

What are some similarities and differences between how a human doctor helps us heal and how God heals us?

What has God promised to you and the people you love in regard to healing?

I am the LORD who heals you.
EXODUS 15:26

Jesus traveled through all the towns and villages of that area, teaching in the synagogues and announcing the Good News about the Kingdom. And he healed every kind of disease and illness.
MATTHEW 9:35

A man with leprosy approached him and knelt before him. "Lord," the man said, "if you are willing, you can heal me and make me clean."

Jesus reached out and touched him. "I am willing," he said. "Be healed!" And instantly the leprosy disappeared.
MATTHEW 8:2-3

Why Not Run Up a Big Tab?

Let's say you're staying in a high-priced hotel and the room service menu catches your eye. You remember that someone else is paying your hotel bill, so you think, *Why not order some snacks? some dessert? a steak?* After all, you're not the one paying.

That's what worries some people about the idea of sin and grace. They see that Jesus has paid the debt for sin—past, present, and future—and that he offers salvation as a gift. They're afraid that some people will take advantage of God's grace and run up a big tab of sin, knowing that Jesus will pay for it. They see that God has left himself open to be taken advantage of. And he has. If we don't believe that, then we don't understand the generosity of grace.

But the truth is, no one who is truly connected to Christ in a saving way wants to continue a life of sin, seeing how much he or she can get away with. The grace of God saves us not just from the punishment and guilt of sin but from the presence and practice of sin, from its destruction in our lives—its false promises, its heartbreak, and its consequences. The person who is connected to Christ doesn't say, "Now I can sin as much as I want to!" but says instead, "If I don't have to sin, I don't want to!"

 | ## DISCUSSION STARTERS

How do people usually respond when something is being given away for free?

What does it mean to take a gift for granted?

When someone sins and says, "God will forgive me" even before he or she sins, what does it say about how the person views God? What does it say about how the person views sin?

Should we keep on sinning so that God can show us more and more of his wonderful grace? Of course not! Since we have died to sin, how can we continue to live in it?
ROMANS 6:1-2

Some ungodly people have wormed their way into your churches, saying that God's marvelous grace allows us to live immoral lives. The condemnation of such people was recorded long ago, for they have denied our only Master and Lord, Jesus Christ.
JUDE 1:4

Some people even slander us by claiming that we say, "The more we sin, the better it is!" Those who say such things deserve to be condemned.
ROMANS 3:8

How Do You Handle Criticism?

Humble yourselves under the mighty power of God, and at the right time he will lift you up in honor.

1 PETER 5:6

When Peter came to Antioch, I had to oppose him to his face, for what he did was very wrong.

GALATIANS 2:11

Whoever learns from correction is wise. . . . If you listen to constructive criticism, you will be at home among the wise.

PROVERB 15:5, 31

What do you do when someone criticizes or corrects you? Do you go with your first instinct to defend your actions or opinions? Do you criticize the other person in return? Do you point out the flaw in the other person's argument or the way it was presented? Or do you listen to it, evaluate it, and learn from it?

Nobody likes to be criticized or corrected. There's a sting to it. But if we quickly dismiss a correction or argue with it, we miss out on an opportunity to learn from what our critics have the courage to say.

As sinful humans, we have an amazing ability to convince ourselves of our own rightness and to justify what we know isn't right. But others can often see what we don't. We can be blind to our own sin, oblivious to our real motives, and unaware of how we might be hurting others. But other people can sometimes see the situation more clearly. And the truth is, sometimes we react most fiercely when we know deep down that they're right. Sometimes the truth hurts, and it's less painful to blame the person who points it out than face the reality of our own sin and failure.

Criticism delivered in a loving manner is a gift to us. But even criticism delivered with the wrong motives in the worst of ways can be a gift too, depending on how we respond to it. So when we're criticized, we should consider it carefully, looking for the truth that needs to be faced and rejecting the untruth that needs to be dismissed. We learn from it, and then we let it go.

 ## | DISCUSSION STARTERS

What does it feel like when someone criticizes you?

How can a person receive and respond to criticism with humility?

How can someone's criticism be a gift from God?

A Message from an Angel

If the first thing someone said to you was, "Don't be afraid!" then it would be logical to assume that seeing that person was scary or startling. Interestingly, whenever the angel Gabriel and other angels in the Bible appeared to people to give them a message, the first thing the angel usually said was, "Don't be afraid!" Evidently angels are startling and scary when you hear them speak or see them appear, unlike the cute cherubs people like to imagine.

Even though the angel Gabriel must have been startling to see, his message was always one announcing something very good to come, something that would help people know they didn't have to fear him or the future. He had very good news. And what was that news?

In the Old Testament book of Daniel, God sent the angel Gabriel to explain to Daniel about the coming of the Anointed One—Jesus. Then in Luke 1, Gabriel came to Zechariah, an elderly priest in the Temple, telling him that his wife would bear a son, John, who would "prepare the people for the coming of the Lord" (1:17). Gabriel also came to Mary, telling her that she would have a son, Jesus, who would "be very great" and would "be called the Son of the Most High" (1:32).

Gabriel's message is always the same. It's Jesus. *Don't be afraid; Jesus is coming.* Whatever frightens us in this life, we can be comforted to know that Jesus is real and that he's coming for us. We don't have to be afraid as we face the future.

> As I was praying, Gabriel, whom I had seen in the earlier vision, came swiftly to me at the time of the evening sacrifice. He explained to me, "Daniel, I have come here to give you insight and understanding."
>
> **DANIEL 9:21-22**

> Gabriel appeared to her. . . . "Don't be afraid, Mary," the angel told her, "for you have found favor with God! You will conceive and give birth to a son, and you will name him Jesus."
>
> **LUKE 1:28, 30-31**

 | DISCUSSION STARTERS

How have you seen angels depicted in movies or artwork?

Why would the promise of Jesus' coming have reassured Daniel, Zechariah, and Mary?

How does it reassure you to know that Jesus is coming?

Jesus replied, "Now the time has come for the Son of Man to enter into his glory. I tell you the truth, unless a kernel of wheat is planted in the soil and dies, it remains alone. But its death will produce many new kernels—a plentiful harvest of new lives."

JOHN 12:23-24

If you try to hang on to your life, you will lose it. But if you give up your life for my sake, you will save it.

MATTHEW 16:25

Since we have been united with him in his death, we will also be raised to life as he was.

ROMANS 6:5

First You Have to Die

When a dormant (the plant version of asleep) seed is planted into the ground for forty days at forty degrees and takes in water, it miraculously begins to expand. The seed coat is broken, and out comes the little roots and the little shoots. Life sprouts! But in order for there to be a plant, the seed itself has to die.

This is the example from nature Jesus used to help prepare his disciples for his coming death on the cross. The kernel of wheat (or seed) is Jesus himself. He is the Son of Man who will be glorified. He is the grain of wheat who must fall to the ground and die in order to bring about a "plentiful harvest."

When Jesus spoke about how it was necessary to die in order to harvest new life, he meant it to be applied in our lives too. If we want to bear fruit or have a lasting impact on our world, first we're going to need to die. When Jesus tells us we need to die, he's talking about dying to self, or to selfishness. It means dying to the attitude that says, *I am going to live for myself; the purpose of my life is to make myself happy and to experience all that life can give me.*

It's hard to die. We fear we'll lose our individuality, our personalities, and our freedoms. But when our lives revolve around ourselves, we aren't really living at all. And when our self-centeredness begins to die, that's when we really begin to live.

 | ## DISCUSSION STARTERS

What does it mean that a seed has to "die" in order to grow a plant?

How did Jesus' death produce a harvest of new lives?

What fruit can be harvested in our lives when we die to ourselves?

Too Young for God to Use?

"**M**ust be four feet tall to ride," says the sign at the entrance to the best roller coaster at the amusement park. When we're young, it can sometimes seem like we'll never be old enough to get to do the cool stuff. But we are never too young to use whatever gifts, talents, and opportunities God has given us to tell other people who he is and what he's doing in our lives. We're never too young to reach out and love others or speak up about the love of God. We might think we don't have the experience we need or the ability to do it like someone else. Or we might be afraid of being criticized or judged harshly. But when the Holy Spirit calls us to do something for him and confirms it through godly people in our lives, we can be confident that he will give us what we need in order to do what he has called us to do. Not only that, but he'll also be right with us, giving us the courage we need, no matter what people say or think.

God has made you for a purpose. His purpose. And you don't have to wait until you are educated enough or experienced enough to start serving him. No one else sees the world the way you do, and no one else has the unique combination of gifts you have. God has designed you uniquely to be an extension of his work in the world. What are you waiting for?

JULY

18

🧂🧂 | DISCUSSION STARTERS

What are some ways you can extend God's love to people at your age?

How can a young person prepare himself or herself for ministry—both now and in the future?

Why do you think young people are sometimes slow to step out to serve God?

"O Sovereign LORD," I said, "I can't speak for you! I'm too young!"

The LORD replied, "Don't say, 'I'm too young,' for you must go wherever I send you and say whatever I tell you."
JEREMIAH 1:6-7

Don't let anyone think less of you because you are young. Be an example to all believers in what you say, in the way you live, in your love, your faith, and your purity.
1 TIMOTHY 4:12

O LORD, our Lord, your majestic name fills the earth! Your glory is higher than the heavens. You have taught children and infants to tell of your strength, silencing your enemies and all who oppose you.
PSALM 8:1-2

A Living Picture of Unfaithfulness

When the LORD first began speaking to Israel through Hosea, he said to him, "Go and marry a prostitute, so that some of her children will be conceived in prostitution. This will illustrate how Israel has acted like a prostitute by turning against the LORD and worshiping other gods."

HOSEA 1:2

Then the LORD said to me, "Go and love your wife again, even though she commits adultery with another lover. This will illustrate that the LORD still loves Israel, even though the people have turned to other gods and love to worship them." So I bought her back.

HOSEA 3:1-2

Imagine that God picked out the person you are to marry. The reason he wants you to marry this person is because he knows he or she will leave you for not just one other person but for many—that this person will sell his or her body to other people and have children with them, even while being married to you.

This is the story of Hosea and his wife, Gomer, in the Old Testament. When we read it, we feel offended that God would ask such a thing of Hosea. But God wanted Hosea to understand what it is like to be married to an unfaithful wife before Hosea spoke God's Word to Israel. Through this real-life illustration, Hosea would not only *understand* the betrayal, he would *feel* it. And we can too, if we are willing to see ourselves in this story and feel God's broken heart.

We see ourselves in Gomer's unfaithfulness, and we see the faithfulness of God in the love of her husband, Hosea. Or at least we should. But we don't really want to see ourselves this way, do we? It seems too extreme. However, God knows we have sold ourselves to many other lovers in this world, and he is still wooing us to himself. He wants to envelop us in his faithful, redeeming love, saying, "I will heal you of your faithlessness; my love will know no bounds, for my anger will be gone forever" (HOSEA 14:4).

 | ## DISCUSSION STARTERS

What does it mean to be faithful to someone?

In what ways are we unfaithful to God?

When we read about how Hosea bought his own wife back, how is this a picture of what God has done for us?

The Search for God's Will

Some people think figuring out God's will for their lives is like a spiritual game of hide-and-seek. They think God has something specific he wants them to do that is hidden from view and that they have to try to find it. It's like a cat and mouse game of guidance, and they have to look for hidden clues to figure out what God wants.

But God's will isn't like that. Certainly God knows the next step in our lives, but there is no place in Scripture that says we're supposed to try to figure that out and follow it. God's will for our lives has been made clear in the Bible. And while it takes some effort on our part to understand and absorb what God wants, his will is not hidden.

The Bible doesn't tell us which person to marry, which car to drive, where to go to college, or what job to take. But as we saturate our minds in the revealed will of God spelled out for us in the Bible, we begin to think more like God and we're better able to discern what God wants for us. So rather than asking God to give us some sort of special sign that will show us what to do, we are to ask God to renew our minds. Our goal is to build our lives on the foundation of what God has clearly told us to do in the Bible. Good students of Scripture become wise decision makers over a lifetime of following God's clear instructions. Our job is not to hunt for the secret will of God, but to do what God has clearly told us to do.

God's will is for you to be holy, so stay away from all sexual sin.
1 THESSALONIANS 4:3

Be thankful in all circumstances, for this is God's will for you who belong to Christ Jesus.
1 THESSALONIANS 5:18

Let God transform you into a new person by changing the way you think. Then you will learn to know God's will for you.
ROMANS 12:2

| DISCUSSION STARTERS

What are some things you know are God's will for your life, based on the clear instructions in the Bible?

Does the success or failure, difficulty or ease of something indicate if it is in God's will?

In what area are you seeking to know the will of God?

JULY

21

Anyone who listens to my teaching and follows it is wise, like a person who builds a house on solid rock. Though the rain comes in torrents and the floodwaters rise and the winds beat against that house, it won't collapse, because it is built on bedrock. But anyone who hears my teaching and doesn't obey it is foolish, like a person who builds a house on sand. When the rains and floods come and the winds beat against that house, it will collapse with a mighty crash.
MATTHEW 7:24-27

If you look carefully into the perfect law that sets you free, and if you do what it says and don't forget what you heard, then God will bless you for doing it.
JAMES 1:25

Are You Listening?

Is the television turned on at your house sometimes when no one is watching? You can hear it, but you're not really listening to it. It is one thing to hear someone talking. It is another thing to listen. And it is still another thing to understand and accept what is being said.

When Jesus sat in the Temple teaching or on the hillside speaking, the people were amazed because, as Matthew recorded, "he taught with real authority—quite unlike their teachers of religious law" (MATTHEW 7:29).

But we can be amazed at what someone says and still reject it or ignore it. We can see that someone speaks with authority and still refuse to submit to it. So it is a worthwhile question to ask ourselves, *Am I listening to what God is saying to me through his commandments in the Bible? Am I taking seriously what Jesus taught with his words and with his life and in his death and resurrection?*

 **DISCUSSION STARTERS**

What actions do you take when you want to listen to someone?

What is the evidence that a person is truly listening to God?

Is there something you've heard God say that you find difficult to accept or obey?

The Good Side of Persecution

Has anyone ever made fun of you because you are a Christian? Have you ever been excluded from an event, mocked for your beliefs, ridiculed for your obedience to Jesus? If so, then you've had a small taste of persecution. And Jesus said that you should be congratulated for it. "God blesses you when people mock you and persecute you and lie about you and say all sorts of evil things against you because you are my followers," Jesus said. "Be happy about it! Be very glad!" (MATTHEW 5:11-12).

Why should you be happy if you are persecuted because of your connection to Jesus? For one thing, it means that your faith is so real and relevant, people can see it in you and it makes them uncomfortable! Jesus said that there is such a tension between living for him and following the ways of the world that this tension is bound to show up in the form of persecution. When you are persecuted, you can enjoy a new kind of connection with Jesus and with all of those who have been banished, beheaded, belittled, or burned at the stake because of their faith.

We know that people in other parts of the world experience far greater persecution than we do. But we can actually be glad rather than resentful or offended when we suffer for the cause of Christ. Sooner or later all Christians will be mistreated for the things they believe or the life they live. It's not something to dread—but something to celebrate.

 | **DISCUSSION STARTERS**

How was Christ treated by people? How about his disciples?

What's the difference between being mistreated and being mistreated because of Christ?

What are your fears regarding persecution?

You will be arrested, persecuted, and killed. You will be hated all over the world because you are my followers.
MATTHEW 24:9

Do you remember what I told you? "A slave is not greater than the master." Since they persecuted me, naturally they will persecute you.
JOHN 15:20

Everyone who wants to live a godly life in Christ Jesus will suffer persecution.
2 TIMOTHY 3:12

Temptation comes from our own desires, which entice us and drag us away.

JAMES 1:14

Throw off your old sinful nature and your former way of life, which is corrupted by lust and deception.

EPHESIANS 4:22

Run from anything that stimulates youthful lusts. Instead, pursue righteous living, faithfulness, love, and peace. Enjoy the companionship of those who call on the Lord with pure hearts.

2 TIMOTHY 2:22

Don't Take the Bait

When a fisherman puts a worm on a hook, he is setting a trap for an unsuspecting fish. The fish comes along and sees the worm, which looks good for food, and doesn't realize until it's too late that it has been hooked.

When the book of James says that temptation comes when our own desires "entice" us, it's not that different from a fish that is enticed and then caught by the bait on a hook. We are tempted when the trap of sin is baited with things that appeal to our desires. Just as fish anticipate the pleasure of grabbing the bait and instead experience the pain of the hook, we anticipate pleasure when we go for what tempts us, only to eventually experience the pain it causes. For example, when we eat too much of what isn't good for us, it tastes delicious in our mouths for a few minutes—and then we experience the pain of bad health or weight gain. Or when we give in to temptation in a relationship, we experience temporary pleasure, which is followed by guilt, shame, and regret over what we've done.

How can we keep from taking the bait of temptation? A fish that has already eaten takes no bait. If we fill up our hearts and thoughts with God's Word and God's presence, and if we develop our sense of finding pleasure in him, we're not nearly as likely to take the bait of sin.

 | **DISCUSSION STARTERS**

What happens when a fish bites the bait on the hook?

What strategies for resisting temptation do you find in 2 Timothy 2:22?

Think through various sins—greed, dishonesty, anger, gluttony. What is the bait, and what do we really get when we bite?

What Does
Goodness Look Like?

"That's good!" we say, talking about our favorite dinner or a new movie or a law that is passed or an experience we have. We see ourselves as judges who determine what is good and what is not. We label things as good or bad based on a standard inside ourselves, one that is often shaped more by personal preferences or the culture around us than anything solid and definitive.

But God has shown us exactly what goodness is. God himself is the standard and the definition of goodness. Moses asked to see God, but God gave him only a glimpse. And what was the essence of what Moses saw? God's goodness. We can't see God without seeing his goodness. And if we don't see his goodness, we haven't seen God.

Sometimes our circumstances seem like anything but evidence of God's goodness. But that's because we tend to define God by what *we* have deemed good. We have to turn that around. We have to learn to define goodness by who God is and what he does. God is completely, abundantly, perfectly, and forever good. God himself is the standard by which we should compare anything we want to label as good.

| DISCUSSION STARTERS

What are some things God says are good? What are some things he says are bad?

What sometimes causes us to question God's goodness?

What difference does it make if God himself becomes our standard for what is good?

Moses responded, "Then show me your glorious presence."

The LORD replied, "I will make all my goodness pass before you, and I will call out my name, Yahweh, before you."

EXODUS 33:18-19

Surely your goodness and unfailing love will pursue me all the days of my life.

PSALM 23:6

How great is the goodness you have stored up for those who fear you.

You lavish it on those who come to you for protection, blessing them before the watching world.

PSALM 31:19

25

The LORD had said to Abram, "Leave your native country, your relatives, and your father's family, and go to the land that I will show you."
GENESIS 12:1

It was by faith that Abraham obeyed when God called him to leave home and go to another land that God would give him as his inheritance. He went without knowing where he was going.
HEBREWS 11:8

That is why I am suffering here in prison. But I am not ashamed of it, for I know the one in whom I trust, and I am sure that he is able to guard what I have entrusted to him until the day of his return.
2 TIMOTHY 1:12

Traveling without a Map

Before you go on a trip, does someone in your family study a map or perhaps print out a map from the computer that tells you every turn to take until you arrive at your destination? Can you imagine heading out on a trip with no idea where you're going or how to get there?

When God called him, Abraham wasn't a nice, godly Jewish boy. He came from a family of idol worshipers who didn't know God. Yet when Abraham heard God telling him to leave his family and move to another country that God would show him later, Abraham just did it. He didn't know where God was leading him, but he went because God told him to. That's faith.

Living by faith is being willing to go when God clearly tells you to go, even when you don't know where or what or when or how before you take your first step in obeying God. To follow Christ wherever he leads means we have to give up control, predictability, ease, and familiarity. Living by faith rarely feels comfortable. It means that we take a step forward in obedience, not because of our confidence in where we're going, but because of our deep confidence in who is calling and leading us.

 | DISCUSSION STARTERS

What if someone told you to move across the country tomorrow? What reasons would you have for not going?

What excuses could Abraham have come up with not to go?

What do we know about God that should make us willing to go when he says to go?

Sweet Meditation

Many of us wake up to the blare of the radio, then we listen to music in the car or on the bus, have the TV on in the background when we're at home, and wear headphones as we exercise or do homework. For most of us, there is a steady stream of noise that takes up space in our heads and shapes our thoughts. We rarely make mental space for quiet reflection. Instead, when things get quiet, we look for something to fill the silence. But do you ever feel like your soul needs a vacation from the noise to get filled up with God? Does your mind ever need a break to think great thoughts about God?

David said, "May my meditation be sweet to Him" (Psalm 104:34, NKJV). Spending time in purposeful contemplation about God wasn't an obligation or a duty for him. It was pleasant. He knew that he would enjoy the time he spent contemplating God, thinking through what God is like, what he has done, and what it means to him to be in a relationship with him. Meditation is when we call to mind, think over, dwell on, and apply what we know about the works, ways, purposes, and promises of God. In some ways it is like talking to ourselves. We talk to ourselves about God, sometimes arguing with our incorrect assumptions or reasoning through our understanding of God's Word. Meditation helps us work into our thought patterns and plans the truths we've heard in a sermon or read in Scripture or discussed in our family devotions, before these truths slip away. It's the purposeful process we use to enjoy God and sense his nearness to us.

> I recall all you have done, O Lord; I remember your wonderful deeds of long ago. They are constantly in my thoughts. I cannot stop thinking about your mighty works.
>
> *PSALM 77:11-12*

> Study this Book of Instruction continually. Meditate on it day and night so you will be sure to obey everything written in it. Only then will you prosper and succeed in all you do.
>
> *JOSHUA 1:8*

🧂🧂 | DISCUSSION STARTERS

Think through your day. What fills up your ears and your thoughts?

Is there a particular time you could use to meditate on a word, phrase, or passage of the Bible, or to simply think about God?

How can meditation help us sense the nearness of God?

How do you know what your life will be like tomorrow? Your life is like the morning fog—it's here a little while, then it's gone. What you ought to say is, "If the Lord wants us to, we will live and do this or that."

JAMES 4:14-15

Then Esther sent this reply to Mordecai: "Go and gather together all the Jews of Susa and fast for me. Do not eat or drink for three days, night or day. My maids and I will do the same. And then, though it is against the law, I will go in to see the king. If I must die, I must die."

ESTHER 4:15-16

My life is worth nothing to me unless I use it for finishing the work assigned me by the Lord Jesus—the work of telling others the Good News about the wonderful grace of God.

ACTS 20:24

Taking a Risk

When you take a risk, you can lose money, lose face, or even lose your life. Is there anything wrong with taking a risk? It depends on *why* you're taking the risk. Would it be worth the risk if your goal was to make a lot of money, to impress people, or just to have fun? Would it be worth the risk to go to a country where you might be put in jail for sharing the gospel?

There are numerous examples in Scripture of believers who took risks for the cause of God and his people. Esther risked being killed when she went before the king to save her people. Daniel risked being thrown in the lions' den when he bowed to pray. Paul kept on preaching, despite the constant risk of beatings and imprisonment.

There is no promise that every effort for the cause of God will succeed, at least not in the short run. Taking a risk for God requires faith—not that God will keep you physically, personally, or financially safe, but that God is sovereign and will do what is right. We can put our confidence in his ultimate protection.

 | **DISCUSSION STARTERS**

Are there any scary things you like to do just for the fun of it? What are some of those things?

What possible risks in living out your commitment to Jesus make you uncomfortable?

What gives you the confidence to take risks for God? What can hold you back from taking those risks?

Joy Ahead

Most of us are willing to do unpleasant things if it means we'll get something we want as a result. We might not like to train for a sport, but we want to be on the team. And though we might not always enjoy going to work, we enjoy getting a paycheck! The Bible says that Jesus endured the Cross—a very unpleasant thing—for the joy awaiting him. What joy was on the other side of the Cross that made it worth the suffering for Jesus?

As Jesus looked ahead, he knew that his endurance of the Cross would mean that the debt for our sin would be paid. It brought him joy that he was completing the work he was sent to do, which would mean we wouldn't have to be separated from him because of our sin. Jesus also anticipated the joy of resurrection. He knew that the shame of the Cross would end and that the result would be the conquering of death forever!

Another joy Jesus looked forward to was the joy of reunion. Jesus had lived in perfect fellowship with the Father from before the foundation of the world, and as he headed toward the Cross, he began to anticipate the joy of being with his Father once again. Jesus also knew that the joy of rest was ahead of him. In heaven, he would sit down at the right hand of God, because his most important work was complete. (But he isn't just resting. He is ruling!)

Jesus is not content to keep this joy to himself! His greatest joy is to share his joy with us! Because we are redeemed, we anticipate our resurrection, which will unite us with him and with the Father. We will join him in a place of rest, where we will rule and reign with him forever. This joy ahead makes the hard things here worth enduring!

JULY

28

Because of the joy awaiting him, he endured the cross, disregarding its shame. Now he is seated in the place of honor beside God's throne.

HEBREWS 12:2

Father, bring me into the glory we shared before the world began.

JOHN 17:5

| DISCUSSION STARTERS

What unpleasant tasks are you willing to do for something pleasant?

Jesus was willing to endure shame. Whose shame did he endure, and what was that shame?

How can it help us endure hard things here and now if we anticipate the joy that's ahead for us in heaven?

JULY

29

Should not the Judge of all the earth do what is right?
GENESIS 18:25

You have all wisdom and do great and mighty miracles. You see the conduct of all people, and you give them what they deserve.
JEREMIAH 32:19

The Lord is still there in the city, and he does no wrong.

Day by day he hands down justice, and he does not fail.
ZEPHANIAH 3:5

You Are Right!

There are three little words we love to hear people say to us: "You were right!" Somehow it satisfies that desire in us to be the smartest person in the room—the one who saw things clearly before anybody else did.

The opposite of the joy that comes from saying, "I was right!" is the agony of acknowledging, "I was wrong." We all have to admit it at some point. But God never does. God is right all the time. He always does what is right.

The Bible uses the same word for righteousness (or rightness) as it does for justice. Justice is the righteous way God rules over every part of the universe. While human judges can't help but be swayed by prejudices and limitations in their knowledge, God is a righteous judge. He can't be anything other than perfectly just.

When the justice of God works its way into our understanding of the circumstances in our lives, we can stand back and say, "God, you were right. Everything you do is right." But this is not what comes naturally to us. Because we don't know God as well as we should, we're more likely to point our fingers at God, accusing him of unfairness, questioning his timing, and doubting his love. But the more we know him, the more confidence we have in his justice. We can begin to say to him about everything he does, "You are right!"

 | **DISCUSSION STARTERS**

Why do you think it feels so good to be right?

When we think God has not done the right thing, what is our judgment based on?

How can you be sure God is always right?

Who's Accusing You?

We all make mistakes that we have to ask forgiveness for. Isn't it a relief when someone gives you the gift of forgiveness? But have you ever had someone tell you that you are forgiven and then bring up your offense again just to rub it in or make sure you haven't forgotten what you did?

That's something God never does. The Bible says that when God forgives us, he will never again remember our sins. It's not that our all-knowing Father forgets, but rather that he chooses not to bring up our sin to hold it against us. So when we hear a voice reminding us of past failures that we've already confessed to God and received forgiveness for, we can be confident that it is not God's voice we're hearing, but Satan's. It is Satan, who is called "the Accuser," who reminds us of our past sins to make us feel guilty.

But why should you listen to his bringing up your past if God does not do so? You have to choose who you are going to listen to. Will you listen to your enemy, the Accuser, who wants to ruin you and use you and deceive you by whispering in your ear reminders of your failures? Or will you listen to God, who reminds you of his abundant forgiveness?

Through this man Jesus there is forgiveness for your sins. Everyone who believes in him is declared right with God.
ACTS 13:38-39

He has reconciled you to himself through the death of Christ in his physical body. As a result, he has brought you into his own presence, and you are holy and blameless as you stand before him without a single fault.
COLOSSIANS 1:22

The Accuser, Satan, . . . replied to the LORD, . . . "A man will give up everything he has to save his life. But reach out and take away his health, and he will surely curse you to your face!"
JOB 2:1, 4-5

 | **DISCUSSION STARTERS**

What is it like to feel guilty?

What's the difference between the feeling of guilt and the feeling of conviction?

Why would Satan want to accuse you? What is he trying to do?

The Plumb Line

Have you ever hung wallpaper or watched someone who has? One of the most important things to do when hanging wallpaper is to use a plumb line. You put a weight on the end of a piece of string and hang it from the ceiling to use as a guide for marking straight lines. Without the help of a plumb line, the edges of the wallpaper won't match up, and everything will be crooked.

God uses a plumb line too—a clear standard that shows us how we should live. He knows that we have the tendency to compare ourselves to other people and that using other people as our standard causes us to end up "crooked." His plumb line is his own perfect holiness.

We don't have to wonder what God expects of us. He has given us a plumb line that shows us when we're wandering off course. We see it in the Ten Commandments and even more clearly in the only one who ever lived a life lined up with the plumb line—Jesus Christ. And because God knows we will never live up to his standard of holiness, he has given us a gift—the gift of the perfect righteousness of Jesus. So when God looks at our lives, instead of seeing our crookedness, he sees Jesus' holiness.

I saw the Lord standing beside a wall that had been built using a plumb line. He was using a plumb line to see if it was still straight. . . . And the Lord replied, "I will test my people with this plumb line. I will no longer ignore all their sins."
AMOS 7:7-8

Look! I am placing a foundation stone in Jerusalem, a firm and tested stone. It is a precious cornerstone that is safe to build on. Whoever believes need never be shaken. I will test you with the measuring line of justice and the plumb line of righteousness.
ISAIAH 28:16-17

Everyone has sinned; we all fall short of God's glorious standard.
ROMANS 3:23

 | **DISCUSSION STARTERS**

When a teacher or a boss gives you an assignment, how does it feel when there are no clear guidelines about what he or she expects?

What Scripture verses can you think of that provide a plumb line for us—something to keep us headed in the right direction?

How do we keep from feeling defeated by our inability to live up to the perfection of the plumb line?

May I Serve You?

When you see a Help Wanted sign in the window of a business, you know that the business is looking for someone to go to work for them. But Jesus doesn't hang a Help Wanted sign in the window of the world. Instead, he holds up a big sign that says Help Available!

Jesus didn't come to earth to recruit workers. He came to do a great work for us, which he accomplished by living a perfect life and dying in our place. He didn't come because he needs us but because we need him.

We tend to rush up to God so certain that he will be delighted with all we've done and intend to do for him. And certainly he loves a heart that desires to please him. But first, we have to see that his greatest aim is not to be served by us but to serve us. He wants us to place our faith not in what we can do for him but in what he has done for us. And then he wants us, out of love for him and a desire to be like him, to serve people around us.

The Christian life is not about doing for God. It is about receiving from God. God serves us by giving us acceptance, forgiveness, freedom, and joy—so much so that these qualities spill out of us into the lives of other people as we serve them the way Christ has served us.

 | ## DISCUSSION STARTERS

What does it mean to serve somebody?

Would the other people in your family say that you are most often a person who looks for ways to serve, or do you look to be served?

What are some ways you see family members and friends serving others?

Who is more important, the one who sits at the table or the one who serves? The one who sits at the table, of course. But not here! For I am among you as one who serves.

LUKE 22:27

Even the Son of Man came not to be served but to serve others and to give his life as a ransom for many.

MARK 10:45

Human hands can't serve his needs—for he has no needs. He himself gives life and breath to everything, and he satisfies every need.

ACTS 17:25

Kind and Severe

Did you ever play the game Red Rover? "Red Rover, Red Rover, send Mary right over!" one side says in unison. And Mary comes running.

When the Bible tells us that God is both kind and severe, we can think of it a bit like the two sides of the Red Rover game. Both sides are real. But God calls us for a different reason: kindness. The kindness of God calls out to each one of us, saying, "Come over!" And who wouldn't want to run away from the severity of God—a place of certain judgment—into the arms of abundant forgiveness, generosity, freedom, and joy?

God wants us to see how kind he is. But he also wants us to see how severely he punishes sin. Since he is holy, he can't just ignore the seriousness of sin. Behind every display of divine goodness stands the severity of judgment if that goodness is scorned. That's why he gives us time. He's patient. He's calling out to us to run toward his kindness. And even though he will be severe with those who don't run to him, everyone who does run to him never has to worry about being the target of his severity.

 | ## DISCUSSION STARTERS

How do you see both God's kindness and severity in these verses?

Why do you suppose we only like to think about God's kindness?

Why is it good for people—even believers—to think about God's severity?

I am slow to anger and filled with unfailing love and faithfulness. I lavish unfailing love to a thousand generations. I forgive iniquity, rebellion, and sin. But I do not excuse the guilty. I lay the sins of the parents upon their children and grandchildren; the entire family is affected—even children in the third and fourth generations.
EXODUS 34:6-7

Don't you see how wonderfully kind, tolerant, and patient God is with you? . . . Can't you see that his kindness is intended to turn you from your sin? But because you are stubborn and refuse to turn from your sin, you are storing up terrible punishment for yourself.
ROMANS 2:4-5

God is both kind and severe. He is severe toward those who disobeyed, but kind to you if you continue to trust in his kindness.
ROMANS 11:22

Honoring God with Your Body

Isn't it amazing how billions of people on this earth are made up of all the same body parts, and yet we all look so different? Some people's bodies are strong and firm; some are weak and feeble. Some are large; some are small. Some are young and some are old. And amazingly, no matter the size or shape or age of our bodies, we can all use our bodies to honor God.

How do we honor God with our bodies? Does it mean we try to look good or that we do what we can do to stay healthy?

All of us are stewards, or managers, of the bodies God has given us. We're to use every resource at our disposal—including our bodies—to bring honor to God. Giving your body to God for his use means that you give him your eyes, your tongue, your hands, and your feet rather than giving your eyes, your tongue, your hands, and your feet to sin. Everything you do with your body shows that Christ is more precious to you than anything else. Don't think that you can give your heart to God and not give every part of your body to him too. Either you belong to God—heart, soul, and body—or you don't really belong to him at all.

🧂🧂 | DISCUSSION STARTERS

Think through the various parts of your body. What can you do with those parts of your body to honor God? What actions would dishonor him?

Do you think a focus on wise eating habits and good health is honoring to God? At what point does it become dishonoring to him?

Why do you think God wants our bodies, too, and not just our hearts?

Do not let any part of your body become an instrument of evil to serve sin. Instead, give yourselves completely to God, for you were dead, but now you have new life. So use your whole body as an instrument to do what is right for the glory of God.
ROMANS 6:13

Give your bodies to God because of all he has done for you. Let them be a living and holy sacrifice—the kind he will find acceptable.
ROMANS 12:1

Don't you realize that your body is the temple of the Holy Spirit, who lives in you and was given to you by God? You do not belong to yourself, for God bought you with a high price. So you must honor God with your body.
1 CORINTHIANS 6:19-20

Investment Advice

Investment advice. Like most other kinds of advice, there are usually lots of people willing to offer it. Investment counselors point out the potential risks and rewards of various stocks, bonds, accounts, and businesses.

Jesus offered investment advice too. He said that we have a choice. We can live with a view toward accumulating things of value here on earth, which we will leave behind when we die. Or we can live with a view toward accumulating valuable things in heaven, which we will enjoy forever. He instructed us to "store your treasures in heaven."

Jesus offers us sound investment advice—showing us how we can invest our lives in the cause of heaven. We can give out the gospel, send missionaries to hard places in the world, feed the hungry in the name of Jesus, take care of widows and orphans as the Bible instructs, translate the Bible into new languages, and train pastors to teach the Word. Jesus wants us to see that the only investments that will pay eternal dividends of joy are what we invest in the cause of Christ right now.

Sometimes we think of the money we give to God's cause—or any other resource, such as time and energy—as a sacrifice. But Jesus helps us to see that it is the only investment that will follow us beyond the grave. Every other investment is something we'll eventually let go of.

Don't store up treasures here on earth, where moths eat them and rust destroys them, and where thieves break in and steal. Store your treasures in heaven, where moths and rust cannot destroy, and thieves do not break in and steal. Wherever your treasure is, there the desires of your heart will also be.
MATTHEW 6:19-21

God said to him, "You fool! You will die this very night. Then who will get everything you worked for?"

Yes, a person is a fool to store up earthly wealth but not have a rich relationship with God.
LUKE 12:20-22

 | **DISCUSSION STARTERS**

What is the difference between spending money and investing money?

When we invest our treasure in heaven, how does that reveal our faith?

What are some ways your family is storing up treasure in heaven?

Provide and Protect

Most of us understand what the word *husband* means—it's a man who is married to a woman. But do you know what *to husband* means as an action—in the verb form of the word? It's kind of a farm word. To husband is to nurture (as in crops or animals), preserve, protect, and care for. So for a husband (noun) to husband (verb) his wife means that he will nurture her and protect her and care for her.

This is exactly what the Bible tells us about the role of a husband in marriage. As the head of the family, the husband has the responsibility of protecting and providing for his family. God calls the husband to provide for his family physically (giving food and shelter), emotionally (connecting with them in meaningful ways), and spiritually (offering godly guidance and encouragement). God also calls the husband to protect his family physically (by keeping them safe), emotionally (by setting wise relational boundaries), and spiritually (through prayer and guarding against harmful influences).

Husbanding is not about a right to command or control. It is a man's responsibility to love like Christ—to lay down his life for his family.

 | **DISCUSSION STARTERS**

What are some of the qualities that make a great husband?

Who are some husbands you have observed who do an excellent job providing for and protecting their families—physically, emotionally, and spiritually?

How is the biblical understanding of a husband's role different from how our culture thinks a husband and a wife should interact?

AUGUST

5

Husbands, love your wives and never treat them harshly.
COLOSSIANS 3:19

Husbands ought to love their wives as they love their own bodies. For a man who loves his wife actually shows love for himself. No one hates his own body but feeds and cares for it, just as Christ cares for the church.
EPHESIANS 5:28-29

You husbands must give honor to your wives. Treat your wife with understanding as you live together. She may be weaker than you are, but she is your equal partner in God's gift of new life. Treat her as you should so your prayers will not be hindered.
1 PETER 3:7

Written on Stone

A covenant is an agreement or mutual promise made between two parties. It's through covenants that God chose to commit himself to his people with solemn promises. God made five promises for his side of the covenant with Abram, which he later reaffirmed to Moses:

1. Israel would be God's special possession.
2. Israel would be a kingdom of priests to God.
3. Israel would be a holy nation.
4. God would fight for Israel and overcome all its enemies.
5. God would treat Israel with grace and mercy and forgive the people's sins.

All these divine promises depended on certain conditions being fulfilled by the people, as Exodus 19:5 says: "If you will obey me and keep my covenant, you will" experience all these divine blessings. God wrote his conditions in stone on Mount Sinai in the Ten Commandments. In Exodus 24:3 we read that the people accepted the covenant: "We will do everything the LORD has commanded."

God doesn't have to obligate or commit himself to anyone. But he does. He obligates himself to his people in relationship, purpose, privilege, victory, and forgiveness. No other god does that. Other gods only make demands. God makes promises. And he makes good on them.

I am confirming my covenant with you. Never again will floodwaters kill all living creatures; never again will a flood destroy the earth.
GENESIS 9:11

Abram fell face down on the ground. Then God said to him, "This is my covenant with you: I will make you the father of a multitude of nations!"
GENESIS 17:3-4

The LORD said, "I have made a covenant with David, my chosen servant. I have sworn this oath to him: 'I will establish your descendants as kings forever; they will sit on your throne from now until eternity.'"
PSALM 89:3-4

 | ## DISCUSSION STARTERS

What did God promise to Noah, Abram, and David in the verses above?

Why do you think God made this covenant expecting obedience when he knew that people couldn't keep the Commandments?

Has God fulfilled the promises he made in the verses above? How do you know?

Written on Hearts

If you bought a new car and it just wouldn't start, you might read through the manual and go through all the steps to get the car going. But if there was no gas in the tank, the car still wouldn't start!

The people of Israel had God's instruction manual—the Ten Commandments. But there was no gas in their tank to obey. They knew what to do, but they didn't have the power or the want-to inside to obey. The Ten Commandments were just a list of external rules.

That's why God promised he would make a new covenant with his people someday. It would be better than the old one that he'd made at Mount Sinai, because in the new covenant, God would put his Spirit inside his people. Rather than being written on tablets of stone like they were at Mount Sinai, the new covenant would be written by God on the hearts of his people. In this way, he gave us a love for his will and his ways. God deals with the power of sin by writing his law on our hearts so that we hate sin from the inside. His desire is for us to love his will and walk in his ways because we want to, not just because it's his law.

 | ## DISCUSSION STARTERS

Look around the room. What needs power to make it operate?

How and when did God give believers power to obey?

In what ways is it better to live under the new covenant instead of the old one?

> "I will make a new covenant with the people of Israel and Judah. This covenant will not be like the one I made with their ancestors when I took them by the hand and brought them out of the land of Egypt. They broke that covenant, though I loved them as a husband loves his wife," says the LORD. "But this is the new covenant I will make with the people of Israel on that day," says the LORD. "I will put my instructions deep within them, and I will write them on their hearts. I will be their God, and they will be my people."
>
> *JEREMIAH 31:31-33*

> I will give you a new heart, and I will put a new spirit in you. I will take out your stony, stubborn heart and give you a tender, responsive heart. And I will put my Spirit in you so that you will follow my decrees and be careful to obey my regulations.
>
> *EZEKIEL 36:26-27*

219

Take your son, your only son—yes, Isaac, whom you love so much—and go to the land of Moriah. Go and sacrifice him as a burnt offering on one of the mountains, which I will show you.

GENESIS 22:2

It was by faith that Abraham offered Isaac as a sacrifice when God was testing him. Abraham, who had received God's promises, was ready to sacrifice his only son, Isaac, even though God had told him, "Isaac is the son through whom your descendants will be counted." Abraham reasoned that if Isaac died, God was able to bring him back to life again.

HEBREWS 11:17-19

Reasoning Faith

Have you ever put together a big five hundred–piece puzzle and been convinced at some point that there must be some pieces missing because you just couldn't find the ones you need? Sometimes walking with God feels like that. We look at our circumstances and then look at God's promises, and we think, *This just doesn't seem to fit together.*

Certainly Abraham must have had those thoughts when he heard God telling him to put his son Isaac to death. Yet Genesis records that "early the next morning Abraham got up and saddled his donkey" and headed up the mountain with young Isaac (GENESIS 22:3, NIV). It's not clear in Genesis what gave Abraham the confidence to tell his servants, "*We* will worship . . . and then *we* will come right back" (GENESIS 22:5, emphasis added). But Hebrews tells us that Abraham "reasoned" from who God is, and it empowered him to obey. Abraham must have thought, *I don't like this at all. But for God to fail me, he'd have to stop being God, and that's impossible. God is doing something here I don't understand, but I know he will provide. My life is a front-row seat for watching God keep his promises.*

That kind of reasoning is faith. It helps us put together the puzzle in our minds when our circumstances seem to be saying that God is not good or that he has failed us or that he isn't living up to his promises. We have to reason it through from what we know is true about God's character and power and purposes.

 | **DISCUSSION STARTERS**

When your parents tell you to do something that you don't understand, how do you respond? What do you know about your parents that could help you to obey?

What does "early the next morning" say about Abraham's obedience?

What do you think was the purpose of Abraham's test?

Planning for Retirement?

You've seen the advertisements on television—gray-haired couples swinging on a porch swing, playing a round of golf, taking a cruise, while the announcer talks about saving money for retirement. It has become a way of life in our culture, working thirty or forty years and planning to spend the remaining years fishing, gardening, traveling, and playing.

But while this has become an accepted goal of life in our culture, we don't see it in the Bible. King David pleaded with God to continue to use him for ministry even in his old age. John was banished to Patmos around the age of ninety for preaching the gospel. Anna was still prophesying in the Temple when she was very old. Paul wrote to Philemon from his prison cell as an old man in chains for preaching the gospel.

The way we as believers plan for our later years should stand in stark contrast to the way the world plans for retirement. Our attitudes should be more like this: *My professional career may end at sixty-five, but then I'll be on call for full-time work for God.* It's a time not for rewarding ourselves but for working to further the Kingdom. Even if you're still young, it's not too early to think about how you want to live when you get older. No Christian exists merely to make an honest living, raise a family, enjoy retirement, and then die. We are all called to ministry as long as we live.

 | ## DISCUSSION STARTERS

What are some ways older people can serve God in ministry?

What excuses do we use to avoid ministry as students? as parents of young children? as middle-aged people with teenagers and aging parents? as retirees?

What do 1 Peter 4:10 and 1 Corinthians 12:7 say about every Christian's call to ministry?

Now that I am old and gray,
do not abandon me, O God.
Let me proclaim your power
to this new generation,
your mighty miracles to
all who come after me.
PSALM 71:18

I will praise the LORD as long
as I live. I will sing praises to
my God with my dying breath.
PSALM 146:2

To me, living means living
for Christ, and dying is even
better. But if I live, I can do
more fruitful work for Christ.
PHILIPPIANS 1:22-23

Do You Have a Guardian Angel?

He will order his angels to protect you wherever you go. They will hold you up with their hands so you won't even hurt your foot on a stone.

PSALM 91:11-12

Angels are only servants— spirits sent to care for people who will inherit salvation.

HEBREWS 1:14

Last night an angel of the God to whom I belong and whom I serve stood beside me, and he said, "Don't be afraid, Paul, for you will surely stand trial before Caesar! What's more, God in his goodness has granted safety to everyone sailing with you."

ACTS 27:23-24

Lots of people like to think they have a guardian angel protecting them. Whenever they narrowly avoid an accident or life-threatening situation, they say their guardian angel must be looking after them. But is it their guardian angel who's taking care of them, or someone else?

Throughout Scripture we find angels personally involved in protecting God's people in times of great need. When they minister to people, it's because God has directed them to do so. Our God uses his awesome power in compassionate, loving ways to help us when we're hurting or in trouble.

The Bible never says to pray directly to angels for help. And there are no instances in Scripture of people even asking God to send an angel to protect them. The only instance in Scripture of someone trying to persuade someone else to seek help from an angel was Satan, who quoted Psalm 91 about angelic protection while tempting Jesus in the wilderness.

We are grateful for angels and how they help us, but when we focus only on angels and what they can or cannot do, it takes our focus off Jesus. As we think of guardian angels watching over us, we have to be sure to keep our eyes on the one who sent them—to put our trust in God, not angels.

 | **DISCUSSION STARTERS**

Have you ever sensed that an angel has taken care of you? When?

Why do you think many people would rather give credit to an angel for helping them than to God?

Who is our one and only true source of help and protection?

True Beauty

There is a saying that has been around since the third century BC: "Beauty is in the eye of the beholder." If this is true, then there is no objective source for deciding if something is beautiful or ugly—it is all a matter of personal preference or opinion. But is that true?

Built into each one of us is a longing for beauty. We get pleasure from seeing beauty in a green valley, a marble statue, or the perfect golf swing. We experience the beauty of a piece of music, words well spoken, or the taste of a ripe, red strawberry. Seeing and experiencing beauty all around us adds joy to life. But all these things are just reflections or pointers to a greater beauty.

God himself is ultimate beauty. He's the definition of beauty, the standard of beauty that we judge everything against. And our longing for beauty is really a longing for God himself.

A great painting is beautiful not because of the isolated colors or shapes or textures but because of the way all those elements interact with each other. It is the same with the person of God. What makes God beautiful is not just his attributes but their relationship to each other—their perfect harmony and balance and completeness. All his perfections are on display, and when we are able to catch a glimpse of how they relate to one another, it takes our breath away. And we fall down to worship true beauty.

🧂🧂 | DISCUSSION STARTERS

What or who is beautiful to you?

How does what we see as beautiful affect what we become?

Why do you think it seems a little strange to say that God is beautiful?

There was nothing beautiful or majestic about his appearance, nothing to attract us to him.
ISAIAH 53:2

You should clothe yourselves instead with the beauty that comes from within, the unfading beauty of a gentle and quiet spirit, which is so precious to God.
1 PETER 3:4

One thing I ask of the LORD, this is what I seek: that I may dwell in the house of the LORD all the days of my life, to gaze upon the beauty of the LORD and to seek him in his temple.
PSALM 27:4, NIV

Your Father knows exactly what you need even before you ask him! Pray like this: Our Father in heaven, may your name be kept holy. May your Kingdom come soon. May your will be done on earth, as it is in heaven.
MATTHEW 6:8-10

Jesus went up on a mountain to pray, and he prayed to God all night.
LUKE 6:12

The Holy Spirit helps us in our weakness. For example, we don't know what God wants us to pray for. But the Holy Spirit prays for us with groanings that cannot be expressed in words.
ROMANS 8:26

A Conversation with Your Father

Imagine a relationship between a parent and a child in which the only time they talk is when the child asks the parent for what he or she wants. The child is uninterested in hearing what the parent wants or getting wise input or pouring out his or her thoughts and feelings to mom or dad.

That's what it's like when our prayers to God are only a list of what we want or what we want God to do. It's easy to get into the habit of praying that way—asking him for what we want and need, without talking to him about what he thinks is important. God our Father wants prayer to be more than a wish list; he wants it to be a conversation. He wants to hear what's on our hearts—what we're concerned about, what we're happy about, what we're confused about. But he doesn't want us to do all the talking. He wants us to listen to him speak through his Word and sometimes directly to our hearts as we pray. He wants us to set aside our self-focus and talk about what he is doing in the world—and to welcome it and celebrate it. He wants us to offer ourselves to him to be used for his purposes.

When we pray the way Jesus shows us to pray, acknowledging our relationship to him, we find that welcoming his work comes ahead of giving him our list of wants. Praying this way puts our wants into proper perspective.

 | ## DISCUSSION STARTERS

What is prayer?

If God knows our needs before we ask, why does he want us to ask?

How might your family pray together differently if you used Jesus' model for prayer (see Matthew 6)?

Losses and Gains

An accounting ledger has two columns—one for income or assets, and another one for payments or losses. In a way, our relationship with Jesus is like that. Part of growing in our relationship with him is understanding the things in our lives that are true assets—the things that add to our relationship with him—and the things that take away from it.

Paul had this sense of an accounting ledger in his life. In his column of gains or assets, he listed all the advantages of his insider religious status. At one time he saw his religious connections as something valuable. But then he had a life-transforming experience with Jesus, and what went in each ledger column was completely reversed.

Paul saw that his religious experience was not an asset at all but a liability or a loss. Instead of moving him closer to knowing God in an intimate and authentic way, it gave him a false sense of rightness. In the spiritual accounting of his life, he realized that if anything was feeding his self-righteousness and keeping him from an awareness of his deep need for real relationship with God, it was hurting him more than helping him.

Have you grown up in church? Are you blessed with a family that has a long tradition and legacy of faith? It can create a strong foundation of faith for you—an asset. Or it can be a liability. Which is it for you?

 | ## DISCUSSION STARTERS

How have your church and your family helped you know Jesus better?

How can someone's religious history or background work against him or her?

What is the difference between religion and a relationship with Jesus?

I was circumcised when I was eight days old. I am a pure-blooded citizen of Israel and a member of the tribe of Benjamin—a real Hebrew if there ever was one! I was a member of the Pharisees, who demand the strictest obedience to the Jewish law. I was so zealous that I harshly persecuted the church. And as for righteousness, I obeyed the law without fault.

I once thought these things were valuable, but now I consider them worthless because of what Christ has done. Yes, everything else is worthless when compared with the infinite value of knowing Christ Jesus my Lord. For his sake I have discarded everything else, counting it all as garbage, so that I could gain Christ.

PHILIPPIANS 3:5-8

This left Jacob all alone in the camp, and a man came and wrestled with him until the dawn began to break. When the man saw that he would not win the match, he touched Jacob's hip and wrenched it out of its socket. Then the man said, "Let me go, for the dawn is breaking!"

But Jacob said, "I will not let you go unless you bless me."
GENESIS 32:24-26

Yes, he wrestled with the angel and won. He wept and pleaded for a blessing from him. There at Bethel he met God face to face, and God spoke to him.
HOSEA 12:4

Wrestling with God

How does someone win a wrestling match? The winner is usually the one who overpowers the other, pinning him to the mat. But Genesis tells us about a wrestling match between Jacob and God that Jacob won—not by pinning his opponent on the ground but by his desperate desire for God.

Jacob was at the end of his rope. That's when a man came and began a wrestling match that lasted all night. Finally, the man touched Jacob's hip and threw his leg out, and Jacob recognized that the man was actually God. That's when Jacob prayed one of the greatest prayers in the Bible: "I will not let you go unless you bless me."

Many people talk about wrestling with God when really they're talking about rebelling against God. But we don't wrestle with God to argue with him or to make him prove himself to us. Wrestling with God is not about pinning God down. It's about experiencing his power and enjoying his presence. Redemptive wrestling with God is when we can't bear to think about living without his blessing in our lives, when we value his blessing so much it is worth fighting for. It's going hard after him, longing for *his* will and *his* glory and *his* blessing upon us, so that we are living proof of what God can do with people who are at the end of themselves.

 | **DISCUSSION STARTERS**

In what way did Jacob "win" the wrestling match?

Why do you think God purposely left Jacob with a limp?

In what ways might we need to "fight" to enjoy God's blessing?

The Devil's Defeat

AUGUST 15

Have you ever been playing a card game or some other game, confident you are winning, only to find out someone else has a trump card or a secret play that makes him or her the winner?

When Jesus was on the cross, the devil thought he was winning. He thought that if he could kill Jesus, that would be the end, and he would be victorious. But it was a terrible miscalculation on the devil's part. He didn't realize that in orchestrating the evil that would bring Jesus to the Cross, he was bringing defeat on himself.

What was Jesus' secret winning play? Colossians 2:14-15 describes it this way: "He canceled the record of the charges against us and took it away by nailing it to the cross. In this way, he disarmed the spiritual rulers and authorities. He shamed them publicly by his victory over them on the cross." Jesus disarmed the devil. He took away the weapon of death from the devil's hand. And while the devil is still active in this world, the day is coming when his defeat, which is already certain, will be complete. One day Jesus will not only defeat the devil for good—he will *destroy* the devil for good.

 | **DISCUSSION STARTERS**

What does it mean to disarm an opponent?

How does Jesus' death fulfill God's words to the serpent in Genesis 3:15: "He will strike your head, and you will strike his heel"?

What does it mean that the devil is defeated—for today and for the future?

Because God's children are human beings—made of flesh and blood—the Son also became flesh and blood. For only as a human being could he die, and only by dying could he break the power of the devil, who had the power of death.
HEBREWS 2:14

He has rescued us from the kingdom of darkness and transferred us into the Kingdom of his dear Son.
COLOSSIANS 1:13

Then the devil, who had deceived them, was thrown into the fiery lake of burning sulfur, joining the beast and the false prophet. There they will be tormented day and night forever and ever.
REVELATION 20:10

What Are
You Going to Wear?

Clothe yourself with the presence of the Lord Jesus Christ.
ROMANS 13:14

You must clothe yourselves with tenderhearted mercy, kindness, humility, gentleness, and patience.
COLOSSIANS 3:12

Don't be concerned about the outward beauty of fancy hairstyles, expensive jewelry, or beautiful clothes. You should clothe yourselves instead with the beauty that comes from within, the unfading beauty of a gentle and quiet spirit, which is so precious to God.
1 PETER 3:3-4

It is that back-to-school season for many families, a time when new fall fashions are showing up in the store windows, and it's hard not to think about getting some new clothes. While clothes don't tell the whole story about a person, certainly the clothes we wear say something about us—how we approach life, where we want to fit in, what we want other people to notice about us.

Just as we make choices about how we want to clothe our bodies, we also make choices about how we want to clothe ourselves spiritually. We can clothe ourselves with mercy, kindness, humility, gentleness, and patience. We can cover ourselves with a way of interacting with people on the outside that is evidence that the Holy Spirit is working on us and changing us on the inside. We can clothe ourselves with a gentle and quiet spirit, which is not a particular personality type but a choice to stop trying to always get our own way. And perhaps the most beautiful way we can clothe ourselves is with God's very presence in our lives. Rather than shouting to the world that we want to fit in here and get our needs met here, we live life welcoming the presence of God into every situation, into every relationship, so that we have a sense of God with us, as close to us as the shirts on our backs.

 | **DISCUSSION STARTERS**

What is your favorite outfit? What do you think it says about you?

As you read through the three verses on the left, which set of clothes would you most like to put on today?

In practical terms, how can you clothe yourself with God's presence?

Because I Love You . . .

One of the things that happens on the first day of school is that you learn the rules. Sometimes it can seem that classroom rules, playground rules, house rules, every kind of rules are just meant to ruin our fun. Some people see the rules God gave us for living in the same way—as unreasonable rules set by a strict God that are meant to take the fun out of life. But the rules God gave us in the Ten Commandments aren't meant to take anything from us. They're a gift to us, an expression of God's love toward us.

God did not lean out of heaven one day thinking, *These people are having too much fun*, and then proceed to give us a to-do list to make us miserable. God saw people continually ruining their lives by chasing after what they thought would make them happy apart from him. So he gave us a light that points out what will hurt us, a set of boundaries that keep us close to him, and a clear standard for judging our thinking and behavior. The Ten Commandments are the most complete description of absolute good that people have ever been given. Through them we learn that we need to bend our lives to conform to that goodness, not redefine *good* to fit our crookedness. The law is like a mirror that shows us what we really are— lawbreakers who desperately need forgiveness for our failures and who need a perfection that we can't get on our own. Without the law, we wouldn't see how much we need Jesus and how much he loves us.

The LORD our God commanded us to obey all these decrees and to fear him so he can continue to bless us and preserve our lives, as he has done to this day.

DEUTERONOMY 6:24

How joyful are those who fear the LORD and delight in obeying his commands. Their children will be successful everywhere; an entire generation of godly people will be blessed.

PSALM 112:1-2

Open my eyes to see the wonderful truths in your instructions.

PSALM 119:18

 | DISCUSSION STARTERS

What loving purpose can you see in the rules in your classroom or at home?

What do God's rules tell us about God himself?

Do you take the Ten Commandments seriously? What shows that?

You must not have any other god but me.
EXODUS 20:3

Do not love this world nor the things it offers you, for when you love the world, you do not have the love of the Father in you.
1 JOHN 2:15

You say, "That's not true! I haven't worshiped the images of Baal!" But how can you say that? Go and look in any valley in the land! Face the awful sins you have done. You are like a restless female camel desperately searching for a mate.
JEREMIAH 2:23

An Exclusive Relationship

"I, _____, take you, _____, to be my wedded husband. To have and to hold, from this day forward, for better, for worse, for richer, for poorer, in sickness or in health, to love and to cherish till death do us part. And hereto I pledge you my faithfulness." These are the words a bride says to her groom at the altar. It's not a promise she makes to many men—just one. Theirs is an exclusive love relationship.

That's what God wants and expects from each of us—an exclusive love relationship. He doesn't want anything to take his rightful place in our lives. In the first commandment God is saying, "I am giving myself to you in grace, and I don't want anything to come between us. I want to be the sole object of your affection, loyalty, and worship."

One of the ways the Bible describes sin is spiritual adultery. God is our husband and covenant partner and the one we are to love exclusively. Every time we sin, we are saying to God, "God, you don't love me. You're not providing for me. So I have to go off to someone or something else for love and provision and protection. You're not enough." But the good news is that God forgives and restores spiritually unfaithful people. He invites us back into a loving, exclusive relationship.

 | ### DISCUSSION STARTERS

Do you know someone who is faithful? How is that person's faithfulness evident?

What are some things or people we sometimes turn to in an attempt to replace God?

How can we restore and nurture our love relationship with God if we find that we've been unfaithful to our exclusive relationship with him?

When Desires Become Demands

work hard all week. Don't I deserve a little peace and quiet when I come home?" "I work two jobs to put you through school; I deserve your respect." "All my friends have a car to drive to school. I get good grades. I deserve a car too." Does this kind of thinking sound familiar?

The more we want something, the more we think of it as something we need and deserve. And the more we think we are entitled to it, the more convinced we are that we can't be happy without it. That's how a desire becomes a demand and creates an idol. What we want is not always the problem; the problem is that we want it too much.

While we may think of an idol as a statue of wood, stone, or metal worshiped by pagans, in reality an idol is anything besides God that we depend on to make us happy, fulfilled, or secure. It is anything other than God that motivates and masters us, anything we love and pursue in place of God. Idols begin with desires—often good and healthy desires. But when a desire becomes a demand, when it begins to control our thoughts and behavior, that thing we want has become an idol.

Growing in the Christian life is a process of identifying and confessing our idols one by one. It means cooperating with God as he removes them, bit by bit, from our hearts, until finally we're convinced that he is all we need to make us happy.

You must not make for yourself an idol of any kind or an image of anything in the heavens or on the earth or in the sea.
EXODUS 20:4

I will heal you of your faithlessness; my love will know no bounds, for my anger will be gone forever.
HOSEA 14:4

Dear children, keep away from anything that might take God's place in your hearts.
1 JOHN 5:21

🧂🧂 | DISCUSSION STARTERS

Can you think of anything you wanted so much you moved from desiring it to demanding it?

How does a person change what he or she wants or how much he or she wants it?

What are some of the common idols in our society today?

You must not misuse the name of the LORD your God. The LORD will not let you go unpunished if you misuse his name.
DEUTERONOMY 5:11

You can ask for anything in my name, and I will do it, so that the Son can bring glory to the Father.
JOHN 14:13

On judgment day many will say to me, "Lord! Lord! We prophesied in your name and cast out demons in your name and performed many miracles in your name." But I will reply, "I never knew you. Get away from me, you who break God's laws."
MATTHEW 7:22-23

Using God's Name

"Oh God!" "Jeez!" "Gosh darn!" These are some of the "acceptable" phrases our culture has come up with to add emphasis or express frustration using a vague form of God's name. Though we may not mean it this way or think of it this way, these expressions take the holy name of God and make it common—even disrespected. And when we think about it that way, if we love God, we realize we don't want to do that to his name.

There are other ways we misuse God's name. When we pray using Jesus' name and we're really just trying to manipulate God's power to meet our own selfish desires, we're misusing God's name. When we flash our spiritual credentials in situations where using God's name will advance our agenda or put us in a positive light with someone we want to impress, we're stealing God's glory and misusing his name. Some people use God's name by saying, "God told me . . ." just to make themselves seem more spiritual or to try to manipulate someone else. We always need to be examining ourselves, asking, *Am I bringing glory to God's name, or am I using God's name for my own glory?*

 | **DISCUSSION STARTERS**

What words do people use that are really a form of God's name?

How can we know if someone who claims to have heard from God is authentic?

What are some appropriate ways we can use God's name?

Sabbath Rest

"I can't be there; I have an appointment." That's what you say when someone asks you to do something and you have a previous commitment. Have you ever thought about the Sabbath as an appointment with God—an appointment you won't let anything else interfere with? Or is Sunday just a second Saturday to you, a day that you go to church and then do as you please, or get caught up on whatever homework or housework you haven't gotten done during the week? What makes the Sabbath special at your house? Anything?

God said to "*be careful* to keep my Sabbath day." To be careful is to be intentional. If we're going to treat Sunday as a special holy day (a day set apart, different from all other days), we have to make some plans or set some boundaries for how we will or will not spend the day. Now that can sound like making rules that will sap all the joy out of the day. But really the Sabbath is a gift to us from God. To enjoy that gift requires that we set some plans in place to intentionally rest from the work we do on other days. That gives us a chance to think about, talk to, celebrate, and enjoy God. We have a Sunday appointment with him that we would not think of canceling for anything ordinary.

 | ## DISCUSSION STARTERS

What could your family do to make Sundays special and set apart from other days?

How can we keep the Sabbath faithfully without becoming legalistic?

What can you or your family eliminate from Sundays so that you can focus more on resting and relating to God?

Be careful to keep my Sabbath day, for the Sabbath is a sign of the covenant between me and you from generation to generation. It is given so you may know that I am the LORD, who makes you holy. You have six days each week for your ordinary work, but the seventh day must be a Sabbath day of complete rest, a holy day dedicated to the LORD.
EXODUS 31:13, 15

Honor the Sabbath in everything you do on that day, and don't follow your own desires or talk idly. Then the LORD will be your delight.
ISAIAH 58:13-14

It was the Lord's Day, and I was worshiping in the Spirit.
REVELATION 1:10

Honor your father and mother, as the LORD your God commanded you. Then you will live a long, full life in the land the LORD your God is giving you.

DEUTERONOMY 5:16

Children, obey your parents because you belong to the Lord, for this is the right thing to do. "Honor your father and mother." This is the first commandment with a promise: If you honor your father and mother, "things will go well for you, and you will have a long life on the earth."

EPHESIANS 6:1-3

Mom and Dad, You Matter

"**M**y parents are so cool. I can't wait to talk to them about this to get their opinion and advice." Can you imagine hearing someone in high school say this? A college student? Even an adult?

It can be terribly uncool to honor your parents. If you refuse to join in the discussion with your peers about how ridiculous your parents are, you will probably get some strange looks, at the very least. And it doesn't really stop when we're out of school. We live in a culture where parent-bashing is the norm. Parents who "just don't get it" are the constant butt of jokes on sitcoms and in movies.

Confronting this norm of disrespect comes the fifth commandment—to honor our fathers and mothers. The word *honor* comes from a Hebrew word meaning "to be heavy" or "to give weight." It involves seriously taking someone into account, offering that person profound respect and a place of importance and reverence. The opposite of honoring someone is trivializing, despising, or forgetting him or her, or treating the person as if he or she doesn't matter.

Honoring your parents is an attitude, but it's also accompanied by actions. It's a way of saying, "You are worthy. You have value. You are someone God has sovereignly placed in my life. You may have failed me, hurt me, and disappointed me at times, but I choose to look at you with compassion—as people with needs, concerns, and scars of your own—and treat you with respect."

 | **DISCUSSION STARTERS**

What are some ways you have observed your parents honoring their own parents?

What are some specific actions and attitudes that honor parents?

Why do you think honoring parents is important to God?

Are You a Murderer?

Have you ever heard anybody say, "If looks could kill . . ."? What did that person mean? Most likely it was a reference to the hateful look on someone's face. Unless we're very good actors, most of us can't help but let what's in our hearts show on our faces. Sometimes we have murder in our hearts, and it shows. This doesn't necessarily mean we want to physically kill the person we are angry with. But we might want to damage the person's reputation, hurt his or her feelings, or injure his or her relationships with others.

If we think we're doing okay on the sixth commandment because we haven't physically killed anybody, we're not looking deep enough. Jesus said that we break this commandment when we have a murderous motive in our hearts that comes out in hateful words. God commands us never to harm another person with our actions, thoughts, words, or indifference. But he expects even more than that. He not only wants us not to be life takers; he wants us to be life givers. Just as we can be murderous with words, we can be life giving with words. We can offer words of encouragement instead of cynicism, words of affirmation instead of criticism, words of truth instead of deceit, words of love instead of hate.

 | ## DISCUSSION STARTERS

Make your worst mean, ugly, "if looks could kill" face. What does that expression say to others?

What words and phrases could you say that are life giving to others?

Is there someone you need to ask forgiveness of for "murdering" him or her with words?

You must not murder.
DEUTERONOMY 5:17

You have heard that our ancestors were told, "You must not murder. If you commit murder, you are subject to judgment." But I say, if you are even angry with someone, you are subject to judgment! If you call someone an idiot, you are in danger of being brought before the court. And if you curse someone, you are in danger of the fires of hell.
MATTHEW 5:21-22

Anyone who hates another brother or sister is really a murderer at heart. And you know that murderers don't have eternal life within them.
1 JOHN 3:15

You must not commit adultery.
DEUTERONOMY 5:18

Give honor to marriage, and remain faithful to one another in marriage. God will surely judge people who are immoral and those who commit adultery.
HEBREWS 13:4

You have heard the commandment that says, "You must not commit adultery." But I say, anyone who even looks at a woman with lust has already committed adultery with her in his heart.
MATTHEW 5:27-28

Sticking Together

Have you ever sealed an envelope and then tried to open it again? As you try to pry it open, it rips and tears, with some parts of the flap still sticking to the envelope. This is similar to what happens when a person has sex outside of marriage: It's like two people attach and then get ripped apart. And nothing attaches people as deeply as sexual intercourse does. When they "pull apart," there are pieces of them left behind, creating a lot of damage, pain, and regret. And later, this makes it difficult for them to fully attach to someone else.

God wants to save us from this pain. His design is for us to become "attached" to one person we can be completely committed to for life. Jesus said, "'A man leaves his father and mother and is joined to his wife, and the two are united into one.' Since they are no longer two but one, let no one split apart what God has joined together" (MATTHEW 19:5-6). He knows that a marriage with two people seeking to be faithful to each other is what will make us deeply happy, and that attaching ourselves to people outside of marriage will ultimately bring only misery.

Not only does God want us to avoid the heartache and regret of betrayal, he wants marriage to be a living illustration of the kind of faithful love relationship Christ wants to have with us. He wants the world to be able to see the way Jesus loves his people reflected in how we love each other.

 | DISCUSSION STARTERS

How does it hurt a relationship when one person breaks his or her promises?

In addition to sexual faithfulness, what does it mean to be faithful in marriage?

How does adultery show selfishness as well as a lack of trust in God?

Are You a Taker?

One of the first words most of us learned is "Mine!" followed closely by "Give me" and "I want." As toddlers we saw something we wanted and we reached out for it—it didn't matter whose it was. As we grow, if God does not change us, we become grown-up takers who continue to reach out for what we want, refusing to rest in what God has provided for us.

Stealing is not just taking something that doesn't belong to us. Plenty of nonmaterial things can be stolen: time from an employer, credit for someone else's work or accomplishment, a service that you use but don't pay for. We also steal when we don't pay what we owe, whether it is money, belongings, affection, courtesy, appreciation, or time. We steal from our parents when we waste things they've paid for us to have—education, food, opportunities. We steal from our employers not only by taking things home that belong to the company, but by wasting time on the job when we're being paid to contribute.

When God says, "You must not steal," he's telling us to be honest in our dealings with others. We're to stop sponging off others or demanding that others meet our needs. The real issue is not so much actual theft, which most of us recognize is wrong. It's about the heart attitude behind stealing. It's having a taker's attitude about life. More than that, it's an attitude toward God that says, "You have not given me enough. I can't trust you to provide what I need to feel satisfied. I have to take things into my own hands so that I can maintain the lifestyle I need to." God has promised to give us everything we need. Will you take him at his word?

> You must not steal.
> *DEUTERONOMY 5:19*

> If you are a thief, quit stealing. Instead, use your hands for good hard work, and then give generously to others in need.
> *EPHESIANS 4:28*

> Give to anyone who asks; and when things are taken away from you, don't try to get them back.
> *LUKE 6:30*

 | ## DISCUSSION STARTERS

What is the difference between a giver and a taker?

Is there anything you or your family uses but doesn't pay for, any debts you owe but aren't paying?

What are the advantages and disadvantages of being a giver instead of a taker?

You must not testify falsely against your neighbor.
DEUTERONOMY 5:20

So stop telling lies. Let us tell our neighbors the truth, for we are all parts of the same body.
EPHESIANS 4:25

If you want to enjoy life and see many happy days, keep your tongue from speaking evil and your lips from telling lies. Turn away from evil and do good. Search for peace, and work to maintain it.
1 PETER 3:10-11

Who Me, a Liar?

"Sticks and stones will break my bones, but words will never hurt me!" Have you ever said that little rhyme when someone said something mean or unkind to you? If only it were true. Because words do hurt people—especially when those words are not true. They hurt both the person who speaks the lie and the person who is lied about.

We don't like to think of ourselves as liars, but all of us would have to admit that we have told outright lies in our lifetime. Or perhaps we've lied by twisting the truth or allowing a falsehood to go unchallenged. But while the ninth commandment prohibits lying, it specifically refers to saying something false about someone else. What does it mean to "testify falsely"? It is when a child spins the story of what happened in order to get a sibling in trouble, when a teenager withholds the truth about a friend's character so Mom and Dad won't prevent him or her from hanging out with this person. It's a mom who criticizes someone else to make herself look better. It's a dad who unfairly allows a coworker to look bad in the boss's eyes so he can get a leg up.

The Heidelberg Catechism tells what to do instead. It says, "I should love the truth, speak it candidly, and openly acknowledge it. And I should do what I can to guard and advance my neighbor's good name."

 | **DISCUSSION STARTERS**

How does it feel when someone says something about you that isn't true?

Is there a difference between putting spin on a story and lying? How about between a little white lie and an outright whopper? How about between telling an untruth and allowing an untruth to go unchallenged?

Why do you think God takes lying so seriously?

I Wish I Had . . .

I wish I had his sports car. I wish I had her flat stomach. I wish I had his athletic talent. I wish I were as popular as she is. We can't help noticing things other people have that we wish we had. That wanting becomes coveting when our heart fixates on or obsesses over something we think we must have to be happy. We believe we are more deserving than that other person is, and we resent the fact that we can't have that thing ourselves. Wanting what we don't have—and dissatisfaction with what we do have—is like a monster that is constantly being fed by the consumer culture we live in.

So how can we feed a growing sense of contentment instead of a growing desire for what someone else has? We can't just decide one day that we won't covet anymore. It is too much a part of our hearts. In fact, our hearts are organs of deep desire. The cure for coveting is to learn to covet the right things.

The psalmist knew the right things to covet in order to find satisfaction and deep contentment. In Psalm 73:25 the psalmist says to God, "I desire you more than anything on earth." The more we value Jesus and the more we marinate in the truth that he is everything we need, the less we become obsessed with desires for what other people have that we don't.

DISCUSSION STARTERS

Have you ever observed someone who went without something he or she really wanted out of a desire to be content with what he or she had?

What happens to our relationships when we give in to coveting?

What does coveting say about our faith in God?

You must not covet your neighbor's wife. You must not covet your neighbor's house or land, male or female servant, ox or donkey, or anything else that belongs to your neighbor.
DEUTERONOMY 5:21

I have learned how to be content with whatever I have.
PHILIPPIANS 4:11

True godliness with contentment is itself great wealth. After all, we brought nothing with us when we came into the world, and we can't take anything with us when we leave it. So if we have enough food and clothing, let us be content.
1 TIMOTHY 6:6-8

The Smartest Person Who Ever Lived

AUGUST

28

I want them to have complete confidence that they understand God's mysterious plan, which is Christ himself. In him lie hidden all the treasures of wisdom and knowledge.
COLOSSIANS 2:2-3

The people were amazed at his teaching, for he taught with real authority— quite unlike the teachers of religious law.
MARK 1:22

To those who listen to my teaching, more understanding will be given, and they will have an abundance of knowledge. But for those who are not listening, even what little understanding they have will be taken away from them.
MATTHEW 13:12

Who is the smartest person you know? Do you know anyone who knows the answer to every question when you watch a game show on TV, or someone who uses big words you've never heard before and actually understands what they mean?

Who would you say is the smartest person who ever lived? We don't necessarily think about Jesus as being brilliant intellectually—perhaps because we read in the Gospels of his ordinary upbringing and his interaction with common people. He didn't go to college or have advanced degrees. The idea that Jesus is a master of algebra, economics, physics, or French literature may have never crossed our minds.

But could Jesus be Lord of this universe if he weren't smart? Could he be unintelligent or uninformed and still be divine? If you think about it, how could we truly worship him if we didn't respect him as the smartest person who ever lived, the one person with the best information on the most important subjects? Jesus is worthy of being our teacher. Under his instruction, we can learn how to think, what to do, and what really matters.

 | ## DISCUSSION STARTERS

What kinds of things cause you to think that a person is smart?

How could thinking of Jesus as the smartest person who ever lived change how you interact with him and how you worship him?

Think through various areas of knowledge and expertise, and then discuss what it means that Jesus knows more about those areas than any other person.

Everything? Even This?

Turn on the television and you will hear some TV preachers tell you that if you put your faith in God, he will make you healthy and even wealthy.

But God doesn't promise that. He doesn't say that if you follow him you will never have to suffer. What he does promise is that when you suffer, it won't be meaningless. He promises that your suffering will not be wasted—that he'll take the hard, hurtful experiences and realities in your life and use them for good purposes in your life and the lives of others.

But this is hard to believe when difficult things happen. We wonder, *What possible good could come out of this?* When we struggle to make sense of the truth that God can use bad things for good purposes, considering what happened at the Cross helps us. The Cross is the ultimate example of God's ability to work all things together for good. He even brought good from the most wicked thing darkness ever did—putting innocent Jesus to death. If God can use the cruel death and enormous suffering of his innocent Son on the cross to bring about the greatest good of all time, then we can be confident that he can do something good in and through the suffering in our lives too.

Either everything works for good or nothing makes sense. It is the "everything" in Romans 8:28 that makes this hard to accept but also fills us with hope. *Everything* means there is not one thing that falls outside of this promise—not suicide, not murder, not permanent injury, not divorce. God is not saying these things are good. But he does promise that if you love him, he will use even the worst thing you can imagine for your ultimate good. He will use the most bitter experience in your life to bless you.

> We know that God causes everything to work together for the good of those who love God and are called according to his purpose for them.
>
> **ROMANS 8:28**

> My suffering was good for me, for it taught me to pay attention to your decrees.
>
> **PSALM 119:71**

✄ | DISCUSSION STARTERS

What are some good things that came from Jesus' dying on the cross?

What is the difference between saying that everything is good and everything works together for good?

How can believing that God can bring good out of everything change how we respond to suffering?

O God, you have taught me from my earliest childhood, and I constantly tell others about the wonderful things you do.
PSALM 71:17

Intelligent people are always ready to learn. Their ears are open for knowledge.
PROVERBS 18:15

Anyone who hears my teaching and doesn't obey it is foolish, like a person who builds a house on sand.
MATTHEW 7:26

Are You Teachable?

"Will you teach me?" Maybe you don't say those words, but do you want to learn? Are you open to being taught? Are you a person who is teachable? Or are you satisfied with what you already know? Do you resent it when someone suggests that you might not know something or that he or she could teach you something?

Some people are too prideful to be taught. They don't want to admit that there is something they don't know, something they don't understand or haven't mastered. Some people simply stop being learners at some point along the way. They seem to suffocate any natural curiosity. Other people settle for filling their minds with insignificant things so that they have no hunger to think great thoughts or learn new things.

To be teachable requires a spirit of humility. For some people, pride gets in the way, and they remain stuck where they are. No one can become increasingly more like Jesus if he or she is not teachable. God gives us the Holy Spirit to lead us into truth. The Holy Spirit makes us willing to learn. And then God gives us so many ways to learn more about him, like the world he has made and his purposes in this world. We can learn from studying the Bible, from listening intently in church or youth group (perhaps by taking notes to stay tuned in), by observing others who are further along in faith, and by having conversations with godly people. All that is required is to be teachable.

 | **DISCUSSION STARTERS**

When you want to learn something (like how to throw a fastball, do algebra, remember people's names, or cook), what do you have to do?

What people has God placed around you whom you'd like to learn from?

What thought patterns or sin tendencies keep us from staying teachable?

True Greatness

Who do you think is the greatest sports star who ever competed? How about the greatest inventor? the greatest military strategist?

Can you imagine Jesus pointing you out as the greatest prophet of all time? That's what Jesus said about John the Baptist, his cousin. Jesus said, "I tell you the truth, of all who have ever lived, none is greater than John the Baptist" (MATTHEW 11:11).

What was it that made John the Baptist great? John was the first prophet who actually saw Jesus—the fulfillment of those prophecies—with his own eyes. Perhaps it was also something about the heart of John the Baptist that made him great. He said about Jesus: "He must become greater and greater, and I must become less and less" (JOHN 3:30). John wanted Jesus to become greater in other people's eyes. He wanted Jesus to get greater attention, greater affection. He wanted more people to tune in to who Jesus is and the life he offers.

True greatness is found in wanting Jesus to shine brighter and be seen for who he is, rather than wanting people to see us as stars. The more we seek to shine the spotlight on Jesus instead of on ourselves, the more content we'll be in who we are. It's in humbling ourselves that we become great.

 | ## DISCUSSION STARTERS

In your opinion, who are some of the greatest people who ever lived? Why?

How can you intentionally humble yourself and "become less and less"?

How does humbling yourself show faith in God?

The greatest among you must be a servant. But those who exalt themselves will be humbled, and those who humble themselves will be exalted.
MATTHEW 23:11-12

Humble yourselves under the mighty power of God, and at the right time he will lift you up in honor.
1 PETER 5:6

He must become greater and greater, and I must become less and less.
JOHN 3:30

The First Adam and the Last Adam

When Adam sinned, sin entered the world. Adam's sin brought death, so death spread to everyone, for everyone sinned.
ROMANS 5:12

Adam's one sin brings condemnation for everyone, but Christ's one act of righteousness brings a right relationship with God and new life for everyone. Because one person disobeyed God, many became sinners. But because one other person obeyed God, many will be made righteous.
ROMANS 5:18-19

The Scriptures tell us, "The first man, Adam, became a living person." But the last Adam—that is, Christ —is a life-giving Spirit.
1 CORINTHIANS 15:45

Have you ever had a teacher who punished the whole class for something one person in the class did? It doesn't feel fair, does it? Likewise, when we first confront the idea that we are all held accountable for Adam's sin and are paying the price for it, we want to protest because it seems unfair. Why should we experience the consequences of his bad choice?

The truth is, we were all "in Adam" as his descendents. So in a way, when he sinned, it is as if we all sinned. His sin transformed his inner nature, and that sin nature has been passed on to us. We're kidding ourselves to think that if we had been in Adam's shoes we would have resisted temptation and made a better choice.

If we don't think it is fair that Adam's sin counts against us, then neither should we accept that Christ's righteousness will work in our favor. But it does.

The good news is that what Christ has done through his obedience for all who are connected to him by faith is far greater than what Adam did through his disobedience for all who are connected to him by birth. In a deep and mysterious way, we were united to Adam in his sinning. But now we've been deeply and mysteriously united to Jesus so that his obedience has the final redeeming word in our lives.

 | **DISCUSSION STARTERS**

How were Adam and Jesus different? How were they similar?

What do those who stay "in Adam" (because they never become connected to Jesus through faith) receive through Adam's disobedience?

What do all those "in Christ" receive through his obedience?

Satan Has to Ask Permission

You know God is powerful, and you believe that God is more powerful than Satan, right? But the bigger truth is that Satan has absolutely no power that God doesn't grant to him. That is how "in charge" God is over the universe and how limited Satan is in the world.

God is in charge, and Satan knows it. The only power that Satan has is what God gives to him. He can only do what God permits him to do. When he wants to do anything—including anything that will cause pain to one of God's children—he has to ask God's permission.

In Luke, we read of Satan asking permission to harm one of God's own. Jesus said, "Simon, Simon, Satan has asked to sift each of you like wheat. But I have pleaded in prayer for you, Simon, that your faith should not fail" (22:31-32). The "each of you" Satan wants to sift (or put through the wringer of suffering) includes you and me. Satan's sifting is an effort to destroy our faith. And while God may give Satan permission to sift us, he will never allow our faith to fail permanently or our hope to be destroyed in the end. The almighty God will never grant Satan permission to destroy the faith that makes you his and keeps you his forever (SEE JUDE 1:1).

 | ## DISCUSSION STARTERS

Who are some people you have to ask permission from for things?

In what ways does it help you to know that Satan has to ask God's permission to bring suffering into your life?

In what ways does it bother you that God sometimes gives Satan permission to bring suffering into your life?

"All right, you may test him," the LORD said to Satan. "Do whatever you want with everything he possesses, but don't harm him physically." So Satan left the LORD's presence.

JOB 1:12

The demons kept begging Jesus not to send them into the bottomless pit. There happened to be a large herd of pigs feeding on the hillside nearby, and the demons begged him to let them enter into the pigs. So Jesus gave them permission.

LUKE 8:31-32

Simon, Simon, Satan has asked to sift each of you like wheat. But I have pleaded in prayer for you, Simon, that your faith should not fail. So when you have repented and turned to me again, strengthen your brothers.

LUKE 22:31-32

Better than Saving Your Life

I am sending you out as sheep among wolves. So be as shrewd as snakes and harmless as doves. But beware! For you will be handed over to the courts and will be flogged with whips in the synagogues. . . . Don't be afraid of those who want to kill your body; they cannot touch your soul. Fear only God, who can destroy both soul and body in hell.

MATTHEW 10:16-17, 28

You will be arrested, persecuted, and killed. You will be hated all over the world because you are my followers.

MATTHEW 24:9

Most of us want to be safe. So we wear our seat belts and take our vitamins and lock our doors. And those things are part of being wise. But Jesus didn't seem to place a high priority on personal physical safety—at least not when the choice was between being safe and being persecuted for devotion to Jesus.

Imagine the scene as Jesus prepared to send his disciples out in twos for ministry. Far from giving a pump-you-up pep talk to reassure them, he seemed to be preparing them for the worst. "When you are arrested, don't worry about how to respond or what to say," he instructed (MATTHEW 10:19). "All nations will hate you because you are my followers," he predicted (MATTHEW 10:22). And then he encouraged them not to fear those who wanted to kill them, saying, "Don't be afraid of those who want to kill your body; they cannot touch your soul."

Excuse me? we want to say in response. *They can only kill my body? And this should be a relief to me?*

God has not promised us that he will protect us from physical harm. In fact, he has promised us that as his followers, we should expect to be persecuted. And he promises that when we are, we will be rewarded generously for everything we've endured to make his name known.

 | **DISCUSSION STARTERS**

What do you know about how followers of Jesus in the New Testament were treated?

Why do you think God considers the safety and security of our souls to be more important than the safety and security of our bodies?

Can people who are ministering in foreign countries, inner-city neighborhoods, or anywhere else expect to always be physically safe?

A Day Person or a Night Person?

Some people are night people. Their energy just gets going when the sun goes down, and they love to stay up late. Other people are morning people. They like to get up early and get things done and go to bed early for a good night's sleep. The Bible talks about day people and night people. But it is not referring to their sleep habits. It is referring to whether or not they've embraced Jesus and the new way of living he brings.

Our culture is uncomfortable making a clear distinction between people when it comes to eternity. But according to Scripture, the world is divided into two kinds of people—night people and day people. And while we might not be able to identify who is who, God can. At the end of time, the people who have chosen darkness will enter into eternal darkness. And the people who have chosen light will enter into the eternal light of heaven, where "the city has no need of sun or moon, for the glory of God illuminates the city, and the Lamb is its light" (REVELATION 21:23). So are you a day person or a night person?

🧂🧂 | DISCUSSION STARTERS

Who at your house is a morning person? Who is a night person?

Is it possible for people of the light to get sucked into doing deeds of darkness? Can people who love darkness do the deeds of light?

Why do you think our culture is uncomfortable with the reality that all people are either people of the darkness or people of light?

God's light came into the world, but people loved the darkness more than the light, for their actions were evil.
JOHN 3:19

You are all children of the light and of the day; we don't belong to darkness and night. . . . Night is the time when people sleep and drinkers get drunk. But let us who live in the light be clearheaded, protected by the armor of faith and love, and wearing as our helmet the confidence of our salvation.
1 THESSALONIANS 5:5, 7-8

Once you were full of darkness, but now you have light from the Lord. So live as people of light! For this light within you produces only what is good and right and true.
EPHESIANS 5:8-9

God made Christ, who never sinned, to be the offering for our sin, so that we could be made right with God through Christ.

2 CORINTHIANS 5:21

It was the LORD's good plan to crush him and cause him grief.

ISAIAH 53:10

Since he did not spare even his own Son but gave him up for us all, won't he also give us everything else?

ROMANS 8:32

An Innocent Man Punished

Many nights on the news we see footage of someone who is on trial for a crime. We see the person in the courtroom standing next to his or her attorney or advocate while the case is tried before a judge or jury. And if the verdict is guilty, the defendant is usually led away from the courtroom to pay the penalty for his or her crime.

Imagine if, when the defendant is pronounced guilty, the lawyer is taken off to jail to be punished for the defendant's crime. We would want to talk back to the television, saying, "That's wrong! You've got the wrong man! He shouldn't have to pay!"

And yet that is exactly what happened to Jesus, our sinless advocate. He did nothing wrong. Ever. He is absolutely innocent, while we are absolutely guilty. We deserve the death penalty for our rebellion toward God and our rejection of him. But instead of our paying that penalty with our own lives, Jesus, the one who is pleading our case before God, paid it. Jesus, the sinless one, offered himself up to receive the punishment we, who are guilty, deserve. All the sin of all people for all time—Jesus paid for all of it.

 | **DISCUSSION STARTERS**

What does it mean to be guilty? What does it mean to be innocent?

If you were guilty and someone else paid your penalty, what would be an appropriate response toward that person?

Why do you think Jesus was willing to pay the penalty for our sin?

Time for Work

It is interesting to observe how people respond when they win the lottery. Some of them never go back to work; they see the money as their ticket to a life of ease. Others report for work the next day and keep on working. They recognize that meaningful work is about more than a paycheck.

Did you know working is a very godlike thing to do? We read in Genesis that God worked for six days and then rested on the seventh day. When he made Adam, he immediately gave him a job in the Garden—a job he was perfectly suited for, a job that was fulfilling.

We tend to categorize work into spiritual work, like being a missionary or a minister, and secular work, like being a doctor, an engineer, a salesperson, a teacher, or a student. But to God, all work is a calling from him and has dignity. Martin Luther said, "A dairymaid can milk cows to the glory of God." We live in a day and age where certain professions are honored above others. (Have you ever seen "Oscars" given out to police officers or lunchroom cooks or accountants?) And yet if you do what you do for the glory of God, it has eternal value in God's book.

 | **DISCUSSION STARTERS**

What jobs or professions have always fascinated you? How could a person do those jobs to the glory of God?

Are there some professions that could never bring glory to God?

Who are some people you know who set a good example of working hard and using their gifts to serve God in their professions?

You have six days each week for your ordinary work.
EXODUS 20:9

Make it your goal to live a quiet life, minding your own business and working with your hands, just as we instructed you before. Then people who are not Christians will respect the way you live, and you will not need to depend on others.
1 THESSALONIANS 4:11-12

We hear that some of you are living idle lives, refusing to work and meddling in other people's business. We command such people and urge them in the name of the Lord Jesus Christ to settle down and work to earn their own living.
2 THESSALONIANS 3:11-12

Work willingly at whatever you do, as though you were working for the Lord rather than for people. Remember that the Lord will give you an inheritance as your reward, and that the Master you are serving is Christ.

COLOSSIANS 3:23-24

Jesus came and told his disciples, "I have been given all authority in heaven and on earth."

MATTHEW 28:18

All authority comes from God, and those in positions of authority have been placed there by God.

ROMANS 13:1

Who's the Boss?

What would it be like if you showed up for a job one day and your boss was Jesus? How would you treat your boss? How would you interact with your coworkers? How would it affect the quality of the work you do and your attitude as you do it? The truth is, no matter who our human boss or authority is, no matter what we're doing, whether it is volunteer work or schoolwork or paid work, we are really working for Jesus.

And this truth really helps us when we don't like what we've been asked to do. Because if we see Jesus as our boss, we want to please him. That gives us the extra push to complete unpleasant tasks. Knowing Jesus is our real boss also helps us when we don't like our human bosses or leaders. We're able to treat those in authority over us with respect, whether they've earned it or not, because we know that God has placed them in those positions. We can relax knowing those people are accountable to God for how they use their power. Seeing Jesus as our boss also helps us to do the right thing when we're tempted to cut corners, not finish the job, or take credit we don't deserve. We know that Jesus is always with us. He sees what we do and what we don't do. He can see our disrespectful thoughts and self-serving motives. So whatever we're doing—school, work, or other activities—we can remind ourselves that he's the one we're ultimately responsible to.

 | ### DISCUSSION STARTERS

Think through different jobs people have. What would it mean for each person to do his or her job as "working for the Lord"?

If you are a student and your work is your schoolwork, what do you think it would look like to consider Jesus the boss of your class time and homework?

Do you need to change any work habits or attitudes based on the truth that you are working for the Lord?

What Did Jesus Have to Learn?

Usually when we talk about learning, we mean gaining knowledge or information about something we didn't know before. When we learn how to tie our shoes or water-ski, we're able to do something we couldn't do before.

So when the Bible tells us that Jesus "learned obedience," our first instinct is to think that Jesus was perhaps disobedient, and then he learned to obey. But is that really the case? Was he in some way disobedient before?

No. The Bible doesn't say that Jesus learned to obey; it says that he learned obedience. This means that Jesus learned obedience when he *experienced* it. And it was while enduring the agony of the Cross that Jesus experienced his most costly obedience. Jesus went from obeying without any physical suffering to obeying through unspeakable suffering.

We might think that it was somehow easier for Jesus to obey God in hard things because he was God. But he was also fully human. He felt the temptation to disobey, the urge to give in to what would have been easier. Jesus learned through his own experience what it feels like for obedience to God to cost something—something that hurts.

> Even though Jesus was God's Son, he learned obedience from the things he suffered.
> *HEBREWS 5:8*

> He humbled himself in obedience to God and died a criminal's death on a cross.
> *PHILIPPIANS 2:8*

> I used to wander off until you disciplined me; but now I closely follow your word.
> *PSALM 119:67*

 | **DISCUSSION STARTERS**

When do you find it especially hard to obey your parents, your teacher, your boss, or God? What do you think makes that especially difficult?

How does it help you to know that Jesus understands what it is like to obey in doing something very difficult?

In what ways can you learn obedience from the suffering or difficult situations in your life?

You are free, yet you are God's slaves, so don't use your freedom as an excuse to do evil.

1 PETER 2:16

Obviously, I'm not trying to win the approval of people, but of God. If pleasing people were my goal, I would not be Christ's servant.

GALATIANS 1:10

A servant of the Lord must not quarrel but must be kind to everyone, be able to teach, and be patient with difficult people.

2 TIMOTHY 2:24

Slaves by Choice

"Hello, I'm Bill Jones. I'm a real estate agent in Springfield."

"I'm Christopher. I'm on the varsity basketball team."

"Hello, I'm Ashley Smith. I'm friends with Taylor."

These are the ways we typically introduce ourselves to people we are meeting for the first time. We try to figure out what to tell the other person about ourselves that will give us a sense of identity and credibility in their eyes.

The first thing we say about ourselves or the way we identify ourselves when we meet someone new makes a strong statement about how we see ourselves. It says a lot about what we believe is important about us. This helps us understand the significance of the way Paul, James, Peter, and John introduce themselves at the beginning of their letters. Each of these writers introduces himself the same way—as a bond servant or slave of Jesus Christ (SEE ROMANS 1:1; JAMES 1:1; 2 PETER 1:1; AND REVELATION 1:1). It's as if each writer is saying, "The most important thing about me is that I've made Jesus Christ my master. Obeying him is the focus of my life. He is so precious to me that I've willingly bonded myself to him as his servant for life." *Bond servant* doesn't just describe them; it defines them. It shows they know they've been bought by Christ and are owned by him. They have submitted themselves completely to do whatever pleases him.

Becoming a bond servant is not just for super-saints. It is the calling of every believer—to define ourselves as servants of Jesus.

 | DISCUSSION STARTERS

Think about a recent time when you introduced yourself. What did your choice of words show about what you see as significant about yourself?

What would be difficult about being a slave? How is it different to be a slave of Christ compared to being a slave of another person?

How might seeing yourself as a bond servant to Christ impact how you pray?

Hell

Eternal punishment is not a topic most people really want to talk about. And if anyone can discuss it casually with no sense of sadness, he or she must not have considered its realities. The Bible describes hell as a place of blackest darkness, unrelenting torment, unquenchable thirst, and burning fires.

Hell is so horrible that some people have come to the conclusion that a loving God would not send people there. But Jesus spoke often of hell and the people who will go there. Thirteen percent of his teachings refer to eternal judgment and hell. Two-thirds of his parables relate to resurrection and judgment. Jesus wasn't being cruel or dramatic. He was telling the truth that people need to hear about hell.

Gehenna was the name of a rubbish dump outside the walls of Jerusalem, infamous for its unending smolder and decay. People threw their trash—including garbage and animal carcasses—into this pit, where a fire was continually burning. Jesus used Gehenna as a word picture of hell, the place where the "worm does not die, and the fire is not quenched" (MARK 9:48, NIV). Jesus described the duration of heaven and hell with the same adjective: *eternal.* "They will go away into eternal punishment, but the righteous will go into eternal life" (MATTHEW 25:46). Hell lasts as long as heaven.

God doesn't want people to go to hell—that's why he provided a way of salvation for us. But a just God cannot allow evil to go unpunished. Hell is the place where evil will be punished. And the greatest evil in the universe is for a person to choose not to trust God—to deny him and reject his offer of salvation.

> They will go away into eternal punishment, but the righteous will go into eternal life.
> **MATTHEW 25:46**

> The rich man shouted, "Father Abraham, have some pity! Send Lazarus over here to dip the tip of his finger in water and cool my tongue. I am in anguish in these flames."
> **LUKE 16:24**

> The smoke of their torment will rise forever and ever, and they will have no relief day or night.
> **REVELATION 14:11**

| DISCUSSION STARTERS

What are some ways you picture hell in your mind?

Who will go to hell?

When Paul thought about those who had not embraced Christ, he said, "My heart is filled with bitter sorrow and unending grief" (Romans 9:2). How do you feel about the eternal future of those you know who have rejected Christ?

He's Got
the Whole World . . .

"**H**e's got the whole world in his hands. He's got the whole world in his hands. . . ." Have you ever sung that song? If God has the whole world in his hands, then he can do whatever he wants with it, right? He's in charge. Jesus affirmed this when he prayed to his father, "May your will be done on earth, as it is in heaven" (MATTHEW 6:10).

People talk about God's will a lot, and really there are two aspects about the will of God we need to grasp. Both are true, and both are important to understand and believe in. There is the sovereign will of God—what God has planned for history that always comes to pass, without fail. Then there is the revealed will of God—the way God wants us to live—which is clearly revealed in the Bible. This part of the will of God does not always come to pass because of the fallenness of this world and our disobedience.

The will of God is the way he works out his divine plan for all things. That includes small things: "Not a single sparrow can fall to the ground without your Father knowing it" (MATTHEW 10:29). And it includes big things: "The king's heart is like a stream of water directed by the LORD; he guides it wherever he pleases" (PROVERBS 21:1). Nothing and no one can hinder God's sovereign will.

All the people of the earth are nothing compared to him. He does as he pleases among the angels of heaven and among the people of the earth.
DANIEL 4:35

The LORD of Heaven's Armies has sworn this oath: "It will all happen as I have planned. It will be as I have decided. . . . I have a plan for the whole earth, a hand of judgment upon all the nations.
ISAIAH 14:24, 26

Because we are united with Christ, we have received an inheritance from God, for he chose us in advance, and he makes everything work out according to his plan.
EPHESIANS 1:11

 | ## DISCUSSION STARTERS

Can you think of anything that God does not have in his hands or is not in charge of?

Can people look back at choices they made or things they did in the past and say that they missed God's will?

If God is working out his sovereign plan, what is he working all things toward?

Names You Should Never Forget

When you meet someone new, is it easy for you to remember that person's name? Or do you struggle to remember people's names and then feel embarrassed when you forget?

God has many names for himself that he wants us to remember. Each of his names tells us something about who he is. And the more we remember them, the more precious he becomes to us—the more we see how he is able to provide for our every need.

When we are in need and God's resources are at hand, we experience *Yahweh-Yireh*: the Lord provides (SEE GENESIS 22:14). When we are sick and God brings relief, we experience *Yahweh-Rophi*: the Lord who heals (SEE EXODUS 15:26). When we find ourselves in a spiritual battle and God gives us victory, we experience *Yahweh-Nissi*: the Lord our banner (SEE EXODUS 17:15). When God gives us a desire for holiness, we experience *Yahweh-M'Kaddesh*: the Lord who sanctifies (SEE EXODUS 31:13). When our anxiety is overcome by God's peace, we experience *Yahweh-Shalom*: the Lord is peace (SEE JUDGES 6:24). When God gives us victory over any evil that threatens us, we experience *Yahweh-Sabaoth*: the Lord of hosts (SEE 1 SAMUEL 17:45). When God lovingly brings us back into the fold from our wanderings, we experience *Yahweh-Rohi*: the Lord my shepherd (SEE PSALM 23). When we accept the sinless perfection of Christ in place of our own sinfulness, we experience *Yahweh-Tsidkenu*: the Lord our righteousness (SEE JEREMIAH 23:6). When we feel lonely and find God reaching out to us, we experience *Yahweh-Shammah*: the Lord who is there (SEE EZEKIEL 48:35). We don't want to forget God's names! They each tell us something special about who God is and how he wants to give himself to us.

> The LORD is a shelter for the oppressed, a refuge in times of trouble. Those who know your name trust in you.
>
> **PSALM 9:9-10**

> The name of the LORD is a strong fortress; the godly run to him and are safe.
>
> **PROVERBS 18:10**

> Everyone who calls on the name of the LORD will be saved.
>
> **ROMANS 10:13**

♟♟ | DISCUSSION STARTERS

What are some of the most unusual or interesting names you've ever heard of?

Which name of God shows you something you haven't known or experienced with God?

Which name of God is most precious to you? Why?

Making Something of Ourselves

Did you know that there are more than 6,800 known languages spoken in the two hundred countries of the world? Where do all the languages in the world come from—and all the people groups? The Bible tells us in Genesis.

God had given clear instructions after the Flood for people to "be fruitful and multiply. Fill the earth" (GENESIS 9:1). But they weren't spreading. They were clustering. They were refusing to scatter and fill the earth, and they were trying to make something of themselves that would be impressive. They were trying to make themselves feel safe and secure by building an immense tower and by grouping together instead of spreading out. It was a classic example of human pride and rebellion toward God's specific instruction.

So God came down and dealt a blow to their disobedience and made their clustering impossible. They began speaking different languages and couldn't understand each other, so they stopped building their city and scattered all over the world. Humanity was broken into many peoples and languages, and all the alienation and conflict throughout history has been the result.

We're not meant to find our security in our connection to other people but in our connection to God. And God doesn't intend for us to look for praise for ourselves. He wants us to find our fulfillment and joy in praising him and making him famous.

At one time all the people of the world spoke the same language and used the same words. . . . They said, "Come, let's build a great city for ourselves with a tower that reaches into the sky. This will make us famous and keep us from being scattered all over the world."
GENESIS 11:1, 4

Everyone present was filled with the Holy Spirit and began speaking in other languages, as the Holy Spirit gave them this ability.
ACTS 2:4

I saw a vast crowd, too great to count, from every nation and tribe and people and language, standing in front of the throne and before the Lamb . . . shouting with a great roar, "Salvation comes from our God who sits on the throne and from the Lamb!"
REVELATION 7:9-10

 | **DISCUSSION STARTERS**

Have you ever tried to communicate with someone who speaks another language? What made it difficult?

We might not try to build a city with a huge tower to make us feel secure. But what are some things people today look to for security instead of putting their hope in God?

Looking at the three verses on the left, how has God already begun to restore and redeem his judgment on the tower builders? How will he complete it?

Why Do You Eat and Drink?

What did you have for dinner tonight? Was it roast beef or spaghetti or tacos? Did you drink water or milk or lemonade? And more important, did you eat and drink to the glory of God?

That's kind of a hard question to answer, isn't it? Maybe you would say, "I just ate it. I didn't know it had anything to do with God." But God wants to be involved and considered in even the most ordinary aspects of our lives. Sin is not just a list of bad things people do (like stealing and lying and killing). Sin is anything we do that we don't do for the glory of God. It is living life apart from him with no thought of him. To do all things for the glory of God is to reorient everything about our lives so they revolve around him. It is to consider him and his Kingdom purposes in everything we do.

So how do you eat spaghetti and drink lemonade to the glory of God? You begin by receiving it as a gift from him, offering a prayer of gratitude. You put others first—which may mean you don't take the biggest, best meatball for yourself. You make choices about what you eat, how you eat, and who you eat with based not on what pleases you but on what pleases God. You see your meal as God providing you with what you need so you can live all out for him.

 | ## DISCUSSION STARTERS

What is your favorite meal? How can you eat it to God's glory?

Does doing everything to God's glory have more to do with what we do, how we do it, or why we do it?

What are some ways your family can bring glory to God at your dinner table?

> Whether you eat or drink, or whatever you do, do it all for the glory of God.
> *1 CORINTHIANS 10:31*

> God has given each of you a gift from his great variety of spiritual gifts. Use them well to serve one another. . . . Then everything you do will bring glory to God through Jesus Christ.
> *1 PETER 4:10-11*

> Since everything God created is good, we should not reject any of it but receive it with thanks. For we know it is made acceptable by the word of God and prayer.
> *1 TIMOTHY 4:4-5*

Enough

I was given a thorn in my flesh, a messenger from Satan to torment me and keep me from getting proud. Three different times I begged the Lord to take it away. Each time he said, "My grace is all you need. My power works best in weakness."

2 CORINTHIANS 12:7-9

I can do everything through Christ, who gives me strength.

PHILIPPIANS 4:13

Is there something you really, really want that you think you can't live without? Something that you think, *If only I had it, I could be happy?*

Paul had something he really, really wanted. He asked God three times to take away a "thorn" in his flesh. We don't know what it was. It might have been something physical, like blindness. It might have been something relational, like a person who always criticized him.

While we don't know what the problem was, we know how God responded to his request. Jesus spoke to Paul, but he didn't tell him that he would do what Paul had asked. Instead, Jesus assured him that he would be enough for Paul even if he didn't remove the thorn.

What Jesus was saying to Paul—and what he says to us—is "If you have me, you have everything you need. In me you will find everything you need to endure anything. I will provide what you need in the form, amount, and timing that you need it. I am enough for you."

When we start to believe that Jesus is enough for us, we can begin to let go of some of the other things we hold on to for security. We can let go of our fear that somehow we are going to end up cheated or deprived—that someone else is going to get more than we are or that we won't have what we need to make it in life. If we believe Jesus is enough for us, we don't have to fear loneliness, weakness, sickness, poverty, or failure. We take him at his word that his gracious favor is all that we need. It will be enough. Jesus is enough.

 | ## DISCUSSION STARTERS

Is there anything you think you don't have enough of right now? Toys? Technology? Savings? Clothes? Affirmation? Respect? Opportunities?

Is there something that feels like a "thorn" in your life—something you want God to take away?

How could it change your circumstances or your attitude about your circumstances to believe that God's grace is enough for you?

What Will You Do with Your Gift?

Have you ever watched someone make a campfire? If so, you know that it can burn strong for a while, but then it gets reduced to a pile of glowing pieces of wood. Eventually, these embers will become cold and hard if left alone. But if you want to get the fire roaring again, you can use a stick to stir up the embers, gently blow or fan them, and add additional wood, and the flame will burn strong again.

The gifts God gives to us are like a fire that frequently needs to be stirred up and fanned as well as fed with fuel. Every believer has a gift that he or she is responsible to use for God's glory and for the good of other people. It's our responsibility to examine ourselves to find the ember of ability or inclination that God has uniquely given to us and then figure out what it will take to fan that gift into a roaring flame of service to God. You might need someone you trust who knows you well to help you identify your gift. And perhaps you'll need to develop your gift through study or practice or discipline. What you don't want to do is ignore it.

Jesus said, "Whoever would be great among you must be your servant" (MARK 10:43, ESV). True greatness in the Kingdom of God is servanthood. God intends for you to serve by using your unique gift for the benefit of others. So if you have any desire to be truly great, find out what your gift is and use it to serve the world around you—for Jesus' sake.

 | **DISCUSSION STARTERS**

What gifts or special abilities do you see people using for God?

What gifts has God given you that can be used for him? (Remember, if it's a gift from God, it's not prideful to identify it, and it's foolish to hide it!)

How could you "fan into flames" the gifts you've been given?

This is why I remind you to fan into flames the spiritual gift God gave you when I laid my hands on you.
2 TIMOTHY 1:6

God's gifts and his call can never be withdrawn.
ROMANS 11:29

God has given each of you a gift from his great variety of spiritual gifts. Use them well to serve one another. Do you have the gift of speaking? Then speak as though God himself were speaking through you. Do you have the gift of helping others? Do it with all the strength and energy that God supplies.
1 PETER 4:10-11

God is Spirit, so those who worship him must worship in spirit and in truth.

JOHN 4:24

The person who is joined to the Lord is one spirit with him.

1 CORINTHIANS 6:17

Then the dust will return to the earth, and the spirit will return to God who gave it.

ECCLESIASTES 12:7

What Is God Made Of?

We often look on the packaging of food we buy to see the list of ingredients. We want to see what the food is made of. And we look at the labels on our clothes to see what kind of fibers have been woven into the fabric.

Have you ever wondered what God is made of? We know he doesn't have a body of flesh and blood like we do. But what kind of matter or material forms his being? Is he just a ball of energy or merely an idea in people's minds?

Jesus told us what God is made of. He is spirit. What does it mean that God is spirit? It means that he exists as a being that isn't made of any matter; he has no parts or dimensions. We can't detect him with our bodily senses, and he doesn't have a size or shape. He is more excellent than any other kind of existence. His very being is unlike anything else in creation. Anything we try to compare him to falls short.

God is fully spirit and we are not, but he has still made us in his own image. God has given us spirits so we can worship him and unite with his spirit even while we're here on earth. And when we die and go from this life into the presence of God, it is our spirits, not our bodies, that will return to God.

 | **DISCUSSION STARTERS**

Look at the items that are sitting on your table. What are they made of?

What are some of the ways people try to define what God is like or what he's made of?

What do you think it means to be "one spirit with him" (1 Corinthians 6:17)?

Boasting

"I can top that!" Do you ever catch yourself saying or thinking that sentence when someone else tells you about an exciting experience or shows you a prized possession or describes a successful accomplishment? Everybody is tempted to one-up the other person—to have a better story, to show more knowledge, to be more impressive, or to be better connected. And when we give in to that temptation to make ourselves look good, it is called boasting.

Boasting about yourself—your accomplishments, your possessions, your looks, your connections—is taking credit for the distinctive abilities, gifts, and opportunities God has given you.

But there is a good kind of boasting. It is boasting in God. You can never exaggerate the greatness of God, because he is infinitely greater than we could ever imagine or describe. When we boast in the Lord, we say through our words and actions that we're relying on who Jesus is and what he has done for us rather than on our own strength. We see every good thing in our lives as a gift from him. We realize we have done nothing to earn or deserve the favor of God, but he has chosen to love us. And that is our only boast: "Jesus loves me, this I know."

> What do you have that God hasn't given you? And if everything you have is from God, why boast as though it were not a gift?
> **1 CORINTHIANS 4:7**

> If I must boast, I would rather boast about the things that show how weak I am.
> **2 CORINTHIANS 11:30**

> As for me, may I never boast about anything except the cross of our Lord Jesus Christ.
> **GALATIANS 6:14**

🥛 | DISCUSSION STARTERS

Think about recent conversations with your friends. What did you or the other people boast about?

How can we use the gifts God has given us with confidence and humility, and without boasting?

What verse from the Bible would you like to think about when you are tempted to boast?

On the first day of the appointed month in early autumn, you are to observe a day of complete rest. It will be an official day for holy assembly, a day commemorated with loud blasts of a trumpet.

LEVITICUS 23:24

When you have eaten your fill, be sure to praise the LORD your God for the good land he has given you. But that is the time to be careful! Beware that in your plenty you do not forget the LORD your God and disobey his commands, regulations, and decrees that I am giving you today.

DEUTERONOMY 8:10-11

The Lord himself will come down from heaven with a commanding shout, with the voice of the archangel, and with the trumpet call of God.

1 THESSALONIANS 4:16

Sound the Alarm

When a tornado siren goes off, it warns us to take cover. When a smoke detector goes off, it alerts us there might be a fire. When a trumpet was blasted in Old Testament times, it was sounding an alarm, giving a warning to the people of Israel. Why did Israel need to be alarmed?

The people in ancient Israel needed to be periodically awakened from their apathy and careless attitudes toward God. God knew that as his people experienced his goodness, they would have the tendency to drift away and think that their comfortable lives were the result of their own efforts rather than God's blessing. He also knew that when things were going fine in their lives, they would become less sensitive to sin. So God set up a yearly holiday called the Festival of Trumpets to blast the people out of their spiritual laziness. The sound of the trumpet served as a reminder for the people to examine themselves and recognize God's provision in their lives as well as their need for God's grace.

Sometimes we, too, need to be alarmed by our shallow spiritual conditions. We need to wake up from our spiritual sleep and get rid of the sin that is threatening to take over our hearts and lives.

 | **DISCUSSION STARTERS**

What are the consequences of ignoring warning sirens or alarms?

What kinds of things does God use to "sound the alarm" about sin in our lives?

What are some ways you can make sure you don't forget God in the midst of your blessings?

I Can Do It Myself

"I don't need any help. I can do it myself." Have you ever said that? At one time or another, most of us want to prove that we are capable enough, smart enough, or strong enough to do things on our own. We don't want to be seen as weak or needy.

The Bible calls this determined self-sufficiency *pride*. It also tells us that God hates pride (*hate* is a pretty strong word, isn't it?) and that God opposes the proud. Rather than applauding the person who has an "I can do it myself" attitude, God actually turns away from or goes against that person.

So what is God looking for instead of pride and self-sufficiency? He wants us to admit that we can't go through life without him, that we don't have what it takes to create a meaningful life on our own. We need to acknowledge that we aren't strong enough to overcome our sinful desires and we aren't smart enough to understand what is right and true. In other words, God wants us to admit that we need him. Faith is an ongoing dependence on God in place of dependence on ourselves. Rather than hearing us say, "I can do it myself," God longs to hear, "God, I need you. I can't do it on my own."

🧂🧂 | DISCUSSION STARTERS

When are some times you need the help of others or the help of God?

Why do you think God hates pride?

What are some practical ways we can battle pride and cultivate humility in our lives?

SEPTEMBER 20

Haughty eyes, a proud heart, and evil actions are all sin.
PROVERBS 21:4

You say, "I am rich. I have everything I want. I don't need a thing!" And you don't realize that you are wretched and miserable and poor and blind and naked.
REVELATION 3:17

"God opposes the proud but favors the humble." So humble yourselves under the mighty power of God, and at the right time he will lift you up in honor.
1 PETER 5:5–6

You're at War

I love God's law with all my heart. But there is another power within me that is at war with my mind. This power makes me a slave to the sin that is still within me. Oh, what a miserable person I am! Who will free me from this life that is dominated by sin and death?

ROMANS 7:22-24

We are human, but we don't wage war as humans do. We use God's mighty weapons, not worldly weapons, to knock down the strongholds of human reasoning and to destroy false arguments.

2 CORINTHIANS 10:3-4

Who can win this battle against the world? Only those who believe that Jesus is the Son of God.

1 JOHN 5:5

Imagine what it would be like to wake up to gunfire and exploding grenades all around you. One minute you were comfortable in your bed, and the next you were under attack!

That's what happens to us as believers. We can be going along enjoying life when suddenly we find ourselves assaulted by a flurry of doubts, attacked by gripping fears, or burned by difficulty or suffering. But it shouldn't surprise us. The Bible says we're in a war "against evil rulers and authorities of the unseen world, against mighty powers in this dark world, and against evil spirits in the heavenly places" (EPHESIANS 6:12). When you leave behind a life of death and slavery to sin and enter into a new life with Jesus, Satan declares war against you. He uses every means he can to urge you to satisfy yourself with anything other than Christ, and to tempt you to doubt God's goodness.

If you are a Christian, there's a war going on inside of you. You're going to be victorious in the end, but not without many battles, occasional defeats, wounds, and scars. The Spirit inside you will win against the powers of darkness in this world, but know that you've got a fight on your hands.

 | **DISCUSSION STARTERS**

How does a person who's at war live differently from someone who isn't?

What are some of the tactics Satan uses in his war against your soul?

What is your part in fighting this battle? What is God's part?

264

Weapons of Warfare

Imagine heading into a battle with no armor to protect you and no weapons to fight with. You would be a sitting duck—an easy target—for the enemy. But God has not sent us into battle without any weapons. He has given us everything we need to fight the spiritual battles in our lives.

In ancient Rome, a soldier used a belt to cinch up the loosely hanging material of his tunic or robe. He would pull in the loose ends as a way to prepare for battle. The belt of truth pulls together all the spiritual loose ends in our lives. It deals with confusion and error. The body armor of righteousness is the increasing reality of holy living that makes us less vulnerable to flaming arrows of temptation. We wear shoes of peace, showing that we are no longer enemies of God but friends because of what Jesus has done for us. This gives us confidence to confront any accusations the devil might whisper in our ears to defeat us. The shield of faith is our continual trust in God to fulfill his promises to us. It deflects the lies that try to convince us that the world will satisfy us more than God will. The biblical truths about salvation are a helmet, preserving our confidence and protecting us from doubt and discouragement. Spiritual warfare is fought in the mind, the emotions, and the will, and the truth of God's words is our weapon of defense.

 | ## DISCUSSION STARTERS

In movies, TV shows, or books, what kind of armor do soldiers use to protect themselves?

How does a person put on spiritual armor?

When we lose a spiritual battle, is it because our armor has failed?

We are not fighting against flesh-and-blood enemies, but against evil rulers and authorities of the unseen world, against mighty powers in this dark world, and against evil spirits in the heavenly places. Therefore, put on every piece of God's armor so you will be able to resist the enemy in the time of evil. Then after the battle you will still be standing firm. Stand your ground, putting on the belt of truth and the body armor of God's righteousness. For shoes, put on the peace that comes from the Good News so that you will be fully prepared. In addition to all of these, hold up the shield of faith to stop the fiery arrows of the devil. Put on salvation as your helmet, and take the sword of the Spirit, which is the word of God.

EPHESIANS 6:12-17

God is greater than our feelings, and he knows everything.

1 JOHN 3:20

O LORD, you have examined my heart and know everything about me. You know when I sit down or stand up. You know my thoughts even when I'm far away. You see me when I travel and when I rest at home. You know everything I do. You know what I am going to say even before I say it, LORD. You go before me and follow me. You place your hand of blessing on my head. Such knowledge is too wonderful for me, too great for me to understand!

PSALM 139:1-6

God Knows

There used to be a commercial on television where a guy sitting in front of his computer screen gets this message: "You have now reached the end of the Internet." We laugh at the thought of it because we can't imagine ever coming to the point that we've seen everything there is to see on the Internet, let alone *knowing* everything that is there.

If the Internet is that vast, what does that say about the knowledge of God? Because God knows literally everything there is to know. Nothing has escaped him. God fully knows everything about himself and about all things in creation, not to mention all possible things, including events that might happen but don't.

If God wanted to tell us how many grains of sand are on the seashore or how many stars are in the sky or how many hairs are on our heads, he wouldn't have to count them quickly or compute the answer on some sort of massive computer. He doesn't have to try to get his mind working to remember or do some calculations to come to any conclusions. He never learns anything new that he didn't already know. And he never forgets anything.

Perhaps the most amazing part of God's knowledge is his knowledge of us. He knows everything about us—how we think, what we want, where we're headed. He knows our pasts as well as our futures. And he loves us.

DISCUSSION STARTERS

What is something you know now that you didn't know last week?

How do you feel about being so intimately known by God?

What would it mean if there were something God did not know?

Will Your Work Survive?

What happens if you throw a bunch of wood or hay on a fire? It will burn, right? And soon there will be nothing left. But what happens if you throw a gold brick or a chunk of silver or a diamond into the fire? The fire may burn around it, but it won't consume the gold, silver, or jewels.

Paul used this picture to help us understand what is going to happen on the Day of Judgment. He said that all of us will stand before the Judge—Jesus—and that all our "good works" will be put to the test in the fire. It won't be our beliefs that will be tested that day, and our deeds won't determine whether we're in or out of heaven. But on that day Jesus will test our works—not only what we did but also how and why we did those things. Any good works we've done on our own to build our reputation rather than God's, anything done with a secret motive of getting something in return, will burn up.

One day each of us will give an account to God for how we've used what he has entrusted to us to build his Kingdom. And on that day, everything we've done for Christ to the glory of God will add to our eternal joy.

 | ## DISCUSSION STARTERS

What kinds of things burn up quickly when you put them in a fire?

On the Day of Judgment, what kinds of things do you think will burn up quickly in the test of our good works? What will make it through the fire?

Do you think it's possible for us to tell if someone else's good works will survive the fire? Why or why not?

Who will be able to endure it when he comes? Who will be able to stand and face him when he appears? For he will be like a blazing fire that refines metal, or like a strong soap that bleaches clothes. He will sit like a refiner of silver, burning away the dross.
MALACHI 3:2-3

On the judgment day, fire will reveal what kind of work each builder has done. The fire will show if a person's work has any value. If the work survives, that builder will receive a reward. But if the work is burned up, the builder will suffer great loss. The builder will be saved, but like someone barely escaping through a wall of flames.
1 CORINTHIANS 3:13-15

Forgiving Those Who Don't Get It

When someone does something that hurts you, what is your first reaction? Do you want to hurt that person back? Do you want to make him or her pay, or at least make sure the person understands what he or she has done wrong? Most of us do. In fact, everything in us rebels against forgiving someone who just doesn't get what he or she has done or simply is not sorry.

But Jesus proposed a radical way to respond to people who hurt us. He suggested that we pray for them. Jesus himself went beyond preaching this radical forgiveness. He lived it out at the lowest, hardest moment of his life—as he was being nailed to the cross. Hanging on the cross, he asked God the Father to forgive the people who didn't get it when they rejected and killed their only source of salvation—the Son of God.

And for all the people who didn't get it, the day is coming when they will. They will feel the pain of regret over their rejection of and hatred toward Jesus. Revelation 1:7 describes the scene: "Look! He comes with the clouds of heaven. And everyone will see him—even those who pierced him. And all the nations of the world will mourn for him."

We don't have enough love on our own to forgive like Jesus. But he can fill us with his love so that we, too, can forgive those who hurt us—even when they're not sorry and don't even get how they've hurt us.

You have heard the law that says, "Love your neighbor" and hate your enemy. But I say, love your enemies! Pray for those who persecute you! In that way, you will be acting as true children of your Father in heaven.
MATTHEW 5:43-45

Jesus said, "Father, forgive them, for they don't know what they are doing."
LUKE 23:34

The wisdom we speak of is the mystery of God—his plan that was previously hidden, even though he made it for our ultimate glory before the world began. But the rulers of this world have not understood it; if they had, they would not have crucified our glorious Lord.
1 CORINTHIANS 2:7-8

 | DISCUSSION STARTERS

Does someone have to be sorry in order for you to be willing to forgive him or her?

When Jesus said, "They don't know what they are doing," what do you think he meant?

What does Jesus' example tell us about how to respond to those who don't deserve our forgiveness?

Escape Clause

Most airplanes and submarines have an escape hatch. It's a door that opens to provide a way out in an emergency. Similarly, many legal contracts have what is called an escape clause. It describes a way out of the contract without having to fulfill the agreement.

Some people think that to pray passionately for something and then to follow it with "if it be your will" is giving God an escape clause—a way out of doing what we're asking him to do. But saying "if it be your will" is not giving God an escape clause or helping him save face. It is a humble recognition that we can't presume to know what God will do. It's a commitment to trust God regardless of what he does.

Shadrach, Meshach, and Abednego didn't pretend that they knew what God would do in their situation when they were thrown into a blazing hot furnace, and there is no evidence that they cried out to God telling him what they thought he *should* do. Because they knew God and trusted God, they believed he would do what was right, even if it resulted in their deaths. Their commitment was to remain true to God no matter what. They knew God needs no escape clause. He can be trusted to always do what is right.

 | **DISCUSSION STARTERS**

Have you ever felt trapped inside a space and in need of a way out?

Which do you think would have required more genuine faith for Shadrach, Meshach, and Abednego—to believe God would save them from a fiery death or to commit to love him even if he didn't?

Read about some people of faith in Hebrews 11:29-39. What does this list show us about what faith looks like when God saves and when he does not?

Even though the fig trees have no blossoms, and there are no grapes on the vines; even though the olive crop fails, and the fields lie empty and barren; even though the flocks die in the fields, and the cattle barns are empty, yet I will rejoice in the LORD! I will be joyful in the God of my salvation!

HABAKKUK 3:17-18

Shadrach, Meshach, and Abednego replied, "O Nebuchadnezzar, we do not need to defend ourselves before you. If we are thrown into the blazing furnace, the God whom we serve is able to save us. He will rescue us from your power, Your Majesty. But even if he doesn't, we want to make it clear to you, Your Majesty, that we will never serve your gods or worship the gold statue you have set up."

DANIEL 3:16-18

On the tenth day of the appointed month in early autumn, you must deny yourselves. . . . On that day offerings of purification will be made for you, and you will be purified in the LORD's presence from all your sins.
LEVITICUS 16:29-30

It's your sins that have cut you off from God. Because of your sins, he has turned away and will not listen anymore.
ISAIAH 59:2

Unlike those other high priests, he does not need to offer sacrifices every day. They did this for their own sins first and then for the sins of the people. But Jesus did this once for all when he offered himself as the sacrifice for the people's sins.
HEBREWS 7:27

Cleaning Day

Some people are pickier about cleanliness than others. While some of us can live in a messy room or eat in an unsanitary kitchen, others can't. Cleanliness is very important to God. Not so much personal cleanliness, but spiritual cleanliness. God cannot tolerate the filthiness of sin in his presence.

To help us understand this, in Old Testament times God made himself at home in the Holy of Holies, a special room in the Jewish Temple that could only be entered by the high priest once a year. And even the high priest could enter only after he had cleansed himself carefully. God instructed the people of Israel to do an annual cleaning— a day set aside to cleanse God's holy dwelling place—by making sacrifices for their sin. It wasn't dust and dirt that God wanted cleaned out. It was the uncleanness of his people's sinful attitudes and actions.

On that solemn day, the people of Israel fasted and prayed to God for forgiveness while the priest offered sacrifices. The sacrifices would cover the impurity of their sin for another year. But it was no permanent solution to the problem of sin. That special day foreshadowed and anticipated a greater, permanent cleansing of God's people and of his dwelling place—the hearts and lives of believers. The day of cleansing to come would be accomplished by a special priest—Jesus—who did not need a cleansing ceremony. He was already perfectly clean. Christ's death took care of our sin problem for good. He washed away our sin with his blood so we can become holy enough to live in God's home with him forever.

☕ | DISCUSSION STARTERS

How much mess and dirt can you tolerate?

Why do you think God set aside a special day of cleansing for his people?

This special day was a time to reflect and mourn over sin. Would you and your family benefit from a time set aside for this?

The Scapegoat

Have you ever heard someone described as a scapegoat? It's someone who takes the blame that really belongs to someone else. For example, when the teacher demands to know who turned all the desks upside down while she was gone and one student steps up and says he did it, when really a large group of students participated, he's the scapegoat.

The Bible says that all of us have sinned. We're all guilty. And the punishment for sin is death. But God has provided a scapegoat—someone who will take on himself all the blame for our sin. He gave us a visible picture of this in the Old Testament observance of the annual Day of Atonement. On that day, two goats were chosen. One goat was killed to provide a picture of the death of a substitute for sin. The priest put his hands on the other goat—the scapegoat—and confessed the people's sins. By doing this, he ceremonially transferred the sin to the goat. Then the scapegoat was sent out into the wilderness to take the sin away from the community.

When Jesus died, he became the scapegoat for all the wrongs we've done. Like the goat in Old Testament times, he was innocent but he took the blame for our sin on himself. And through his death, he carried our sin far away so that we don't have to live under a heavy weight of guilt and shame. Just as the guilt for sin was placed on the scapegoat and it went off into the wilderness never to be seen again, so Christ has taken on our sin and removed it so that it can never be thrown back in our faces. Now we can enjoy the complete forgiveness of God.

> He will lay both of his hands on the goat's head and confess over it all the wickedness, rebellion, and sins of the people of Israel. In this way, he will transfer the people's sins to the head of the goat. Then a man specially chosen for the task will drive the goat into the wilderness. As the goat goes into the wilderness, it will carry all the people's sins upon itself into a desolate land.
>
> *LEVITICUS 16:21-22*

> He has removed our sins as far from us as the east is from the west.
>
> *PSALM 103:12*

🧂 | DISCUSSION STARTERS

Have you ever observed a person or group be made into a scapegoat?

In what ways is Jesus as our scapegoat better than the scapegoat the Israelites had in Old Testament times?

What difference does it make in your life to truly understand that your sin is gone?

Seventy Times Seven

Forgiveness is not easy. When someone hurts you, it's hard to resist becoming resentful or trying to make the other person pay. But when that person does the same thing to you a second time, it is even harder to forgive. You feel like that person is not at all sorry and is taking advantage of you.

The religious leaders in Jesus' day taught that you should forgive someone two times, but if the person hurts you a third time, you were not obligated to forgive. So when Peter suggested that perhaps you should forgive up to seven times, he thought he was going far beyond what could be expected of anybody. He thought it only reasonable to set some limits on forgiveness to avoid being taken advantage of. And he was sure Jesus would give him a pat on the back for his generosity.

But Jesus said he should forgive not seven times but seventy times seven times. Jesus said to keep on forgiving beyond what is reasonable. In other words, forgive others the way you've been forgiven—because God has forgiven you far more than seven times. He's forgiven too many times to count! You see, when God offers us forgiveness, he is opening himself up to being taken advantage of. And he keeps on forgiving.

To be in Christ is to live in an atmosphere of overflowing forgiveness. And our willingness—or our resistance—to generously forgive others reveals whether or not we're really breathing in that air.

Peter came to him and asked, "Lord, how often should I forgive someone who sins against me? Seven times?"

"No, not seven times," Jesus replied, "but seventy times seven!"

MATTHEW 18:21-22

Where is another God like you, who pardons the guilt of the remnant, overlooking the sins of his special people? You will not stay angry with your people forever, because you delight in showing unfailing love.

MICAH 7:18

 | DISCUSSION STARTERS

How does it feel when someone hurts you the same way more than once?

What do you think Jesus meant when he said we should forgive seventy times seven times?

How can seeing God as a generous forgiver help us to forgive those who have hurt us?

Showing Respect

Have you ever given an older woman your seat or listened to an older man tell stories about his childhood? Have you ever invited an older couple to join you for a meal or asked for advice from a grandparent or mentor? Whether you have or not, do you think these actions are just good, old-fashioned manners, or are they more than that?

Showing respect and giving honor to older people are more than good manners; they are based on God's Word and honor God himself. The respect we show (or don't show) to older people is a window into the respect (or lack of respect) we have for God. We show respect in our body language—the way we sit, stand up straight, and look an older person in the eye when he or she speaks. We avoid using disrespectful tones of voice. We show interest in what the person has to say rather than ridiculing it or simply tuning it out. These are the ways we show respect to older people and, in doing so, show respect for God.

As we grow in our respect for the Lord, our growth should show itself in respect and honor for these people he has made in his image and put in our lives for a purpose. Any disregard—like rolling our eyes at what older people say or ignoring their requests or instructions—reveals that we think we are smarter and more with it than they are, and that we think their opinions, preferences, and experiences have little value. But when we seek to brighten the lives of older people by giving them the respect they deserve, we honor what they have to offer us and the world.

Stand up in the presence of the elderly, and show respect for the aged. Fear your God. I am the Lord.
LEVITICUS 19:32

The glory of the young is their strength; the gray hair of experience is the splendor of the old.
PROVERBS 20:29

Listen to your father, who gave you life, and don't despise your mother when she is old.
PROVERBS 23:22

 | ## DISCUSSION STARTERS

What are some ways God has blessed you through having older people in your life? How have you benefited from their experience, wisdom, and love?

Why do you think older people tend to be disrespected in our society? How does it make any person feel to be ignored, ridiculed, or forgotten?

How could you be a blessing to some older people you know?

Bodies and Souls

Have you ever noticed how some salad dressings separate in the bottle? The vinegar is heavier so it settles in the bottom, while the lighter oil and seasonings sit on top. When we shake it up, it comes out mixed together. But if it sits for a while again, it will separate again.

Here on earth, we have bodies and souls that are intertwined. But the day is coming when our bodies and souls will separate. When we die, our bodies will become lifeless shells. But we will continue to exist as souls—either with Jesus in heaven or separated from him in hell.

The Bible says that when the believer's soul leaves his or her body, this person is immediately "at home with the Lord." While there is much we don't understand about heaven, we do know that when we're there, we'll feel like we've finally arrived at home. We'll be very content there as souls without bodies. But we won't be like that forever.

As great as it will be in heaven after we die, God has something even better in mind for our eternal future. He will not leave our dead bodies in the ground forever—he will raise up our bodies from the dead. But our new bodies will be so much better than our old ones—they'll be given a divine makeover so they'll be perfect and completely pleasing to God. Our souls and bodies will be reunited to live forever in the new heaven and new earth. We will live with Christ forever—with glorified bodies and souls.

I long, yes, I faint with longing to enter the courts of the LORD. With my whole being, body and soul, I will shout joyfully to the living God.
PSALM 84:2

Don't be afraid of those who want to kill your body; they cannot touch your soul. Fear only God, who can destroy both soul and body in hell.
MATTHEW 10:28

We are fully confident, and we would rather be away from these earthly bodies, for then we will be at home with the Lord.
2 CORINTHIANS 5:8

 | ### DISCUSSION STARTERS

What does it mean to feel "at home" somewhere? What are some places where you feel most at home?

Jesus had a glorified body—like ours will be someday—when he rose from the dead. What do we know about his body from things he did after he rose from the dead? (See Luke 24:13-53 and John 20–21.)

How can it give you hope now, while you're here on earth, to know that your soul will never die?

Your Inheritance

A "last will and testament" is an important and official legal document that a person writes to let people know what should be done with his or her possessions after that person dies. The people who get that person's belongings or money after he or she dies are the heirs.

God, too, has made up a will and named his heirs. "God promised everything to the Son as an inheritance," says Hebrews 1:2. In the end, Jesus will have all things under his complete control and ownership—all natural resources, all governmental power, all human intelligence, all the riches of the earth. Everything will be under his authority and command.

And while Jesus doesn't have to share the inheritance with anyone, he will! Romans 8:17 calls us "co-heirs with Christ" (NIV). Jesus will not keep his inheritance to himself. He has promised that he will share all he inherits with anyone who will trust in him. Scripture says that God's children will inherit a home in heaven, an eternal body made for us by God himself, all God's promises, and all the good things of heaven. Someday each one of us will leave this earth and let go of everyone we have loved and everything we have enjoyed. We'll be left with only our eternal inheritance. But we will not be disappointed. It will be everything we've anticipated and more.

 | **DISCUSSION STARTERS**

What kinds of things do people inherit from other people?

Wills go into effect only after death. On a spiritual level, whose death put our inheritance into effect?

How can knowing about our inheritance in heaven help us in our battle with materialism? How can it help us endure suffering?

You are no longer a slave but God's own child. And since you are his child, God has made you his heir.
GALATIANS 4:7

Since we are his children, we are his heirs. In fact, together with Christ we are heirs of God's glory.
ROMANS 8:17

The Spirit is God's guarantee that he will give us the inheritance he promised and that he has purchased us to be his own people. He did this so we would praise and glorify him.
EPHESIANS 1:14

For seven days you must live outside in little shelters. All native-born Israelites must live in shelters. This will remind each new generation of Israelites that I made their ancestors live in shelters when I rescued them from the land of Egypt. I am the LORD your God.
LEVITICUS 23:42-43

The Word became human and made his home among us.
JOHN 1:14

I heard a loud shout from the throne, saying, "Look, God's home is now among his people! He will live with them, and they will be his people. God himself will be with them."
REVELATION 21:3

Living in Tents

Spending a night or two in a tent out in the backyard or at a campground can be fun. But much longer than that and most people find themselves dreaming of the comfortable surroundings of home. Camping in a tent can remind us to be grateful for a soft bed, a hot shower, and four solid walls.

In Old Testament times, God set up a special holiday for the Jewish people—the Festival of Shelters (or Feast of Tabernacles)—to remind them of how he provided for their ancestors and was with them during the forty years they wandered in the desert after leaving Egypt. For this special holiday, he told them to make little shelters out in the open or on their rooftops and live in them for seven days. Living in the tents or shelters was a reminder of what it was like for the people in Moses' day to live in tents in the wilderness without homes to return to. It reminded them of how God provided their ancestors with manna (a breadlike food that miraculously appeared on the ground every day in the desert) and guided them from place to place with the cloud of his presence.

Living in a comfortable house with plenty of food in the refrigerator, we can forget that God is providing for us. It is easy to start thinking that our jobs give us the money we need or that we can take care of ourselves. It's easy to forget that we are dependent on God, that our homes, our jobs, our food—everything we have—all come from him. The Festival of Shelters serves as a reminder that life here is only temporary, and this earth will not be our home forever.

 | ## DISCUSSION STARTERS

What are the fun parts and not-so-fun parts of sleeping outside in a tent?

What are some ways we can celebrate and remind ourselves of God's provision and presence?

When do you find yourself forgetting your dependence on God and living like this world is your home?

Come and Drink

Humans can live for several weeks without food, but we can live for only three days without water. So drinking water is truly a matter of life and death. But water has not always been as easy to come by as it is for us today.

As part of the annual Festival of Shelters, the Jewish people celebrated God's provision of water. The priests would go down to the pool of Siloam and fill up their pitchers with water and take them back to the Temple. They would pour the water into silver containers while people shouted, "With joy you will draw water from the wells of salvation!"

It was on this day, as crowds of people were watching the priests pour the water into the containers in the Temple, that Jesus made a big announcement. He stood up and shouted for everyone to hear, "Anyone who is thirsty may come to me! Anyone who believes in me may come and drink!" He chose the most dramatic moment of the festival to make an important statement about himself. He was saying that just as God had sustained and satisfied his people with water from a rock in the wilderness in the days of Moses, he would satisfy the spiritual thirst of anyone who comes to him. In other words, he was the living fulfillment of everything this feast celebrated. Just as no one can live without drinking water, it is only by taking in the living water of Jesus that a person can live forever.

OCTOBER

4

With joy you will drink deeply from the fountain of salvation!
ISAIAH 12:3

On the last day, the climax of the festival, Jesus stood and shouted to the crowds, "Anyone who is thirsty may come to me! Anyone who believes in me may come and drink! For the Scriptures declare, 'Rivers of living water will flow from his heart.'"
JOHN 7:37-38

They drank from the spiritual rock that traveled with them, and that rock was Christ.
1 CORINTHIANS 10:4

| DISCUSSION STARTERS

During Bible times, people had to get all their water from a city well or a river and carry it back to their homes in pots. How would your attitude toward water change if this were something you had to do every day?

Try to imagine the scene from the festival when Jesus shouted out that he was the living water. Why do you think he chose that time to say this? How do you think people responded?

What do you think it means to be spiritually thirsty?

OCTOBER

5

Arise, shine, for your light has come.

ISAIAH 60:1, NIV

Jesus spoke to the people once more and said, "I am the light of the world. If you follow me, you won't have to walk in darkness, because you will have the light that leads to life."

JOHN 8:12

The city has no need of sun or moon, for the glory of God illuminates the city, and the Lamb is its light. The nations will walk in its light, and the kings of the world will enter the city in all their glory.

REVELATION 21:23-24

I Am the Light

There's a big difference in the impact of a match that is lit in the middle of the day and one lit in the dark. In the darkness, the flame is bright and its light is unavoidable, piercing through the shadows.

In Jesus' day, on six special nights during the Festival of Shelters, candles in four giant candleholders in the Temple court were set aflame. The candles illuminated the night sky all around Jerusalem. People danced through the night, holding burning torches in their hands, singing, and celebrating the way God led his people throughout history. In particular, they were remembering how, in Moses' day, God gave the Israelites a pillar of fire by night. This light guided the Israelites through the darkness of the desert as they journeyed to the Promised Land.

Jesus used this dramatic backdrop to make an astounding claim. With the candles burning bright, Jesus said for all the people to hear: "I am the light of the world. If you follow me, you won't have to walk in darkness, because you will have the light that leads to life" (JOHN 8:12). Throughout the Old Testament the promise of light was connected to the coming of the Messiah who would set things right in this dark world. And now Jesus was saying to them, *The Light is here—I am the Light you've been looking for.*

 | ## DISCUSSION STARTERS

Have you ever shone a flashlight in the nighttime? How about in the daytime? What is the difference?

In what ways was there spiritual darkness during Jesus' time? What are some ways our world today is spiritually dark?

Try to imagine the scene of the festival with all the burning torches lighting up the night sky. Why do you think Jesus chose this particular time to shout out, "I am the light of the world"?

Playing Favorites

We all have favorite people—particular friends and types of people we enjoy getting to know and spending time with more than others. We usually find it easy to be kind and caring toward these people. But the Bible says that a test of whether or not God is really at work in us is how we respond to people who are different from us—different in ways we don't like or aren't comfortable with, or in ways we think of as beneath us.

Favoritism is when we allow outward things about people to determine who we'll mistreat and who we'll flatter, who we'll pay attention to and who we'll ignore. Sometimes we show favoritism based on external things like appearance, race, wealth, popularity, or social status. This kind of unfair treatment flows out of our natural tendency to be takers instead of givers, users instead of servants. Until we are changed by the Holy Spirit into people who love like God loves—showing no favoritism—we will be nicer to people we see as having something to offer us. But when we begin to see people the way Jesus sees them, we start treating all people with respect and compassion. We start preferring all people above ourselves, regardless of where they come from, how they look, or who they are.

🧂🧂 | DISCUSSION STARTERS

Who are some of your favorite people? Why?

What types of people are you tempted to show favoritism toward? What types of people are you tempted to overlook or treat disrespectfully?

What kind of "evil motives" could James 2:4 be talking about?

Peter replied, "I see very clearly that God shows no favoritism. In every nation he accepts those who fear him and do what is right."

ACTS 10:34-35

My dear brothers and sisters, how can you claim to have faith in our glorious Lord Jesus Christ if you favor some people over others?

Suppose someone comes into your meeting dressed in fancy clothes and expensive jewelry, and another comes in who is poor and dressed in dirty clothes. If you give special attention and a good seat to the rich person, but you say to the poor one, "You can stand over there, or else sit on the floor"—well, doesn't this discrimination show that your judgments are guided by evil motives?

JAMES 2:1-4

When you give to someone in need, don't do as the hypocrites do—blowing trumpets in the synagogues and streets to call attention to their acts of charity! I tell you the truth, they have received all the reward they will ever get. . . . Give your gifts in private, and your Father, who sees everything, will reward you.

MATTHEW 6:2, 4

He will bring our darkest secrets to light and will reveal our private motives. Then God will give to each one whatever praise is due.

1 CORINTHIANS 4:5

Pleasing God or People?

Think about the last time you did something nice for someone else. Maybe you raised money for a good cause or volunteered your time to help the needy or fixed a meal for someone who was sick. Afterward, did you find a way to let people around you know what you had done? Do you like it when people see you put your money into the offering plate? Do you sometimes find yourself praying in public in a way that will make those listening think you are very spiritual?

If we're honest, we have to admit that it feels good to be admired by other people and applauded for our good works and spirituality. Jesus understood that we are tempted to practice our faith and do our good works in a way that will capture the attention of others. That's why he talked specifically about giving, praying, and fasting. He said that if the approval of people is what we're giving for and living for when we do these things, then we'd better enjoy it thoroughly, because it's all we can expect to get.

However, if our motive is to please *him* and we do these things in ways that don't draw attention to ourselves, we can be confident that he will reward us fully and eternally someday. When we turn away from the public applause of people and instead look for the private approval of God, we enjoy the secret satisfaction of his pleasure now. And we can look forward to the ultimate reward of hearing him say one day, "Well done, my good and faithful servant" (MATTHEW 25:21).

 | **DISCUSSION STARTERS**

What does it mean to give in secret, pray in secret, and fast in secret?

Why do we like for people to know about our generosity and spirituality?

What are the benefits now of keeping our giving, praying, and fasting a secret? What will be the benefits later?

What Makes for Good Worship?

For many families, the Sunday dinner table sometimes becomes an evaluation session of the morning's worship service. We give excuses for why we just couldn't worship that day. "The music was too loud." "The music was too boring." "I can't relate to that preacher." "All those kids were running in and out." "There wasn't enough liturgy." "It was too informal." "Did you see that lady dancing in the aisle?"

In reality, there is only one evaluation of worship that matters. And it is not ours. The real question is not, "Did that church experience help *me* to worship?" The real question is, "Did I worship God today in a way that is worthy of *him*?" Rather than, "Was *I* pleased with the worship experience today?" we should ask, "Was *God* pleased with my worship today?"

Worship is an authentic experience from the heart with God, or it is nothing. And true worshipers do not view songs and prayers and sermons as mere traditions or duties. They see them as ways to enjoy God and celebrate his greatness. The purpose of life is to show how valuable Christ is every day of our lives. Worship means using our minds and hearts and bodies to express the worth of God and all he is for us in Jesus. So how are you doing? Is God pleased with your worship?

 | DISCUSSION STARTERS

What makes the weekly event at your church a true worship service?

According to the verses above, when is worship displeasing to God?

How do you think God evaluated the worship you offered at church last Sunday? How about on Monday, Tuesday, and Wednesday?

OCTOBER

8

The time is coming—indeed it's here now—when true worshipers will worship the Father in spirit and in truth. The Father is looking for those who will worship him that way.
JOHN 4:23

These people honor me with their lips, but their hearts are far from me.
MATTHEW 15:8

When you lift up your hands in prayer, I will not look. Though you offer many prayers, I will not listen, for your hands are covered with the blood of innocent victims.
ISAIAH 1:15

Faith is the assurance of things hoped for, the conviction of things not seen. For by it the men of old gained approval. By faith we understand that the worlds were prepared by the word of God, so that what is seen was not made out of things which are visible.

HEBREWS 11:1-3, NASB

Without faith it is impossible to please Him, for he who comes to God must believe that He is and that He is a rewarder of those who seek Him.

HEBREWS 11:6, NASB

At last everyone will say, "There truly is a reward for those who live for God; surely there is a God who judges justly here on earth."

PSALM 58:11

Impossible to Please?

Some bosses and teachers are impossible to please. They seem to always find some fault with a person's work or effort. It can be disheartening and discouraging, making that person just want to give up trying.

Some people see God like that—impossible to please. They feel like their efforts to be good enough or do enough for God are never sufficient. But Hebrews 11 tells us clearly how people gain God's approval: by faith. Hebrews describes faith as being sure of God's promises—confident that they are worth looking forward to and living for. Faith is also believing that the one true God who made the world (not just some sort of "higher power") exists. Hebrews 11 says there is something specific we need to believe about this God: "that He is a rewarder of those who seek Him."

God is not a stingy, hard-to-please tyrant or bully. He is a generous rewarder. He gives us the desire to go after him, and then he rewards us for our pursuit of him. What is the reward God gives us? He gives grace and forgiveness. He rewards us with the righteousness of Jesus in place of our failed attempts at being right with God. But the most prized reward he gives us is himself—in closer relationship and clearer understanding.

 | ## DISCUSSION STARTERS

What kinds of things do people usually have to do to get a reward?

Do you see God as difficult to please or as a generous giver? Why?

What does it mean to seek him, as Hebrews 11:6 tells us to do?

Caring Enough to Confront

We see something in someone else that bothers us—maybe that person said or did something wrong, or maybe he or she has a habit or an attitude that is unflattering or annoying. Oftentimes our first urge is to tell someone else about it—and maybe laugh a little or start running down a list of that person's faults. But is that what a person does who loves as Christ loves?

When we see or hear about something another person did wrong and we're tempted to talk to someone else about it rather than talking to that person directly, we have the opportunity to live out Christ's love. If we've seen another person's weakness or fault, we should give that person our encouragement and support, not critical gossip. When someone we have a relationship with sins, he or she needs someone who cares enough to lovingly confront that sin with humble biblical counsel.

Talking to someone about another person's faults brings only a short-lived sense of satisfaction to our sinful human nature. Satan fools us into thinking that as we try to knock someone else down, it somehow makes us look better. But it doesn't work that way. Instead, our gossip hurts us, the person we shared it with, and the person we gossiped about. While it might feel safer to talk about people rather than talking to them, it's really not safe at all. Gossip destroys relationships and reputations. So what's the alternative? Instead of gossiping, we can choose to lovingly confront someone. It will take courage and humility, but it will be worth it.

 | ## DISCUSSION STARTERS

What does it mean to gossip?

Jesus was often blunt in confronting people about sin, yet we know he did so in perfect love. Can you think of some examples of times he did this?

Why do you think gossip is so harmful? What are some things you can do when you feel tempted to spread or listen to gossip?

OCTOBER 10

We urge you to warn those who are lazy. Encourage those who are timid. Take tender care of those who are weak. Be patient with everyone.
1 THESSALONIANS 5:14

When Peter came to Antioch, I had to oppose him to his face, for what he did was very wrong.
GALATIANS 2:11

If another believer is overcome by some sin, you who are godly should gently and humbly help that person back onto the right path.
GALATIANS 6:1

Mockers

The LORD, the God of their ancestors, repeatedly sent his prophets to warn them, for he had compassion on his people and his Temple. But the people mocked these messengers of God and despised their words. They scoffed at the prophets until the LORD's anger could no longer be restrained and nothing could be done.

2 CHRONICLES 36:15-16

Oh, the joys of those who do not follow the advice of the wicked, or stand around with sinners, or join in with mockers.

PSALM 1:1

Do you know what it means to mock someone? Mocking is ridiculing something or someone. It's being skeptical and critical, or making fun of something that's important to someone else.

Some people mock faith in God. They see it as something for unintelligent or unsophisticated people. Some mock Christianity because they look at the lives of certain Christians and don't see much difference from their own lives. They see that Christians struggle with some of the same sins they do, so they label all believers as hypocrites. Some people see faith as arrogant, saying, "So you think you've got a corner on truth?" Some see it as fanatical or over the top, suggesting that a little faith is a good thing, but there's a danger of going off the deep end. Some see faith as something people use to impress others or to get what they want. Some people get a mocking tone when they see a believer suffering, and ask, "What good is God if he doesn't keep that from happening?"

The day will come when people who mock God will discover that they missed the most valuable truth in the universe. On that day you'll be glad that you stood up for Jesus, but you won't feel any pleasurable sense of "I told you so." There will be no joy in seeing those who arrogantly and foolishly made fun of God enter a reality completely without God. It hurts when someone mocks what is precious to us, but we can follow the example of Christ, who chose to love and forgive those who mocked him. Rather than being sensitive about what hurts us, we can allow our hearts to be broken by the reality that the mocker has not yet seen God for who he truly is.

 | **DISCUSSION STARTERS**

Have you ever heard someone make fun of God or Christians (either in real life or on TV)?

Jesus said that God blesses us when people mock us because we follow Jesus (see Matthew 5:10-12). What form do you think this blessing will come in?

How would you answer or respond to some of the mocking attitudes toward God or Christians mentioned above?

Plugged In

Have you ever gotten frustrated with a piece of equipment or a machine that didn't seem to work, only to find out that someone had unplugged it from the electrical outlet? Then when it was plugged in, it worked just fine.

Jesus said that if we are not plugged in to him, we can't do *anything*. Nothing. No power, no life, no meaning. Wasted effort. He meant that anything we do with our own power apart from him is worthless. But Paul said that through Christ he could do *everything*. And for Paul that meant he could suffer in prison and preach in Rome and be cold and hungry yet still have joy. His connectedness to Jesus made it possible to face whatever life brought his way.

Our connectedness to Jesus is the secret to doing anything—in fact, everything. Remaining in Christ means entering into his presence as we roll out of bed in the morning. It means breathing out prayers of trust throughout the day. It means drawing strength from him and finding joy in him until our heads hit our pillows at the end of the day.

When we feel overwhelmed and feel like giving up, we can remember that Jesus is enough for even this. And when we start thinking, *I don't need to ask for God's help; I can handle this myself,* we can remember that for anything to be worthwhile, we need Jesus to do it through us.

Remain in me, and I will remain in you. For a branch cannot produce fruit if it is severed from the vine, and you cannot be fruitful unless you remain in me. Yes, I am the vine; you are the branches. Those who remain in me, and I in them, will produce much fruit. For apart from me you can do nothing.
JOHN 15:4-5

I can do everything through Christ, who gives me strength.
PHILIPPIANS 4:13

🥤 | DISCUSSION STARTERS

What does a vine provide for a branch? How long would a branch live on its own apart from the vine?

What is the difference between doing something by our own power and doing it through Christ?

What are some ways you can nurture connectedness to Jesus throughout your typical day?

Watch out for your great enemy, the devil. He prowls around like a roaring lion, looking for someone to devour.
1 PETER 5:8

The devil—the commander of the powers in the unseen world . . . is the spirit at work in the hearts of those who refuse to obey God.
EPHESIANS 2:2

You are the children of your father the devil, and you love to do the evil things he does. He was a murderer from the beginning. He has always hated the truth, because there is no truth in him. When he lies, it is consistent with his character; for he is a liar and the father of lies.
JOHN 8:44

The Devil

Bring up the topic of the devil, and some people will look for a way to turn the matter into a joke. The cartoonish picture of a red character with horns and a tail leads people to associate everything they hear about the devil with superstition and humor. But we confuse fact with fiction. The devil is very real; he is our invisible enemy, and he is out to hurt us, deceive us, and ruin us in any way he can.

The devil is called many things throughout Scripture, and just as the names of God reveal much about God's character and conduct, so do the names for Satan. He is called a murderer from the beginning, the father of lies, a roaring lion, the evil one, the dragon, a serpent, the prince of this world, the enemy, an accuser of our brothers, our adversary, the power of darkness, the tempter, and the wicked one.

To laugh off the reality of Satan is to open the door for his lies to deceive you, his accusations to attack you, and his evil to overpower you. He wants to trick you and tempt you, to destroy and devour you. So "put on all of God's armor so that you will be able to stand firm against all strategies of the devil" (EPHESIANS 6:11). Satan is very real and very powerful, but Christ in you is the power that defeats him.

 | **DISCUSSION STARTERS**

What are some things people believe about the devil? Are these things true?

Look over the list of names for the devil. Which ones make you hate him more, just like names for God help us to love God more?

Why is it important to recognize that the devil is real?

A Work of Art

Have you ever seen an artist in the process of making a piece of art—maybe a drawing or a painting or a quilt? Or maybe you've watched a potter take a lump of wet, messy clay and put it on a potter's wheel. The clay gets spun around while the potter shapes the clay with his or her hands and makes it into a bowl or plate or some other container. Throughout Scripture, God uses the picture of a potter making something out of clay to show us how he is shaping us into what he wants us to be.

How ridiculous would it be for the clay to tell the potter how it should be shaped and what it should be used for? Or how strange would it be for the canvas to tell the painter what to draw or the fabric to tell the tailor what to sew? That's for the creator to decide! But sometimes we just don't like how our Creator has made us, do we? We think, *Why did God give me this body? Why didn't he give me that ability? Why isn't he using me that way?* So we have to ask ourselves, *Does God have the right to shape my life according to his own wise purposes, or not?* Though we are tempted to resist, or at least to give him our input and opinion, our answer should be, "Yes! Potter, I give you this lump of clay called my life. Use whatever pressure is needed to shape me into something of great worth and beauty in your sight, something ready to display your glory!

🧂🧂 | DISCUSSION STARTERS

What's the most impressive work of art you've seen? What made it so good?

A potter applies pressure to shape the clay. What pressures has God applied to your life to shape you into someone he can use?

Is being in God's hands a safe place to be? How do you know?

> Will the one who contends with the Almighty correct him? Let him who accuses God answer him!
> **JOB 40:2, NIV**

> Who are you, a mere human being, to argue with God? Should the thing that was created say to the one who created it, "Why have you made me like this?"
> **ROMANS 9:20**

> I . . . found the potter working at his wheel. But the jar he was making did not turn out as he had hoped, so he crushed it into a lump of clay again and started over. Then the LORD gave me this message: "O Israel, can I not do to you as this potter has done to his clay? As the clay is in the potter's hand, so are you in my hand."
> **JEREMIAH 18:3-6**

God said, "Let us make human beings in our image, to be like us."
GENESIS 1:26

The Lord—who is the Spirit—makes us more and more like him as we are changed into his glorious image.
2 CORINTHIANS 3:18

Just as we are now like the earthly man, we will someday be like the heavenly man.
1 CORINTHIANS 15:49

In the Image of God

When you look in a mirror, are you looking at yourself? Not really. You're looking at an image of yourself—a reflection of who you are.

Similarly, when God looks at us, he sees an image of himself, a reflection of who he is. This isn't an identical image, but he does see creatures similar to himself in many ways. We are God's image in our ability to think and feel and love, in our ability to know right from wrong, and in our ability to make choices. We're like him in that he is Spirit and we have a spirit.

God made humans in his image beginning with Adam and Eve in the Garden of Eden, but something terrible happened to that image when they sinned. The image got distorted and damaged. So now, while we are still made in God's image, some part of that image has gotten lost and twisted along the way.

That is why Jesus came. In Jesus we see what human likeness to God was intended to be. He is the perfect image bearer of God in human form. And one day we, too, will look like Jesus, when we are "conformed to the image of [God's] Son" (ROMANS 8:29, NASB). In fact, the process of becoming more like him has already started. Paul says that we are to "put on the new self, which is being renewed in knowledge in the image of its Creator" (COLOSSIANS 3:10, NIV). Even now, as we grow in godliness, we are becoming better and better reflections of God. When God looks at us, we are getting closer to reflecting his image.

 | DISCUSSION STARTERS

Who do you know who looks amazingly similar to his or her parents?

What are some ways we are like God? What are some ways we are not like him?

In what ways would you like to look more like Jesus?

The Kingdom

Fairy tales and stories often center on kings and their kingdoms. And what we know from these tales is that in a kingdom, the king is in charge. What he says goes.

Jesus talked a lot about his Kingdom—but the kind of Kingdom he spoke of is different from any other kingdom we've heard of. Jesus told people that the Kingdom of God "is already among you," but he also talked about it as something that is coming in the future. It was confusing to people in his day, and it can be for us, too.

So which is it? Is the Kingdom of God something in the future that we are waiting for, or are we living in it now? The answer is yes. The Kingdom of God has come—but only partly. The fulfillment of the Kingdom came in part when Jesus entered our world and lived out God's purposes for him. But the coming of his Kingdom will be complete only when Jesus returns and destroys evil and its deadly effects on this world for good.

The Kingdom of God is a reality in our lives to the extent that Jesus rules in our hearts. His Kingdom comes to us like a small seed that must be planted so it can blossom. It does not come like a military overthrow that takes power by force. His Kingdom is somewhat hidden now, but we can become a part of it by making him the King of our hearts and lives. And one day God's Kingdom will not be hidden. Everyone will see Jesus as King and bow before him.

 | **DISCUSSION STARTERS**

What stories can you think of that include kings and kingdoms?

In what ways is Jesus the same as other kings? In what ways is he different?

What can we do now to welcome God's Kingdom in the world and in our hearts while we wait for it to be fully completed?

One day the Pharisees asked Jesus, "When will the Kingdom of God come?"

Jesus replied, "The Kingdom of God can't be detected by visible signs. You won't be able to say, 'Here it is!' or 'It's over there!' For the Kingdom of God is already among you."
LUKE 17:20-21

Seek the Kingdom of God above all else, and live righteously, and he will give you everything you need.
MATTHEW 6:33

The Kingdom of God is not just a lot of talk; it is living by God's power.
1 CORINTHIANS 4:20

Are All Sins the Same?

What do you think is worse: borrowing a dollar and not giving it back or robbing a bank at gunpoint? Is it worse for a Christian leader to lie on his or her tax return than for someone who makes no claim of Christianity to do the same thing? Are all sins the same?

Well, it depends on what we mean by *the same*. All sins break our relationship with God, which is a serious issue. All sins are forgivable only on the basis of the death of Christ. But that doesn't mean all sins are exactly the same. And all sins are not the same in their effects or their judgment.

Jesus said that a person who lusts has committed adultery in his or her heart. In terms of being an offense against God's holiness, having impure thoughts and cheating on a spouse are the same. However, the sin of lust in your heart does not have the same effect on you or other people as the sin of physically committing adultery. Some sins have far more devastating consequences and greater punishments. And some sins are more serious because of who commits them. People in positions of responsibility and those who have had more exposure to God's Word are held to a higher standard by God.

But the good news is that in the Bible we can't find one instance where God refused to forgive a truly repentant person, no matter how serious his or her sin was. God's forgiveness is big enough to cover any and all sin.

A servant who knows what the master wants, but isn't prepared and doesn't carry out those instructions, will be severely punished. But someone who does not know, and then does something wrong, will be punished only lightly. When someone has been given much, much will be required in return; and when someone has been entrusted with much, even more will be required.

LUKE 12:47-48

Dear brothers and sisters, not many of you should become teachers in the church, for we who teach will be judged more strictly.

JAMES 3:1

 | ## DISCUSSION STARTERS

The Bible tells about people who were forgiven for lying, murdering, committing adultery, and even killing Christians. Can you tell about some of those people?

What sins can you think of that have more serious consequences?

What do you think it means in Luke 12:48 that "when someone has been given much, much will be required in return"? What has God entrusted to you for which he will require much in return?

One Flesh

"How do I love thee? Let me count the ways. . . ." "Roses are red, violets are blue. . . ." Have you ever noticed how love seems to express itself in poetry? In fact, the very first recorded human words are love poetry. When Adam saw Eve for the first time, his words came out in a poem:

> *This one is bone from my bone,*
> *and flesh from my flesh!*
> *She will be called "woman,"*
> *because she was taken from "man."*

Genesis tells us where love between a man and a woman comes from. In fact, the Bible says that romantic love is "the very flame of the LORD" (SONG OF SOLOMON 8:6, ESV). Throughout the Bible we see that God uses marriage to show us something about the ultimate romance—the way God loves us. Why do men and women tend to pair off and get married? Is it just something that society has developed over time? No, marriage is something God created to show us how he wants to be intimate with us and committed to us—and how he wants us to love him and be faithful to him. Marriage is God's gift to people to help us understand his passionate love toward us in a way nothing else can.

 | ## DISCUSSION STARTERS

How can you tell when someone is really in love?

What do you think it means to be "united into one"?

In what ways does married love help us understand the relationship between Christ and the church?

The LORD God said, "It is not good for the man to be alone. I will make a helper who is just right for him." . . .

So the LORD God caused the man to fall into a deep sleep. While the man slept, the LORD God took out one of the man's ribs and closed up the opening. Then the LORD God made a woman from the rib, and he brought her to the man.

"At last!" the man exclaimed, "This one is bone from my bone, and flesh from my flesh! She will be called 'woman,' because she was taken from 'man.'"

GENESIS 2:18, 21-23

As the Scriptures say, "A man leaves his father and mother and is joined to his wife, and the two are united into one." This is a great mystery, but it is an illustration of the way Christ and the church are one.

EPHESIANS 5:31-32

Falling Down

Is there anything more embarrassing than falling down in public? Have you ever slipped on the sidewalk or in the middle of the school cafeteria with everyone watching? How humiliating! Falling down makes us feel out of control. And don't we love to be cool and in control?

It is interesting to note that whenever people in the Bible got a glimpse of God, they fell down before him. And they weren't at all embarrassed by it. For example, when John saw the resurrected Jesus, Revelation 1 says he "fell at his feet like a dead man." A dead person is silent— no more negotiating, no more arguing, no more excuses. A dead person is still. No more wrestling with God's will, no more running ahead of him or away from him.

When John saw Jesus, he had no desire to be in control. He wanted to surrender all control. He fell down before Jesus in worship and wonder, in submission and stillness. To worship facedown is the ultimate outward sign of inner surrender.

Falling before Jesus is the one place where falling is not embarrassing. To fall at the feet of Jesus is to finally come to the place where your reputation doesn't matter anymore. Your appropriateness doesn't matter anymore. In this place *Jesus* is all that matters.

Such was the appearance of the likeness of the glory of the LORD. And when I saw it, I fell on my face.
EZEKIEL 1:28, ESV

Ezra praised the LORD, the great God, and all the people chanted, "Amen! Amen!" as they lifted their hands. Then they bowed down and worshiped the LORD with their faces to the ground.
NEHEMIAH 8:6

When I saw Him, I fell at His feet like a dead man.
REVELATION 1:17, NASB

 | ## DISCUSSION STARTERS

Have you ever fallen down in public or seen someone else fall down? What happened?

Why do you think so many biblical characters fell down before God?

Would you ever consider praying to God facedown? How might that impact your heart?

Your Spiritual Birthday

Some people can give the exact date they became a Christian. Perhaps you are one of those people, and maybe you have the date written in your Bible as your spiritual birthday. But other people have a hard time pinpointing a specific day when they went from being spiritually dead to spiritually alive. But just because they can't nail down the date doesn't mean they haven't been born again.

We know that God does something inside us that gives us new spiritual life. But exactly how that happens is a mystery to us. When God gives us this new life, it is an instantaneous event. It happens only once. At one moment we are spiritually dead, and then at the next moment we have new spiritual life from God. But we don't always know when this instantaneous change occurs.

For many people, their new spiritual life starts at a definable time when they realize they are separated from God and they turn to Jesus. For some people it happens when they're alone in their rooms, and for others it happens in a crowded stadium or in a church. For children who grow up in a home where Jesus is taught about and loved or for those who attend a Bible study and gradually grow in their understanding of the gospel, there may not be a dramatic event. But there will be an instantaneous change. The change will become evident over time in the way they live and think, and in the way they want to please God. It may not be definable, but it will be unmistakable.

The wind blows wherever it wants. Just as you can hear the wind but can't tell where it comes from or where it is going, so you can't explain how people are born of the Spirit.
JOHN 3:8

Anyone who belongs to Christ has become a new person. The old life is gone; a new life has begun!
2 CORINTHIANS 5:17

I know this: I was blind, and now I can see!
JOHN 9:25

 | **DISCUSSION STARTERS**

When did your new spiritual life begin? Can you pinpoint a date that this happened?

If you can't identify a date you were saved, how can you know for sure that God has given you new life?

What does God do to cause us to turn to him?

OCTOBER

21

If anyone gives you even a cup of water because you belong to the Messiah, I tell you the truth, that person will surely be rewarded.

MARK 9:41

God blesses you when people mock you and persecute you and lie about you and say all sorts of evil things against you because you are my followers. Be happy about it! Be very glad! For a great reward awaits you in heaven.

MATTHEW 5:11-12

Look, I am coming soon, bringing my reward with me to repay all people according to their deeds.

REVELATION 22:12

A Great Reward Is Waiting

That's not fair! we think when someone else is paid more than we are for the work we've done or gets more than we do when birthdays roll around. And most of us are a bit uncomfortable with the idea that there could be a difference in the amount of reward people experience in heaven. At first glance, this can seem a bit unfair. We think that heaven should be and will be identical for everyone.

But while heaven will be wonderful for everyone there, Scripture makes it clear that not every believer's position and experience in heaven will be the same. The Bible teaches that believers will receive differing rewards according to how much their faith expresses itself in acts of service, sacrifice, suffering, and submission. Paul says, "Each will be rewarded according to his own labor" (1 CORINTHIANS 3:8, NIV).

How will heaven's rewards be different? One way to think of it is that everyone's cup will be full—but some will have larger cups than others. All of us will be full of joy, but some may have more joy because their capacity for joy will be larger, having been stretched through their trust in God and obedience to him in their earthly life.

 | ## DISCUSSION STARTERS

Does the idea of people receiving different levels of rewards seem unfair to you? Why or why not?

What kinds of things did Jesus promise would be rewarded?

Read the parable of the ten servants in Luke 19:11-27. What does it teach about how our actions affect our eternal rewards?

Now Everything Is Ruined

Have you ever put something red with a load of white clothes in the washing machine? You pull the clothes out of the washer only to find that everything is ruined. Everything has been tainted with red.

This is what happened when the darkness of sin entered the pure atmosphere of the Garden of Eden. And when sin entered this perfect world, it wasn't only humans who felt the effects. All of creation became cursed. The animal kingdom was no longer tame; the ground became full of thorns and weeds; and the atmosphere produced deadly weather conditions. Sin ruined everything, and everything changed. Nothing is the way it was created to be.

Death, disease, and destruction are the realities of a world that is under a curse. We regularly experience the brokenness of this cursed world in the form of natural disasters, an environment that is deteriorating, and bodies that die. Romans 8:22 says that "all creation has been groaning" under this curse. But the day is coming when that groaning will end. "Creation looks forward to the day when it will join God's children in glorious freedom from death and decay" (ROMANS 8:21). This is what all of history is moving toward—when God restores his entire creation to the way it was before sin ruined everything.

🎲 | DISCUSSION STARTERS

What do you think it was like to live in the Garden of Eden?

What are some of the ways you experience sin's curse on the world?

What will be some of the best things about the day described in Revelation 22:3 when "no longer will there be a curse upon anything"?

He said to the woman, "I will sharpen the pain of your pregnancy, and in pain you will give birth. And you will desire to control your husband, but he will rule over you."

And to the man he said, "Since you listened to your wife and ate from the tree whose fruit I commanded you not to eat, the ground is cursed because of you. All your life you will struggle to scratch a living from it. It will grow thorns and thistles for you, though you will eat of its grains. . . . For you were made from dust, and to dust you will return."

GENESIS 3:16-19

Against its will, all creation was subjected to God's curse.

ROMANS 8:20

OCTOBER 23

The LORD is merciful and compassionate,

slow to get angry and filled with unfailing love.

The LORD is good to everyone.

He showers compassion on all his creation.

All of your works will thank you, LORD,

and your faithful followers will praise you.

They will speak of the glory of your kingdom;

they will give examples of your power.

They will tell about your mighty deeds

and about the majesty and glory of your reign.

For your kingdom is an everlasting kingdom.

You rule throughout all generations.

PSALM 145:8-13

God's Greatness A–Z

When an office-supply store runs an ad that says it has everything you need for back-to-school A–Z, what does it mean? It means that it has a complete selection of school supplies. Anything and everything you can think of that you might need—the store has it.

When King David wrote his last psalm in the book of Psalms, he wanted to express how completely worthy God is of praise. And so in Psalm 145 he told about God's greatness—in a sense, from A to Z. David's way of expressing this was not just by stating the greatness of God. He wrote what is called an alphabetic psalm. He began with the Hebrew *A* and wrote a line for each of the twenty-two letters in the Hebrew alphabet. Each line celebrates a different aspect of God's greatness. It was his way of saying, "God is everything good and wonderful. He is great and glorious from A to Z!"

David saw in the greatness of God a huge expanse to explore and discover and celebrate, so he stretched out his praises as far as he could. At the end of his psalm, he called everyone everywhere to join him in praising God forever (SEE VERSE 21). God has no limits but can be explored forever. We can never exhaust all the details of his greatness.

 | **DISCUSSION STARTERS**

Work your way through the alphabet as a family, naming things that make God great from A to Z.

Nobody's Perfect

Nobody's perfect, right? So why did Jesus say, "You are to be perfect, even as your Father in heaven is perfect" (MATTHEW 5:48)? And why did Paul say that he was pressing on to possess that perfection? It sounds impossible. Is it worth it to even try?

If you belong to Jesus, you are perfect right now in the sense that God has taken away all your sin. You stand before God in perfection—not on your own, but on the perfection of Jesus. He has taken your sin and given you his perfection as a gift. In this way, you're perfect.

But while Jesus has made you perfect, he is still at work in you to make you holy in the way you live day to day. This is what the writer of Hebrews means when he says that Jesus "made perfect those who are being made holy." This is an ongoing process as you move away from your lingering imperfection toward holiness.

You will never have a perfect life to offer God on your own. Your perfection before God will always depend on the perfection of Jesus offered in your place. But the day is coming when Jesus will make you completely perfect in eternity. And every step you take now toward holiness is a taste of that coming perfection.

 | ## DISCUSSION STARTERS

Typically, why does someone say, "Nobody's perfect"?

In what ways will we be perfect in heaven?

What do you think it means to "press on to possess that perfection"? What's one way you could do that this week?

> How foolish can you be? After starting your Christian lives in the Spirit, why are you now trying to become perfect by your own human effort?
> *GALATIANS 3:3*

> By that one offering he forever made perfect those who are being made holy.
> *HEBREWS 10:14*

> I don't mean to say that I have already achieved these things or that I have already reached perfection. But I press on to possess that perfection for which Christ Jesus first possessed me.
> *PHILIPPIANS 3:12*

"Look!" Nebuchadnezzar shouted. "I see four men, unbound, walking around in the fire unharmed! And the fourth looks like a god!"
DANIEL 3:25

When Gideon realized that it was the angel of the LORD, he cried out, "Oh, Sovereign LORD, I'm doomed! I have seen the angel of the LORD face to face!"
JUDGES 6:22

"Why do you ask my name?" the angel of the LORD replied. "It is too wonderful for you to understand."
JUDGES 13:18

The Angel of the Lord

Did you know that some authors use pen names—names other than their own—when they write books? They do it for a variety of reasons—sometimes to avoid confusion with someone who has a similar name, sometimes because they simply like the sound of another name, sometimes because they want to mask their identity so they can write something completely different from what people expect from them.

The Son of God actually made some personal appearances on earth with a different name and in a different form before he was born as a baby. When the Bible records these appearances, Jesus is referred to as the angel of the Lord. Hagar met this angel in the desert, and he comforted her with predictions concerning her son and their future. Abraham heard the angel of the Lord's voice on Mount Moriah telling him not to kill his son Isaac. Jacob spent the night wrestling with the angel of the Lord. Moses saw and heard the angel of the Lord in the form of a burning bush.

This angel seems not just to be *from* God but actually to *be* God, and he's not like other angels. Though Scripture doesn't specifically spell it out, various passages seem to indicate that the angel of the Lord was the preincarnate Son of God (Jesus before he took on flesh). Centuries before Jesus was born in Bethlehem as a baby, he came to earth as an angel with a mission. God was here in the form of this angel, providing his loving guidance and careful protection, actively involved in the lives of his people.

 | ## DISCUSSION STARTERS

Look up the following passages in the Bible. What does the angel of the Lord do in these Old Testament appearances? What evidence do you see that the angel is really God?

- Hagar (Genesis 16:7-14)
- Abraham (Genesis 22:9-18)
- Gideon (Judges 6:11-14)
- Daniel (Daniel 3:22-25)

The Ones God Has Chosen

Perhaps one reason some people are turned off by Christianity is that they've talked to some Christians who seem very proud that they are "in" while others are "out." Some Christians act as if they are better or smarter than those who haven't come to Christ, and that turns people off.

But if we really understand what God does and what we do for our salvation, there's no room for pride—just gratitude. We don't turn to Christ because we are savvy enough to figure out on our own that we need to. We respond to God when he gets ahold of us and draws us to himself through his gift of grace. "God saved you by his grace when you believed. And you can't take credit for this; it is a gift from God" (EPHESIANS 2:8).

We see this calling from God numerous times in the Old Testament when he says he will preserve a remnant. The remnant is a small number from the whole nation that he will keep faithful to him. He was saying, in other words, that while the majority of people may reject or refuse him, he will always preserve at least a few faithful followers who will not turn away from him. He can do this because he is the one enabling people to respond to him. This shows us that he is the initiator. He is the one who calls us to him in the first place, and he's the one who makes sure we make it all the way home.

 | ## DISCUSSION STARTERS

Are there some things you have saved that you want to keep for yourself because you love and enjoy those things?

What are ways Christians can come across as arrogant to unbelievers?

How is God's ability to preserve a remnant obvious throughout history?

> I will preserve a remnant of the people of Israel and of Judah to possess my land. Those I choose will inherit it, and my servants will live there.
> *ISAIAH 65:9*

> It is the same today, for a few of the people of Israel have remained faithful because of God's grace—his undeserved kindness in choosing them. And since it is through God's kindness, then it is not by their good works. For in that case, God's grace would not be what it really is—free and undeserved.

> So this is the situation: Most of the people of Israel have not found the favor of God they are looking for so earnestly. A few have—the ones God has chosen—but the hearts of the rest were hardened.
> *ROMANS 11:5-7*

You Remind Me of Someone I Know

Have you ever seen someone who looks so much like someone else you know it seems hard to believe? Or have you ever tapped someone on the shoulder thinking it was someone you knew, only to discover it was a complete stranger?

When Jesus came to the Jewish people to show them what God is like, he had some striking resemblances to some of their most cherished Jewish ancestors. These weren't really physical similarities. God planned that those ancestors would give people a preview of the character and purpose of Jesus so people would recognize him when he came. Aspects of each of those ancestors' lives pointed to who Jesus is and what he came to do.

For example, Romans 5:14 describes Adam as "a pattern of the one to come" (NIV). Adam's sin brought death, while Jesus' sinlessness brought life. Or look at the example of Joseph. God worked behind the scenes to use the evil done against Joseph for good. And God worked behind the scenes to use the evil done against Christ on the cross for the ultimate good of those who believe in him. As Moses was the deliverer of his people from slavery in Egypt, Jesus delivered his people from their slavery to sin. And just as Jonah was sent to people who had rejected God, so Jesus was sent to people who rejected him as God's Son. Each of these people in the Old Testament showed the Jewish people a little bit about what Jesus would be like and what he would do.

The Scriptures tell us, "The first man, Adam, became a living person." But the last Adam—that is, Christ— is a life-giving Spirit.
1 CORINTHIANS 15:45

The law was given through Moses, but God's unfailing love and faithfulness came through Jesus Christ.
JOHN 1:17

Jesus said, "I tell you the truth, Moses didn't give you bread from heaven. My Father did. And now he offers you the true bread from heaven."
JOHN 6:32

 | **DISCUSSION STARTERS**

Have you ever been told that you remind someone of another person in the way you look or act?

Think about some of the other Old Testament figures, like Abraham, Isaac, Jacob, and David. What preview did they give of Jesus?

Some people think of the Bible as a collection of moral stories or instructions for living. In what ways is it more than that?

Something Worth Being Afraid Of

Throughout the Bible we read over and over that we shouldn't be afraid—that we should fear only God. So that makes it especially interesting when we read that there is something we *should* be afraid of—something that should make us tremble with fear. What is it? Here's what the writer of Hebrews wrote: "God's promise of entering his rest still stands, so we ought to tremble with fear that some of you might fail to experience it" (4:1). God holds out to us the gift of rest—the kind of rest only he can provide—and the fact that some of us fail to reach out and take it should cause us to tremble with fear.

Entering God's rest means being at peace with God, free from real guilt and from feelings of guilt. Entering God's rest means that our aimless search for the source of truth is over. We've found truth in the person of Jesus, and we can be at rest. Entering God's rest means we surrender our "self-effort" salvation—our attempts to be right with God by our own efforts. God's rest means being at peace in the grace and provision of God.

Why would anybody not take the gift of rest that God holds out? For most people, the reason is unbelief. Some people simply don't believe that the rest God offers is as good as God says it is. Some people trust more in their own abilities to create an enjoyable life than they do in God's promise of a full and unending life. And that's not just sad; it's scary.

There's really only one thing in this world to be afraid of—not trusting God. We should have a healthy fear of what will happen if we see what God is offering to us in himself and then choose not to take it, if we see the door open to rest and refuse to enter in.

> Jesus said, "Come to me, all of you who are weary and carry heavy burdens, and I will give you rest."
> **MATTHEW 11:28**

> Because of their unbelief they were not able to enter his rest.
> **HEBREWS 3:19**

> God set another time for entering his rest, and that time is today.
> **HEBREWS 4:7**

🥛 | DISCUSSION STARTERS

What does God's rest mean to you? What is your favorite part of resting?

Do you think of coming to God as rest or work? Why?

Why should a person be afraid of not trusting God?

You intended to harm me, but God intended it all for good. He brought me to this position so I could save the lives of many people.
GENESIS 50:20

Job replied, "You talk like a foolish woman. Should we accept only good things from the hand of God and never anything bad?" So in all this, Job said nothing wrong.
JOB 2:10

God knew what would happen, and his prearranged plan was carried out when Jesus was betrayed. With the help of lawless Gentiles, you nailed him to a cross and killed him.
ACTS 2:23

Does God Do Evil?

Lots of television shows fall into the genre of whodunits. These are usually crime stories or mysteries, which unfold over the course of an hour to reveal who committed the crime.

When we are trying to figure out who is responsible for the evil in the world, it can be confusing, because the Bible indicates that God himself allows evil events and evil deeds: Joseph's being sold into slavery, Job's losing his family, even Jesus' being crucified—the Bible tells us that God knew about these evil deeds in advance. But at the same time, it is clear that nowhere in Scripture do we see God directly doing anything evil.

While God has ordained history to include evil events, he doesn't *do* anything evil. If we were to say that God himself does evil, we would have to conclude that he is not a good and righteous God, and therefore that he is not really God at all. On the other hand, if we believe that God does not use evil to fulfill his purposes, then we would have to admit that there is evil in the universe that is not under God's control and might not fulfill his purposes. Neither of these conclusions is true. When we're faced with evil, we can trust that God is good and powerful and that he uses all things to fulfill his good purposes—even evil.

 | **DISCUSSION STARTERS**

Have you ever gotten a shot that hurt or put medicine on a sore that made it sting? How is this painful experience actually something good?

The Bible doesn't explain to us exactly what role God plays in the evil that happens in the world. How can we trust God with this mystery?

What evil circumstance has God used for good in your life or in the life of someone you know?

Demons

Sometimes in movies or TV shows the hero is confronted by an enemy who has brought along plenty of backup. The hero is seriously outnumbered and out-weaponed, and it looks like he will be defeated.

When it comes to our spiritual battle, we could easily think the same thing about ourselves. Satan is not alone in his efforts to destroy and devour us. He has thousands of cohorts—demons. Demons are angels who were once servants of God until they rebelled against him and lost their place and privilege of serving him. Now they work continually to bring about evil in the world. Demons use lies, deception, and every other kind of destructive activity to try to cause people to turn away from God and bring themselves to ruin. Demons try to keep people in slavery to things that separate them from God. They also try to damage the witness of Christians by using temptation, doubt, guilt, fear, confusion, sickness, envy, and pride to trip them up.

But as members of God's family, we don't have to be afraid of demons. We are not outnumbered or out-weaponed. The truth is, the Spirit who lives in us is greater than the spirit who lives in the world (SEE 1 JOHN 4:4). We can resist the devil and he and his demons will flee from us (SEE JAMES 4:7) because of the power of the Holy Spirit at work in our lives.

OCTOBER
30

God did not spare even the angels who sinned. He threw them into hell, in gloomy pits of darkness, where they are being held until the day of judgment.
2 PETER 2:4

We are not fighting against flesh-and-blood enemies, but against evil rulers and authorities of the unseen world, against mighty powers in this dark world, and against evil spirits in the heavenly places.
EPHESIANS 6:12

He disarmed the spiritual rulers and authorities. He shamed them publicly by his victory over them on the cross.
COLOSSIANS 2:15

🧂🧂 | DISCUSSION STARTERS

What is the difference between an angel and a demon?

One of the weapons that demons use is unforgiven sin. How did Jesus take that weapon away at the Cross?

What does it mean to resist the devil? What's one specific way you can do that this week?

The people who sat in darkness have seen a great light. And for those who lived in the land where death casts its shadow, a light has shined.
MATTHEW 4:16

Make sure that the light you think you have is not actually darkness.
LUKE 11:35

Don't let evil conquer you, but conquer evil by doing good.
ROMANS 12:21

After Darkness, Light

Quick—what holiday is today? Did you think of Halloween? Today is also a much more significant holiday. It is Reformation Day. On October 31, 1517, Martin Luther nailed his 95 Theses (or topics for debate) to the door of a church in Wittenberg. At the time, the church was telling people they had to pay money to the church for their sins to be forgiven. People were forced to buy pieces of paper called pardons or indulgences from the church if they wanted the church to forgive their sins.

Luther knew that repentance is an inward experience and that indulgences had no spiritual value. He loved the truth from the Bible, and he wanted others to learn that truth. He and other reformers—people like John Calvin, William Tyndale, John Knox, and John Wycliffe— changed the world through their courageous and costly commitment. They believed strongly in allowing people to read the Bible for themselves, and they helped people understand that salvation is a gift of God, not something we earn. They taught that every Christian has their own personal relationship with God and doesn't need another person to go to God for them.

On Reformation Day, we celebrate what God did to shine the light on the true gospel through these reformers. One of the Latin sayings of the Reformers was "Post Tenebras Lux." This saying means, "After darkness, light." The centuries prior to the Reformation were very dark, with people being ignorant of simple biblical truths. The Reformation brought light into the darkness. And that is worth celebrating!

 | ## DISCUSSION STARTERS

What is the difference between Halloween and Reformation Day in terms of what is being celebrated?

How would your faith be different if you couldn't read the Bible in your own language?

The Reformers faced punishment and even death for bringing light to some of the dark places in the church. What do you think gave them the courage to stand up for the truth?

A Spiritual Sweet Tooth

What is the sweetest thing you can think of? Your favorite kind of ice cream? Your favorite candy? Or maybe a rich chocolate cake?

In the time before there was refined sugar, honey was the sweetest taste people ever enjoyed. So when the psalmist was looking for a metaphor that would describe how good the Word of God is, he reached for the best example of sweetness that people knew at that time: honey.

He was saying that the Word of God tastes like the sweetest thing he'd ever tasted.

The Bible is not meant to be drudgery you force-feed yourself because you know it's good for you (maybe like brussels sprouts!). God intends for his Word to be an invigorating taste sensation, a treat. But we so easily turn what he has given as a delightful gift into a guilt-inducing demand.

If you find that the Word of God often seems tasteless or unenjoyable, perhaps you want to ask God to give you a spiritual sweet tooth. He can give you that desire . . . and he can fulfill it.

 | **DISCUSSION STARTERS**

What is your favorite sweet food?

Do you really believe you could get as much pleasure from the Bible as you get from your favorite dessert? How?

How do you think you will know if God answers your prayer for a spiritual sweet tooth?

The laws of the LORD are true; each one is fair.

They are more desirable than gold, even the finest gold.

They are sweeter than honey, even honey dripping from the comb.

PSALM 19:9-10

When I discovered your words, I devoured them. They are my joy and my heart's delight, for I bear your name, O LORD God of Heaven's Armies.

JEREMIAH 15:16

My child, eat honey, for it is good, and the honeycomb is sweet to the taste. In the same way, wisdom is sweet to your soul. If you find it, you will have a bright future, and your hopes will not be cut short.

PROVERBS 24:13-14

Do not judge others, and you will not be judged. For you will be treated as you treat others. The standard you use in judging is the standard by which you will be judged.

MATTHEW 7:1-2

How can you think of saying to your friend, "Let me help you get rid of that speck in your eye," when you can't see past the log in your own eye? Hypocrite! First get rid of the log in your own eye; then you will see well enough to deal with the speck in your friend's eye.

MATTHEW 7:4-5

It is the Lord himself who will examine me and decide.

1 CORINTHIANS 4:4

Who Am I to Judge?

"Do not judge others, and you will not be judged." These are some of the most well-known but also misunderstood and misapplied words Jesus ever spoke. What did Jesus mean when he said not to judge? Was he suggesting a "mind your own business" policy for those who follow him?

When Jesus said, "Do not judge others," he wasn't saying we should never label something in another person's life as sin. He wasn't saying we shouldn't care about what other people do or what they believe.

Jesus was talking about having a condemning attitude toward others while refusing to see our own faults in light of God's standards. He was talking about an attitude that shows no mercy to someone who has done wrong—an attitude that finds pleasure in criticizing the person rather than in extending mercy and compassion. The way we think and speak about someone who sins or fails in some way reveals how much we've truly experienced God's grace ourselves.

Jesus says that instead of being quick to judge others, we need to examine ourselves. He says, "Get rid of the log in your own eye." How do we do that? Careful self-examination. We fully repent of our own sins. Then we seek to have a broken heart over the sin of others.

 | **DISCUSSION STARTERS**

What does it mean to judge another person?

On what basis can we label something as sinful or wrong in another person's life? How and when should we express that to the person?

What does it feel like to be judged by another person?

God's Picture Book

When we learn to read, we don't start out with thick novels or heavy textbooks. First we're taught letters, then words, and then sentences.

Similarly, in God's desire for human beings to know him, he started with a "picture book"—the types and ceremonies and prophecies that are described in the Old Testament. He began giving us a picture of who he is through the Law, the Prophets, and the books of poetry— through the story of the Israelites. The sacrifices and offerings, the detailed designs on the Temple—they were all preparation for the more complete, definitive revelation of God that later came in the person and work of Jesus Christ. God has been showing himself to us from the very beginning, but at first it was in bits and pieces, forms and shadows. It wasn't untrue; it just wasn't complete until Jesus fulfilled it all.

Jesus is the key that unlocks the door of understanding to the picture book of the Old Testament. Jesus Christ is the tree of life in the Garden of Eden. He's the clothing God gave Adam and Eve, providing covering for their shame. He's the ark that carried Noah through the flood of judgment. He's the goat that took on all the sins of the people on the Day of Atonement. He's the hero who killed the giant. He's the priest who brings sinners close to God. Everywhere we look in the Old Testament, we find glimpses of Jesus, pictures that prepare us to understand and embrace Jesus himself.

 | **DISCUSSION STARTERS**

Look up these verses to discover the Old Testament pictures Jesus fulfilled:

- Genesis 28:12 and John 1:51
- Numbers 21:9 and John 3:14-15
- Exodus 16:4 and John 6:32
- Leviticus 1:3 and 1 Peter 1:18-19

Jesus took them through the writings of Moses and all the prophets, explaining from all the Scriptures the things concerning himself.
LUKE 24:27

Christ, our Passover Lamb, has been sacrificed for us.
1 CORINTHIANS 5:7

Jesus replied. "Destroy this temple, and in three days I will raise it up."

"What!" they exclaimed. "It has taken forty-six years to build this Temple, and you can rebuild it in three days?" But when Jesus said "this temple," he meant his own body.
JOHN 2:19-21

Jesus told him, "If you want to be perfect, go and sell all your possessions and give the money to the poor, and you will have treasure in heaven. Then come, follow me."

MATTHEW 19:21

Zacchaeus stood before the Lord and said, "I will give half my wealth to the poor, Lord, and if I have cheated people on their taxes, I will give them back four times as much!"

LUKE 19:8

"Yes, Lord, I will follow you, but first let me say good-bye to my family." But Jesus told him, "Anyone who puts a hand to the plow and then looks back is not fit for the Kingdom of God."

LUKE 9:61-62

Too Much to Ask?

What would you say is the most important thing in your life? It's a hard question to answer. Because there is what we think *should be* the most important thing, and then there's what truly *is* the most important thing, whether or not we realize it.

Jesus had the ability to see inside people's lives and know exactly what was important to them. And so often when people told Jesus they wanted to follow him, he pointed to what was most important to them and told them, "This is what following me is going to cost you."

Jesus was testing them—testing to see if he was really their treasure, their joy, their security, their hope, their home. And Jesus will test us in this way too, because he knows exactly what is competing in our hearts for our affection.

When God asks us to let go of what is most precious to us, it's not because he wants to take away our happiness. It's because he wants to add to it. He knows that we will be happiest when we've given him everything. Then we will be able to get more of him and enjoy him more.

 | **DISCUSSION STARTERS**

What are some things you would never want to lose?

What are signs that we value and desire something more than we value or desire Jesus?

How can we learn to let go of things we love so we can enjoy Jesus more?

What Does God Pour Out?

Some sinks have one spout that produces hot and cold water mixed. Other sinks have two spouts—one for hot and one for cold, and you have to decide which one you're going to put your hands under.

In a similar way, there are two streams flowing from the heart of God—mercy and wrath—and you are standing under one of them. Both streams flow from God's perfection. God is perfect in love, and he is equally perfect in judgment. Since he is holy, he cannot tolerate evil—in fact, he hates it. "You love justice and hate evil" (HEBREWS 1:9).

The wrath of God is not irrational rage from an out-of-control deity. It is the righteous, pure, and perfectly appropriate expression of God's justice toward evil. The greatest demonstration of God's wrath was when his own Son, Jesus, took our sin upon himself on the cross and God poured out his full fury of judgment on sin. That same wrath will be poured out on all those who choose a life away from God. But for those who choose to find protection in Jesus, there is no need to fear the wrath of God. God poured out his wrath on his Son, and as we hide ourselves in him, we experience the stream of mercy from God instead of the stream of his wrath. "For God chose to save us through our Lord Jesus Christ, not to pour out his anger on us" (1 THESSALONIANS 5:9).

 | ## DISCUSSION STARTERS

What does our society tend to think about the idea of a wrathful God? Why do you think we are uncomfortable with God's wrath?

What does each verse above say about what God wants to pour out on us instead of wrath? Which of these things have you experienced?

Is there any comfort in knowing that God will pour out his wrath on evil someday?

God has every right to exercise his judgment and his power, but he also has the right to be very patient with those who are the objects of his judgment and are fit only for destruction. He also has the right to pour out the riches of his glory upon those he prepared to be the objects of his mercy.
ROMANS 9:22-23

God has poured out his love into our hearts by the Holy Spirit, whom he has given us.
ROMANS 5:5, NIV

The grace of our Lord was poured out on me abundantly, along with the faith and love that are in Christ Jesus.
1 TIMOTHY 1:14, NIV

NOVEMBER

6

They were severely beaten, and then they were thrown into prison. The jailer was ordered to make sure they didn't escape. So the jailer put them into the inner dungeon and clamped their feet in the stocks. Around midnight Paul and Silas were praying and singing hymns to God.
ACTS 16:23-25

I have learned how to be content with whatever I have. I know how to live on almost nothing or with everything. I have learned the secret of living in every situation, whether it is with a full stomach or empty, with plenty or little. For I can do everything through Christ, who gives me strength.
PHILIPPIANS 4:11-13

Complaining or Content?

Some people focus on their misery. They can recount in full detail to anyone who'll listen every ache, pain, and inconvenience. In fact, if nothing is going wrong, they can barely find anything to talk about.

Paul and Silas had every reason to complain. They had been wrongly accused and beaten with rods until their bodies throbbed with pain. They were locked up in the darkest, gloomiest section of the prison, under the constant supervision of a hardened jailer. They had everything they needed for a great big pity party! Paul could have complained, "God, I have served you for years, and I have been persecuted and beaten almost to death. I have this thorn in the flesh that won't go away. And the reward I get for these years of devoted work for you is finding myself under the threat of execution in a Roman prison, chained to soldiers? Where are the blessings you promised me?"

But Paul and Silas didn't focus on the misery of their situation. They focused on the sufficiency of God to help them endure their difficult circumstances. Even in the face of hunger and discomfort and cold and maybe sores that needed medication, Paul could say, "I can endure this. I won't be bitter or angry with God. I won't walk away from God. I can honor God and enjoy God even in this." Instead of complaining, Paul was content in God and confident that God would give him the strength he needed to endure faithfully.

 | ## DISCUSSION STARTERS

What do you think it would have been like to be imprisoned in Paul's day?

What does it look like to be content even in difficult situations?

What is something you need to endure without complaining, as God gives you strength?

Many Hats

Have you ever heard it said of someone that he or she "wears a lot of hats"? When we use that expression, it's not meant literally—we're talking about a person who fills several different roles or functions. For example, one man might be a husband, a father, a sales manager, a baseball coach, and a church elder. A girl might be a student, a sister, a daughter, a friend, an athlete, and a musician.

We could say that Jesus wore many hats. The Bible describes him as a Prophet, a Priest, and a King. Each of these roles played a part in expressing God's nature and fulfilling God's plan for our salvation. To help us understand each of these roles, God gave us "pictures" of them in the Old Testament.

Old Testament prophets were people called to carry out God's covenant: They warned of the judgment to come and paved the way for grace—the new way God would deal with people when Jesus came. Jesus came as a Prophet who was a living, breathing embodiment of God's judgment of the world and grace for his people.

Priests stood in the presence of God to mediate between God and his people. Jesus came as our Priest who was both sacrificer and sacrifice, whose blood alone forgives sins.

Kings reigned over God's people as earthly representations of the heavenly King. Jesus came as a King, the true Son of King David. His Kingdom is forever, and his rule will never end.

Jesus is the one the Old Testament prophets, priests, and kings all pointed to. As Prophet, he announces salvation. As Priest, he earns salvation on our behalf. As King, he rules over us in love and purity.

🧂 | DISCUSSION STARTERS

What are some of the hats people around your table wear?

Who were some of the Old Testament prophets? priests? kings?

How do we benefit from Jesus' perfectly fulfilling each role?

> Moses continued, "The Lord your God will raise up for you a prophet like me from among your fellow Israelites. You must listen to him."
> *DEUTERONOMY 18:15*

> A different priest, who is like Melchizedek, has appeared. Jesus became a priest, not by meeting the physical requirement of belonging to the tribe of Levi, but by the power of a life that cannot be destroyed.
> *HEBREWS 7:15-16*

> I will raise up one of your descendants, your own offspring, and I will make his kingdom strong.... And I will secure his royal throne forever.
> *2 SAMUEL 7:12-13*

"I am confirming my covenant with you. Never again will floodwaters kill all living creatures; never again will a flood destroy the earth."

Then God said, "I am giving you a sign of my covenant with you and with all living creatures, for all generations to come. I have placed my rainbow in the clouds. It is the sign of my covenant with you and with all the earth."
GENESIS 9:11-13

The one sitting on the throne was as brilliant as gemstones—like jasper and carnelian. And the glow of an emerald circled his throne like a rainbow.
REVELATION 4:3

Rainbow

A rainbow occurs when raindrops and sunshine cross paths. When sunlight enters water drops, it reflects off their inside surfaces and separates into the component colors, which is similar to what happens with a glass prism.

God uses rainbows as a special sign to remind us of something important about himself. God told Noah, in essence, "When you see the rainbow, you will remember that I remember I am committed to you." The rainbow was a sign to Noah of God's mercy and commitment. So when we see a rainbow, it should remind us of God's mercy even in judgment and his commitment to living up to his promises.

The rainbow appears another time in the Bible. But this time it is not merely an arc across the sky. The rainbow that John, the author of Revelation, sees in heaven is even better than the one that Noah saw. This rainbow encircles the throne that Jesus sits on in heaven. It is a full circle. In other words, John sees the reality of God's faithfulness in its unending completeness.

If the rainbow in the sky reminds us of God's faithfulness in showing mercy toward us, just think how much more this full-circle rainbow around God's throne reveals about his complete, all-encompassing, unending faithfulness to us! This rainbow shows us in brilliant, living color that God will keep all his promises to us.

 | **DISCUSSION STARTERS**

What should we think about when we see a rainbow?

A rainbow is a sign of God's covenant with Noah. What sign did God give for these other covenants?
- Abraham (Genesis 17:10)
- Moses (Exodus 31:13)
- The New Covenant (1 Corinthians 11:23-26)

Divine Discipline

Some parents let their children do whatever they want to do—never punishing the children when they need it or prodding them in the right direction. Other parents are so strict, with so many rules or such harsh punishments, that their children live in constant fear of being in trouble.

God doesn't go to these extremes in how he parents us. He's the perfect parent. His discipline flows out of his love, not his anger. He does not lose his temper and lash out. He knows exactly what we need, and he disciplines us just right. When he disciplines us—by setting wise boundaries, allowing us to experience the natural consequences of our bad choices, and helping us to see the wrong in what we've done—he is loving us. It's good for us to learn that sin hurts us, so God may allow us to experience the pain sin causes. It is good for us to learn that disobedience leads to emptiness and regret, so he may allow us to feel the pain of that regret.

God takes no pleasure in the pain we experience when disciplined. He's like the parent who says, "This is going to hurt me more than it hurts you." But because he loves us, he does what is best for us.

 | ## DISCUSSION STARTERS

What would it be like to be in a family where the parents never discipline their children?

What is God's goal when he disciplines his children?

How should we respond to God's discipline in our lives?

As you endure this divine discipline, remember that God is treating you as his own children. Who ever heard of a child who is never disciplined by its father? If God doesn't discipline you as he does all of his children, it means that you are illegitimate and are not really his children at all. Since we respected our earthly fathers who disciplined us, shouldn't we submit even more to the discipline of the Father of our spirits, and live forever?

For our earthly fathers disciplined us for a few years, doing the best they knew how. But God's discipline is always good for us, so that we might share in his holiness. No discipline is enjoyable while it is happening—it's painful! But afterward there will be a peaceful harvest of right living for those who are trained in this way.

HEBREWS 12:7-11

The Lord of Time

Have you ever watched a TV show or movie or read a book about people who travel back or forward in time? It is the stuff of science fiction, because we know it is impossible. As humans, we are bound by time. We can't stop it. The clock is always ticking, and the calendar is always moving forward.

But God is not limited by time the way we are—just like he is not bound by gravity or space as we are. He doesn't age like we do. God exists apart from time, or outside time. And while he sees events in time and acts at particular times in the past and the present and the future, time to him is not a succession of moments or a progression of days. He sees all time as if it just happened. It's hard to understand, isn't it? Because it is so different from how we experience time, it's hard to wrap our minds around it.

Although God is not bound by time the way we are, the Bible from Genesis to Revelation is a record of the way God has acted over time to redeem his people. Paul writes, "When the right time came, God sent his Son" (GALATIANS 4:4). He is the Lord who created time. And he is the Lord who rules over time and uses it for his own purposes.

Remember the things I have done in the past. For I alone am God! I am God, and there is none like me. Only I can tell you the future before it even happens. Everything I plan will come to pass.
ISAIAH 46:9-10

You must not forget this one thing, dear friends: A day is like a thousand years to the Lord, and a thousand years is like a day.
2 PETER 3:8

"I am the Alpha and the Omega—the beginning and the end," says the Lord God. "I am the one who is, who always was, and who is still to come—the Almighty One."
REVELATION 1:8

 | ## DISCUSSION STARTERS

If you were like God and could see all events as if they just happened, what past or future event would you most like to see?

How does understanding God's timelessness increase our confidence in what he says about what is ahead for believers?

How does this knowledge about God being outside of time help us understand Ephesians 1:4: "Even before he made the world, God loved us and chose us in Christ to be holy"?

Everywhere at Once

Have you ever wished you could be in two places at the same time—maybe at the soccer game and the concert because both are happening at the same time? Human bodies can't do that. We can only be in one place at a time. But God is not limited like we are. God is everywhere, with his whole being.

God cannot be defined in terms of size or dimensions, and he cannot be contained by any space. We might think he is everywhere in the same way a smell diffuses throughout a house when a scented candle is burning—with molecules spread all around. But there are not parts of God everywhere. He's present with his whole being in every part of space.

While God is present in all places in his creation, he is *distinct* from his creation. It's kind of like a sponge. Water is present everywhere in the sponge, but the water is still completely separate from the sponge.

Wherever we are, God is with us—fully present with us. We can't hide from him; we can't get lost from him. He will never leave us or forsake us. He is with us wherever we are.

 | **DISCUSSION STARTERS**

Where are some places you would never want to go? Do you think God is there?

Who are some people in the Bible who tried to hide from God or run away from him? What made them want to escape God's presence?

What difference does it make that God is fully present with you?

"Am I a God who is only close at hand?" says the LORD. "No, I am far away at the same time. Can anyone hide from me in a secret place? Am I not everywhere in all the heavens and earth?" says the LORD.
JEREMIAH 23:23-24

Will God really live on earth? Why, even the highest heavens cannot contain you. How much less this Temple I have built!
1 KINGS 8:27

I can never get away from your presence! If I go up to heaven, you are there; if I go down to the grave, you are there. If I ride the wings of the morning, if I dwell by the farthest oceans, even there your hand will guide me, and your strength will support me.
PSALM 139:7-10

Love from the center of who you are; don't fake it. Run for dear life from evil; hold on for dear life to good. Be good friends who love deeply; practice playing second fiddle.

ROMANS 12:9, *The Message*

Don't look out only for your own interests, but take an interest in others, too.

PHILIPPIANS 2:4

The whole law can be summed up in this one command: "Love your neighbor as yourself."

GALATIANS 5:14

Second Fiddle

In an orchestra, the first-chair violinist—the most prominent and high-profile member of the orchestra—leads out by playing the main melody. While there are other violinists in the string section, they are not as honored as the lead violinist. This is where we get the expression "playing second fiddle."

If you play second fiddle to someone else, it means that the other person is in a stronger position or is seen as more important than you. And most of us don't like feeling that way. We are all born with the inner drive to be seen as important and the desire to be honored. We love to be served rather than to serve others. We feel jealous when someone else gets more attention or more praise than we do. We are usually scoping out situations to figure out how we can get the best seat or the biggest slice, not looking for ways to play second fiddle.

When we allow other people to get their needs or desires met while ours go unmet, when we give someone else preferred treatment while we are ignored, when we put the focus on another's achievements or hardships while we stay in the shadows . . . that's what it means to die to ourselves. It is a sure sign that the Holy Spirit is meeting our need for significance in the deepest places of our souls. Only then will we be content with playing second fiddle.

 | DISCUSSION STARTERS

Paul says to practice playing second fiddle. How can we do that?

Have you ever observed someone who showed contentedness and grace in playing second fiddle?

What are the good things about playing second fiddle?

Judgment Day

How would you live if you thought it didn't really matter—if you thought no one would ever check up on what you do, where you go, what you consume, or how you think? Would it make a difference?

The reality is, nobody gets by without being held accountable for how he or she lives. The Bible says that each one of us will give a personal account of our lives to God. Does that make you squirm? Are you embarrassed at the thought of it—or are you fearful at the thought of standing before the judgment seat of God? And perhaps more important, should you be?

The Bible says that we are saved through faith—and that this is a gift of God. It is not something we earn through good deeds. But our actions are the evidence that our faith is there. The record of our deeds will testify before the Judge about how genuine—or absent—our faith has been in our lives. It's not that our actions earn our salvation; it's that they demonstrate it.

For the believer, Judgment Day is not an event to dread. It is a day to anticipate with confidence that "there is no condemnation for those who belong to Christ Jesus" (Romans 8:1). If the Holy Spirit is in you, on that day when the spotlight shines on your life, all will see the attitudes and actions of a person in love with Jesus and used by Jesus. His work in you and through you will be on display.

> Christ Jesus . . . will someday judge the living and the dead when he appears to set up his Kingdom.
> *2 TIMOTHY 4:1*

> We must all stand before Christ to be judged. We will each receive whatever we deserve for the good or evil we have done in this earthly body.
> *2 CORINTHIANS 5:10*

> He will judge or reward you according to what you do. So you must live in reverent fear of him.
> *1 PETER 1:17*

 | ## DISCUSSION STARTERS

What is the job of a judge?

What are your thoughts and feelings about Judgment Day?

What would you like the record of evidence to reveal about you?

God said, "Let us make human beings in our image, to be like us."
GENESIS 1:26

Go and make disciples of all the nations, baptizing them in the name of the Father and the Son and the Holy Spirit.
MATTHEW 28:19

May the grace of the Lord Jesus Christ, the love of God, and the fellowship of the Holy Spirit be with you all.
2 CORINTHIANS 13:14

Can 1 + 1 + 1 = 1?

In your math class, if you tried to tell your teacher that 1 + 1 + 1 = 1, you probably wouldn't get a very good grade. But in exploring the mystery and wonder of who God is, we discover that where he is concerned, 1 + 1 + 1 really does equal 1. This is the holy mystery called the Trinity.

The Trinity means that there is one God who exists as three distinct persons—the Father, the Son, and the Holy Spirit. Or to say it another way, God is one in essence and three in person. Essence is *what* you are; person is *who* you are. So God is one "what" but three "whos."

The Bible says that we were chosen by God the Father and made holy by the Spirit for obedience to Jesus Christ. Are the three parts of the Trinity just three different ways of looking at God or simply ways of referring to three roles he plays? The answer must be no, because the Bible is clear that the Father, the Son, and the Holy Spirit are distinct persons.

Since the Father sent the Son into the world, he can't be the same person as the Son. And after the Son returned to the Father, the Father and the Son sent the Holy Spirit into the world. Therefore, the Holy Spirit must be distinct from the Father and the Son.

The Trinity can be hard to understand, but it is important because God and his character are important. There might be some things about him we can't grasp, but we do know the most important things: The Father, the Son, and the Holy Spirit are distinct persons. Each person is fully God. And there is only one God. Seeking to understand God more fully is a way we honor him.

 | **DISCUSSION STARTERS**

What does each verse at the beginning of today's devotion reveal to us about the Trinity?

What are things Jesus said or did that point to the reality of the Trinity?

How can embracing the Trinity help us to love God more fully? What is something you especially appreciate about each person of the Trinity?

God Is with You

Brother Lawrence was a French monk who lived during the 1600s. Because his sense of inner peace was so profound, people were drawn to him. He explained to them his efforts to keep his attention riveted on God, no matter what he was doing, and how that filled him with peace and joy. He called it the practice of the presence of God. "We should establish ourselves in a sense of God's Presence, by continually conversing with Him. It's a shameful thing to quit His conversation to think of trifles and fooleries," he said. "We need only to recognize God intimately present with us and to address ourselves to Him every moment."[1]

If we're honest, we have to admit that the promise that God is with us doesn't always seem like such a great deal! Often we don't want God to simply *be* with us. We want him to *do* something for us. The truth is, sometimes we want *what he has to offer* more than we want *him*. We work through our Bible studies to get the answers, and we pray through our lists until our minds wander. Too quickly, we're on to "more important" matters than simply experiencing and enjoying the very real presence of God. He's here, but we've missed him.

God's generous offer of his very presence is his most precious gift to us. The God who made us walks beside us in the highest and lowest points of life. He's there at big events, and he's with us on ordinary afternoons.

> I know the LORD is always with me. I will not be shaken, for he is right beside me.
> **PSALM 16:8**

> Even when I walk through the darkest valley, I will not be afraid, for you are close beside me. Your rod and your staff protect and comfort me.
> **PSALM 23:4**

> Come close to God, and God will come close to you.
> **JAMES 4:8**

🧂🧂 | DISCUSSION STARTERS

When are some times you'd rather have someone with you than be alone?

When is it easiest for you to "practice" God's presence? When is it most difficult?

How could you enjoy and appreciate the presence of God more?

---

1. For more on Brother Lawrence, see *Practicing the Presence of God* (Orleans, MA: Paraclete Press, 2007).

Natural Causes

If you've ever planted a garden, you know the basic steps required: You plant seeds in the ground and water them, and the sun shines on them. In time, the seeds become sprouts that grow into plants. We might know why this happens, and we might know all the natural factors behind what makes things grow and why clouds pour out rain and how animals and people eventually feed on plants. But is that all there is to it?

We think of many things in creation as merely natural occurrences. But actually they are the work of God. Psalm 148:8 says that weather patterns occur at the command of God: "Fire and hail, snow and clouds, wind and weather . . . obey him." God directs the stars in the heavens and the sun rising in the morning. God even tells the grass when to grow: "You cause grass to grow for the livestock" (PSALM 104:14).

There's a "natural" explanation for all these things, yet the Bible says God causes them to happen. God is the primary cause because he planned and initiated everything that takes place in creation. He is the secondary cause because the created order acts in ways that are consistent with how God created it. So we can't assume that if we know the "natural" cause of something in this world, God did not cause it. According to the Bible, all these natural events are entirely caused by God.

God's breath sends the ice, freezing wide expanses of water.

He loads the clouds with moisture, and they flash with his lightning.
JOB 37:10-11

He gives his sunlight to both the evil and the good, and he sends rain on the just and the unjust alike.
MATTHEW 5:45

Look at the birds. They don't plant or harvest or store food in barns, for your heavenly Father feeds them.
MATTHEW 6:26

 | ### DISCUSSION STARTERS

What do you know about why and how the sun comes up in the morning?

Think about some wonders of nature. Do these things make sense without a Creator who set them in motion and keeps them going?

Think of three things you usually take for granted as a part of "natural" events, and thank God for these things.

Two-Edged Sword

What do you do with a sword? Protect or defend yourself or someone else? Cut something open?

The Bible describes God's Word as a sword. It has the power to cut us to the core—spiritually speaking. What God says about us and about himself penetrates deeply into the inner parts of us. It cuts through the surface of our words and actions to reveal our deepest thoughts and attitudes. It cuts through our outward religious acts to show what we truly love and worship.

But God's Word is not simply a sword. It is described as a two-edged sword. What does that mean? That means it cuts both ways. The same God who speaks comfort to his children also speaks words of judgment against his enemies. The words of Jesus at once offer salvation for the believer and pronounce destruction for the unbeliever. His words offer conviction and comfort, commands and promises, punishments and rewards. He speaks grace to his people and destruction to his enemies.

Some people come to the Bible looking for comfort and encouragement. They don't really want to read anything that makes them uncomfortable or challenges them to change. But what God's Word has to say to us is not always a comforting word. Sometimes it confronts and corrects. His word is a two-edged sword, and we need both sides.

 | **DISCUSSION STARTERS**

What does it feel like to be cut?

Read Revelation 1:16 again. Why do you think Jesus is described as having a two-edged sword coming out of his mouth?

Why should you welcome rather than defend yourself from Jesus' sword?

The word of God is alive and powerful. It is sharper than the sharpest two-edged sword, cutting between soul and spirit, between joint and marrow. It exposes our innermost thoughts and desires.
HEBREWS 4:12

A sharp two-edged sword came from his mouth.
REVELATION 1:16

Put on salvation as your helmet, and take the sword of the Spirit, which is the word of God.
EPHESIANS 6:17

NOVEMBER

18

If you confess with your mouth that Jesus is Lord and believe in your heart that God raised him from the dead, you will be saved. For it is by believing in your heart that you are made right with God, and it is by confessing with your mouth that you are saved.

ROMANS 10:9-10

Everyone who acknowledges me publicly here on earth, I will also acknowledge before my Father in heaven. But everyone who denies me here on earth, I will also deny before my Father in heaven.

MATTHEW 10:32-33

Private Faith?

Occasionally we hear someone's faith described as "very private"—something that person is not comfortable talking about. But the Bible doesn't recognize even the possibility of having genuine faith but keeping it private and never talking about it with others. According to Paul, true followers of Jesus talk with other people about their love for God and their commitment to him—and they do so openly and boldly. Christianity is personal, but it was never intended to be private.

No one would expect to have a conversation with Tiger Woods without talking about golf. We would never imagine having a conversation with a NASCAR driver without talking about racing. Neither should we expect to talk with someone who's in love with Jesus without ever getting to the subject of Jesus. We don't have to have lots of theological training or be ready to answer every question or win every debate to talk about him. We simply talk about what and who is most important to us.

Paul said we are to confess with our mouths that Jesus is Lord. When we confess that Jesus is Lord, we're not just saying that Jesus is a significant religious figure or just that Jesus is the only way to know God (although he is both of those things). We're saying, "Jesus is *my* Lord. The aim of my life is to submit to him as my authority and proclaim how good he is to the whole world."

 | **DISCUSSION STARTERS**

What are some of your favorite topics to talk to people about?

What does it mean to "confess with your mouth"? Why do you think some people want to keep faith "private"?

Paul wrote in Philippians 2:11 that one day every tongue will confess that Jesus is Lord. How can that give us confidence now?

Your Royal Crown

Did you know that the Imperial Crown of India has more than six thousand diamonds on it? Or that the Imperial Crown of Russia weighs nine pounds? And England's Imperial State Crown has diamonds, pearls, sapphires, emeralds, and rubies on it! But as amazing as those crowns might be, they won't compare with the one the Bible tells us we'll receive someday from Jesus himself. This crown symbolizes the reward for our faithfulness in resisting temptation. The crown is our reward for perseverance in the face of persecution because of our love for Christ. The crown is the gift God will give us for loving him more than the things of this world. This crown will be precious to us, because it will have cost us something—maybe everything.

This is not a mere piece of headgear we could thoughtlessly part with. It will be too precious. Only one thing—one person—could cause us to give away our crown. Only someone who is more worthy of it. Revelation 4:10-11 tells us what we'll do with our crowns when we see Jesus on the throne in heaven: "They lay their crowns before the throne and say, 'You are worthy, O Lord our God, to receive glory and honor and power.'"

On that day, when we see Jesus on the throne, our sacrifices won't seem so sacrificial, and our suffering won't seem so significant. We will say to him, "You are the one who is worthy of glory. You gave me the faith, you gave me the perseverance, you created in me everything that earned this crown. It all came from you, and I want to give it back to you! I want you to have all the glory you deserve. I have no desire to keep it to myself because now I see that you are truly worthy!"

> Now the prize awaits me—the crown of righteousness, which the Lord, the righteous Judge, will give me on the day of his return. And the prize is not just for me but for all who eagerly look forward to his appearing.
>
> *2 TIMOTHY 4:8*

> God blesses those who patiently endure testing and temptation. Afterward they will receive the crown of life that God has promised to those who love him.
>
> *JAMES 1:12*

 | **DISCUSSION STARTERS**

What does a crown tell you about the person who is wearing it?

Think about the two kinds of crowns Jesus has been given: the crown of thorns and the crowns from those who worship him. What does each kind of crown tell you about him?

From the verses above, who does God reward with a crown?

323

Long ago you laid the foundation of the earth and made the heavens with your hands. They will perish, but you remain forever; they will wear out like old clothing. You will change them like a garment and discard them.

But you are always the same; you will live forever.
PSALM 102:25-27

I am the LORD, and I do not change.
MALACHI 3:6

Whatever is good and perfect comes down to us from God our Father, who created all the lights in the heavens. He never changes or casts a shifting shadow.
JAMES 1:17

No Shifting Shadow

Let's say you're walking along the sidewalk, and you can see your shadow in front of you. But then later your shadow is behind you or there's no shadow at all. Why is that? Because your shadow is determined by the sun, which is always moving around the earth. So your shadow is always changing.

When James said that God never casts a "shifting shadow," he was saying that God never changes. He is steadfast and dependable. What difference does it make that God doesn't change? Well, think for a minute what it would be like if God could change. If he could change, it would be either for the better or for the worse. If God could change for the better, then it would mean he is not perfect now. And if God could change for the worse, then wouldn't that mean he would become a little bit evil? We could never really trust a God who changed.

We don't have to wonder if God is going to change his mind about his plans for redeeming us or this world. We don't have to be concerned that he might go back on the promises he's made. We don't have to be afraid his love will lessen, his holiness will be spoiled, or his goodness will be corrupted. God never changes.

 | **DISCUSSION STARTERS**

In what ways have you changed in the last year?

Are there ways you've been hurt by people or institutions or plans that have changed? How does it reassure you that God will never change?

What are some of God's characteristics that you're glad will never change?

Why So Much Blood?

Those of us who have grown up in the era of supermarkets where we buy boneless, skinless chicken breasts wrapped in plastic have never had to deal much with the reality of animal slaughter. For most of us, the closest we come to dealing with the carcass of a dead animal is after Thanksgiving dinner. So it is difficult for us to accept and understand the sacrificial slaughter of thousands of animals described in the Old Testament.

We could estimate that there were more than a million animals sacrificed during the thousand-plus years of the Old Covenant. So considering that each bull's sacrifice spilled a gallon or two of blood, and each goat's a quart, it is mind boggling to think of all that blood and all those burning carcasses. If we're honest, most of us would just rather not talk about all this blood sacrifice stuff. It seems too primitive. And certainly it is messy and unsightly. We wonder why blood was so important to God.

But all that blood served as an unavoidable megaphone, shouting about the seriousness of sin and reminding the people that sin both brings and demands death. The blood was like a constantly flashing neon sign in the window of the Israelites' minds: Sin brings death. . . . Sin brings death. . . . Sin brings death. That megaphone of sacrifice also pointed to the need for a perfect sacrifice that would end the need for the animal sacrifices. Jesus was that perfect sacrifice. Our sin was dealt with by his death.

DISCUSSION STARTERS

What do you think it would be like to sacrifice a goat or lamb in an ongoing effort to deal with your sin?

Why do we no longer need to sacrifice animals as payment for sin?

In what way does sin both bring and demand death?

Under the old system, the blood of goats and bulls and the ashes of a young cow could cleanse people's bodies from ceremonial impurity. Just think how much more the blood of Christ will purify our consciences from sinful deeds so that we can worship the living God.
HEBREWS 9:13-14

Those sacrifices actually reminded them of their sins year after year. For it is not possible for the blood of bulls and goats to take away sins. That is why, when Christ came into the world, he said to God, "You did not want animal sacrifices or sin offerings. But you have given me a body to offer."
HEBREWS 10:3-5

This is what the LORD says: "What did your ancestors find wrong with me that led them to stray so far from me? They worshiped worthless idols, only to become worthless themselves."

JEREMIAH 2:5

What do you benefit if you gain the whole world but lose your own soul? Is anything worth more than your soul?

MATTHEW 16:26

Everything else is worthless when compared with the infinite value of knowing Christ Jesus my Lord.

PHILIPPIANS 3:8

Worth It or a Waste?

Do you ever find yourself doing something and wondering, *Will this really be worth it?* Will being on the team be worth all the hours of practice? Will getting good grades be worth the study time? Will the promotion be worth the overtime? Will the flat stomach be worth the nightly sit-ups?

We come to Jesus with the same question, although we probably wouldn't say it quite so bluntly. *Jesus, are you worth it?* Jesus, are you worth the bother, the commitment, the potential ridicule, the perseverance? What is in the future that will make it worth my while to trust you now?

Revelation 5 describes the end of time, when the final accounting is done, when we finally discover what was worthy of our best energies and investment. Verse 12 says, "They sang in a mighty chorus: 'Worthy is the Lamb who was slaughtered—to receive power and riches and wisdom and strength and honor and glory and blessing.'"

Of course, we can hardly imagine that day now, and sometimes it doesn't seem real. But we can be confident of what Scripture tells us. One day we will discover, if we haven't already, that the Lamb is worthy. Jesus is worth it. Jesus is worth seeking after. He's worth the sacrifice and the suffering. We won't be disappointed. He's worth it.

 | ## DISCUSSION STARTERS

What is something that requires a lot of your time now, and what makes it worth it?

In what ways would you say it is worth it right now to follow Jesus?

In what ways do you think it will be worth it in eternity to follow Jesus now?

An Anchor of Hope

Ever since there have been boats on the water, there have been anchors. The earliest anchors were probably rocks with a pair of wooden arms that sunk into the seafloor to keep a ship in a specific place. When an anchor is firm, a ship—and the people on it—are secure. Even if the winds blow hard, the ship won't crash against the rocks or float out into the rough seas.

Hebrews describes our hope in Jesus and his promises as an "anchor for our souls." This anchor isn't hurled into the depths of the sea but rises through the heights into heaven—into the very throne room of God. This anchor embeds itself in the pure soil of heaven. Because God has given us this anchor, nothing can throw us off course or destroy us.

This confidence in our security is meant to give us hope. Not optimism or good feelings, but solid confidence. In other words, our hope in Jesus is not risky or uncertain. It is "strong and trustworthy," like a boat held in place by a solid anchor. We don't have to be afraid that God won't keep his promises to us, and we don't have to be afraid that the difficulties of this world will throw our lives off course or crush us. Our security isn't found in our bank accounts, our good grades, our insurance policies, or our own abilities. Our security is in Jesus alone, and we're safe. Jesus offers himself to us as an "anchor for the soul."

🧂🧂 | DISCUSSION STARTERS

What would it be like to be on a ship in a storm—with no anchor?

What are some things we often look to for security instead of putting our hope in Jesus?

What is one way you can "hold to the hope" this week?

I pray that God, the source of hope, will fill you completely with joy and peace because you trust in him. Then you will overflow with confident hope through the power of the Holy Spirit.
ROMANS 15:13

We who have fled to him for refuge can have great confidence as we hold to the hope that lies before us. This hope is a strong and trustworthy anchor for our souls.
HEBREWS 6:18-19

You have been called to one glorious hope for the future.
EPHESIANS 4:4

As Jesus was walking along, he saw a man who had been blind from birth. "Rabbi," his disciples asked him, "why was this man born blind? Was it because of his own sins or his parents' sins?"

"It was not because of his sins or his parents' sins," Jesus answered. "This happened so the power of God could be seen in him."

JOHN 9:1-3

When Jesus heard about it he said, "Lazarus's sickness will not end in death. No, it happened for the glory of God so that the Son of God will receive glory from this."

JOHN 11:4

Why Did This Happen?

When something bad or difficult happens, people's first response is often to ask God, "Why?" We want God to explain his reasoning behind why he has allowed hurt into our lives or the lives of those we love. When the disciples asked Jesus to explain why a blind man was born without sight, they were asking him the same question we all ask when we suffer: Whose fault is this? Who is to blame? Why did this happen?

They wanted to know the reason for the suffering, but that wasn't what Jesus wanted to focus on. It was the purpose of his suffering. "It was not because of his sins or his parents' sins," Jesus said. "This happened so the power of God could be seen in him."

God uniquely uses suffering as the backdrop to put his character on display in and through our lives. True, we can put God on display in the successes we achieve. But not in the way we can in the sufferings we experience. God receives glory when he miraculously intervenes with his healing power. But he also receives glory when people endure their suffering through the grace God gives them. That grace allows us to see the broken and hurt places in our lives not as punishment, but as a platform. Then we recognize that in our weakness, God can be shown to be strong.

 | **DISCUSSION STARTERS**

How was the power of God shown in the blind man's life (see John 9)?

Is there someone you know who has suffered in a way that caused you to see the glory of God more clearly?

What does it mean to put the glory of God on display in your life?

The Lord Will Provide

"**B**ut Mom, I *neeeed* it!" we plead when there's something we really want. And if it's something we really do need, most moms will do whatever it takes to provide it.

But even if Mom delivers what you think you need, your real provider always has been and always will be God. God sees what you need even before you know you need it, and he puts everything in place to provide it. That's what Abraham discovered thousands of years ago. He had been instructed to sacrifice his son Isaac, whom he loved immensely, as a test of his love for God. But at just the last moment, God kept him from sacrificing his son. Abraham looked up and saw a ram provided by God to sacrifice in place of Isaac. In his gratitude, Abraham spoke a new name for God that day—*Yahweh-Yireh*—which means "the Lord will provide."

The provision God made for Abraham that day was really just a preview of a greater provision God would make for every person of faith. In order to save Isaac, God provided a ram. But in order to save us, God provided himself—in the person of Jesus. And as Jesus suffered on the cross, he endured what Isaac avoided. Whereas Abraham went home with Isaac, God the Father turned away from his Son. This is God's ultimate and most significant provision for us—an acceptable substitute who took on our sin and died in our place.

 | ## DISCUSSION STARTERS

Do you know people who are really generous? What kinds of things do they provide for other people?

What needs do you have that God has provided for?

What do you need to trust God to provide for you?

"We have the fire and the wood," the boy said, "but where is the sheep for the burnt offering?"

"God will provide a sheep for the burnt offering, my son," Abraham answered. . . .

Then Abraham looked up and saw a ram caught by its horns in a thicket. So he took the ram and sacrificed it as a burnt offering in place of his son. Abraham named the place Yahweh-Yireh (which means "the LORD will provide").

GENESIS 22:7-8, 13-14

Since he did not spare even his own Son but gave him up for us all, won't he also give us everything else?

ROMANS 8:32

The LORD is my strength and shield. I trust him with all my heart. He helps me, and my heart is filled with joy. I burst out in songs of thanksgiving.
PSALM 28:7

Let your roots grow down into him, and let your lives be built on him. Then your faith will grow strong in the truth you were taught, and you will overflow with thankfulness.
COLOSSIANS 2:7

Obscene stories, foolish talk, and coarse jokes—these are not for you. Instead, let there be thankfulness to God.
EPHESIANS 5:4

Gratitude on Guard

One of the favorite tourist stops for people visiting London, England, is to watch the changing of the guard at Buckingham Palace. Besides putting on a grand show, the guard actively protects the palace and the queen from anything and anyone who might seek to penetrate the walls of the palace and harm her.

Likewise, there are many harmful attitudes that would like to penetrate the walls of our hearts and minds. Greed. Self-centeredness. Addiction. The feeling that the world owes us. Once inside, these thought patterns wreak havoc on our relationships and steal our joy. So if we want to keep them out, we have to place a guard on watch to protect us. And that guard is gratitude—chosen intentionally in the words we speak and the way we think. This kind of ongoing gratitude is like a guard against sinful, harmful attitudes that attack us and try to make themselves at home in us.

It is hard for shallow whining to find a foothold in the heart of a grateful person. There's no room for demanding behavior in the life of a grateful person. The same lips that offer thanksgiving are less likely to complain or blame or gossip. Voicing our gratitude humbles us, leaving no room for pride. Expressing gratitude to God builds our faith and confidence in him, making doubt take a backseat. Gratitude guards us from what would destroy us.

 **| DISCUSSION STARTERS**

What are you especially grateful for?

When you are grateful for the material things you have, the family you have, and the spiritual blessings you have, how can that help guard against sin?

How does expressing gratitude out loud help it make its way into our hearts?

The Scale for Suffering

How many different kinds of scales have you used or seen? There are all kinds of different scales you can use depending on what you're weighing, but one type is called a balance scale. It has two bowls on opposite ends of a beam.

This might have been the type of scale Paul had in mind when he described the suffering of this life as "small" and "momentary." Because those who have suffered in terms of their bodies, their emotions, their relationships, or their faith might have a hard time describing that suffering as insignificant or temporary. We might wonder if Paul really knew what it is like to suffer. But the truth is that Paul's suffering included being imprisoned, beaten, stoned, shipwrecked, robbed, hungry, thirsty, cold, and naked—none of which we would describe as small or momentary. So how could Paul describe his experiences that way?

Paul saw a set of balance scales. On one side of the scale is the suffering of this life—the temporary pains and short-term losses. On the other side of the scales is the glory we will experience in heaven—the satisfying joy of being with Jesus, the overflowing inheritance of our eternal reward, and the unending pleasure of heaven. When Paul said his trials were light, he didn't mean they were easy or painless. He meant that compared to what was coming they were small and insignificant. All our hard times now are like feathers on one side of the scale compared to the weight of glory ahead in heaven.

What we suffer now is nothing compared to the glory he will reveal to us later.
ROMANS 8:18

Our present troubles are small and won't last very long. Yet they produce for us a glory that vastly outweighs them and will last forever!
2 CORINTHIANS 4:17

These trials make you partners with Christ in his suffering, so that you will have the wonderful joy of seeing his glory.
1 PETER 4:13

 | ## DISCUSSION STARTERS

Do you have any scales to weigh things in your house? Bathroom scales? Kitchen scales? A postal scale? How do they work?

What perspective on suffering and glory does each of the verses on the right give us?

What can we do to remember that the glory ahead is weightier than our suffering now?

Would You Want to Be in Heaven if Jesus Weren't There?

NOVEMBER 28

Whom have I in heaven but you? I desire you more than anything on earth. My health may fail, and my spirit may grow weak, but God remains the strength of my heart; he is mine forever.

PSALM 73:25-26

Everything else is worthless when compared with the infinite value of knowing Christ Jesus my Lord. For his sake I have discarded everything else, counting it all as garbage, so that I could gain Christ.

PHILIPPIANS 3:8

LORD, you alone are my inheritance, my cup of blessing.

PSALM 16:5

ots of people look forward to heaven. They want to see people they love who have died. They don't want to have any more pain. They want to live in a place where the struggles of life are over. But for many people, if they're honest, seeing Jesus in heaven is optional. Since they don't really know him and they haven't really come to love him and value him, they have no particular longing to be with him for eternity.

It's a little bit like someone offering you the use of his or her vacation home for the week, and then telling you later that the owner is going to be there too. Your response to the second piece of news indicates if you have genuine affection for the owner or if you are just glad to be on the receiving end of the stuff he or she is handing out.

Before Jesus went to the cross, he prayed for all the people who would believe in him. Jesus knew just what to pray for us; he knew exactly what we'd need. So he prayed, "Father, I want these whom you have given me to be with me where I am. Then they can see all the glory you gave me because you loved me even before the world began!" (JOHN 17:24). Jesus wants us to experience what we were made for—to see him and know him as he truly is. Jesus wants us to see how much God loves him and what makes him worthy of that love and honor. In heaven we'll be filled with joy and surrounded by everything good. But without Jesus, heaven just wouldn't be heaven.

 | DISCUSSION STARTERS

When you think about heaven, what are some of the things you look forward to?

What longings do you think Jesus will fulfill in heaven?

How can we nurture our longing for being with Jesus in heaven?

That Smells Good

What smells bring a smile to your face? Is it the smell of a chocolate cake coming out of the oven or onions simmering on the stove? Do you love the smell of a fresh-cut Christmas tree or a bouquet of roses?

Did you know there's a smell that brings a smile to the face of God? The Bible tells us that God is pleased by the smell of the sacrifice Jesus made on the cross. Now that is hard for us to understand because we can't imagine that smelling good. And we know that when Jesus was on the cross with all our sin laid on him, God actually had to turn away from him—almost as if he had to get away from the stench of all that sin.

So why would the Bible say that Jesus' sacrifice was a "pleasing aroma" to the Lord? Because that sacrifice on the cross demonstrated the love of God in the most complete and perfect way possible. It was a tangible, unmistakable, worldwide demonstration of the way God loves sinners.

Likewise, when we love other people sacrificially—when we love with the kind of depth and self-giving that Jesus demonstrated on the cross—it is like a sweet perfume that God can smell, and it makes him smile. As more and more people know and experience the love of Jesus, the smell gets stronger and stronger, and God is pleased.

| DISCUSSION STARTERS

What is the worst thing you have ever smelled? What's the best?

What do the three verses on this page tell you about what smells good to God?

What expressions of sacrificial love have you seen from your family members? What is something you can do to love someone sacrificially this week?

> The priest will burn the entire sacrifice on the altar as a burnt offering. It is a special gift, a pleasing aroma to the LORD.
> *LEVITICUS 1:9*

> Live a life filled with love, following the example of Christ. He loved us and offered himself as a sacrifice for us, a pleasing aroma to God.
> *EPHESIANS 5:2*

> He uses us to spread the knowledge of Christ everywhere, like a sweet perfume. Our lives are a Christ-like fragrance rising up to God.
> *2 CORINTHIANS 2:14-15*

Getting and Giving

This is the season our mailboxes are filled with stacks of mail-order catalogs. Through their colorful pictures and creative words, they seek to convince us that we don't have enough stuff—that we need more, newer, better. They go beyond supplying our needs; they appeal to our greed—the desire to get and keep more than we really need.

We have a choice. We can give in to greed and keep collecting more stuff and spending more money on ourselves. Or we can break out of the cycle of believing the lie that more will satisfy us. How? By giving. The only way to do battle with the greed in our hearts is to give—to become outrageous givers. God can turn greedy, grasping, fearful hoarders into generous, honest, trustworthy givers.

To become givers, we have to decide not to listen to the voice inside us that asks, *If I let this go, who will take care of me? What will satisfy me?* We have to face our fear that God will not be able to take care of us, protect us, or at least make sure we maintain the lifestyle we think we need to make us happy. We tell ourselves the truth about God—that because he has been so generous in giving us Jesus, we can be confident that he will give us everything we need. We take him at his word that he can satisfy us and that he will bless us as we give to others. We test his promise that it is "more blessed to give than to receive" (ACTS 20:35).

Some people are always greedy for more, but the godly love to give!
PROVERBS 21:26

Beware! Guard against every kind of greed. Life is not measured by how much you own.
LUKE 12:15

You can be sure that no immoral, impure, or greedy person will inherit the Kingdom of Christ and of God. For a greedy person is an idolater, worshiping the things of this world.
EPHESIANS 5:5

 | ## DISCUSSION STARTERS

What do you find yourself dreaming of getting? What do you find yourself dreaming of giving?

When have you experienced or observed someone else enjoying the happiness that comes from outrageous giving?

What does our greed or generosity say about what we think of God?

His Two Comings

Throughout Old Testament times, God spoke through the prophets, giving the people of Israel details about what to look for in the coming Messiah. These previews were given so people would long for his coming and recognize him when he arrived. In light of the prophecies, the people looked forward to one great day of the Lord when the Messiah would come, defeat his enemies, save his people, establish his Kingdom, and rule in peace and righteousness forever. As the Israelites saw it, the coming of the Messiah meant the end of this age and the beginning of the age to come. It meant the establishment of the eternal Kingdom of God on earth. And it meant the fulfillment of all God's promises.

What the people didn't expect was that the fulfillment of the prophecies would be split into two comings of the Messiah—once as a Lamb to give himself as a sacrifice for sin, and again as a Lion to defeat his enemies and establish his eternal Kingdom. Many of the Old Testament prophecies about the Messiah are still awaiting fulfillment. So just as the people of Israel longed for the Messiah to come, we long for him to come again. And because we can see that all the prophecies related to his first coming were fulfilled exactly, we have confidence that all the remaining promises about Jesus will be fulfilled when he comes again.

🏸 | DISCUSSION STARTERS

Look up the following prophecies and discuss whether they refer to Jesus' first coming, his second coming, or both.

- Genesis 3:15
- Isaiah 9:1-7
- Isaiah 52:13–53:12
- Jeremiah 23:5-6
- Daniel 7:13-14
- Zechariah 9:9

The LORD has sent this message to every land: "Tell the people of Israel, 'Look, your Savior is coming. See, he brings his reward with him as he comes.'"
ISAIAH 62:11

The virgin will conceive a child! She will give birth to a son and will call him Immanuel (which means "God is with us").
ISAIAH 7:14

The woman said, "I know the Messiah is coming—the one who is called Christ. When he comes, he will explain everything to us."
JOHN 4:25

Pilate said, "So you are a king?"

Jesus responded, "You say I am a king. Actually, I was born and came into the world to testify to the truth. All who love the truth recognize that what I say is true."

"What is truth?" Pilate asked.
JOHN 18:37-38

Jesus told him, "I am the way, the truth, and the life. No one can come to the Father except through me."
JOHN 14:6

I Was Born for This

Every year Christmas poses the question, Why did Jesus come? When he was on trial near the end of his life, Jesus himself answered this question clearly. He said, "I was born and came into the world to testify to the truth." Christmas exists because Jesus came to show us that there is ultimate truth and that truth can be known.

But evidently, from what Jesus said, not everyone recognizes the truth. According to Jesus, "Everyone who is of the truth hears My voice" (JOHN 18:37, NASB). He didn't mean that only a certain group of people can hear the sound of his voice. He meant that only some people who hear his voice recognize that what he is saying is true.

In 2 Thessalonians 2:10, Paul writes that Satan uses every kind of evil deception to fool people who "refuse to love and accept the truth that would save them." Many people have been deceived into thinking that individuals can decide for themselves what God is like. Some people say about Jesus, "That may be your truth, but that's not my truth." Some people think those who believe in an absolute truth—something everyone should believe and follow—are unintelligent and even dangerous.

But Jesus said that there is a truth that comes from God outside the world we know, and it is this truth that gives the world meaning. This is a truth that should be pursued, believed, and enjoyed. This truth is Jesus.

 | **DISCUSSION STARTERS**

What are some things you believe are absolutely true? How do you know these things are true?

When you talk to people who don't believe there are things that are true for everyone, how can you respond?

What does John 16:12-15 tell us about how we can know truth?

Family Matters

Do you know people who can trace their ancestries to someone famous—a war hero, an inventor, a sports legend, or a Hollywood actor? People who are related to someone famous usually like to talk about it. But it is different when people can trace their ancestry to someone infamous—a mass murderer, an unethical businessperson, a cruel dictator. These descendants are not usually so quick to want to talk about their ancestors.

Matthew and Luke both include a genealogy in their Gospels—a record of the human ancestry of Jesus. Jewish people were looking for a Messiah who would fulfill the prophecies by being a legal heir to the throne of David. So Matthew's genealogy traces the ancestors of Joseph, the legal father of Jesus, all the way back not only to David but to Abraham. Luke's Greek readers were less concerned about the fulfillment of Jewish prophecy but needed to see the humanity of Jesus, so Luke traced Jesus' ancestry all the way back to Adam.

But perhaps the most important thing we learn in the genealogies of these Gospels is that Jesus redeems all kinds of people. If you look through the list of people in Jesus' ancestral line, you'll see people famous for their faith and people infamous for their failures. There were Jews and Gentiles, men and women, and all of them needed a Savior. This gives us hope that no matter what we've done or where we come from, Jesus is not ashamed to have us in his family.

> This is a record of the ancestors of Jesus the Messiah, a descendant of David and of Abraham. . . . Jacob was the father of Joseph, the husband of Mary. Mary gave birth to Jesus, who is called the Messiah.
>
> *MATTHEW 1:1, 16*

> Jesus was known as the son of Joseph. . . . Adam was the son of God.
>
> *LUKE 3:23, 38*

| DISCUSSION STARTERS

What does your family's ancestry say about you?

What does Luke 3:23 tell us about the birth of Jesus?

Look through the genealogies of Jesus in Matthew 1 and Luke 3. Who are you surprised to see there because of what you know about them?

Praise the Lord, the God of Israel, because he has visited and redeemed his people. He has sent us a mighty Savior from the royal line of his servant David, just as he promised through his holy prophets long ago.

LUKE 1:68-70

Remember that Christ came as a servant to the Jews to show that God is true to the promises he made to their ancestors.

ROMANS 15:8

All of God's promises have been fulfilled in Christ with a resounding "Yes!"

2 CORINTHIANS 1:20

The Promised One

Have you ever had to wait for someone to fulfill a promise to you—a promise to take you somewhere or give you something or let you do something? It can be hard to wait for a promise to be fulfilled.

God made a promise to us. In fact, he has made many promises. But God's most important promise—the promise all his other promises depend on—was that he would send his Son to save us from our sin. Many years and many generations passed before what God promised became a reality. The people he made the promise to had to wait, and waiting can be hard.

But waiting patiently for God to fulfill his promises is what it means to have faith. We don't become Christians just by believing what God has done for us in the past through Jesus. Saving faith means putting all our hopes in what God is going to do for us in the future because of what Jesus accomplished on the Cross.

Putting your faith in God's promises is not something you do one time on the day you become a Christian. The essence of being a Christian is placing all your hopes in the promises of God and being willing to wait, trusting that, "God's way is perfect. All the LORD's promises prove true" (PSALM 18:30).

 | **DISCUSSION STARTERS**

What does it mean to make a promise?

What promises has God made in his Word that you are holding on to?

In what way are all God's promises fulfilled in Jesus?

Right on Time

Have you ever tried to talk to somebody who wouldn't talk back to you? Most of us give up pretty quickly on a conversation when the other person is silent.

The Jewish people had been waiting a long time to hear from God when Jesus was born. It had been more than four hundred years since they had last heard God speak to them through one of his prophets. It seemed like God had gone silent, and some people had grown weary of keeping up their hopes that God would come through for them. While they were waiting, the Romans occupied their country and ruled over them. This made them long even more for a great deliverer who would save them from their misery and rule with justice and peace.

But God knew when the time was just right to send Jesus, the Messiah, into the world. He knew when the exact religious, cultural, and political conditions demanded by his perfect plan were in place. You see, God is not making up plans as he goes. All the grand events of God's plan for our redemption have been scheduled in advance, from Creation to the final judgment. In fact, "he has set a day for judging the world" (ACTS 17:31). The course of history is not a mystery to God. Time is in his hands. And he will bring about his plans and purposes in our world and in our lives right on time.

When the right time came, God sent his Son, born of a woman, subject to the law.
GALATIANS 4:4

Before John came, all the prophets and the law of Moses looked forward to this present time.
MATTHEW 11:13

"The time promised by God has come at last!" he announced. "The Kingdom of God is near! Repent of your sins and believe the Good News!"
MARK 1:15

 | ## DISCUSSION STARTERS

How does it make you feel when you talk to someone who doesn't talk back?

Why do you think God decided Jesus would be born in the place and the time he was? What does this show us about God's careful timing?

What do you need to trust God's perfect timing for in your own life?

I Am the Lord's Servant

It's hard to imagine how frightening it must have been for teenage Mary to see an angel and hear him speaking to her. No wonder she was "confused and disturbed." It must have been even more frightening for her to process what the angel was telling her—that she was going to become pregnant even though she had never slept with a man. And yet Mary responded to the angel with submission. In a sense she said to God, "I'm yours. You can do anything you want with me."

It requires faith to see the hard things in our lives as gifts of God's grace—faith to rest in who God is and his love for us so we can be confident he is doing something good in and through our circumstances. It's easy to label what we would consider "good things" in our lives as gifts from God, and we welcome them with gratitude. But Mary's example shows us how to welcome those things we would not label as good, confident that God's gifts sometimes come in perplexing and even painful packages. Somehow, in God's mysterious ways, these things, too, are gifts of his grace toward us.

Gabriel appeared to her and said, "Greetings, favored woman! The Lord is with you!" Confused and disturbed, Mary tried to think what the angel could mean. "Don't be afraid, Mary," the angel told her, "for you have found favor with God!"
LUKE 1:28-30

Mary responded, "I am the Lord's servant. May everything you have said about me come true."
LUKE 1:38

How my spirit rejoices in God my Savior! For he took notice of his lowly servant girl, and from now on all generations will call me blessed.
LUKE 1:47-48

 | ## DISCUSSION STARTERS

What do you think went through Mary's mind when the angel was speaking to her?

What did Mary believe about God that caused her to respond with a song of praise?

Are there things you know God has asked you to do or endure that you find difficult to say yes to?

Name Him Jesus

Most parents spend a lot of time thinking about what they will name their babies. They think through names with special meanings, traditional family names, and names they just like the sound of.

Mary and Joseph didn't have to wonder what to name the baby Mary was carrying. The angel who appeared to Mary and Joseph separately told them both what to name the baby: Jesus. And this was no random name, though it was an ordinary name for a Jewish boy in that day. The name *Jesus* was rich with meaning about who this child would be and what he would do.

Jesus, or *Yeshua* in Hebrew, means "the Lord saves." It is a combination of *Yahu*, a personal name for God, and *shua*, which means "a cry for help" or "a saving cry." So in a sense, the angel was telling Joseph and Mary by the name he was to be given that this child would be a rescuer, a savior—someone who would be no less than God himself in the body of a baby.

| DISCUSSION STARTERS

What does your name mean? Why did your parents choose it for you?

Read Luke 1:31-33. Can you name five things the angel told Mary about her child?

What do you think it was like for Mary to take in what the angel told her about what her baby would do and who he would be?

DECEMBER

7

You will conceive and give birth to a son, and you will name him Jesus. He will be very great and will be called the Son of the Most High. The Lord God will give him the throne of his ancestor David. And he will reign over Israel forever; his Kingdom will never end!

LUKE 1:31-33

An angel of the Lord appeared to him in a dream. "Joseph, son of David," the angel said, "do not be afraid to take Mary as your wife. For the child within her was conceived by the Holy Spirit. And she will have a son, and you are to name him Jesus, for he will save his people from their sins."

MATTHEW 1:20-21

The earth was formless and empty, and darkness covered the deep waters. And the Spirit of God was hovering over the surface of the waters.
GENESIS 1:2

The angel replied, "The Holy Spirit will come upon you, and the power of the Most High will overshadow you. So the baby to be born will be holy, and he will be called the Son of God."
LUKE 1:35

You will receive power when the Holy Spirit comes upon you. And you will be my witnesses, telling people about me everywhere—in Jerusalem, throughout Judea, in Samaria, and to the ends of the earth.
ACTS 1:8

Overshadowed

Have you ever driven through thick fog—so thick you could barely see what was in front of you? Fog is basically a cloud that is close to the ground. In several places in the Bible, the presence and power of God in the person of the Holy Spirit is described as a cloud, like the cloud that led the Israelites in the desert and the bright, shining cloud that came down at the Transfiguration.

We get that sense of an enveloping cloud when we read the words the angel said to Mary—that the Holy Spirit would "come upon" her and "overshadow" her like a cloud. God, in the person of the Holy Spirit, would come over her and do a creative work in her womb, making new life.

We all desperately need the same thing—for the Holy Spirit to come upon us and overshadow us. We need him to make new life where there is none, to bring light where there is darkness. We need the Holy Spirit to enter into the chaos of our inner thoughts, emotions, and desires and change us from the inside out. We can't create new spiritual life on our own. We need the power of God to work inside us so that Christ can be born in us.

 | **DISCUSSION STARTERS**

What is it like to be in the middle of a cloud in the form of fog?

How is the Holy Spirit always involved in creating life?

In what ways do you need the creative power of the Holy Spirit to come upon you?

Jump for Joy

One of the most exciting times in a woman's pregnancy is when she begins to feel her child move inside her. It all becomes more real as the mother begins to feel the baby shift positions, stick out an arm, or even hiccup.

When the angel told Zechariah that his wife, Elizabeth, would have a son, he said that this baby would be filled with the Holy Spirit, even before his birth. And when Elizabeth was six months pregnant, her relative Mary came to visit. When Mary, carrying Jesus in her womb, walked in the door, something happened. The baby inside Elizabeth jumped for joy. It must have taken Elizabeth's breath away. She could feel her baby's excitement, and she knew why he was excited. "Elizabeth was filled with the Holy Spirit," says Luke 1:41. Both mother and child were filled with the Holy Spirit, and the Spirit enabled them to sense the presence of the Messiah.

We all need the Holy Spirit to cause us to recognize Jesus. And when the Holy Spirit does this, we want to jump for joy too.

🧂🧂 | DISCUSSION STARTERS

Can you remember a time when you have been so happy and excited that you jumped for joy (or wished you could)?

What do you think the conversations between Elizabeth and Mary would have been like when Mary came to visit?

What other examples can you think of from the Bible when the Spirit gave someone the ability to recognize who Jesus was?

The angel said, "Don't be afraid, Zechariah! God has heard your prayer. Your wife, Elizabeth, will give you a son, and you are to name him John. You will have great joy and gladness, and many will rejoice at his birth. . . . He will be filled with the Holy Spirit, even before his birth."

LUKE 1:13-15

At the sound of Mary's greeting, Elizabeth's child leaped within her, and Elizabeth was filled with the Holy Spirit. Elizabeth gave a glad cry and exclaimed to Mary, "God has blessed you above all women, and your child is blessed. Why am I so honored, that the mother of my Lord should visit me? When I heard your greeting, the baby in my womb jumped for joy."

LUKE 1:41-44

Magnification

Have you ever looked at something through a magnifying glass? A magnifying glass makes something look much bigger than it actually is. Is that what Mary meant when she said, "My soul magnifies the Lord"? Was she trying to make God look bigger than he actually is?

We can never make God bigger or greater than he actually is. The truth is, we can never fully take in or understand his actual greatness. But we can magnify him. We magnify God not by making him bigger than he is but by making him greater in our thoughts, in our affections, in our memories, and in our expectations. We magnify him by having higher, larger, and truer thoughts and understandings of him. We magnify him by praising him and telling others about his greatness so they can have bigger thoughts about him too.

Sometimes we wonder why we aren't happy, why we make sinful choices, why we feel distant from God. Often it's because we have small thoughts about God and magnified thoughts of ourselves, our wants, our rights, our accomplishments. Mary, the one God chose to be the mother of his Son, could have easily allowed her thoughts of herself to become inflated. But instead of magnifying herself, she magnified the Lord.

Mary said: "My soul magnifies the Lord, and my spirit has rejoiced in God my Savior. For He has regarded the lowly state of His maidservant; for behold, henceforth all generations will call me blessed."

LUKE 1:46-48, NKJV

Oh, magnify the LORD with me, and let us exalt His name together.

PSALM 34:3, NKJV

Because he is righteous, the LORD has exalted his glorious law.

ISAIAH 42:21

 | ## DISCUSSION STARTERS

What is the most interesting thing you've looked at through a magnifying glass?

Read Luke 1:46-55. What are some phrases that show Mary's humble thoughts about herself and her big thoughts about God?

What's one way you can magnify God this week?

Bethlehem's Baby

Bethlehem was a small and unimpressive village. And though the Jewish people remembered Micah's prophecy that the Messiah would come from Bethlehem as a descendant of King David, they were not expecting their Savior to be born in such a humble place.

We are often a little surprised when someone from a small town accomplishes something of true greatness. We have a tendency to think that for something or someone to be significant, the idea, the business, or the person must be birthed in a major city or well-known place.

When God sent Jesus, he turned every expectation of what people thought would make him great upside down. Jesus came as a baby instead of a grown man. He was born to ordinary parents, not people of prominence or power. He came as a humble teacher rather than a conquering king. And he was born in an obscure little town rather than one of the great cities of the day.

This tells us something important about how God chooses whom and what he will use and bless. He doesn't choose on the basis of accomplishments or reputation or worldly value. God chooses to use simple, ordinary things and people so that he is the one who gets all the glory.

 | DISCUSSION STARTERS

Are there some great companies or organizations or people who come from the city or town you live in?

What are some of the ways we show that we believe bigger is better?

Bethlehem means "house of bread," and it is King David's hometown. Why are these two things significant for the place of Jesus' birth?

You, O Bethlehem Ephrathah, are only a small village among all the people of Judah. Yet a ruler of Israel will come from you, one whose origins are from the distant past.... And he will stand to lead his flock with the LORD's strength.

MICAH 5:2, 4

The Scriptures clearly state that the Messiah will be born of the royal line of David, in Bethlehem, the village where King David was born.

JOHN 7:42

Jesus was born in the town of Bethlehem in Judea.

MATTHEW 2:1

Prepare the Way

What happens at your house when guests are coming? Do you clean up things that are messy, fix things that are broken, make plans for how you will welcome your visitors? As God prepared to send his Son into this world, he sent someone ahead to get things ready. He had promised that he would do that, so some people were watching for that individual. Two Old Testament prophets (Malachi and Isaiah) had prophesied that before the Messiah came, a messenger would come who was sent by God.

John the Baptist was the person God sent to prepare his people for Jesus. It wasn't food or beds that needed to be prepared; it was hearts. It was John's mission to call people to repent—to leave behind their sin and turn back to God. John prepared the people for Jesus by helping them get their hearts ready.

God knows our hearts need to be prepared to receive Jesus. You're probably busy preparing for Christmas with parties and programs and presents. But are you preparing your heart to receive Jesus? Have you cleaned out the clutter of sinful attitudes and selfishness? Are you looking expectantly for Jesus to make himself known to you?

It began just as the prophet Isaiah had written: "Look, I am sending my messenger ahead of you, and he will prepare your way. He is a voice shouting in the wilderness, 'Prepare the way for the LORD's coming! Clear the road for him!'" This messenger was John the Baptist.
MARK 1:1-4

He will be a man with the spirit and power of Elijah. He will prepare the people for the coming of the Lord. He will turn the hearts of the fathers to their children, and he will cause those who are rebellious to accept the wisdom of the godly.
LUKE 1:17

 | **DISCUSSION STARTERS**

Think through what you do to prepare for company at your house. How can you do similar things to prepare for Jesus?

When Luke says that John came in the "spirit and power of Elijah," it means he proclaimed judgment. How does an awareness of our sin help prepare us for Jesus?

What are some practical ways we can prepare to welcome Jesus into our celebration of his birth?

No Room for Him

When all the people who were descendants of David arrived in the tiny town of Bethlehem to be counted, people made room in their houses for relatives, and the places for travelers to stay filled up quickly. So when Mary and Joseph arrived in Bethlehem, they had to nestle themselves into a stall in a barn or perhaps in a cave that was used as a stable.

We might think that since God could orchestrate an empire-wide census to bring Mary and Joseph to Bethlehem, surely he could have made sure there was a room available for Jesus to be born in. But somehow it seems appropriate that his life on earth would begin this way. Jesus never had a home of his own, and his own people rejected and finally crucified him.

Jesus never forces himself on anyone or into any area of our lives where we do not welcome him. So if we want Jesus to move in, we have to make room for him by clearing out many other things. It's only when we open the door to him and receive him that he makes himself at home in our hearts.

 | ## DISCUSSION STARTERS

What do you think it would be like to spend the night in a barn?

Why do you think Jesus had to live a life of poverty?

What would it mean to make more room for Jesus in your schedule, your heart, your home?

While they were there, the time came for her baby to be born. She gave birth to her first child, a son. She . . . laid him in a manger, because there was no lodging available for them.

LUKE 2:6-7

Jesus replied, "Foxes have dens to live in, and birds have nests, but the Son of Man has no place even to lay his head."

MATTHEW 8:20

He came into the very world he created, but the world didn't recognize him. He came to his own people, and even they rejected him. But to all who believed him and accepted him, he gave the right to become children of God.

JOHN 1:10-12

She gave birth to her first child, a son. She wrapped him snugly in strips of cloth and laid him in a manger.

LUKE 2:7

He got up from the table, took off his robe, wrapped a towel around his waist, and poured water into a basin. Then he began to wash the disciples' feet, drying them with the towel he had around him.

JOHN 13:4-5

He took the body down from the cross and wrapped it in a long sheet of linen cloth and laid it in a new tomb that had been carved out of rock.

LUKE 23:53

Clothed in Humility

Most of us like to look good. We like to impress other people, and we realize that what we wear sends a message about ourselves. So we look for clothes that will tell people what we want to say about who we are.

From the day he was born, Jesus' clothing told us something significant about him. The way he dressed reflected the attitude of his heart: humility. Mary didn't have nice clothes to put on Jesus. In fact, there were no clothes at all for him— just strips of cloth that were wrapped around him.

Jesus chose to take off the robes of glory that were his in heaven. He laid them aside to be wrapped in rags. He "took the humble position of a slave" (PHILIPPIANS 2:7) instead of seeking to impress.

We see this same picture in another scene much later in Jesus' life. The night before he died, Jesus took off his robe and wrapped a towel around his waist. Then he began to wash the dusty feet of his disciples. And when he finished he told them, "I have given you an example to follow" (JOHN 13:15).

Jesus shows us what it looks like to clothe ourselves in humility. With this kind of wardrobe, our intent will not be to impress but to serve.

 | **DISCUSSION STARTERS**

Think about your favorite outfit. What does it say about you?

Think through Jesus' life and lifestyle. In addition to the way he dressed, what were some other signs that showed his humility?

What does Philippians 2:3-8 teach us about the humility of Jesus? how we can dress the same way?

Good News of Great Joy

Some people think anything having to do with God is very serious. If God has anything to do with it they assume it'll be really boring and they won't have any fun. But Jesus is not a bore or a burden; he's not a drag or drudgery. Jesus is the greatest joy in the universe. He's the best news anyone has ever heard.

That's what the angel came to tell the shepherds who were taking care of their sheep on that dark night outside Bethlehem. Initially, instead of being excited, the shepherds were afraid—terrified, even. Evidently the angel was right there with them and radiated a bright light like they had never seen.

But the Good News of Jesus replaces our fear with joy. What is this Good News? "The Savior—yes, the Messiah, the Lord—has been born today." When they checked it out for themselves, the shepherds found that the angel had told them the truth, so they returned to their flocks, "glorifying and praising God for all they had heard and seen. It was just as the angel had told them." They couldn't keep what they had seen to themselves. They told everyone what happened. "And all who heard it wondered at what the shepherds told them" (LUKE 2:18). That word *wondered* means that the people who heard about it marveled—they were blown away. When we look for ourselves to see if the news we've heard about Jesus is really true, we get to experience that same joy and wonder.

 | **DISCUSSION STARTERS**

What do you think it would be like to see an angel?

What made the coming of Jesus such good news?

Why do you think it is sometimes hard to be filled with joy at the Good News of Jesus?

That night there were shepherds staying in the fields nearby, guarding their flocks of sheep. Suddenly, an angel of the Lord appeared among them, and the radiance of the Lord's glory surrounded them. They were terrified, but the angel reassured them. "Don't be afraid!" he said. "I bring you good news that will bring great joy to all people. The Savior—yes, the Messiah, the Lord—has been born today in Bethlehem, the city of David!" . . .

They hurried to the village and found Mary and Joseph. And there was the baby, lying in the manger. After seeing him, the shepherds told everyone what had happened and what the angel had said to them about this child. . . .

The shepherds went back to their flocks, glorifying and praising God for all they had heard and seen. It was just as the angel had told them.

LUKE 2:8-11, 16-17, 20

Glory Revealed

Are there any wrapped packages under the Christmas tree at your house yet? Won't it be fun to tear off the paper so that what's inside will be revealed for everybody to see?

That night so long ago when the shepherds were guarding their sheep seemed like an ordinary night—just like so many nights before out in the fields. But then the wrapping of heaven was torn open, revealing its glory. God made his glory visible—in fact it surrounded the shepherds. It was as if God pulled back the curtain of the heavens so that it spilled out and around those simple shepherds. What they saw was a glory that has always been there but is usually hidden from human view.

What is the glory of the Lord that surrounded them? The glory of the Lord is the expression of who God is, the demonstration of his character. When the writer to the Hebrews says that Jesus "radiates" God's own glory, he means that the glory is to God what the brightness is to the sun. The glory of God is the product of his presence, the revelation of himself. The fullness of God is seen in Jesus Christ as it has never been seen before. In Jesus' judgment, justice, love, wisdom, power, and knowledge we see God himself. The birth of Christ was the revelation—or the unwrapping—of the glory of the Lord. Have you seen it?

The glory of the LORD will be revealed, and all people will see it together.
ISAIAH 40:5

Suddenly, an angel of the Lord appeared among them, and the radiance of the Lord's glory surrounded them.
LUKE 2:9

The Son radiates God's own glory and expresses the very character of God.
HEBREWS 1:3

 | ## DISCUSSION STARTERS

Luke wrote that the shepherds were terrified when God's glory was revealed. Have you ever been terrified when something was uncovered or opened up?

Why do you think God's glory is usually hidden from human view?

Read 2 Corinthians 3:18. Where is the glory of God being revealed, and what does that mean?

Peace on Earth

When the angel appeared to the shepherds to tell them about the Savior born in Bethlehem, he was not alone. He brought an army with him. But it wasn't an army of soldiers; it was an army of angels.

Usually when we think about an army, we think of war, not peace, right? But that night heaven began to invade earth, not to fight against us or destroy us, but to save us. Jesus didn't come to destroy his enemies. He came to make them his friends. And whether we realize it or not, all of us, at one point, were God's enemies. Left on our own, we fight against God.

But God has not left us on our own. Even though we have declared war on him deep in our hearts, he has declared peace on us. He has reached out to us, making the first move toward peace. God gives us the grace to overcome our natural resistance toward him so that we can experience peace with him. He gives us the faith to trust in him, making us one of "those with whom God is pleased."

🎲 | DISCUSSION STARTERS

What is the difference between a friend and an enemy?

In what way did Jesus bring peace on earth?

What are some evidences you see that people (including yourself) are naturally against God?

Suddenly, the angel was joined by a vast host of others—the armies of heaven—praising God and saying, "Glory to God in highest heaven, and peace on earth to those with whom God is pleased."

LUKE 2:13-14

To us a child is born, to us a son is given; and the government shall be upon his shoulder, and his name shall be called Wonderful Counselor, Mighty God, Everlasting Father, Prince of Peace. Of the increase of his government and of peace there will be no end.

ISAIAH 9:6-7, ESV

Since our friendship with God was restored by the death of his Son while we were still his enemies, we will certainly be saved through the life of his Son.

ROMANS 5:10

He Became Poor

Has anyone asked you what you want for Christmas this year? Since we are asked this question from an early age, it is easy for Christmas to become all about getting rather than giving. Wouldn't a better question to ask each other be, "What are you *giving* for Christmas?" Because giving is what Christmas is all about, and we see that when we look at what Jesus did in coming to earth.

Jesus is the one who made the universe. Everything is his. The glory and joy of heaven are his. He has power and privilege. He is rich in his relationship with his Father and the Spirit. Yet in coming to earth, he set it all aside. He gave up the riches of heaven to become poor on earth. And his poverty had a purpose: to make us rich. Not rich financially, but rich spiritually. Though he was rich, he became poor so that we can have the riches he let go of. What are those riches? The riches of an eternity in heaven with God, enjoying a satisfying, saving relationship with God.

It is seeing this generosity of Jesus that turns selfish people into joyful givers. We tend toward selfishness because we believe the lie that keeping more for ourselves will make us happy. But Jesus shows us that what will truly make us happy is to become generous givers—like he is.

You know the generous grace of our Lord Jesus Christ. Though he was rich, yet for your sakes he became poor, so that by his poverty he could make you rich.
2 CORINTHIANS 8:9

God blesses those who are poor and realize their need for him.
MATTHEW 5:3

Sell your possessions and give to those in need. This will store up treasure for you in heaven!
LUKE 12:33

 | **DISCUSSION STARTERS**

What does it mean to be rich? What does it mean to be poor?

What are some of the ways the Son enjoyed being rich in heaven, and in what ways was he poor while on earth?

How does the generosity of Jesus make you want to be more generous this Christmas season?

Seeing and Believing

Has anyone ever told you something that seemed so incredible you said, "I have to see it to believe it"? It must have been that sense of amazement and curiosity that caused the shepherds to hurry to Bethlehem.

Don't we wish there had been a modern-day news crew on the scene so we could see with our eyes what they saw? Mary, the young Jewish mother, might have been pretty, or maybe she wasn't. And the baby looked like an ordinary infant. But it was just as the angels had told the shepherds, and that was enough for them. The shepherds believed what the angels had told them about this baby and the baby became their Savior.

But the shepherds must have run into a tremendous dilemma when they "told everyone what had happened and what the angel had said to them about this child" (Luke 2:17). Apparently "all who heard the shepherds' story were astonished" (Luke 2:18). Those astonished people were likely divided into two camps. Some believed, while others did not. Some probably said, "That sounds crazy." And some probably shrugged their shoulders in apathy, saying, "That's interesting, but I don't need a Savior."

What has been your response to seeing Jesus? Like the shepherds, have you believed? Like the shepherds, have you told others about him? Like the shepherds, have you glorified and praised God for Jesus?

 | ## DISCUSSION STARTERS

What do you think it looked like, felt like, and smelled like in the stable where Jesus was born?

What are some of the things we believe in without seeing?

Imagine what kinds of things people who listened to the shepherds might have said about their story. What would you have said in response?

DECEMBER

19

When the angels had returned to heaven, the shepherds said to each other, "Let's go to Bethlehem! Let's see this thing that has happened, which the Lord has told us about."

They hurried to the village and found Mary and Joseph. And there was the baby, lying in the manger. After seeing him, the shepherds told everyone what had happened and what the angel had said to them about this child. . . .

The shepherds went back to their flocks, glorifying and praising God for all they had heard and seen.

LUKE 2:15-17, 20

Eight days later, when the baby was circumcised, he was named Jesus, the name given him by the angel even before he was conceived.
LUKE 2:21

When the right time came, God sent his Son, born of a woman, subject to the law.
GALATIANS 4:4

Don't misunderstand why I have come. I did not come to abolish the law of Moses or the writings of the prophets. No, I came to accomplish their purpose.
MATTHEW 5:17

Perfect Obedience

Most people who are married wear wedding rings. The rings aren't what make them married, but are outward signs of a commitment to each other. In the same way, circumcision was instituted by God as an outward sign of his committed relationship with Abraham and his descendants. Circumcision was commanded for all males who were of Abraham's household. It was an intimate and important sign that marked Jewish men as belonging to God.

Jesus was circumcised when he was eight days old. If he had not been circumcised, he would not have fulfilled the law's requirements, and he would not have been recognized as the son of David and the descendant of Abraham. But Jesus' circumcision meant more than just doing what it took to be a Jewish man. It was not a meaningless ritual. It was the beginning of Jesus' life of completely fulfilling God's laws and living in perfect obedience to him. He did this so all of us who cannot live up to the law can find salvation in the gift of his perfect righteousness. You see, we not only need the atoning death of Jesus to pay the penalty for our sin, we also need the perfect life of Jesus to provide the righteousness acceptable to God. We can claim his perfect law-keeping as our own through faith. What a gift!

 | DISCUSSION STARTERS

Why do you think it is so hard to always obey the rules perfectly?

What do you think Jesus meant when he said he came to fulfill the law?

How does it encourage you to know that through his entire life, Jesus did what was necessary to provide you with perfect righteousness?

A Birthday Present for Jesus

Most of us have a little list going this time of year—if not on paper, then in our heads. It's that list of what we're hoping someone might give us for Christmas. But isn't it interesting that at Christmas we get gifts on someone else's birthday? Jesus is the real birthday boy. Have you ever thought about what Jesus might want for his birthday—this Christmas?

The Bible tells us about wise men who brought gifts to Jesus after he was born. They were led to where he was by a star. Matthew wrote that "when they saw the star, they rejoiced exceedingly with great joy" (MATTHEW 2:10, NASB). It's almost as if there aren't enough words to express how much joy they felt over finding Jesus.

When the wise men saw Jesus, they bowed down and worshiped him. And they gave him costly gifts. Giving is part of worship. Those who worship Christ love to give themselves and what they have to him.

Perhaps the gift you could give to Jesus this Christmas is to say to him, from your heart, "I'm so happy you brought me to you, Jesus! I see that you are worthy of my worship, and I want you to be the King of my life. You are more precious to me than anything I own, and I gladly give you the honor you deserve."

 | ## DISCUSSION STARTERS

Instead of thinking only about what you want to get this Christmas, what gifts would you like to *give*?

Can you think of a time in your life when you felt a lot of joy in finding Jesus?

What gift would you like to give Jesus this Christmas?

> Jesus was born in Bethlehem in Judea, during the reign of King Herod. About that time some wise men from eastern lands arrived in Jerusalem, asking, "Where is the newborn king of the Jews? We saw his star as it rose, and we have come to worship him."
>
> *MATTHEW 2:1-2*

> They entered the house and saw the child with his mother, Mary, and they bowed down and worshiped him. Then they opened their treasure chests and gave him gifts of gold, frankincense, and myrrh.
>
> *MATTHEW 2:11*

Born to Die

DECEMBER 22

They entered the house and saw the child with his mother, Mary, and they opened their treasure chests and gave him gifts of gold, frankincense, and myrrh.

MATTHEW 2:11

He brought about seventy-five pounds of perfumed ointment made from myrrh and aloes. Following Jewish burial custom, they wrapped Jesus' body with the spices in long sheets of linen cloth.

JOHN 19:39-40

When babies are born, there is usually a celebration, and everyone is thinking about the long life ahead for that child. But from his birth—even before his birth—there was a cloud of death looming over the baby Jesus. This was a baby who was born to die.

When the wise men came to see Jesus, Matthew records that they brought him gifts of gold, frankincense, and myrrh. These are unusual gifts for a baby. Gold was a gift suited to a king. And the wise men bowed down to Jesus, recognizing him as King. Frankincense was used in the Temple as part of the ceremony for worshiping God. The wise men recognized that Jesus was no ordinary human. Perhaps they had read Isaiah's prophecy about the Messiah that "mighty kings will come to see your radiance. . . . [They] will bring gold and frankincense and will come worshiping the LORD" (ISAIAH 60:3, 6). But the myrrh they brought to Jesus was an especially unusual gift. Myrrh is a sweet-smelling substance that was used on dead bodies to preserve them and overcome the smell of decay. Why give myrrh to a baby?

Perhaps the wise men also understood Isaiah's prophecy that "it was the LORD's good plan to crush him and cause him grief. Yet when his life is made an offering for sin, he will have many descendants" (53:10). If we're wise, we'll see that the reason to celebrate the baby Jesus is because he was born to die so that we can live.

 | DISCUSSION STARTERS

What kind of gifts do people usually give to newborn babies?

Read Luke 2:34-35. How do Simeon's words to Mary also reveal that Jesus was born to die?

Why do you think the Gospel writers gave us details that point to the death of Jesus from the very beginning of his life?

Eagerly Waiting

It's hard to wait—especially when you really want something and you've been disappointed over and over while waiting for it. That makes you want to give up and stop wanting it so much. That's what many people did before Jesus came—they gave up waiting for and wanting a Messiah to come and deliver them. They got tired of the wait, so they stopped looking and longing. They stopped expecting that God would fulfill his promise.

But not everybody got tired of waiting. Luke 2 tells about two people—Simeon and Anna—who were still eagerly waiting and watching for the promised Messiah. When Simeon saw the baby Jesus, he knew the wait was over. He said, "Sovereign Lord, now let your servant die in peace, as you have promised. I have seen your salvation" (VERSES 29-30). And when Anna heard what Simeon said, she shared it with everyone else she knew who was waiting expectantly.

Once again we are in a period of waiting—waiting for Jesus to come a second time. And we can expect that, like the first time, Jesus will be revealed to those who are waiting eagerly to see him. It might seem like it will never happen, and the world can tell us we are ridiculous to be looking for Jesus' arrival. But don't stop waiting and watching. God has promised, and Jesus will return.

 | ## DISCUSSION STARTERS

When have you found it especially hard to wait?

What does Simeon celebrate about Jesus? What does he prophecy about Jesus (see Luke 2:25-40)?

What are things that drain us of longing for Jesus to return? How can we nurture an eager longing for his return?

DECEMBER

23

At that time there was a man in Jerusalem named Simeon. He was righteous and devout and was eagerly waiting for the Messiah to come and rescue Israel.

LUKE 2:25

Now the prize awaits me—the crown of righteousness, which the Lord, the righteous Judge, will give me on the day of his return. And the prize is not just for me but for all who eagerly look forward to his appearing.

2 TIMOTHY 4:8

For a child is born to us,
a son is given to us.

The government will rest
on his shoulders.

And he will be called:
Wonderful Counselor,
Mighty God, Everlasting
Father, Prince of Peace.

His government and its
peace will never end.

He will rule with fairness and
justice from the throne of his
ancestor David for all eternity.

The passionate commitment
of the LORD of Heaven's Armies
will make this happen!

ISAIAH 9:6-7

A Real Hero

When you're really in trouble, you want someone strong to show up to save you—a real hero. And as people living in this world, we are really in trouble, really in need of someone who can save us from our slavery to sin. And God sent someone to save us. But this Savior didn't seem strong. He seemed ordinary and weak. God sent us a Savior in the form of a baby.

The prophet Isaiah assured us that was no ordinary baby, and he grew up to be no ordinary man. As the Wonderful Counselor, he has the best ideas and strategies; he's the wisest and most perfect teacher. If we listen to him, we'll know what to do. It is good that he is strong and mighty, because the enemy of sin overpowers us. As the Mighty God, he uses his power on our behalf, helping us overcome sin. We can find protection in him when we're tempted. As the Everlasting Father, he cares for us lovingly, with affection that has no limits. We can entrust ourselves to him. As the Prince of Peace, he invites us into his Kingdom of full and perfect happiness, giving us the assurance of safety and security. If we submit to him, we will live lives of blessed obedience to him.

Who could ask for more at Christmas than a baby who became our strong deliverer and our source of security and satisfaction forever?

 | **DISCUSSION STARTERS**

How are the heroes in some of your favorite stories
like Jesus?

Why do you think God chose to have the powerful Savior
come to earth in the form of a helpless baby?

Wonderful Counselor, Mighty God, Everlasting Father, Prince
of Peace. How is each one of these names a special gift to
you personally? Which one do you especially need in your life
right now?

The Greatest Gift

What's the best gift you were given this Christmas? Can you hardly wait to leave the dinner table to play with it, put it on, or figure it out?

At Christmas, one of the ways we celebrate the best gift we've ever been given is by giving each other gifts. God is the ultimate gift giver—the most generous giver in the universe. He knows just what to give to us, just what we need most. And he has given us Jesus. Whether or not we realize it, Jesus is the greatest gift we've ever been given.

When we realize how generous the gift of Jesus is, we can be confident that whatever else God gives us will be good, and that he will, in fact, give us everything good. It only makes sense. Why would God give us the most precious, costly gift of his own Son, who died for us, and then be stingy with us in other ways, holding out on giving us what we need? Why would God pour out his love on us through Jesus and then refuse to provide for every other need we might have?

Today is a day to celebrate the best gift ever from the best gift giver ever—Jesus, the gift we will enjoy forever.

Since [God] did not spare even his own Son but gave him up for us all, won't he also give us everything else?
ROMANS 8:32

From his abundance we have all received one gracious blessing after another.
JOHN 1:16

Thank God for this gift too wonderful for words!
2 CORINTHIANS 9:15

📖 | DISCUSSION STARTERS

What are some of your favorite gifts that you received? How do these gifts show that the people who gave them knew what you wanted or needed?

How have you enjoyed the generosity of God over this past year?

How does Romans 8:32 encourage you as you think about needs you have in the coming year?

All who heard the shepherds' story were astonished, but Mary kept all these things in her heart and thought about them often.

LUKE 2:18-19

He returned to Nazareth with them and was obedient to them. And his mother stored all these things in her heart.

LUKE 2:51

Pondering

Pretty soon it will be time to take down the Christmas lights and put away the decorations. January will be here, and this Christmas will be a memory. If we're not careful, ordinary life can cause us to lose our sense of wonder over Jesus' coming.

That might have happened on the first Christmas too. Though it seems like everyone would keep their eyes on a baby whose birth had been announced by a sky full of angels, evidently people lost interest. The shepherds had to go back to taking care of their sheep. The wise men went back to their own country. It seems as if most people set aside their hopes that this baby could make a difference in the world.

But Mary didn't. She "treasured up all these things and pondered them in her heart" (LUKE 2:19, NIV). It was as if she said to herself, *I won't forget hearing the angel, having the Spirit come over me, seeing Jesus worshiped by the wise men.* Evidently Mary didn't understand everything about Jesus, but she wanted to, so she began a process of "connecting the dots" in her own mind, adding up the prophecies fulfilled by her son and all the miracles surrounding his birth. She thought through everything again and again while others lost interest.

Don't let your life slip back into ordinary days with few thoughts of wonder over Jesus' coming. Ponder him in your heart.

 | **DISCUSSION STARTERS**

What has been your favorite part of celebrating Christmas this year?

What thoughts do you imagine went through Mary's mind as she tried to make sense of all she'd experienced and witnessed?

What are some ways you can ponder Jesus when you find he is not in your thoughts throughout the day?

The Family Business

Many young men and women grow up thinking about whether or not they want to join the "family business" when they are an adult. Many follow in their father's or mother's footsteps professionally or join with their parents in business. That's what Jesus did. Until he was thirty years old, he worked as a carpenter like his earthly father. But he also knew he was born for a higher purpose—to fulfill the work his Father in heaven had given him to do.

When Jesus was twelve years old, his parents were frantically searching for him. They finally found him in the Temple talking to the religious leaders about what the Scriptures teach. Mary said, "Your father and I have been frantic, searching for you everywhere." Jesus answered, "Didn't you know that I must be in my Father's house?" In other words, Jesus had chosen this crucial stage in his life, on the brink of adulthood, to tell his parents in an unforgettable way that he knew who his real Father was and what it would mean for his life. Even though he was young, he recognized that he was God's unique Son and that his mission would require a devotion to God that would take priority over his devotion to his earthly family.

 | **DISCUSSION STARTERS**

Have you ever gotten separated from your parents in a busy place? How did you feel?

What do you think it was like for Joseph to be an earthly father to Jesus?

What do you think it would have been like to listen in to Jesus discussing the Scripture with the rabbis?

Jesus was known as the son of Joseph.
LUKE 3:23

Three days later they finally discovered him in the Temple, sitting among the religious teachers, listening to them and asking questions. All who heard him were amazed at his understanding and his answers.

His parents didn't know what to think. "Son," his mother said to him, "why have you done this to us? Your father and I have been frantic, searching for you everywhere."

"But why did you need to search?" he asked. "Didn't you know that I must be in my Father's house?" But they didn't understand what he meant.
LUKE 2:46-50

Since the Beginning

While Matthew and Luke started their Gospels with the genealogies of Jesus, wanting us to see his humanness, John wanted us to see that the Son of God's first appearance on the scene was not as a baby in Bethlehem. He has, in fact, always existed—since the beginning of time. Before the world was created or time began, the Word, who was God, was already there with God.

The word *Word* is a translation of the Greek word *logos*. It was used in Greek philosophy to indicate the "first cause." It referred to the great unknown reason, will, and power behind the universe. John was telling us that Jesus is that first cause. He is the one who started everything, and nothing got its start without him. Jesus was the agent or the means by which God made everything in the world—from the outer galaxies in the heavens to the smallest atom.

John wanted us to know that this one who chose to enter the world is the one who made the world. This truth fills us with wonder and amazement. The God who made the world and everything in it willingly reduced himself to Mary's womb to be born into this world.

In the beginning the Word already existed. The Word was with God, and the Word was God. He existed in the beginning with God. God created everything through him, and nothing was created except through him.
JOHN 1:1-3

Through him God created everything in the heavenly realms and on earth. . . . Everything was created through him and for him.
COLOSSIANS 1:16

Now in these final days, he has spoken to us through his Son. God promised everything to the Son as an inheritance, and through the Son he created the universe.
HEBREWS 1:2

 | **DISCUSSION STARTERS**

What do you think Jesus enjoyed most about the world he created?

What does the Genesis 1 account of how the world was created tell us about the power of the Word of God?

If Jesus is the Word, what is God saying to us through Jesus?

The Word Became Flesh

Have you ever seen someone on TV who was wearing a fat suit or who dressed up as an elderly person to play a different role? When people put on costumes, it is usually for a brief time and then they go back to being who they really are.

We might assume that's what Jesus did—that he put on a "costume" of skin to be a human for the thirty-three years he spent on this earth, and then went back to his "usual" self when he returned to heaven. But Jesus went much further than that. When the Word became flesh, he became flesh forever. He didn't just appear to be human; he *became* human—not just for his brief life on earth, but for eternity. Even now, Jesus, who is God, is in heaven at the right hand of God, the Father, in his glorified human body.

When the Word became flesh, he became capable of new experiences. He entered the world through a mother's body. He had to learn how to walk. He went through puberty. He got splinters in his hands in the carpenter's shop and rocks in his sandals as he walked. But the most important experience he went through as a human was physical death. This was his ultimate purpose in becoming flesh—so he could die in our place.

 | **DISCUSSION STARTERS**

What costumes have you worn? What would it be like to actually become the person you dressed up as?

What other aspects of being human did Jesus experience?

How does it help you to know that Jesus understands what life in this world is like?

The Word became human and made his home among us.
JOHN 1:14

In Christ lives all the fullness of God in a human body.
COLOSSIANS 2:9

Because God's children are human beings—made of flesh and blood—the Son also became flesh and blood. For only as a human being could he die, and only by dying could he break the power of the devil, who had the power of death.
HEBREWS 2:14

The Word became human and made his home among us. He was full of unfailing love and faithfulness. And we have seen his glory, the glory of the Father's one and only Son.
JOHN 1:14

Abram moved his tent and came and dwelt by the oaks of Mamre, which are in Hebron, and there he built an altar to the LORD.
GENESIS 13:18, NASB

I heard a loud shout from the throne, saying, "Look, God's home is now among his people! He will live with them, and they will be his people. God himself will be with them."
REVELATION 21:3

God Pitched His Tent

Have you ever put up a tent in your backyard to play in or sleep in? Imagine if another family were to put up a tent in your backyard to live in. They would probably use your bathroom and have their meals with you. They would be with you almost all the time, and no doubt their lives would intertwine with yours.

John 1 says, "The Word became flesh, and dwelt among us" (VERSE 14, NASB). The Greek word that is translated *dwelt* is the word for "set up a tent." This verse is saying that God became a person who has set up his tent in our backyard. He did this so that his life will be intertwined with ours—so that we will share our lives with him and so we can see him up close and really know him.

And when we see him up close, what do we see? John tells us: unfailing love and faithfulness. Doesn't that seem like the kind of person you would want to have making his home with your family?

 | **DISCUSSION STARTERS**

When someone wants to sit by you at an event or spend the night at your house, what does that say about how they feel about you?

John describes God in the flesh as full of unfailing love and faithfulness. Do you think that is how most people see Jesus?

What difference do you think it would make if your family lived as if Jesus had made himself "at home" in your house?

Pressing On

God has given us the gift of memory, and it is one of those gifts we can use in a way that hurts us or in a way that helps us. Memories of our successes can fill us with sinful pride or with gratitude for God's provision and help. Memories of sins and failures can burden us with hopelessness or prompt us to become more like God. As we look back over the past year, we should give thanks for our successes and make humble confessions for failures. Then we turn toward the future.

As Paul looked toward the future, he was determined to "press on." What would it look like to press on as you enter another year? The kind of straining forward Paul writes about means implementing the self-discipline and self-denial of a serious athlete. It means making plans and setting goals for yourself in the areas of worshiping, studying God's Word, developing your prayer life, and sharing Christ, so that by next year at this time you will be closer to Jesus.

Today is a good day to look back, look forward, and look inward. We want to see ourselves and our lives as Christ sees us and be willing to face hard truths. But more important than looking inward is looking upward to Christ. Looking at Christ gives us a goal to pursue, a person to enjoy, a passion to feed. Looking to Christ orients the direction of the coming year—and of our entire lives.

DISCUSSION STARTERS

Think back over the past year. What accomplishments are you pleased with? What experiences were especially fun or meaningful?

Look ahead into the coming year. What habits do you want to break? What skills would you like to master? What would you like to experience? Where would you like to go?

DECEMBER
31

I focus on this one thing: Forgetting the past and looking forward to what lies ahead, I press on to reach the end of the race and receive the heavenly prize for which God, through Christ Jesus, is calling us.

PHILIPPIANS 3:13-14

The one thing I ask of the LORD—the thing I seek most—is to live in the house of the LORD all the days of my life, delighting in the LORD's perfections and meditating in his Temple.

PSALM 27:4

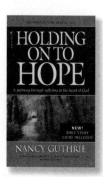
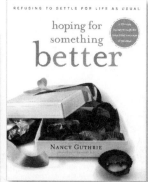